Labyrinths of Power

Political Recruitment
in Twentieth-Century Mexico

Peter H. Smith

PRINCETON UNIVERSITY PRESS
Princeton, New Jersey

Copyright © 1979 by Princeton University Press

Published by Princeton University Press, Princeton, New Jersey
In the United Kingdom: Princeton University Press,
Guildford, Surrey

All Rights Reserved

Library of Congress Cataloging in Publication Data will be
found on the last printed page of this book

This book has been composed in linotype Baskerville

Clothbound editions of Princeton University Press books
are printed on acid-free paper, and binding materials are
chosen for strength and durability.

Printed in the United States of America
by Princeton University Press, Princeton, New Jersey

IN MEMORY OF
don Daniel Cosío Villegas
AND
IN ADMIRATION OF
THE GENERATIONS HE INSPIRED

CONTENTS

ACKNOWLEDGMENTS

This book has been a long time in the making, and I have accumulated countless professional debts and obligations. Financial support has, over the years, come from varied sources: the Joint Committee on Latin American Studies of the Social Science Research Council-American Council of Learned Societies, the ACLS program in Aid to Computer-Oriented Research in the Humanities, the National Endowment for the Humanities (Grant No. RO-6848-72), the Institute for Advanced Study at Princeton, the John Simon Guggenheim Memorial Foundation, and, at the University of Wisconsin-Madison, the Ibero-American Studies Program and the Research Committee of the Graduate School.

Grants from these organizations gave me the opportunity to carry on the research for a number of years, and I would like to record my thanks to staff members at the following libraries and institutions: the Archivo de la Cámara de Diputados, the Archivo de la Cámara de Senadores, the Archivo General de la Nación, the Asociación de Diputados Constituyentes de 1917, the Banco Nacional de Crédito Ejidal, the Biblioteca de México, the Biblioteca de Nacional Financiera, the Biblioteca de la Secretaría de Relaciones Exteriores, the Biblioteca del Banco de México, the Biblioteca Nacional, the Comisión Federal de Electricidad, Condumex, S.A., the Departamento de Archivo e Información of the newspaper *Excélsior*, the Hemeroteca Nacional, and the Oficina de Información de Asuntos Económicos de los Estados y Territorios de México, all in Mexico City. In the United States I have found much information in the Latin American Collection at the University of Texas and in the Memorial Library at the University of Wisconsin.

I have been fortunate to have the help of careful and capable assistants, and this project has had much the flavor of a collective enterprise. James Bauknecht, Stanley Cravens, Peter De Shazo, Mary Grant, James Gary Linn, Soledad Loaeza, Denise Mery-Sanson, Valerie Poellnitz, Joette Reuter, Jeanne Schroeder, and Margaret Schwertfeger helped with aspects of the data-gathering. Margaret Brush, Anne del Carmen Hartwig, Magdalena León de Leal, and Alberto Rábago assisted with the coding; Natalie Aikins did the keypunching; Hans Luis Fetter, Nita Rome, and Ted Hartwig handled the computer programming. Cher Leszczewicz typed successive drafts of the manuscript and assisted in the composition of the index with cheer, efficiency, and skill. Staff members of the Cartographic Laboratory at the University of Wisconsin did the graphic work for the figures.

ACKNOWLEDGMENTS

Permission to reproduce the cartoons that grace the text has been kindly granted by the artists Rogelio Naranjo and Abel Quezada; by the publishers of the Mexico City newspapers *Excélsior* and *El Universal*; and by the management of the publishing houses of B. Costa-Amic and Ediciones de Cultura Popular.

Professional colleagues have consistently lent moral and intellectual support. Friends and associates at the Instituto Mexicano de Estudios Políticos, A. C., and at the Departamento de Investigaciones Históricas of the Instituto Nacional de Antropología e Historia, have been generous with facts and ideas; I would like to express my special gratitude to colleagues at El Colegio de México, where I had the honor of being an Investigador Visitante in 1969-70 and where I have since returned on subsequent visits to Mexico. Roger Anderson, Mary Armstrong, Adolfo Rodríguez Gallardo, John Nagle, and Robert Service shared valuable information with me, and Roderic Ai Camp kindly provided me with complete access to his own storehouse of data on Mexican politicians.

Fellow colleagues have been kind enough to read through earlier versions of the manuscript, in whole or in part, and give me comments and suggestions. For their supportiveness—and their insistence on high standards—I am profoundly grateful to Douglas Bennett, Roderic Ai Camp, Susan Eckstein, Frances Gouda, John Hamilton, Alicia Hernández, Donald J. Mabry, Lorenzo Meyer, Susan Kaufman Purcell, Rafael Segovia, Carole Shammas, Kenneth Sharpe, Richard N. Sinkin, and Mark Wasserman. I have incorporated many of their ideas, and the final product is much the better for their efforts. I alone am responsible for errors of fact or interpretation.

Finally, I want to acknowledge the warmth, guidance, and encouragement of the late Daniel Cosío Villegas, to whose memory this book is dedicated. A man of vision and commitment, he saw the study of the past as an integral part of the search for human priorities. Through his example and his work, in both his teaching and his writing, he has reminded us what history is all about.

Madison, Wisconsin
February 1978

LIST OF ILLUSTRATIONS

LIST OF TABLES

LIST OF FIGURES

LIST OF ABBREVIATIONS

ASA	Aeropuertos y Servicios Auxiliares
CANACINTRA	Cámara Nacional de Industrias de Transformación
CNC	Confederación Nacional Campesina
CNOP	Confederación Nacional de Organizaciones Populares
CONCAMIN	Confederación de Cámaras de Industria
CONASUPO	Compañía Nacional de Subsistencias Populares
COPARMEX	Confederación Patronal de la República de México
CTM	Confederación de Trabajadores Mexicanos
FSTSE	Federación de Sindicatos de Trabajadores en el Servicio del Estado
IEPES	Instituto de Estudios Políticos, Económicos y Sociales
IMSS	Instituto Mexicano del Seguro Social
ISSSTE	Instituto de Servicios y Seguros Sociales de Trabajadores del Estado
PAN	Partido de Acción Nacional
PARM	Partido Auténtico de la Revolución Mexicana
PEMEX	Petróleos Mexicanos
PIPSA	Productora e Importadora de Papel, Sociedad Anónima
PNR	Partido Nacional Revolucionario
PPS	Partido Popular Socialista
PRI	Partido Revolucionario Institucional
PRM	Partido de la Revolución Mexicana
SOMEX	Sociedad Mexicana de Crédito Industrial
SRH	Secretaría de Recursos Hidraúlicos
UNAM	Universidad Nacional Autónoma de México

PART I

INTRODUCTION

· 1 ·

THE LINES OF
INQUIRY

One of the most critical sets of questions about any political system concerns the composition of its leadership: Who governs? Who has access to power, and what are the social conditions of rule? Such issues have direct bearing on the representativeness of political leadership, a continuing concern of democratic theorists, and on the extent to which those in power emerge from the ranks of "the people"—or from an exclusive oligarchy. These themes also relate to the role of the political system within society at large, and to the ways in which careers in public life offer meaningful opportunities for vertical (usually upward) social mobility. In addition, these questions focus attention upon the patterns of political careers—that is, the timing, sequence, and duration of tenure in public offices—patterns which can in turn provide important clues about the operative codes that guide and affect the behavior of the leaders of the system.

Consideration of these problems is highly relevant to an understanding of political change in twentieth-century Mexico, and Mexico offers an exceptionally promising laboratory for a study of them. In the first place, Mexico underwent an extended, violent, and ultimately mass-based revolution in the decade from 1910 to 1920. It is therefore possible to examine, with substantial historical perspective, the long-run impact that the Mexican Revolution may (or may not) have exerted upon the composition of the country's political elite. Did it really alter the social background of the ruling groups, or did it merely reallocate power to differing segments of the same class? Any thorough assessment of the meaning of the Mexican Revolution, and its significance for Mexican society, obviously demands an answer to this question.

In the second place, Mexico has created and maintained an unquestionably "authoritarian" regime—a system that is characterized by "limited pluralism," in Juan Linz's phrase, and one that is identifiably and analytically distinct from democratic or totalitarian types of rule.[1] Authoritarianism is a widespread phenomenon, especially in countries

---

[1] See Juan J. Linz, "An Authoritarian Regime: Spain," most easily consulted in *Mass Politics: Studies in Political Sociology*, ed. Erik Allardt and Stein Rokkan (New York: The Free Press, 1970), pp. 251-283 and 374-381.

throughout the Third World,[2] and an appreciation of its variety and complexity calls for the study of elites. For if authoritarianism consists of limited pluralism, it becomes necessary to determine who falls on which side of the limits—who does (and does not) have the functional right to organize and compete for power. There is an equally urgent need to gain some understanding of the behavior of authoritarian elites and the "rules" of their political game. Ironically enough, the qualities that set off the Mexican regime from so many of its authoritarian counterparts—its apparent stability, and its domination by civilians—also make it an extraordinarily useful case study, since the recruitment and selection processes have endured for many years without a military coup or any other major interruption. To put the question in its simplest form: If you don't attain high office by amassing a popular vote (as in a democratic system), or by ascending the military hierarchy (as in countless places), then how do you do it?

Third, Mexico has undergone rapid and profound socioeconomic change during the course of this century. Industries have flourished, cities have grown, literacy has spread, the population has boomed—and the gap between the rich and poor has steadily increased. The situation thus affords an opportunity to analyze the relationship, if any, between alterations in society at large and in the composition of the ruling groups. For it is at least conceivable that socioeconomic trends, rather than political events or processes, have exercised primary influence upon the patterns of leadership recruitment.

In an effort to confront these issues I focus, in this study, upon the changing characteristics of the national political elite in twentieth-century Mexico. Specifically, as explained in some detail below, I explore the personal biographies of more than 6,000 individuals who held national office in Mexico at any time between 1900 and 1976—before, during, and since the Mexican Revolution. My intent is to analyze the structure and, more important, the transformation of elites over a substantial stretch of time. Straightforward as this purpose seems, it raises a series of complex conceptual problems, not the least of which concerns the very notion of a political elite.

THE CONCEPT OF ELITES

A study of this kind draws heavily upon the intellectual legacy of the classical elite theorists: Gaetano Mosca, Vilfredo Pareto, and Robert

[2] According to Jean Blondel, who does not follow Linz's definitions, about 30 percent of the world's political systems were "authoritarian" as of 1972—and another 30 percent were "populist" (including Mexico). Blondel, *Comparing Political Systems* (New York: Praeger, 1972), Appendix.

4

Michels. Writing in the late nineteenth century, when Europe's hereditary aristocracies were waning and burgeoning labor movements were promoting Marxist visions of stateless utopias, these thinkers argued forcefully that in all societies, no matter what the political system, power would always be controlled by a small minority.[3] "Among the constant facts and tendencies that are to be found in all political organisms," declared Mosca in his famous treatise,

> one is so obvious that it is apparent to the most casual eye. In all societies—from societies that are very meagerly developed and have barely attained the dawnings of civilization, down to the most advanced and powerful societies—two classes of people appear—a class that rules and a class that is ruled. The first class, always the less numerous, performs all political functions, monopolizes power and enjoys the advantages that power brings, whereas the second, the more numerous class, is directed and controlled by the first, in a manner that is now more or less legal, now more or less arbitrary and violent, and supplies the first, in appearance at least, with material means of subsistence and with the instrumentalities that are essential to the vitality of the political organism.[4]

The distribution of power was highly skewed and bimodal, and the minority which possessed it comprised a "ruling class." To this dominant stratum Pareto gave the label that has since remained in common use: the governing, or political, elite.[5]

This emphasis upon a ruling elite seems, at face value, unexceptionable. Political power is unequally (if not bimodally) distributed in all societies; those who have the greatest shares can properly be regarded as an elite, and it is in that sense only that I employ the term throughout this book. Whether power *must* be so concentrated, as Michels gloomily concluded ("Who says organization, says oligarchy"),[6] is a separate question. The fact is that it *has* been so, at least in all societies observed to date, and it applies to twentieth-century Mexico as well as to other situations.

The difficulty with classical elite theory lies in its extension of this

[3] For an excellent analysis of the political context giving rise to elite theory see James H. Meisel, *The Myth of the Ruling Class: Gaetano Mosca and the Elite* (Ann Arbor: University of Michigan Press, 1962).

[4] Gaetano Mosca, *The Ruling Class*, trans. Hannah D. Kahn, ed. Arthur Livingston (New York and London: McGraw-Hill, 1939), p. 50.

[5] *Vilfredo Pareto: Sociological Writings*, trans. Derek Mirfin, ed. S. E. Finer (London: Pall Mall Press, 1966), pp. 248-249.

[6] Robert Michels, *Political Parties: A Sociological Study of the Oligarchical Tendencies of Modern Democracy*, trans. Eden and Cedar Paul, ed. Seymour Martin Lipset (New York: Collier Books, 1962), p. 365.

basic insight. Beginning with its stark, unnecessarily simplistic dichotomy between the rulers and the ruled, the theory went on to posit that the ruling group comprised a unified, organized, self-conscious, purposeful class "obeying," in Mosca's words, "a single impulse."[7] One problem with this formulation stems from the implicit concept of class, which includes the question of consciousness but ignores the question of socioeconomic influence or status. Another and perhaps more basic problem comes from the assumption of shared consciousness. It may be, in some cases, that the dominant elite pursues a common purpose; it may also be, in other cases, that those possessing power do not have a sense of unity. That is a matter for empirical research, not for a priori definition.

In addition, proponents of the theory tended to argue that members of the elite were somehow superior—"select," as the word itself implies—and that, in an almost Darwinian sense, they held a monopoly of power because they were the fittest for it. As Mosca put it, "ruling minorities are usually so constituted that the individuals who make them up are distinguished from the mass of the governed by qualities that give them a certain material, intellectual or even moral superiority; or else they are the heirs of individuals who possessed such qualities."[8] Pareto, for his part, laid the emphasis on psychological attributes: political leaders had to know how to use appropriate combinations of persuasion and force, and this task called for special kinds of personalities. In either case, the assumption was that individuals acquired power largely because of their own qualities, rather than because of structural inequities or patterns of oppression.[9]

A concomitant part of this view was an idea that political elites, or ruling groups, were essentially autonomous. They could be pressured by the masses, and they needed the support (or acquiescence) of the nonelites, but they were mainly beholden to themselves. Even Harold Lasswell, writing in the early 1950s, defined the political elite as the social stratum from which leadership originates "and to which accountability is maintained."[10] Again, this might be true and it might not be true: there is no inherent reason why it must be so.

Ironically enough, some theorists have constructed interpretations

[7] Mosca, *Ruling Class*, p. 53.   [8] Ibid.

[9] For Michels, it should be noted, individuals attained power because of the imperatives of large-scale organization. Mosca, too, was careful to stress that virtue (or superiority) was in the eye of the beholder, though he did not offer much of an explanation about how or why cultural values change over time.

[10] Harold D. Lasswell, Daniel Lerner, and C. Easton Rothwell, *The Comparative Study of Elites: An Introduction and Bibliography* (Stanford: Stanford University Press, 1952), p. 13.

of political democracy by accepting much or most of elite theory and rejecting just this one assumption. In a democratic system, as Joseph Schumpeter (among others) has maintained, positions of power are in principle open to everyone, but they are in fact sought by members of a tiny minority—that is, by competing factions of a political elite which, in contrast to the classical model, owes accountability to its electorate. Democracy, then, consists of the "institutional arrangement for arriving at political decisions in which individuals acquire the power to decide by means of a competitive struggle for the people's vote."[11] In this conception, democracy is merely a method for the selection of elites.[12]

At any rate, the emphasis on elite autonomy led the classical theorists to find the sources of political change within the ruling group itself. In Mosca's terms, "the varying structure of ruling classes has a preponderant importance in determining the political type, and also the level of civilization, of the different peoples," and a change within the ruling class necessarily meant a change within society at large. (Mosca also conceded that dislocations in the ruling class could result from the emergence of new social forces, as when "a new source of wealth develops in a society"[13]—a position that, as James Meisel observed, brought him "uncomfortably close to Marx,"[14] and one that Mosca himself did not thoroughly develop.)

It was Pareto, of course, who crystallized the idea of the circulation of elites. Leadership demanded a requisite combination of psychological attributes, according to Pareto, and the elite must constantly replenish its supply. "Aristocracies decay not only in number but also in quality, in the sense that energy diminishes and there is a debilitating alteration in the proportion of the residues [sympathies] which originally favored the capture and retention of power. . . ." Therefore the elite should draw upon the nonelite, improving (and protecting) itself by renewing itself. Social mobility would thus maintain high standards of leadership and assure political stability as well. But if circulation stopped, danger then arose: "the accumulation of superior elements in the lower classes and, conversely, of inferior elements in the upper classes, is a potent cause of disturbance in the social equilibrium." In time, most ruling groups lost sight of this fact and eventually

11 Joseph A. Schumpeter, *Capitalism, Socialism, and Democracy*, 3rd edition (New York: Harper and Brothers, 1950), p. 269.

12 For trenchant criticisms of this view see T. B. Bottomore, *Elites and Society* (London: Penguin Books, 1964), ch. vii; and Peter Bachrach, *The Theory of Democratic Elitism: A Critique* (Boston: Little, Brown, 1967).

13 Mosca, *Ruling Class*, pp. 51 and 65.

14 Meisel, *Myth*, p. 303.

7

succumbed to challenges from below. Hence revolutions, and hence Pareto's well-known aphorism: "History is a graveyard of aristocracies."[15]

What Pareto envisioned was a cyclical exchange of political dominance between two psychological types, the foxes and the lions. Foxes, in this scheme, tended to be cunning, shrewd, manipulative, artists of corruption and deception. Lions relied on force instead of persuasion: they were primitive, forceful, and strong. Interestingly enough, Pareto identified these leadership types with differing economic activities— foxes with industrial and commercial interests, lions with agriculture —but he did not pursue this connection at any length. Essentially, he saw elite transformation as the interplay of psychological forces, with excesses of one kind counterbalanced by excesses of another.[16]

At face value, this thesis has a certain plausibility. In the case of Mexico, for instance, there appears to be a fox-lion-fox cycle in the transition from the aging Porfirio Díaz (and his elegant collaborator, José Yves Limantour) to rough-and-tumble types like Pancho Villa to smooth operators like Miguel Alemán. But the scheme is as superficial as it is suggestive. In the first place, political leaders, especially in Mexico, have displayed conspicuous abilities for combining foxlike agility with lionlike power, summoning each trait according to the requirements of the situation, not just because of psychic predilection.[17] Second, the cyclical theory does not easily accommodate patterns of linear, secular change (as will be sometimes encountered below). Besides, I do not have any data on the psychological predisposition of Mexican political leaders and could not classify them even if I wanted to. On the other hand, this book is supposed to be a study of elite transformation: if not psychological forces, what might have been the sources of change?

One set of possibilities deals with political factors. In some societies electoral reform, to take one kind of political event, has contributed to major alterations in the social origin of leadership. In England, the Second Reform Bill of 1867 helped precipitate a sharp decline in the proportion of landowners sitting in the House of Commons.[18] In Argentina, as I have elsewhere shown, the enfranchisement of all adult

---

[15] Pareto, *Writings*, pp. 249-250.

[16] Ibid., pp. 256-258. See also Bottomore, *Elites*, pp. 48-68.

[17] I am presenting, in effect, a crude proposition: that political leaders seek power and, once smitten by this ambition, they will take whatever steps are necessary to fulfill it. For a classification of ambitions that is suggestive, but not particularly applicable to this study, see James L. Payne and Oliver H. Woshinsky, "Incentives for Political Participation," *World Politics* 24, no. 4 (July 1972): 518-546.

[18] Robert D. Putnam, *The Comparative Study of Political Elites* (Englewood Cliffs, N.J.: Prentice-Hall, 1976), pp. 173-175.

male citizens in 1912 prompted a similar decline in the percentage of upper-class "aristocrats" in the Chamber of Deputies, and the rise of the Peronist movement led to their near-complete eclipse in the 1940s.[19] Being a process of violent upheaval, a revolution such as occurred in Mexico could—almost by definition—be expected to bring about profound and sudden changes in the composition of elites. Did it?

A lot of people seem to think it did. An ex-president of Mexico, Emilio Portes Gil, writing in a government-sponsored volume, has expressed what practically amounts to an official view on the subject. In contrast to the aristocratic pretensions of the prerevolutionary elite, said Portes Gil,

> The founders and leaders of the Mexican Revolution were men of humble origin who were always in contact with working-class people in the city and the countryside. Many were farmers and had personally suffered the despotism of the landowners . . . ridiculed, reviled, and persecuted, they belonged to a class which possessed no privilege of any kind, and they viewed the *latifundistas* and representatives of the Porfirian dictatorship with contempt. From these men, the spokesmen and commanders of the Revolution, came the laws for the protection of the worker and the peasant, rural education, the conservation of the culture and traditions of the indigenous race, the assertion of national dominion over the subsoil and natural resources, and the many other and important social and political reforms that have made Mexico into a respected country.[20]

In short, the Revolution meant a change from an urban, urbane, exclusive oligarchy to the political preeminence of poor and rural elements.[21] Thus the Revolution opened the doors to political and social opportunity, drew its leaders from the masses, and created a system that would remain truly representative. Sometimes the argument is cast in racial terms, stipulating that the Revolution passed effective power from white *blancos* to mixed-blood *mestizos* and even to some pure-blood *indios*.[22] Hence a streetcorner slogan, used by regime supporters to demonstrate the system's flexibility and by opponents to indicate its mediocrity: "Anyone can become president."

[19] Peter H. Smith, *Argentina and the Failure of Democracy: Conflict among Political Elites, 1904-1955* (Madison: University of Wisconsin Press, 1974), pp. 26-27.

[20] Emilio Portes Gil, "Sentido y destino de la Revolución Mexicana," in *México: Cincuenta años de Revolución*, vol. III, *La política* (Mexico: Fondo de Cultura Económica, 1961), p. 480.

[21] See also Frank Tannenbaum, *Mexico: The Struggle for Peace and Bread* (New York: Alfred A. Knopf, 1964), pp. 54 and 69-71.

[22] See, for example, Roger D. Hansen, *The Politics of Mexican Development* (Baltimore: Johns Hopkins University Press, 1971), pp. 8-9 and ch. 6.

Whatever the validity of this assertion, it would be excessively simple-minded to assume that all elite transformations are due to political factors. As Karl Marx argued so powerfully, and others have since maintained, alterations in leadership can also result from the changing balance of socioeconomic forces. For Marx, the ruling class consisted of those who controlled the means of production and who consolidated their hegemony through political means. A change in the modes of production necessarily entailed a change in social structure and the conditions of class struggle, and this, in turn, necessarily entailed a change in elite role or composition.[23] Donald Matthews and Robert Putnam have observed that, for a variety of reasons, there might be substantial lags in time between economic change and transformation in the social background of elites,[24] and Nicos Poulantzas has pointed out that the changing *role* of elites might not require a change in social origins of membership.[25] But even then, the similarities and differences in social background and position of the economic and political elites provide important indications about the character and operation of the system, and it is abundantly clear that these relationships can hinge upon the processes of economic change.

Despite its logic and clarity, this view has not found easy application in the Mexican context. As a reflection of the problem, Juan Felipe Leal has offered a richly provocative interpretation of the Mexican state. The original leadership of the Revolution came, he says, not so much from peasants as from a lower-middle rural class ("small farmers [*rancheros*], small businessmen, country school teachers, and others from the middle strata") and from a provincial intelligentsia. These two groupings came together in an uneasy coalition that yielded, in time, a new political force, a military and political bureaucracy "whose plan of action pointed towards the implementation of reforms within the framework of capitalism, and not outside of it. As a result," Leal continues,

the Revolution established itself as a great social upheaval, capable of carrying out important changes in the then-prevailing relationships, institutions, and structures, but never suggesting or implying

[23] On Marx see Bottomore, *Elites*, pp. 24-32.
[24] Donald R. Matthews, *The Social Background of Political Decision-Makers* (New York: Random House, 1954), pp. 42-45; Putnam, *Comparative Study*, pp. 179-183.
[25] Nicos Poulantzas, *Political Power and Social Classes*, trans. Timothy O'Hagan (London: NLB and Sheed and Ward, 1973), esp. pp. 332 and 335. See also Poulantzas, "The Problem of the Capitalist State," *New Left Review* 58 (November-December 1969): 67-78, esp. 72-74; and Ralph Miliband, "Poulantzas and the Capitalist State," *New Left Review* 82 (November-December 1973): 83-92.

the dominance of proletariat over the bourgeoisie. More precisely, the change amounted to the establishment of a new form of capitalistic state, with the reorganization of the bloc in power, under the hegemony of the bureaucracy which emerged from the Revolution, and with the redefinition of the existing relationships between the bloc in power and the mass of the oppressed classes.[26]

Thus the Revolution has never been "betrayed," as critics of the contemporary regime have frequently charged.[27] The slowness and incompleteness of social reform are, instead, entirely compatible with the bourgeois thrust of the movement itself.

One difficulty with this view, especially in relation to Mexico, is that it lacks an empirical foundation. Leal, through no fault of his own, is unable to provide much solid information on the social origin or the functional role of revolutionary leadership or the governmental bureaucracy. Have political leaders come from the same background as the economic elites? Is the state in any way separate from the bourgeoisie, though perhaps in alliance with it? Is there, as some scholars have recently maintained, an identifiable and autonomous "state interest"?[28] Or is the political apparatus run directly by the bourgeoisie?

Observed in a somewhat different light, economic development can also affect the composition of elites by creating demands for special skills. As these needs gain recognition, those who can perform these functions move into ascendancy.[29] In reference to Mexico, this argument is commonly invoked to explain the rise of *técnicos*, or economic technicians, as distinct from *políticos*. Raymond Vernon has spelled out the proposition in detail:

In the development of nations, the economic technician is rapidly coming to be thought of as the indispensable man. By general agree-

[26] Juan Felipe Leal, "The Mexican State: 1915-1973, A Historical Interpretation," *Latin American Perspectives* 2, no. 2 (Summer 1975): 48-63, with quotations on 49-50, though I have altered the translation in places. For the Spanish original see Leal, "El Estado mexicano: 1915-1973 (Una interpretación histórica)," paper presented at the Primer Encuentro Latinoamericano de Historiadores (Universidad Nacional Autónoma de México, Centro de Estudios Latinoamericanos, 1973).

[27] Stanley R. Ross, ed., *Is the Mexican Revolution Dead?* (New York: Alfred A. Knopf, 1967).

[28] See, particularly, John F. H. Purcell and Susan Kaufman Purcell, "Mexican Business and Public Policy," in *Authoritarianism and Corporatism in Latin America*, ed. James Malloy (Pittsburgh: University of Pittsburgh Press, 1977), pp. 191-226; and Douglas Bennett and Kenneth Sharpe, "The State in Late Dependent Industrialization: The Control of Multinational Corporations in Mexico," paper presented at the annual meeting of the American Political Science Association, Chicago, 1976.

[29] Suzanne I. Keller, *Beyond the Ruling Class: Strategic Elites in Modern Society* (New York: Random House, 1963); and Putnam, *Comparative Study*, pp. 169-170.

ment, such subjects as exchange-rate policy, fiscal and monetary policy, investment and saving policy, and similar esoteric matters can no longer be left entirely to the rough-and-ready ministrations of the politician. For one thing, the economic techniques have grown so complex that they are beyond the easy understanding of the amateurs; for another, the increasing flow of communications between nations and with international agencies on these subjects has demanded that every country develop a class of responsible officials which is capable of holding up its end in the interchange. In Mexico the economic technician has become an integral element in the decision-making process on issues affecting Mexico's development.[30]

Empirically, it is not always easy to know a *técnico* when you see one,[31] but the causal proposition stands: the influx of technocrats has resulted from the functional requirements of economic change, not from the course of political events.

In sum, classical elite theory has multitudinous weaknesses. Quite unnecessarily, it imbues elites with a self-conscious cohesiveness that might or might not exist. Either benignly or maliciously, it endows elites with allegedly superior qualities, a position that now seems at best naive. Somewhat shortsightedly, it gives elites an autonomy that appears to ignore the roles of common people. Partly for this reason, it offers relatively little insight into the causes and dynamics of elite transformation. Aside from these conceptual and methodological issues, elite theory also has an ideological burden to bear. Anti-Marxist in inception, it came to furnish the intellectual cornerstone of conservative, not to say reactionary, European political thought. Construing minority rule as inevitable, no matter what the system, elite theorists came to evaluate concentrations of power with admixtures of approval, resignation, and despair. Michels was not the only one who followed Mussolini.

What I take from elite theory is not its unnecessary trappings, and certainly not its ideological propensities, but simply its most elementary insight: that power is distributed unequally, that those who possess it can be identified as an elite, and that the characteristics of the elite offer considerable insight into the operation of society. Specifi-

---

[30] Raymond Vernon, *The Dilemma of Mexico's Development: The Roles of the Private and Public Sectors* (Cambridge: Harvard University Press, 1963), p. 136.

[31] Presumably, *técnicos* are defined by their education, expertise, attitudes, and behavior. In one effort to analyze individuals, Roderic Ai Camp has had to include career patterns as one of the identifying criteria, thus running a risk of circularity. Camp, "The Cabinet and the *Técnico* in Mexico and the United States," *Journal of Comparative Administration* 3, no. 2 (August 1971): 190.

cally, I intend to concentrate my efforts on the transformation of political elites in Mexico, and to this end I shall borrow, in part, from Pareto's notion of elite circulation, but without his stress on cycles or on personality types. I shall attempt to go beyond such internal explanations and examine the external relationships between elite changes, political factors, and economic factors. On a conceptual level, elite composition will here be taken as the dependent variable, and political and economic factors will be considered as different clusters of independent variables. It will not be possible to measure these relationships with any precision, given the paucity of longitudinal data, and I will base most inferences of this kind upon patterns of chronological sequence. Even so, this methodological problem does not diminish the intrinsic value of the enterprise.[32]

Moving beyond the limits of classical theory, I also attempt to speculate, at least in a tentative way, about the possible connections between elite composition and attitudes and behavior. As has been frequently observed, most traditional elite analysis stops short of this question, perhaps because of the premise about elite autonomy: the emphasis has been on who the leaders *are*, not on what they *do*. After all, the essence of politics is action; it lies in decisionmaking, in the formulation and execution of policy, and not in social origin. Who cares who governs?

There are good reasons to care. In the first place, it seems to me that social background is bound to shape, in some important way, the general outlooks of elites (and others)—that is, their fundamental cognitive and normative orientations, as distinct from their preferences on particular policy issues.[33] People from an identifiable social class, for instance, are conditioned by that common experience, and they are inclined to share a set of common assumptions. Other things being equal

[32] For an empirical, cross-national study of some of the determinants of elite composition see William B. Quandt, *The Comparative Study of Political Elites*, Sage Professional Papers in Comparative Politics 01-004 (Beverly Hills, California: Sage Publications, 1970).

[33] See Putnam, *Comparative Study*, pp. 93-94. Empirical studies which have found relatively weak or inconsistent associations between social origins and policy preferences include Lewis J. Edinger and Donald D. Searing, "Social Background in Elite Analysis: A Methodological Inquiry," *American Political Science Reivew* 61, no. 2 (June 1967): 428-445; Allen H. Barton, "Determinants of Leadership Attitudes in a Socialist Society," in *Opinion-Making Elites in Yugoslavia*, ed. Allen H. Barton, Bogdan Denitch, and Charles Kadushin (New York: Praeger, 1973), pp. 220-262; R. Wayne Parsons and Allen H. Barton, "Social Background and Policy Attitudes of American Leaders," paper presented at the annual meeting of the American Political Science Association, Chicago, 1974; and Uwe Schleth, "Once Again: Does It Pay to Study Social Background in Elite Analysis?" in *Sozialwissenschaftliches Jahrbuch für Politik*, ed. Rudolf Wildenmann (Munich: Gunter Olzog Verlag, 1971), pp. 99-118.

(as they rarely are), these assumptions would in turn determine attitudes and hence affect behavior. There are numerous exceptions to this rule—Fidel Castro comes quickly to mind—but that is beside the point. I am merely arguing that, in the most general way, people are more likely to think and act in accordance with class-derived perspectives than against them, and that, *ceteris paribus*, they are unlikely to destroy the class from which they come.

But people also undergo a constant learning process, a never-ending experience of what has come to be known as "socialization." Obviously enough, men and women *acquire* ideas and beliefs, rather than transport them intact from cradle to grave. This explains the focus, in much political analysis, on the socializing roles of institutions and activities, particularly schools and occupations. And I, for one, choose to place strong emphasis on the political system itself. In systems that are highly institutionalized, with rigorous prescriptions for behavior, politicians tend to comply with the rules, regardless of their social background, and more often than not they internalize them too. In systems that are less institutionalized, without such clear-cut norms, leaders may continue to hold their own predispositions and even act upon them. In the contemporary world, indeed, there is some empirical evidence for the notion that social background has more bearing on elite attitudes in the less developed countries than in the more developed ones.[34] In reference to Mexico, I would phrase the hypothesis in longitudinal terms: in periods of greater institutionalization, social background may have less impact on attitudes or behavior than in periods of lesser institutionalization.

Finally, the selection of political leadership is a decisionmaking process, and, in principle, a study of this procedure can capture just as much of the essence of politics as can the study of a bill, decree, or constitutional amendment. To be sure, I do not concentrate in any detail on the socioeconomic policies of Mexican leaders; I merely speculate, and intermittently at that, about the relationship between broad policy outlines and elite composition. Notwithstanding this limitation, and for reasons that should become clear, I believe that the mechanisms of elite recruitment and selection provide especially good material for the analysis and understanding of the Mexican system.[35]

[34] The proposition is from Quandt, *Comparative Study*, pp. 197-198. For supporting evidence see Donald D. Searing, "The Comparative Study of Elite Socialization," *Comparative Political Studies* 1, no. 4 (January 1969): 471-500; and Stanley A. Kochanek, "The Relation between Social Background and Attitudes of Indian Legislators," *Journal of Commonwealth Political Studies* 6, no. 1 (March 1968): 34-53.

[35] Recruitment and selection are usually viewed as distinct phenomena; note that, in the subtitle of this book, I have used the word "recruitment" in the broadest possible sense of the term.

APPROACHING THE DATA

In the effort to uncover trends and regularities in elite recruitment, I have adopted a relentlessly empirical approach. After considering various alternatives, and consulting extensively with colleagues in Mexico, I decided to define the twentieth-century political elite operationally for the bulk of this study as those people who held major national office at any time between 1900 and 1971 (when the first phase of data-gathering came to an end): presidents, vice-presidents (when relevant), cabinet ministers, subcabinet officials, heads of large decentralized agencies and state-supported companies, leaders of the government party, governors, senators, deputies, ambassadors, and delegates at two special congresses—the Sovereign Revolutionary Convention of 1914-15 and the Constitutional Congress of 1916-17—for a grand total of 6,302 individuals. A second phase of research concentrated on the period from 1971 through 1976, and these results are reported separately, in Chapter 10. By taking such a large number of people into account I have sought to move beyond the facile generalities and incidental anecdotes that surround the subject and, through the use of quantitative methods (plus the aid of a computer), to uncover recurrent patterns and regularities. Moreover I have attempted to indicate not only *whether* particular phenomena have existed, but also to pinpoint matters of *degree*: how many, how much, how often, how long. It has thus been my goal to introduce a new level of precision into the discussions of elite formation in twentieth-century Mexico.[36]

[36] The most extensive studies to date have come from Roderic Ai Camp, who has compiled an impressive compendium, *Mexican Political Biographies, 1935-1975* (Tucson: University of Arizona Press, 1976), and written a monograph, *The Education of Mexico's Revolutionary Family* (forthcoming), that analyzes the relationship between educational background and political attainment in the post-1935 period. He has also produced a series of articles on selected specific topics, such as "The Cabinet and the *Técnico* in Mexico and the United States," *Journal of Comparative Administration* 3, no. 2, pp. 188-214; "Education and Political Recruitment in Mexico: The Alemán Generation," *Journal of Interamerican Studies and World Affairs* 18, no. 3 (August 1976): 295-321; "Losers in Mexican Politics: A Comparative Study of Official Party Precandidates for Gubernatorial Elections, 1970-75," in *Quantitative Latin American Studies: Methods and Findings*, ed. James W. Wilkie and Kenneth Ruddle, Supplement 6 (1977) of *Statistical Abstract of Latin America* (Los Angeles: UCLA Latin American Center, 1977), pp. 23-34; "Mexican Governors since Cárdenas: Education and Career Contacts," *Journal of Interamerican Studies and World Affairs* 16, no. 4 (November 1974): 454-481; "The Middle-Level Technocrat in Mexico," *Journal of Developing Areas* 6, no. 4 (July 1972): 571-581; "The National School of Economics and Public Life in Mexico," *Latin American Research Review* 10, no. 3 (Fall 1975): 137-151; "A Re-examination of Political Leadership and the Allocation of Federal Revenues in Mexico," *Journal of Developing Areas* 10, no. 2 (January 1976): 193-212; "El sistema mexicano y las decisiones sobre el personal político," *Foro Internacional* 27, no. 1 (July-September

As a result of the definitional criteria, the research has provided virtually complete information on continuity, turnover, and career patterns among the offices at the national level. To identify people for inclusion in the elite, I have taken down the names of all individuals who, according to official records and newspaper reports, have occupied any of the specified offices at all discernible points in time between 1900 and 1971—and, eventually, on up through 1976. Collating the materials in alphabetical order and matching the records have, in effect, made it possible to reconstruct every individual's career within this pool of offices. The technique is naturally subject to human error, and also demands a bit of guesswork (is R. Gómez at one time and place the same as Ramón Gómez at another time or place?), but because of consistent corroboration from other sources I believe that the record-linkage reached a very high degree of accuracy, in the range of 95 percent or more.

Having selected the members of the elite, I then set out in search of biographical information. My assistants and I consulted several kinds of sources:

    a. biographical dictionaries, of varied type and quality, a total of 60 in all;

1976): 51-83; and "Women and Political Leadership in Mexico: A Comparative Study of Female and Male Political Elites" (unpublished).

Additional works on Mexican elites include two theses presented at UNAM: a remarkable, ambitious, but incomplete and partly flawed analysis by Gustavo Abel Hernández Enríquez, "La movilidad política en México, 1876-1970" (Ciencias Políticas y Administración Pública, UNAM, 1968), and the more narrow study by Eduardo Guerrero del Castillo, "El reclutamiento y la selección del personal en la administración pública mexicana" (Ciencias Políticas y Sociales, UNAM, 1963). Another UNAM researcher, Armando Rendón Corona, has recently produced a monograph, "Los profesionales de la política en México 1940-1970" (mimeo, Instituto de Investigaciones Sociales, UNAM, 1976[?]), concentrating mainly on patterns of continuity and turnover. Other studies include the following: James D. Cochrane, "Mexico's New *Científicos*: The Díaz Ordaz Cabinet," *Inter-American Economic Affairs* 21, no. 1 (Summer 1967): 61-72; Merilee Grindle, "Patrons and Clients in the Bureaucracy: Career Networks in Mexico," *Latin American Research Review* 12, no. 1 (1977): 37-66; Wilfred Gruber, "Career Patterns of Mexico's Political Elites," *Western Political Quarterly* 24, no. 3 (September 1971): 467-482; William P. Tucker, "Las élites mexicanas," *Aportes*, no. 13 (July 1969): 103-106; and William S. Tuohy, "Centralism and Political Elite Behavior in Mexico," in *Development Administration in Latin America*, ed. Clarence E. Thurber and Lawrence S. Graham (Durham, N.C.: Duke University Press, 1973), pp. 260-280.

Most of these works tend to concentrate on relatively recent phenomena, and—with the conspicuous example of the Hernández thesis, plus some of Camp's writings—they tend to concentrate on single points in time (or, as Camp usually does, they collapse their data to form a single chronological unit). Consequently, despite their many virtues, these studies can offer little or no insight into processes of historical change or elite transformation.

b. newspaper and magazine articles, reports, and obituaries;

c. official documents and registers;

d. books, autobiographical and otherwise;

e. official and semiofficial archives;

f. a mail survey, sent out to approximately 300 officeholders in mid-1970 (about 80 answers were received).

(For a full discussion see Bibliography and Sources, particularly Section A.) As a result of these efforts, the dataset contains personal biographical information—such as date or place of birth, education, primary occupation—on approximately 3,000 individuals, depending upon the variable concerned. Obviously, and sadly, the data are far from complete.

Despite these limitations the material can yield some rather precise quantitative statements about the composition of political leadership in twentieth-century Mexico: that X percent came from urban communities, that Y percent attended a university, that Z percent were lawyers. But assertions of this kind, in and of themselves, have absolutely no meaning at all. They are purely descriptive. In order to acquire analytical significance, they must be placed within some kind of comparative context. Only then will it be possible to determine whether a given number is high or low—that is, in relation to some kind of standard—and to interpret the results accordingly. During the course of this study I shall employ five different kinds of comparative techniques.

First, and perhaps foremost, I shall make *longitudinal* comparisons, in search of trends and changes within the Mexican elite over time. One obvious strategy here is to categorize officeholders according to presidential regime and look for differences between regimes. The presidency itself has been a constant driving force in Mexican politics, each president has impressed something of his own personality upon his administration, and the presidential regime clearly emerges as an appropriate unit for chronological analysis. As classified for this study, regimes have varied in duration (from several months to six years) and in size of membership (from 56 to 731, usually ranging from 300 to 600), and these differences can affect the comparability of results. Partly for this reason, and also because of my understanding of prevailing political realities, I have grouped some presidential administrations together—as in the era of the ill-fated Convention (1914-15) and the period when Plutarco Elías Calles exercised de facto power as the *Jefe Máximo de la Revolución*, the so-called *Maximato* (1928-34). Incumbents have been identified with the regime *during* which they took office, even if their tenure stretched beyond the end of the regime itself, as has often been the case for state governors. Those with temporary, provisional, or interim status have also been included, no matter how long or short their stay in office.[37]

To complement the regime-by-regime approach I have also created, for analytical purposes, three separate officeholding cohorts. Individuals in the late Díaz regimes, from 1900 to 1911, have been grouped together in a so-called "prerevolutionary" cohort (N = 610); those who held office between 1917 and 1940 constitute a "revolutionary" cohort (N = 2,289); and those who made any appearance between 1946 and 1971 comprise a "postrevolutionary" cohort (N = 2,008). The cohort analysis is of course less sensitive to short-run changes, and to the timing of such changes, than is the regime-by-regime approach. On the other hand, it cuts the elite into fairly sizable populations and yields correspondingly firm and reliable results. Because of its special characteristics, and because of its importance to this study, I shall give an extended explanation of the cohorts in a later section of this chapter.

A second set of comparisons focuses upon elites in varying *levels of office*. In both the cohort analysis and the regime-by-regime approach, I shall concentrate on men in "upper-level" positions—presidents, vice-presidents, cabinet ministers, heads of the government party, and directors of major state-supported companies and agencies.[38] As officeholders on the topmost level, these were people designated directly by the president (or by the functional leadership of the ruling coalition), and they provide a relatively clear indication of the special attributes and underlying tendencies of each presidential regime. Upper-level offices are exclusively appointive, not subject to quotas for regional representation (as is the legislature), so the composition of the group is virtually unaffected by constitutional requirement.[39] Finally, data on top elites have proved to be much more available than for the total elites.[40] Admittedly the number of upper-level individuals in any single presidential regime tends to be rather small, ranging from 15 to 66, and the computation of proportions and percentages becomes a risky enterprise. Partly for this reason I shall also deal with top elites by cohort as well as by regime: between 1900 and 1911 there were 30

[37] Alternate deputies and senators (*suplentes*) have been included only if they actually took seats in the legislature.

[38] As explained in Appendix A, these are positions with scale values of 7 or 8 for the HIGHEST OFFICE variable (see especially Table A-3).

[39] With the exception of the office of Attorney General, which must be held by a qualified lawyer.

[40] See Figure A-1 and the surrounding discussion in Appendix A.

upper-level officeholders, between 1917 and 1940 there were 185, and from 1946 to 1871 there were 159.

Contrasts and similarities between the total elites and the upper-level elites yield some provocative suggestions, and in Chapter 4 I make a systematic search for differences in elite composition according to level of office attained (as measured on an eight-point scale), by cohort.[41] The question underlying this part of the analysis is: have individuals possessing certain social characteristics (such as a university education) tended to get higher on the political ladder than other individuals, and if so, to what extent?

Third, I shall draw comparisons between elites with differing *spheres of influence*. My own research has concentrated largely on those people who are believed to have exercised power, in one way or another, within the political domain. But what about those who have economic power? Are they the same individuals? If not, are they at least from the same social origin? Such questions receive explicit treatment in Chapter 7.

Fourth, I shall make comparisons between the characteristics of Mexican political elites and the *national population at large*. The purpose here is to identify the social attributes which give individuals advantages (and disadvantages) in the quest for political office. Since the incidence of characteristics in the general populace can be interpreted as the distribution that would be statistically "expected" among political elites, were leaders drawn *at random* from the constituent public, this method furnishes a means of assessing the degree—as well as the direction—of social bias in the recruitment processes.[42] Ideally, I would prefer to compare elite characteristics with those of the literate adult male (LAM) population, rather than the entire population, since it is the LAM stratum that has historically contained most serious aspirants to power: illiterates have been marginal to the system, children have been too young, and women—unfortunately—have held very few political offices. Because of vagaries in Mexican census reports, though, I have been able to isolate the LAM population with consistency only for 1960; for other periods I have made estimates where necessary.[43]

41 See Table A-3 in Appendix A.

42 I am *not* assuming that, in order to be democratic or genuinely representative, the social characteristics of political elites should mirror the population at large. I am seeking, instead, to determine the form and extent of social bias.

43 Note that the purpose of isolating the LAM population is analogous to Robert E. Scott's reason for estimating the proportional size of the "participant" culture in Mexican society, which he gives as 1 to 2 percent of the national total in 1910 and around 10 percent in 1960. The "subject" culture might also be included in the pool of possible aspirants to office; by Scott's guess, it amounted to 8 or 9 percent of the 1910 population and 65 percent of the 1960 population. Scott, "Mex-

Fifth, and finally, I attempt to make some *cross-national* comparisons. Insofar as possible, I have selected other countries according to type of political system, in order to ascertain concomitant patterns of variation. The United States, for instance, provides a (woefully imperfect) example of a democratic polity, at least in a Schumpeterian sense; the Soviet Union furnishes an (equally imperfect) case of totalitarianism; Franco's Spain and Ataturk's Turkey, among other polities, offer additional illustrations of authoritarianism. Needless to say, it is extremely difficult to draw these comparisons in a rigorous way: the roles of institutions vary so much across both time and space that one wonders what (or who) should be compared to what (or whom).[44] Moreover I have had no choice but to rely on secondary literature for the comparative data. Consequently the cross-national findings are more suggestive than definitive, and I have by no means exhausted the possibilities in this regard. Even so, I hope to have accomplished my basic objective: establishing, where plausible, some sort of international benchmark for evaluating tendencies in Mexico's political elite.

DEFINING POLITICAL COHORTS

As stated above, much of the longitudinal analysis of change over time relies on comparisons between three political cohorts. In contrast to the most common procedure, which identifies cohorts according to dates of birth, I have defined these cohorts according to *time of holding office on the national level*.[45] To repeat, the first cohort consists of people holding office between 1900 and 1911 (N = 610); the second includes officeholders between 1917 and 1940 (N = 2,289); and the third contains those in national office at any time between 1946 and 1971 (N = 2,008). Time constraints prevented me from including officeholders between 1971 and 1976 in the computerized dataset; otherwise, they would have belonged to the third cohort. Also, to minimize overlap between the cohorts, I have purposely deleted two other his-

---

ico: The Established Revolution," in *Political Culture and Political Development*, ed. Lucian W. Pye and Sidney Verba (Princeton: Princeton University Press, 1965), pp. 335 and 345.

[44] On these points see Dankwart A. Rustow, "The Study of Elites: Who's Who, When, and How," *World Politics* 18, no. 4 (July 1966): 690-717; and John A. Armstrong, *The European Administrative Elite* (Princeton: Princeton University Press, 1972), ch. 2.

[45] Norman Ryder, "The Cohort as a Concept in the Study of Social Change," *American Sociological Review* 30, no. 6 (December 1965): 843-861; and Alan B. Spitzer, "The Historical Problem of Generations," *American Historical Review* 78, no. 5 (December 1973): 1353-1385.

torical periods: (a) the years of violence and disorder, from 1911 to 1917, when multitudinous factions were competing for supremacy, moving in and out of power; and (b) 1940-46, when Manuel Ávila Camacho presided over an era of transition, with many holdovers from the 1917-40 group still clinging to some office and future leaders of the 1946-71 cohort already on the way up.[46]

There are three sets of criteria behind this categorization. *First,* the political tasks confronting these cohorts were fundamentally different. The 1900-1911 group witnessed, and took part in, the decline of Porfirio Díaz's decades-long dictatorship. The 1917-40 elite assumed responsibility for creating a viable political system in the wake of violent revolution. The third group, from 1946 onward, had to manage and consolidate the system. *Second,* the cohorts governed during different phases of Mexico's economic development. The Díaz group presided over the last years of extensive, outward growth; the 1917-40 group held sway during an era of slow growth; and the 1946-71 elite presided, proudly, over a period of unprecedented industrial and economic development.

One assumption underlying my scheme is that each set of political and economic tasks bound members of these officeholding cohorts together, at least more so than the accident of birth. The question is whether these tasks brought different types of leaders to the fore. In this connection John Kautsky has offered a suggestive distinction between "revolutionary" and "managerial" elites, hypothesizing a transition from the former to the latter over time. I am more inclined to think of revolutionary and managerial *roles* than of elites, given the near-impossibility of classifying individuals with precision, but the analytical point still holds.[47]

The *third* criterion, an accompanying characteristic rather than a defining one, but nonetheless of great importance, refers to historical experience. To a substantial extent these differing political cohorts represent distinct biological cohorts as well. Figure 1-1 illustrates the point by plotting the proportional distribution of known birthdates, by decade, for the three groups. (The relatively small numbers of ob-

[46] As a consequence of these deletions, there is very little overlap between the cohorts. Only 13 of the 610 members of the 1900-1911 group found their way into the 1917-40 elite; as expected, none showed up in 1946-71. A fairly large absolute number (157) of the 2,289 individuals in the 1917-40 group turned up among the 2,008 officeholders in the post-1946 years, but this figure still amounts to less than 8 percent of the total membership in either cohort.

[47] John H. Kautsky, "Revolutionary and Modernizing Elites in Modernizing Regimes," *Comparative Politics* 1, no. 4 (July 1969): 441-467; and Kautsky, "Patterns of Elite Succession in the Process of Development," *Journal of Politics* 31, no. 2 (May 1969): 359-396.

Figure 1-1: Distribution of Dates of Birth for Officeholding Cohorts, by Decade

Prerevolutionary Cohort, 1900-11 (N=177)

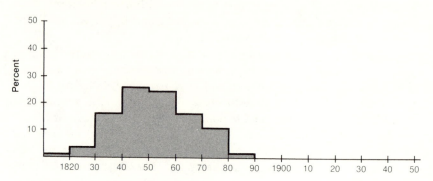

Revolutionary Cohort, 1917-40 (N=626)

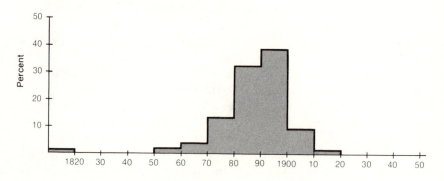

Postrevolutionary Cohort, 1946-71 (N=1,222)

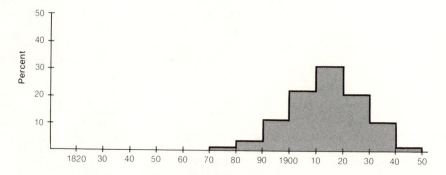

servations, or Ns, aptly illustrate the frequency of missing data.) Members of the 1900-1911 cohort were children of the mid-nineteenth century. Over 80 percent were born in the years between 1830 and 1860, and practically 50 percent were born in the 1840s and 1850s—which means that they reached their majority (and probably developed their political interests) in the 1860s and 1870s, the turbulent era of French intervention, socioeconomic reform, and Díaz's own rise to power. The 1917-40 cohort was an end-of-century group, 70 percent being born in the twenty-year span between 1880 and 1899, thus suggesting that the revolutionary movement had some generational overtones, a possibility to be explored in more detail below. Significantly, members of this elite would have reached adulthood during the revolution itself; to understate the point, this was their decisive common experience. The 1946-71 cohort, by contrast, consists mainly of twentieth-century children. About 70 percent were born between 1900 and 1929, and they and their younger colleagues therefore came into their majority after the conclusion of the Revolution, just around the time that the contemporary authoritarian regime was establishing control of Mexico.

These generational patterns clearly imply variations in political experience, and, specifically, varying relationships to the Revolution. This assumption finds strong support in the data, imperfect though they are, in Table 1-1. Only a handful of the Díaz group, about 3.8 percent in all, is believed to have actively supported any of the revolutionary movements.[48] An overwhelming proportion of the 1917-40 cohort is thought to have participated in the Revolution, more often than not as soldiers (315 are known to have performed military roles; 55 are known to have performed exclusively civilian functions). The third cohort, on the other hand, contains a much smaller share of revolutionary activists, perhaps 11 percent or so. Most of the rest were too young to take part.

Thus, the officeholding cohorts used for analytical purposes in parts of this study reveal sharp differences in composition, birthdates, and political experience. It is in these senses that the 1900-1911 group constitutes what I consider to be a "prerevolutionary" elite. The second cohort, officeholders between 1917 and 1940, will be referred to as the "revolutionary" elite. And the latest group, ascendant from 1946 to 1971, comprises a "postrevolutionary" group. The labels are partly mnemonic devices, a literary shorthand for referring to the separate cohorts; but as I have tried to show, the labels also have a factual and substantive foundation.

[48] Apart from the counterrevolutionary Huerta regime of 1913-14.

TABLE 1-1

Activity during the Revolution, by Cohort

Activity	% among Cohort 1 (N = 610)	% among Cohort 2 (N = 2,289)	% among Cohort 3 (N = 2,008)
Bore arms on side of a revolutionary faction	1.5	13.8	3.6
Performed civilian role on side of a revolutionary faction	0.5	2.4	0.5
Revolutionary activity presumed, but nature unknown	1.8	25.2	7.4
Held office before 1911, presumed to have opposed the Revolution	91.0	0.0	0.0
Born after 1905, presumed to have been too young	0.0	0.7	42.7
Unknown	5.2	58.0	45.7
Totals[a]	100.0	100.1	99.9

[a] May not add up to 100 because of rounding.

It is important to realize that the "revolutionary" cohort (1917-40) does not come even close to providing a random sample of leading participants in the Mexican Revolution as a whole. Because of its stress on officeholding after 1917, it by definition tends to overemphasize the triumphant faction in the struggle for supremacy—that is, the *carrancista* movement. Among the cohort members whose participation in the Revolution is fairly well known, only a handful—less than 10 percent—had ever joined forces with Carranza's major rivals, Pancho Villa or Emiliano Zapata. Hardly any had followed the Flores Magón brothers or Pascual Orozco. Not unexpectedly, quite a few (at least half) claimed to have supported the initial uprising under Madero. But by far the largest share, about 66 percent in all, could be classified as members of the *carrancista* wing. As befits a study of political elites, perhaps, the 1917-40 cohort consists primarily of those who won the Revolution. The subsequent elite inherited that legacy.

In summary, at different points in this study I attempt to locate changes and trends within Mexico's political elite by tracing differences between individual presidential regimes, by drawing comparisons between officeholding cohorts, and by concentrating my attention on upper-level elites as well as on total elites. To clarify the relationships between these strategies, Table 1-2 lists the relevant presidential regimes and gives the size of their total elites and their upper-level elites. On the right-hand side, it presents the chronological location and the size of the three officeholding cohorts, also divided into total and upper-level groups. As the ensuing analysis wears on, it might prove useful to refer back to this table from time to time.

ORGANIZING THE ANALYSIS

Given these various orientations and approaches, the organization of the study bears straightforward correspondence to its purpose. Part I furnishes an introduction, in this chapter by defining the central questions of concern and in Chapter 2 by tracing salient economic, social, and political aspects of Mexico's recent history. Working with the data on leadership from 1900 to 1971, the various sections of Part II focus on component portions of a basic theme: the impact of the Revolution. Chapter 3 examines changes in the social composition of national officeholders and attempts to determine the relative exclusiveness (or openness) of the recruitment process. Chapter 4 raises a corollary question: among those who have gained entrance into the national elite, what have been the social correlates of success within the elite? Have individuals from certain kinds of backgrounds tended to get higher on the political ladder than others, and has this relationship changed over time? Instead of treating political attainment as a function of social background, Chapter 5 explores some hypothetical linkages between institutional offices; according to this perspective, the attainment of a given office might have more to do with the nature of one's previous office than with social-background attributes. Chapter 6 then turns from the shape of political careers to their duration, analyzing rates of continuity and turnover within the national political elite in order to assess the practical implications of the country's renowned "no-reelection" rule. Chapter 6 also brings Part II to a close with a recapitulation of my findings on the "results" of the Revolution.

Part III proceeds to investigate selected aspects of the stable, civilian-dominated authoritarian regime that Mexico had created by 1946. Chapter 7 attempts to explore relationships and interconnections between the country's political and economic elites. Chapter 8 examines the role and composition of a middle-level institution, the national Chamber of Deputies, and of the congressional delegations from the component "sectors" of the governing party, the Partido Revolu-

TABLE 1-2

Regimes, Elites, and Cohorts, 1900-1971

President[a]	Dates	N in total elite	N in upper-level elite	
Porfirio Díaz	1900-1904	393	15	⎤ Prerevolutionary cohort, 1900-1911
Porfirio Díaz	1904-10	438	19	(N in total elite = 610;
Porfirio Díaz	1910-11	317	18	N in upper-level = 30)
Francisco de la Barra	1911	63	16	
Francisco I. Madero	1911-13	376	23	
Victoriano Huerta[b]	1913-14	365	42	
Convention[b]	1914-15	506	45	
Venustiano Carranza as First Chief	1915-17	285	23	⎦
Venustiano Carranza as President	1917-20	583	36	⎤ Revolutionary cohort, 1917-40
Adolfo de la Huerta	1920	56	18	(N in total elite = 2,289;
Álvaro Obregón	1920-24	627	30	N in upper-level = 185)
Plutarco Elías Calles	1924-28	582	30	
Maximato[c]	1928-34	731	66	
Lázaro Cárdenas	1934-40	560	57	⎦
Manuel Ávila Camacho	1940-46	494	43	⎤ Postrevolutionary cohort, 1946-71
Miguel Alemán	1946-52	479	44	(N in total elite = 2,008;
Adolfo Ruiz Cortines	1952-58	496	39	N in upper-level = 159)
Adolfo López Mateos	1958-64	514	40	
Gustavo Díaz Ordaz	1964-70	627	43	
Luis Echeverría[d] (as of 1971)	1970-76	377	38	⎦

[a] The 45-minute term of Pedro Lascuráin, in 1913, has been excluded from all calculations.

[b] Includes the regimes of Francisco Carbajal, Eulalio Gutiérrez, Roque González Garza, and Francisco Lagos Cházaro. (Actually Carbajal did not govern during the "Conventionist" era as such, as he presided over the transition of power from Huerta to the revolutionaries; because it is so small and information is so scarce, his elite is included with this group as a matter of practical convenience.)

[c] Includes the regimes of Emilio Portes Gil, Pascual Ortiz Rubio, and Abelardo Rodríguez.

[d] Here and elsewhere it should be understood that the data on the Echeverría elite are necessarily incomplete.

cionario Institucional (PRI). Taking a summary view of the structural characteristics of Mexico's authoritarian regime, Chapter 9 tries to derive and comprehend the operative "rules of the game" for active politicians; the purpose, especially, is to relate these codes of behavior to the structural environment within which officeholders (and office-seekers) operate. Finally, Chapter 10 moves from macroanalysis to microanalysis, analyzing the presidential succession of 1976 as a case study of the political process, attempting to relate the dynamics of these events to the historical and structural patterns revealed in other sections of the book.

In hopes of maximizing the readability of this study, or at least minimizing its unreadability, I have reserved some discussion of methodology for separate appendices. Appendix A describes, in detail, my criteria and procedures for identifying Mexico's political elite. With particular reference to Chapter 6, Appendix B explicates some issues and problems in the measurement of continuity and turnover. And in amplification of Chapter 8, Appendix C presents some data on membership in the 1964-67 national Chamber of Deputies.

There is nothing definitive about this book. There are problems with the data, and there are problems with the methods. Notwithstanding the emphasis on quantification, with its appearance of mathematical precision, there are questions of interpretation: different people can look at the same facts in different ways, and what is a high number for one person is a low number for another. With this study, I hope to contribute to the literature on elite structures in contemporary Mexico in various ways: by fastening upon some difficult conceptual issues, by bringing large masses of data to bear, by maintaining a concern for methodological rigor, by relating structural system characteristics to observable modes of behavior, and, perhaps above all, by dealing with the historical dynamics of elite transformation over a fairly long period of time, rather than presenting a static picture of elite composition at a single point in time. Of course I may well not have reached these goals, and some readers will doubtless disagree with my premises and my conclusions.[49] Here I raise a lot of complicated questions, and, insofar as possible, I also try to answer them. Enlightenment must come from the attempt, if not from the achievement.

[49] Scholars who wish to challenge, amplify, or refine the findings of this study are welcome to use my machine-readable dataset on the 1900-1971 elites, as has John D. Nagle for his book, *System and Succession: The Social Bases of Political Recruitment* (Austin: University of Texas Press, 1977). For further information see Bibliography and Sources, Section A.

· 2 ·

SOCIETY AND POLITICS
IN MEXICO

The greater the rewards of political office, the more intense the struggle for it. Rewards can differ in kind as well as in degree. Where the state plays a commanding role in the society, access to the political elite confers its members with large shares of power—the opportunity to make binding decisions on key issues, not only in the political realm but also regarding the allocation of socioeconomic goods. Where the government is highly esteemed by the citizenry, where the political system is viewed as legitimate, political office provides incumbents with substantial amounts of prestige. According to a wide variety of circumstances, public office can also open doorways to economic gain and personal wealth. These factors can vary, of course, from time to time and place to place. To comprehend the meaning of elite membership in any given situation, therefore, it is necessary to have some idea of what rewards are prevalent, to what degree, and in what combination.

What has been the case in Mexico? What has been the role of the state, and what has determined the importance and desirability of public office? How have the power, prestige, and emoluments of the elite varied over time? As a means of approaching these questions, and of establishing some basic historical background, this chapter traces some key aspects of social, economic, and political trends in Mexico from the mid-nineteenth century to the present.

In relation to the design of this particular study, I shall also be attempting to describe the behavior of the independent variables that might (or might not) have accounted for patterns of elite transformation in twentieth-century Mexico. As hypothesized in Chapter 1, alterations in the elite might have resulted either from socioeconomic changes (such as industrialization, urbanization) or from political ones (such as the Revolution). Obviously enough, we cannot draw any causal inferences without a general notion, at least, of the relevant social, political, and economic processes.

THE *Porfiriato*

Mexico emerged from a decade of physical destruction during the Wars for Independence (1810-21) in a state of disorder and decay.

With unemployment high, capital scarce, industry in ruins, and roads in near-total disrepair, the level of economic integration was exceedingly low. Nor was there a strong political center. Between 1821 and 1860 Mexico had no less than 50 separate governments, for an average duration of less than one year. The standard means of gaining office was the military coup, an instrument employed so ably, and mischievously, by Antonio López de Santa Anna, who occupied the presidency on nine separate occasions between 1832 and 1855. Underlying this appearance of anarchy, however, there was a system—*caudillismo*, or the hegemony of transient "bosses" or *caudillos* whose main purpose was to sack the treasury.[1] *Caudillo* politics was a source of neither power nor prestige, tending to be the preserve of upwardly mobile *mestizos*, often ex-soldiers from the Wars for Independence. Creole landowners, who formed the social elite, remained on their rural haciendas, where they concentrated on protecting and increasing their own holdings.

The loss of dignity, sovereignty, and territory to the United States—first with Texan independence, then with the war of 1846-48—plunged the country into a major political crisis. Despite many points of agreement, "conservatives" mounted a bitter attack on the "liberals" who had controlled most governments since independence. Led by Lucas Alamán, creole conservatives maintained that Mexico had broken with its own past by trying to imitate, of all things, the values of the aggressor from the north. Invoking Hispanic tradition, they went on to advocate the formation of a constitutional monarchy (in the person of a foreign prince), the preservation of aristocratic ideals, and the juridical protection of the military and the Roman Catholic Church.[2] As the lines of cleavage hardened, the liberals responded, in the mid-1850s, with a series of reforms, known as *La Reforma*, designed to strip power from the army and the Church—and with a new constitution as well. In 1858 the conservatives counterattacked, precipitating nearly twenty years of frightful civil war. From 1863 to 1867, in answer to conservative dreams, Maximilian von Hapsburg came from Austria to rule an ill-starred empire. After capturing and executing Maximilian, Benito Juárez, leader of the liberals, ruled until his death in 1872. A few years later one of his former associates seized the reins of power: General Porfirio Díaz.

For the following 35 years, from 1876 to 1911, Díaz proved himself

[1] For a full elaboration of the model see Eric R. Wolf and Edward C. Hansen, "Caudillo Politics: A Structural Analysis," *Comparative Studies in Society and History* 9 (1966-67): 168-179.

[2] See Charles L. Hale, *Mexican Liberalism in the Age of Mora, 1821-1853* (New Haven: Yale University Press, 1968).

to be a master politician. Beginning with a narrow base, consisting at first of his own military cadre, he managed to create a broad and durable coalition. Convinced that political stability was vital for national growth, whatever the price, he combined systematic repression with the conscious cultivation of a selective clientele. Always ready to avoid unnecessary conflict, he allowed regional *caudillos* to fight among themselves and thereby weaken their collective strength. He built up the army and, to maintain order in the countryside, established the formidable *guardias rurales*. Of liberal background, he did not directly favor the Church, but he took no measures against it, allowing his devoutly Catholic second wife to serve as a symbol of reconciliation. In time, Díaz developed a kind of brain trust, composed of positivistically inclined intellectuals known as the *científicos*. Following the formula of *La Reforma* to the letter, if not entirely in spirit, he ruled that the ban on corporate landholdings should apply to Indian villages—thus opening the land to speculators, ranchers, and political favorites—and in 1894 he curried additional favor among landowners by decreeing that unused lands, or *terrenos baldíos*, were available for private exploitation. Díaz sought and found support among a new group, foreign investors, mainly British and American, whose capital would supply the stimulus for economic progress. Characteristically, too, in order to soften antagonism, he never declared himself to be a dictator; he simply had the constitution amended, time and again, so that he could be reelected to the presidency.

Development there was. After initial (and unsuccessful) efforts to construct railroads with public funds, Díaz gave the concessions to foreign entrepreneurs in late 1880. Within four years, the amount of track had grown from 750 miles to 3,600 miles; by 1910 Mexico had about 12,000 miles of track, most of which were taken over by the government-run National Railways in 1907. The volume of foreign trade increased nine times between 1877 and 1910. Aside from silver and gold, Mexico started exporting other minerals (such as copper and zinc), fiber, and pastoral goods, while the United States became the country's leading partner in trade. Industry grew, with notable advances in cotton, iron, cement, and consumer goods. And by 1895, the national government showed a budget surplus, an unthinkable achievement for earlier generations, and the Díaz regime maintained a balanced budget for the remainder of its tenure. As the centennial celebration approached in 1910, Díaz could proudly boast that the positivistic slogan "order and progress" had become reality in Mexico.

But these advances, if that is what they were, came at a tremendous social cost. While the Porfirian circle accumulated wealth and aped the ways of European aristocracy, Mexico's common people, both urban workers and rural *campesinos*, suffered increasing hardship and exploitation. Notwithstanding the growth of the economy, real wages—never high to begin with—underwent a general decline; by one (certainly exaggerated) estimate, they were in 1910 only one-quarter the value of the 1810 levels. While exporters were sending new products abroad, the production of corn—and other staple goods, including beans (*frijoles*), barely kept pace with population growth.[3] Infant mortality was staggering (as of 1900, about 28.5 percent of all baby boys died within the first year of life),[4] and those children who survived were liable to wind up toiling in sweatshops from 6 a.m. to 6 p.m. More than three-quarters of the population was illiterate[5] and, as of 1910, only 24 percent of the elementary school-age population was in school.[6] Opportunities, to put it mildly, were scarce.

Not surprisingly, the Porfirian order faced a series of popular challenges. Not a year went by without a strike, and the rhythm of worker agitation accelerated over time. Between 1906 and 1908, particularly, there were notable outbreaks in the north, where Mexican workers reacted against wage preferences given to North American laborers by the Cananea Copper Company; among the railroad workers; and at the Río Blanco textile mills. As Ramón Ruiz has recently observed, labor resentment was strongest in the most modern areas of the economy, these being the areas most sharply affected by the international financial crisis of 1906-08.[7] In some localities, such as Morelos, peasants bitterly resented the loss of their land for the mechanized production of sugar and other commercial products; in the north, as well, they protested against the usurpation of land for railway construction.[8]

[3] For data on this period see Charles C. Cumberland, *Mexico: The Struggle for Modernity* (New York: Oxford University Press, 1968), ch. 8, "The Age of Porfirio Díaz"; and John H. Coatsworth, "Anotaciones sobre la producción de alimentos durante el porfiriato," *Historia Mexicana* 26, no. 2 (October-December 1976): 167-187.

[4] Eduardo E. Arriaga, *New Life Tables for Latin American Populations in the Nineteenth and Twentieth Centuries* (Berkeley: Institute of International Studies, University of California, 1968), p. 172.

[5] James W. Wilkie, *The Mexican Revolution: Federal Expenditure and Social Change since 1910* (Berkeley and Los Angeles: University of California Press, 1967), p. 208.

[6] Clark C. Gill, *Education in a Changing Mexico* (Washington: U.S. Government Printing Office, 1969), p. 37.

[7] See Ramón Eduardo Ruiz, *Labor and the Ambivalent Revolutionaries: Mexico, 1911-1923* (Baltimore: Johns Hopkins University Press, 1976), esp. pp. 19-23.

[8] John Womack, Jr., *Zapata and the Mexican Revolution* (New York: Alfred A. Knopf, 1969); and John H. Coatsworth, "Railroads, Landholding, and Agrarian Protest in the Early *Porfiriato*," *Hispanic American Historical Review* 54, no. 1 (February 1974): 48-71.

PART I: INTRODUCTION

The Díaz regime, or *Porfiriato*, centralized political power and greatly strengthened the role of the national state.[9] Key decisions came to be made in Mexico City, usually by Díaz himself, rather than by local or regional *caudillos*. Within the upper echelons of Mexican society, political office became the object of envy and prestige, and membership in the ruling elite was a treasured commodity—partly, perhaps largely, because political stability was seen as the necessary precondition for economic and materialistic growth. Near the end of his regime, Díaz himself explained the rationale: "We were harsh. Sometimes we were harsh to the point of cruelty. But it was necessary then to the life and progress of the nation. If there was cruelty, results have justified it. . . . Education and industry have carried on the task begun by the army."[10] Realizing the implications of this dictum, opponents of Díaz also placed a high value on national power, but for different (and diverse) reasons. Pressure was mounting, and as Díaz and his coterie grew older, it seemed like a matter of time.

THE REVOLUTION

When what has come to be known as the Mexican Revolution began, its direction emerged not from the oppressed strata of society, but from its upper reaches. Francisco Madero, the so-called apostle of Mexican democracy, came from one of the country's wealthiest families, with extensive interests in cattle and mining. His grandfather, Evaristo Madero, was governor of Coahuila from 1880 to 1884, and the family maintained a long and close friendship with Díaz's finance minister, José Y. Limantour. Educated in Paris and at the University of California, Madero pioneered in the application of modern agricultural techniques, especially in cotton cultivation. Something of a mystic, he developed a strong belief in the virtues of political democracy, and of the free-enterprise system as well. Dismayed by the excesses and rigidities of the late Díaz regime (and, according to one writer, stunned by the 1906-08 economic crisis),[11] Madero began voicing opposition to the government. In anticipation of the 1910 elections, he began writing a book called *La sucesión presidencial* in 1908. Its purport was plain (Mexico was ready for liberal democracy) and its formula was simple

---

[9] On the role of the state prior to Díaz see Richard N. Sinkin, *The Mexican Reform, 1848-1876: A Study in Nation-Building* (Austin: Institute of Latin American Studies, University of Texas, forthcoming).

[10] From "President Díaz: Hero of the Americas," by James Creelman, *Pearson's Magazine* 19 (March 1908): 231-277.

[11] James D. Cockcroft, *Intellectual Precursors of the Mexican Revolution, 1900-1913* (Austin: University of Texas Press, 1968), pp. 62-63.

(Díaz himself could run for president in 1910, but he should pick his vice-presidential candidate from outside his immediate circle).[12] Hardly a revolutionary document, *La sucesión presidencial* made barely a reference to the socioeconomic problems and inequalities that were simultaneously being documented by such outstanding intellectuals as Andrés Molina Enríquez.[13]

When Díaz failed to heed the message, Madero entered the 1910 campaign as the candidate of the Anti-Reelectionist Party. And when Díaz was declared the winner, Madero—with himself and 5,000 supporters in jail—refused to recognize the outcome and, in his famous *Plan* of San Luis Potosí, called for armed resistance. The movement rapidly swelled, his troops took Ciudad Juárez (across the border from El Paso), and, in a surprising show of weakness, Díaz capitulated and left the country in May 1911. After an interim period, Madero triumphed in a new election, and in 1912, before delirious crowds in Mexico City, he became the nation's president. Democracy, it seemed, was on its way.

The bubble quickly burst. By November 1911, Emiliano Zapata and his followers in Morelos accused Madero of ignoring the need for land reform. "Having no intentions other than to satisfy his personal ambitions, his boundless instincts as a tyrant, and his profound disrespect" for the Constitution of 1857, they said in their *Plan de Ayala*, Madero "did not carry to a happy end the revolution which gloriously he initiated with the help of God and the people." He had failed to dismantle the Porfirian political machine and revealed disinterest in the plight of the people. For the peasantry, the only alternative was direct action: "We give notice [that] . . . the pueblos or citizens who have the titles corresponding to those properties will immediately enter into possession of that real estate of which they have been despoiled by the bad faith of their oppressors, maintaining at any cost with arms in hand the mentioned possession."[14] Based upon the peasantry around Morelos, *zapatismo* was a local movement, and, as John Womack has shown, it sought to restore a vanished order rather than to build a wholly new world. These people wanted to reclaim their land, and when Madero failed to deliver, they promptly broke with him. Thus began a running conflict between the *zapatista* movement and a succession of governments, a conflict that lasted beyond Zapata's own assassination in 1919.

[12] Francisco I. Madero, *La sucesión presidencial en 1910* (Mexico: Ediciones Los Insurgentes, 1960), first published in 1908.
[13] Andrés Molina Enríquez, *Los grandes problemas nacionales* (Mexico: Carranza e Hijos, 1909).
[14] Womack, *Zapata*, pp. 401-402.

Just as the *zapatistas* claimed, Madero was too timid to eliminate the opposition, and this mistake cost him his life. Early in 1913 his military chief of staff—Victoriano Huerta, a high-ranking general under Díaz—betrayed him, killed him (with the notorious approval of U.S. Ambassador Henry Lane Wilson), and took over presidential power. Attempting to establish a neo-Porfirian regime, Huerta demanded recognition from political authorities throughout the country. Some refused to go along, and armed resistance to the "usurpation" spread. It was at this point, in 1913, that there began the genuinely "revolutionary" phase of the Mexican Revolution.

One of the most powerful centers of resistance to Huerta was the northern state of Chihuahua, where Pancho Villa gained control. Unlike the *zapatista* movement, this was not a peasant rebellion. At least initially, the *villista* forces consisted of small ranchers, unemployed workers, and cowboys: men who clamored primarily for jobs, not small plots of land. So when Villa issued his pronouncement on agrarian reform, in December 1913, it called for confiscation of large haciendas, not for subdivision into plots. The haciendas would be administered by the state, and they would continue to produce commercial crops in order to finance the *villista* military machine. This decision created massive administrative problems, but it also achieved its goal: money flowed in, arms and supplies were obtained (mainly from the United States), Villa's army—the *División del Norte*—became extremely powerful. In fact the army became the principal source of employment for *villista* followers, and as it did so, it took on the quality of a well-paid, professional, mercenary outfit.[15]

Another major challenge to the Huerta usurpation emerged from Coahuila, Madero's own home state, where governor Venustiano Carranza organized a powerful resistance movement. Like Madero, Carranza was a scion of the *porfirista* upper class. Himself a wealthy landowner, he had been an active politician on the local and national levels: under Díaz he became a senator and, in 1908, served as interim governor. In 1910 Carranza first supported the upstart candidacy of Bernardo Reyes for president, and then moved over to the "Anti-Re-electionist" side. In return for his support, Madero rewarded him with the constitutional governorship of Coahuila.

In view of Carranza's personal background, it comes as no surprise to learn that his movement, in its initial phases, lacked ideological commitment. The *Plan de Guadalupe*, issued on March 26, 1913, de-

[15] This interpretation is taken largely from a lecture, "The Development and Structure of the Villista Movement," by Friedrich Katz, Columbia University, April 1973.

nied Huerta's claim to legitimacy and declared, instead, that Carranza should receive recognition as "First Chief of the Constitutionalist Army"; with this authority, Carranza would eventually call for new and fair elections. And that was all. With early support in other northern states, especially Sonora,[16] drawn from an amorphous, largely rural following,[17] the *carrancista* movement lacked social cohesion—or clarity of purpose, other than a determination to unseat Huerta and acquire power.

By mid-1914 the combined opposition of Zapata, Villa, and Carranza led to Huerta's downfall, and opened up a triangular struggle for supremacy. Spokesmen for all three factions gathered at Aguascalientes, hoping to establish a coalition government, but Carranza, sensing an alliance between Villa and Zapata, withdrew from the meeting, refused to recognize the "Conventionist" government, and set up his own regime in Veracruz. The war went on. At stake was the direction, control, and outcome of the Revolution.

It was in this context that, in successive *adiciones* to the *Plan de Guadalupe*, Carranza started to proclaim a social purpose. In December 1914 he promised, in the vaguest of terms, "legislation for the improvement of the condition of the rural peon, the worker, the miner, and in general the proletarian classes."[18] In January 1915, from Mexico City, he issued a pronouncement on agrarian reform, authorizing the restoration or creation of agricultural villages *(ejidos)*, setting up procedures for the reclamation of titles, and establishing a national agrarian commission. The following month he reached a pact with the anarcho-syndicalist *Casa del Obrero Mundial*: in return for favorable labor legislation, the workers would form Red Batallions and place them at the service of the Constitutionalist cause (where they would play a key role in combat against Villa). Within a year the pact was showing signs of strain, as Carranza retaliated against a railroad strike by drafting all strikers into the army, and in 1916 it fell apart.

Notwithstanding its internal weakness, the *carrancista* movement emerged triumphant. The *zapatistas*, local in their character and outlook, withdrew from the national arena and set up a stronghold in Morelos. Villa continued the fight, but was unable to develop a popular base in central Mexico, where peasants wanted land instead of jobs, and in mid-1915 he suffered defeat at the hands of Carranza's brilliant

---

[16] On Sonora see Héctor Aguilar Camín, *La revolución sonorense, 1910-1914* (Mexico: Departamento de Investigaciones Históricas, Instituto Nacional de Antropología e Historia, 1975).

[17] Charles C. Cumberland, *Mexican Revolution: The Constitutionalist Years* (Austin: University of Texas Press, 1972), p. 252.

[18] Ibid., p. 256.

military commander, Álvaro Obregón of Sonora. Thereafter Villa re-
treated to the hills of Chihuahua, waging guerrilla war, but he was no
longer a national threat. With his principal enemies contained, if not
crushed, Carranza confidently convoked a constitutional convention in
late 1916.[19] A few months later, in May of 1917, he became the full-
fledged president of Mexico.

But cleavages persisted and intensified. To Carranza's evident surprise (and presumably dismay), delegates at the constitutional convention rejected his own draft proposal—a pale imitation of the 1857
document—and wrote one of the most progressive charters in the
Western world. Article 27 established the basis for land distribution;
Article 123 affirmed the rights of labor; and others, especially Article 3,
put strict limits on the power of the Church. Splitting into "moderate" and "jacobin" groups, the delegates wrangled over the relationship between centralized power, social policy, and political order, rather than over the fundamental desirability of socioeconomic change,
and in this fashion they revealed a basic outcome of the Revolution.
If for no other reason than military necessity, the mobilization of the
masses had drastically altered the terms (though maybe not the practical result) of the political game.[20] From then on, all serious contenders for power would have to adopt a rhetorical posture in favor of
Mexico's masses, the workers and the peasants.

It is this rhetorical imperative, plus the scale of violence (resulting
in perhaps one million deaths), which has led many observers to accept the "revolutionary" status of the Mexican Revolution without
question, hesitation, or definition. By my own criterion, as well, it
meets the definition of a revolution: it was an illegal seizure of political power, by the threat or use of force, for the purpose of bringing
about a structural change in the distribution of political, social, or economic power. So far so good. But I would also point out that the
Revolution was anything but monolithic, that some factions were more
revlutionary than others, and that it was the moderate wing that carried off the triumph. To be sure, Carranza, and Madero before him,
were committed to basic changes in the procedures for allocating political power, and the "no-reelection" rule stands as testimony to that
fact. Carranza also showed himself to be something of a nationalist,

---

[19] However, this is not the origin of the *constitucionalista* label; that comes from
Carranza's initial promise to uphold the Constitution of 1856-57.

[20] On the convention see E. V. Niemeyer, Jr., *Revolution at Querétaro: The Mexican Constitutional Convention of 1916-1917* (Austin: University of Texas Press,
1974); and Peter H. Smith, "The Making of the Mexican Constitution," in *The
Dimensions of Parliamentary History*, ed. William O. Aydelotte (Princeton: Princeton University Press, 1977), pp. 186-224.

staunchly opposing United States intervention in the struggle against Huerta in 1914. But there the impulse ended. Zapata and Villa were less nationalistic, but each, in his way, was more committed to fundamental socioeconomic change. The *zapatistas* sought far-reaching change in the patterns of land tenure; the *villistas*, though less homogenous, saw unemployment as a problem to be handled by the state. And it was these two groups, the ones driven by socioeconomic concerns, that went down to defeat. Within the *carrancista* ranks there were some revolutionaries genuinely dedicated to the purpose of socioeconomic transformation, but they were not predominant. Whether they would be able to realize their goal is a separate question.

For quite some time, in fact, Mexico's leaders were more concerned with power and stability than with structural transformation. The conclusion of the widespread fighting opened up a political struggle that became a war of physical attrition. Zapata was murdered by *carrancista* troops in 1919; Villa was finally assassinated in 1923. In 1920, when Carranza tried to impose the little-known Ignacio Bonillas as president, Álvaro Obregón launched an uprising that resulted in Carranza's death —and Obregón's accession to the presidency. In 1923 Obregón's close collaborator, Adolfo de la Huerta, mounted another revolt and ended up in exile. During his four-year regime (1924-28) Plutarco Elías Calles waged open war upon the proclerical *Cristero* revolt and put down another coup attempt in 1927. Stretching the interpretation of the "noreelection" clause, Obregón campaigned again for president in 1928, won the election handily—and was assassinated by a religious fanatic before taking the oath of office.

The Obregón murder plunged the country into a political and constitutional crisis, and Calles moved quickly to stabilize the situation. At his behest, leaders of the nation's power groups agreed that a new election should be held the following year, and, more important, they founded an official party of unity, the Partido Nacional Revolucionario (PNR). For several years Calles wielded tremendous power from not-so-far behind the scenes, as so-called *Jefe Máximo de la Revolución*, while a series of short-term presidents—Emilio Portes Gil, Pascual Ortiz Rubio, and Abelardo Rodríguez—occupied the nation's highest formal office. In 1934 Lázaro Cárdenas became president, in 1935 he broke with Calles, and in 1938 he reorganized the party along corporativist lines, renaming it the Partido de la Revolución Mexicana (PRM) and building it around four separate functional groupings: the agricultural (peasant) sector, the labor sector, the military sector, and, as a kind of residual category, the "popular" or middle-class sector. The military lost its status as a formal sector in the 1940s, and when Miguel

Alemán reorganized the party once again in 1946—this time as the Partido Revolucionario Institucional (PRI)—it acquired the form it has had ever since: an utterly dominant official party, composed of three sectors (peasant, worker, popular) and partly responsible for the unity and stability that have come to be the hallmark of the Mexican political system.

One of the most remarkable concomitants of the party-building process has proved to be the alteration, and in general the diminution, of the political role of the Mexican military. Around 1920 there were about 80,000 men under arms, more than twice the number of 1910, and they were led by youthful *arriviste* generals who avidly sought political power. From Obregón through Cárdenas, presidents attempted to contain the army through a succession of tactics: bringing revolutionary generals into the regular army and putting them on the federal payroll, giving governorships and other major posts to allies and dissidents, promoting professional standards among enlisted men and junior officers, frequently switching commands, and reducing the military budget.[21] In reflection of these policies, the military share of actual national government expenditures declined from 53 percent in 1921 to 19.1 percent in 1941 to a mere 5.5 percent in 1961.[22] In recent years the army has continued to perform important residual functions —operating, as David Ronfeldt has shown, as a kind of parallel government structure,[23] frequently containing conflict—but it no longer dominates the political scene as it did during the decade of the twenties.

The resolution of political crisis, and the achievement of institutional stability, established a vital precondition for economic development in Mexico. During the 1960s, in fact, the country's economic performance came to be known as the "Mexican miracle," as foreign observers expressed unbridled admiration at the vision of economic growth and political stability in an area of the developing world. To understand the social and political ramifications of this process, however, it is necessary to gain some analytical perspective on the form, as well as the fact, of economic change in Mexico.

[21] See Edwin Lieuwen, *Mexican Militarism: The Political Rise and Fall of the Revolutionary Army, 1910-1940* (Albuquerque: University of New Mexico Press, 1968); and Jorge Alberto Lozoya, *El ejército mexicano (1911-1965)* (Mexico: El Colegio de México, 1970).

[22] Wilkie, *Mexican Revolution*, pp. 102-103.

[23] David F. Ronfeldt, "The Mexican Army and Political Order since 1940," in *Contemporary Mexico: Papers of the IV International Congress of Mexican History*, ed. James W. Wilkie, Michael C. Meyer, and Edna Monzón de Wilkie (Berkeley and Los Angeles: University of California Press, 1976), pp. 317-336.

ECONOMIC AND SOCIAL CHANGE

Whether or not the Revolution caused, or even prompted, economic transformation, there can be no doubt that the Mexican economy has undergone profound transition throughout the twentieth century, especially during the years since 1940. Table 2-1 reveals that the gross domestic product (GDP) grew from about 8.5 billion pesos in 1900 to 21.7 billion pesos in 1940 (in constant 1950 prices), an average annual increase of 2.4 percent—a rate whose modesty resulted partly from the devastation wrought by revolutionary warfare. Between 1940 and 1960, the GDP jumped from 21.7 billion pesos to 74.3 billion pesos, as the average annual increase went up to 6.4 percent, an impressive figure by any international standard. During the decade of the sixties, Mexico maintained this level of growth, and—with one of the fastest growing populations in the world—achieved a solid per capita growth rate

TABLE 2-1

The Structure of Production: *
1900, 1940, and 1960

Activity	Percentage Distribution		
	1900	1940	1960
Agriculture	—[a]	24.3	18.9
Crop production	14.3	12.6	12.3
Livestock	15.6	10.4	6.1
Forestry	—	1.2	0.3
Fishing	—	0.1	0.2
Manufacturing	13.2	18.0	23.0
Mining	6.4	5.6	2.2
Electric energy	—	1.0	1.4
Petroleum	—	2.9	3.2
Construction	—	3.6	3.5
Transportation	3.1	4.5	4.9
Commerce	—	24.0	25.7
Government	—	3.1	2.7
Unclassified activities	47.4	13.0	14.8
Totals	100.0	100.0	100.0
(Total size of GDP, in millions of pesos of 1950)	8,540	21,658	74,317

SOURCE: Clark W. Reynolds, *The Mexican Economy: Twentieth-Century Structure and Growth* (New Haven: Yale University Press, 1970), pp. 60-61.

[a] Data not available.

of 3.3 percent per year.[24] This pace would slacken in the 1970s, as the "miracle" seemed to have come to an end, but the legacies of growth persist.

With the acceleration in growth, there also came a transformation in the structure of production. Table 2-1 implies that the shift from 1900 to 1940 was fairly moderate, though the paucity of data on the Porfirian economy (and the huge share of "unclassified activities" for 1900) make this judgment tenuous; it appears, however, that the relative contribution of agriculture declined only slightly, from around 30 percent to 24 percent, while the contribution of manufacturing went up from 13 percent to 18 percent. After 1940 the pace of transformation quickened. By 1960 the agricultural share of GDP had slipped to 18.9 percent, and the input from manufacturing was up to 23 percent; the trend was even more apparent by 1970, when agriculture accounted for only 11.4 percent of GDP, while manufacturing and commerce continued to expand.[25] Clearly, Mexico has not become a fully industrialized nation; but just as clearly, it has been undergoing a steady process of industrialization.

This transition has exerted a strong impact on the composition and sectoral distribution of the labor force. As shown in Table 2-2, the proportion of workers engaged in agriculture held around the 68-70 percent level in 1900 and 1930, then dropped to 54.9 percent by 1960 (a decline that continued through the decade of the sixties).[26] Concurrently, the share of workers employed in industry rose rather steadily, from 10.7 percent in 1900 to 12.9 percent by 1930 to 16.8 percent in 1960. Other fields underwent moderate changes, although the increase in the relative role of the government, up from 1.4 percent in 1900 to 3.7 percent in 1960, provides a suggestive reflection of the state's activist participation in the national economy during the postrevolutionary era. Comparison of the data in Tables 2-1 and 2-2 adds another insight: Mexican agriculture has remained employment-intensive, involving over half the work force in 1960 and producing about one-fifth of GDP; industry, broadly defined, has been capital-intensive, with less than 20 percent of the work force producing as much as 33 percent of GDP.[27]

[24] Roger D. Hansen, *The Politics of Mexican Development* (Baltimore: Johns Hopkins University Press, 1971), p. 3.

[25] Banco Nacional de México, *Review of the Economic Situation of Mexico* 47, no. 545 (April 1971): 172.

[26] Dirección General de Estadística, Secretaría de Industria y Comercio, *IX censo general de población, 1970. Resumen general* (Mexico: Talleres Gráficos de la Nación, 1972), pp. 597-598.

[27] See Clark W. Reynolds, *The Mexican Economy: Twentieth-Century Structure and Growth* (New Haven: Yale University Press, 1970), p. 64.

TABLE 2-2

Sectoral Distribution of the Active Work Force:
1900, 1930, and 1960

Sector	1900 (%)	1930[a] (%)	1960[a] (%)
Agriculture	69.5	67.8	54.9
Mining	2.1	1.0	1.2
Manufacturing	10.7	12.9	16.8
Transportation and communication	1.3	2.0	3.7
Commerce and finance	5.2	5.0	7.6
Service (including professionals)	4.4	4.6	7.6
Government (including military)	1.4	2.9	3.7
Other[b]	5.4	3.9	4.6
Totals	100.0	100.1	100.1

SOURCE: Arturo González Cosío, "Clases y estratos sociales," in *México: Cincuenta años de revolución*, vol. II, *La vida social*, by Julio Durán Ochoa et al. (Mexico: Fondo de Cultura Económica, 1961), pp. 56-57.

[a] Totals do not add up to 100 because of rounding.
[b] Includes owners and proprietors.

This pattern of high-technology, low-employment industry is typical of "late-developing" economies, such as Mexico's, which have tended to import manufacturing processes, as well as materials, from the relatively more industrialized countries of the world. This process requires capital and, as I shall emphasize below, one major source of capital has been the Mexican state. Another, not surprisingly, has been foreign investment, especially from the United States. As revealed in Table 2-3, the quantity and allocation of foreign investment in Mexico have undergone important variations. From a total amount of 1.5 billion dollars (of 1970) in 1911, at the end of the *Porfiriato*, direct foreign investment slipped to less than half a billion dollars in 1940—partly because of the turmoil of the Revolution, partly because of Mexican policy (specifically, Cárdenas' expropriation of oil companies in 1938), and partly because of the worldwide Depression. By 1970, however, the figure had soared to 3.8 billion dollars, 80 percent of which came from the United States. And in sharp contrast to previous eras, when mining and communication-transportation were the dominant activities for foreigners, nearly three-quarters (73.8 percent) of this investment was in the manufacturing sector, mostly in critical industries: chemicals, petrochemicals, rubber, machinery and industrial equipment. In this way, as well as through other means (such as trade and tourism), Mexico has obtained a considerable share of the financial resources for economic growth from abroad—and foreigners, notably Americans, have assumed substantial if indirect influence on the direction of economic policy.

TABLE 2-3

Patterns of Foreign Investment:
1911, 1940, and 1970

Activity	Percentage Distribution		
	1911	1940	1970
Mining	28.2	24.1	5.5
Public services, communication, transportation	47.1	63.0	0.4
Manufacturing	4.5	7.1	73.8
Commerce	4.2	3.6	15.5
Other[a]	16.0	2.2	4.8
Totals	100.0	100.0	100.0
(Total amount, in millions of U.S. dollars of 1970)	1,452	449	2,822

SOURCE: Bernardo Sepúlveda and Antonio Chumacero, *La inversión extranjera en México* (Mexico: Fondo de Cultura Económica, 1973), p. 50.

[a] Includes agriculture, construction, petroleum, and "other activities."

Naturally enough, the combined processes of economic growth, industrialization, and demographic increase exerted a profound impact on Mexico's class structure. To indicate both the direction and the magnitude of this change, Table 2-4 offers approximate percentage figures for rural and urban components of the upper, middle, and lower classes for 1900 and 1960.[28] The estimates are based on the aggregate structure of occupations, which are taken to convey indirect notions of two critical dimensions: income levels and social prestige. This correlation is anything but perfect, as recent studies have shown,[29]

[28] Very similar estimates for 1895 and 1940 appear in José E. Iturriaga, *La estructura social y cultural de México* (Mexico: Fondo de Cultura Económica, 1951), p. 28; a general discussion of the theme is in ch. III, "Las clases sociales," pp. 24-89.

[29] See, for instance, Stuart Blumin, "The Historical Study of Vertical Mobility," *Historical Methods Newsletter* 1, no. 4 (September 1968): 1-13; Otis Dudley Duncan, "Social Stratification and Mobility: Problems in the Measurement of Trend," in

but, in the absence of other data, the distribution of occupations can serve to illustrate the basic trends.

TABLE 2-4

Class Structure in 1900 and 1960

Class	1900 (%)	1960 (%)
Upper		
Urban	0.2	0.4
Rural	0.4	0.1
(Subtotal)	(0.6)	(0.5)
Middle		
Urban	1.7	7.2
Rural	6.6	9.9
(Subtotal)	(8.3)	(17.1)
Lower		
Urban	16.3	32.3
Rural	74.8	50.1
(Subtotal)	(91.1)	(82.4)
Total	100.0	100.0

SOURCE: Arturo González Cosío, "Clases y estratos sociales," in *México: Cincuenta años de revolución*, vol. II, *La vida social*, by Julio Durán Ochoa et al. (Mexico: Fondo de Cultura Económica, 1961), p. 55.

The outlines are clear enough. The upper class has remained very small, comprising about one-half of one percent of the population, while shifting its social location from the countryside to the city, as the traditional *hacendado* has given way to bankers and industrialists. The middle class, by contrast, has roughly doubled in relative size, from 8.3 percent to 17.1 percent of the total, with urban and rural components becoming nearly equal in size. I myself find the distinction between upper- and middle-class occupations to be extremely tenuous, since many people in middle-class jobs have upper-class incomes (and vice versa), and it might well be preferable to combine the two into a single social class, the nonmanual class, consisting of those who do not work primarily with their hands. But no matter how you look at it, one

Indicators of Social Change: Concepts and Measurements, ed. Eleanor Bernert Sheldon and Wilbert E. Moore (New York: Russell Sage Foundation, 1968), pp. 695-719; Michael B. Katz, "Occupational Classification in History," *Journal of Interdisciplinary History* 3, no. 1 (Summer 1972): 63-88; and Donald J. Treiman, "A Standard Occupational Prestige Scale for Use with Historical Data," *Journal of Interdisciplinary History* 7, no. 2 (Autumn 1976): 283-304.

fundamental point comes through: relatively speaking, *the middle class is a highly privileged class,* and people with middle-class occupations in 1960 fell into the upper-one fifth of the total population.[30]

The lower class consists of those who perform manual labor and, in my view, it stands unambiguously apart from the upper-middle strata on both conceptual and empirical grounds. As shown in Table 2-4, the lower class has decreased in relative size, declining from 91.1 percent to 82.4 percent, although it has increased in absolute size because of population growth. By 1960, a sizable proportion of this stratum lived in cities, and, although the *campesinos* of the countryside remained the more numerous element, this shift reflected an underlying process that affected all sectors of the population: the secular trend toward urbanization. According to data compiled by James W. Wilkie, more than 70 percent of the Mexican population in 1900 lived in rural communities, defined as those with less than 2,500 inhabitants; by 1960 the proportion was less than half (49.3 percent), and by 1970 it was down to 41.3 percent.[31]

Despite the rhetorical impulses of the Revolution, the nation's social classes have not shared equally the benefits of economic growth. To demonstrate the point, Table 2-5 sets out information on income distribution by population deciles (tenths), ranked from lowest to highest, for selected years from 1950 through 1969. The data convey a picture of sharp, and growing, inequalities. As the "Mexican miracle" progressed, the share of income accruing to the poorest tenth of the population dropped from 2.4 percent to 2.0 percent, while the richest tenth increased its share from 49 percent to 51 percent: that is to say, half the national income went to 10 percent of the families! Even more revealing, perhaps, is the fact that the top two deciles—comprising the upper and middle classes, according to the estimates in Table 2-4—increased their combined share of income from 59.8 percent to 64 percent. This gain came at the explicit expense of the lower class, contained in deciles I through VIII, particularly the lower segments of the lower class (deciles I through IV). As reflected by the steady rise in the Gini coefficient, which provides a summary measure of overall in-

[30] Data in the 1970 census appear to suggest that (1) both the middle and lower classes became much more urbanized during the 1960s, (2) González Cosío overestimated the rural components of these two strata for 1960, or (3) a little bit of both effects occurred. By my standards, in any case, the "middle class" continued to comprise about 20 percent of the total population. See the figures in Dirección General de Estadística, Secretaría de Industria y Comercio, *IX censo general . . . 1970,* pp. 889, 895, 901, and 911.

[31] Wilkie, *Mexican Revolution,* pp. 218-219; and Dirección General de Estadística, Secretaría de Industria y Comercio, *IX censo general . . . 1970,* p. 59.

equality, Mexico's pattern of growth has only tended to exacerbate the maldistribution of income.[32]

TABLE 2-5

Distribution of Family Incomes:
1950, 1958, 1963, and 1969

Decile	Percentage Shares of Income			
	1950	1958	1963	1969
I (poorest)	2.4	2.2	2.0	2.0
II	2.7	2.8	2.2	2.0
III	3.8	3.3	3.2	3.0
IV	4.4	3.9	3.7	3.5
V	4.8	4.5	4.6	4.5
VI	5.5	5.5	5.2	5.0
VII	7.0	6.3	6.6	7.0
VIII	8.6	8.6	9.9	9.0
IX	10.8	13.6	12.7	13.0
X (richest)	49.0	49.3	49.9	51.0
(Top 5%)	(40.2)	(38.6)	(38.3)	(36.0)
Totals	100.0	100.0	100.0	100.0
Gini coefficient of inequality	0.50	0.53	0.55	0.58

SOURCES: Ifigenia M. de Navarrete, "La distribución del ingreso en México: tendencias y perspectivas," in *El perfil de México en 1980*, I (Mexico: Siglo XXI, 1970), p. 37; and David Barkin, "Mexico's Albatross: The United States Economy," *Latin American Perspectives* 2, no. 2 (Summer 1975): 65.

One of the most critical mechanisms in any social structure is the educational system. In Mexico, a central commitment of revolutionary ideology has concerned the expansion of educational opportunity for the purposes of increasing social mobility, augmenting the nation's supply of trained talent, and creating a more just society. To some extent these goals have in fact been realized. In 1910, just before the Revolution, only 24 percent of the elementary school-age population was attending school. By 1930 the figure had gone up to 42 percent, and by 1958 it had risen to 58 percent.[33] Largely because of these trends,

[32] It should be noted, in passing, that changing income distribution is partly a function of changing age structure, since young people tend to have less wealth than older people; Mexico's rapid rate of population growth would thus increase the Gini coefficient over time, but it is hard to measure this effect.

[33] Attendance figures are from Gill, *Education*, p. 37; and Secretaría de la Economía Nacional, Dirección General de Estadística, *Quinto censo de población, 15 de mayo de 1930. Resumen general* (Mexico: Talleres Gráficos de la Nación, 1934), p. 66.

illiteracy experienced a sharp decline, dropping from 76.9 percent in 1910 to 66.6 percent in 1930, 37.8 percent in 1960, and 28.3 percent in 1970.[34]

Despite these accomplishments at the primary-school level, the upper levels of the Mexican educational system (secondary, preparatory, and university) have functioned so as to preserve and even strengthen interclass barriers. In 1926 only 3,860 students were enrolled in the postprimary basic secondary cycle, probably no more than 4 or 5 percent of the available school-age population.[35] Twenty years later, in 1946, the number had risen to 48,376—still about the same percentage as before, and possibly even less, given the effects of population growth.[36] The preparatory cycle, through which students pass on to university, has been even more exclusive; in particular, the Escuela Nacional Preparatoria in Mexico City has remained the bastion of the national elite. A university education has been consistently reserved for only a tiny fraction of the population. According to my best estimate, about 1.7 percent of the literate adult male population had attended a university in 1900; by 1960, several decades after the Revolution, the figure had risen to only 2.7 percent.[37] In this context, higher education could hardly function as a broad avenue to social mobility.

Of all the universities, the most important, by virtually any standard, has been the Universidad Nacional Autónoma de México (UNAM). Originally founded by royal decree in 1551, it entered a period of protracted turbulence after Mexico's acquisition of independence from Spain. Emperor Maximilian closed it down in 1865, and it was not reopened until 1910, when it was renamed the National University. In 1929 the university attained autonomy, and, as a result, a new official name. Situated in Mexico City, with many of the best professors in the country, UNAM has long been the capstone of the Mexican educational system.

Despite its visibility and prominence, UNAM did not have very large enrollments—not until the mid-1960s, when a revised admissions

34 Wilkie, *Mexican Revolution*, pp. 208-209; and Dirección General de Estadística, Secretaría de Industria y Comercio, *IX censo general . . . 1970*, p. 273.

35 Gill, *Education*, p. 52; percentage estimate for the available school-age population based on Departamento de la Estadística Nacional, *Resumen del censo general de habitantes de 30 de noviembre de 1921* (Mexico: Talleres Gráficos de la Nación, 1928), p. 59.

36 Proportional estimate based on data in Secretaría de la Economía Nacional, Dirección de Estadística, *Compendio estadístico* (Mexico: Talleres Gráficos de la Nación, 1947), p. 89.

37 As estimated from data in Secretaría de Economía, Dirección General de Estadística, *Estadísticas sociales del porfiriato 1877-1911* (Mexico: Talleres Gráficos de la Nación, 1956), pp. 52-53; and Dirección General de Estadística, Secretaría de Industria y Comercio, *VIII censo general de población, 1960. Resumen general* (Mexico: Talleres Gráficos de la Nación, 1962), pp. 308-340.

policy turned it into one of the most gigantic universities in the entire world. But in the years before 1950, when virtually all of the political leaders in this study received their education, UNAM was a relatively compact institution. Figure 2-1 reveals that from 1924 to 1950, enrollment in the Escuela Nacional Preparatoria, a dependency of UNAM, barely exceeded 5,000 a year; enrollment in the university-level professional schools (law, engineering, medicine, etc.) ranged from about 7,500 to less than 20,000. Individual classes were often very small, as students and professors got to know one another fairly well. Because of attrition during the course of university careers, the number of people receiving degrees remained small—no more than 200 or 300 a year during the 1920s, about 1,000 a year during the 1940s.[38] To be a UNAM graduate was, throughout this period, to be a member of an exclusive educational club.[39]

Figure 2-1: Student Enrollment at UNAM Professional Schools and Escuela Nacional Preparatoria, 1924-66

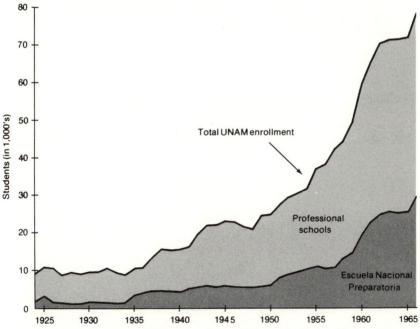

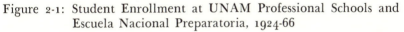

SOURCE: Arturo González Cosío, *Historia estadística de la Universidad, 1910-1967* (Mexico: UNAM, Instituto de Investigaciones Sociales, 1968), Cuadro XXIII. Figures include both men and women.

[38] Arturo González Cosío, *Historia estadística de la Universidad, 1910-1967* (Mexico: UNAM, Instituto de Investigaciones Sociales, 1968), p. 106.
[39] As shown by Alonso Portuondo, "The Universidad Nacional Autónoma de México in the Post-Independence Period: A Political and Structural Review" (M.A. thesis, University of Miami, 1972).

UNAM also had clear social overtones. For some clues on the social composition of the student body, Table 2-6 offers figures on father's occupation for students in UNAM as a whole and also for those in the faculty of law (which produced more politicians than any other faculty). Compiled in 1949, when more than 23,000 students were attending the university, the data presumably reveal the UNAM to be a less socially exclusive institution than in prior years, when the vast majority of leaders under study went to school. But even at that late date, it is abundantly clear that most UNAM students came from middle- or upper-class families. Over 20 percent had fathers engaged in high-status professions (law, medicine, etc.),[40] about 30 percent had fathers in commerce, and practically 90 percent came from white-collar backgrounds of one sort or another. The profile for law students was much the same, with a slightly higher proportion of parents in the professions and a somewhat lower share performing manual tasks as *obreros*.

TABLE 2-6

Fathers' Occupations for UNAM Students, 1949

Occupation, by Category	% for All UNAM students	% for Law Students Only
Professionals	20.6	25.4
Technicians	5.6	5.4
Artists	1.2	0.7
Military	3.8	4.8
Merchants	30.0	27.2
Farmers (*agricultores*)	6.4	11.1
Artisans	2.2	1.5
Employees	20.6	18.3
Workers (*obreros*)	9.5	5.6
Totals	99.9[a]	100.0

SOURCE: Instituto de Investigaciones Sociales, Universidad Nacional Autónoma de México, *Primer censo nacional universitario 1949* (Mexico: UNAM, 1953), pp. 45-47, 181-182.

[a] Does not add up to 100 because of slight omissions in the data.

[40] This is an impressive figure, since only 33,484 men were engaged in "free professions" in 1930, around the time that most UNAM students in the 1949 survey were born. This means that nearly 15 percent of all professionals as of 1930 would have sired children around that time and sent them on to UNAM—an extraordinary figure, given the odds on paternity and survival, and it suggests to me that virtually every professional must have sent his children on to UNAM if at all possible. For the 1930 data see Secretaría de la Economía Nacional, Direccíon General de Estadística, *Quinto censo de población . . . 1930*, p. 72.

48

Like other universities in Mexico,[41] UNAM therefore did not—as of 1949—offer widespread opportunity for children of the working class. To the extent that it furnished chances for mobility, it appears to have enabled sons of merchants and employees to move up into the professions. Generally speaking UNAM did not do much to loosen up the country's social structure; on the contrary, it ratified and emphasized the system of class distinctions.

Mexico's recent process of economic growth, the so-called miracle, has thus led to basic transformation of some aspects of society, particularly in the sectoral allocation of the work force and in the composition of the social classes. But at the same time these trends have coincided with increasing, not decreasing, inequalities, and the educational system has done little to mitigate these effects. As Pablo González Casanova has observed, about 50 to 70 percent of the Mexican population is "marginal" to national life, and receives almost none of the benefits of growth—although they provide much of the labor and resources needed for growth itself. It is the privileged remainder of the population, anywhere from one-third to one-half, which has reaped the rewards of development. This situation, characterized by González Casanova as "internal colonialism," provides the social foundations for Mexico's authoritarian political regime.[42]

MEXICO'S AUTHORITARIAN REGIME

It has been more than a decade since Juan J. Linz offered his pathbreaking definition of political authoritarianism, a form of rule that is conceptually and empirically distinct from democracy (characterized by free and open pluralism) and totalitarianism (characterized by "total" domination of society by the state). In contrast, Linz wrote, "Authoritarian regimes are political systems with limited, not responsible, political pluralism: without elaborate and guiding ideology (but with distinctive mentalities); without intensive nor extensive political mobilization (except at some points in their development); and in which a leader (or occasionally a small group) exercises power within formally ill-defined limits but actually quite predictable ones."[43] Seeking

[41] As of 1949 the social profile of provincial universities was much the same as for UNAM. See Lucio Mendieta y Núñez, "Ensayo sociológico sobre la Universidad," in Instituto de Investigaciones Sociales, Universidad Nacional Autónoma de México, *Primer censo nacional universitario 1949* (Mexico: UNAM, 1953), p. CI.

[42] Pablo González Casanova, *Democracy in Mexico*, trans. Danielle Salti (New York: Oxford University Press, 1970).

[43] Juan J. Linz, "An Authoritarian Regime: Spain," in *Mass Politics: Studies in Political Sociology*, ed. Erik Allardt and Stein Rokkan (New York: The Free Press,

a prototypical case, Linz applied the model to Spain under Franco; with some modification, the model can also fit contemporary Mexico.

PLURALISM

The central and defining characteristic of authoritarianism is limited pluralism, a situation in which there is active competition for political power, but one in which access to the competition is sharply restricted. Of the restrictions on political contestation there can be no doubt. Since 1917 government candidates have completely dominated presidential campaigns, always winning more than 70 percent of the popular vote (according to official tallies) and usually getting more than 90 percent.[44] This pattern held, particularly, in the elections of Alemán (1946), Adolfo Ruiz Cortines (1952), Adolfo López Mateos (1958), Gustavo Díaz Ordaz (1964), Luis Echeverría (1970), and José López Portillo (1976). Opposition parties—in recent years the Partido de Acción Nacional (PAN), the Partido Popular Socialista (PPS), and the Partido Auténtico de la Revolución Mexicana (PARM)—have never provided more than a token challenge, the last two often supporting the PRI candidate for president. In the Chamber of Deputies, too, spokesmen for these parties have put up minimal resistance to government proposals, while PRI delegates have usually voted in unanimous accord with the executive.

So the contest for power is effectively restricted to supporters of the regime, the circle that has come to be known as the "revolutionary family." Within those limits, however, genuine competition exists. For reasons spelled out more fully in Chapter 8, I do not believe that the struggle takes place between the three components of the PRI—the peasant, worker, and popular sectors—or that Mexico has developed (or is developing) a one-party democracy. Rather, the political process entails an unceasing battle between factional *camarillas*, groups bound by loyalty to an individual leader (or *gallo*, cock) who is expected to award patronage in return for their support. Occasionally the *camarillas* possess a set of shared policy preferences that places them on the "left" or "right" of the political spectrum, but they consistently express fealty to the tenets of the Revolution—and their essential bond is more personalistic and instrumental than ideological. Thus politicians acquire the labels of their leaders: this one is a *cardenista*, that one is an *alemanista*, the other one a *diazordacista*, and so on. In important (and

---

1970), p. 255. It is *not* my intent to use the term "authoritarianism" in a normative or pejorative sense; like Linz, I employ it merely as an analytical category.

[44] González Casanova, *Democracy*, pp. 198-200.

revealing) ways, these attachments bear close resemblance to the *caudillismo* of years past.

Since the early 1940s the struggle between *camarillas* has found resolution through accommodation and equilibrium, not elimination or annihilation of contending factions. Consequently, the competition is continuous. The most powerful groups obtain positions in national ministries, where they can try to maximize their leverage, and cabinet appointments are widely viewed as an indication of the prevailing political balance. Note, for instance, the terms in which Francisco Javier Gaxiola described the cabinet first appointed by Manuel Ávila Camacho in December 1940:

Miguel Alemán, Gobernación (Interior): "he had been the head of General Ávila Camacho's political campaign and the governor of Veracruz," one of the most important states in Mexico; "from the very beginning," Gaxiola added, "I think that he viewed this post as the anteroom to his office in the presidential palace";

Ezequiel Padilla, Foreign Relations: "fundamentally a *padillista*," an independent soul who later ran a losing campaign against Alemán in 1946;

Pablo Macías, National Defense: "a loyal revolutionary . . . a genuine representative of the army that came from the people," the same army whose political influence was by then in sharp decline;

Luis Sánchez Pontón, Public Education: "he undoubtedly represented the most leftist tendency within the government," and, paradoxically, his designation revealed the president's intention to initiate more conservative educational policies;

Heriberto Jara, Navy: in recognition "of his well-known revolutionary credentials and his radical activity within the constitutional congress at Querétaro" in 1916-17;

Javier Rojo Gómez, Agriculture: "a representative of the *campesino* class";

Ignacio García Téllez, Labor: "for his close connections with General Lázaro Cárdenas";

Gaxiola himself, National Economy: "because of my friendship with General Abelardo L. Rodríguez," president from 1932 to 1934, a relationship which identified Gaxiola with both the *Maximato* and the *callista* group that was ousted from power by Cárdenas in 1935.[45]

[45] Francisco Javier Gaxiola, *Memorias* (Mexico: Editorial Porrúa, 1975), pp. 251-253.

To be sure, Ávila Camacho was probably making an exceptionally conscious effort to establish a government of national unity in the wake of his election, one of the more bitterly contested in recent history, and he also appointed many of his personal allies, including his brother, to positions of confidence and trust. But the basic point still stands: there was diversity within the upper circles of the ruling group, different factions found representation, and competition ensued. This pattern has held ever since, and it marks, explicitly, the political boundaries of the limited pluralism that obtains in modern Mexico.

MENTALITY VERSUS IDEOLOGY

The Mexican Revolution gave birth to a set of doctrines that has bequeathed watchwords ever since. Embodied in the Constitution of 1917, the principle tenets are: no-reelection, land reform (Article 27), workers' rights (Article 123), and subordination of the Church to the state (Article 3 and elsewhere). In addition, as Frank Brandenburg has observed, the "revolutionary creed" has come to include several other principles: nationalism, perhaps the most prominent of all the doctrines; constitutionalism; political liberalism; racial and religious tolerance; social justice, public responsibility for economic activity; and international prestige.[46]

Though these goals are mutually consistent, for the most part, and though officeholders generally pay explicit homage to them (government correspondence being stamped with the slogan "effective suffrage —no-reelection"), these doctrines do not amount to an ideology in any strict sense of the term. It is an unwritten creed, or set of vague assumptions, that informs but does not prescribe responses to specific situations. As Howard Cline once wrote, in a spirit of unabashed praise:

> It is necessary to stress that the Mexican Revolution boasts no Marx or Engels to provide an ideology in advance and that its doctrines change from time to time without unduly embarrassing Mexicans themselves. A chief function of the official party, as a matter of fact, is to interpret and even pronounce doctrines of the evolving Revolution which are added to the cumulative corpus of attitudes and beliefs that make up its mystique. The ideology of the Mexican Revolution is, thus, eclectic, elastic, pragmatic. In this, it somewhat resembles the incremental growth of English common law, which is

[46] Frank R. Brandenburg, *The Making of Modern Mexico* (Englewood Cliffs, N.J.: Prentice-Hall, 1964), pp. 7-18.

built on case histories and mindful of precedents, but not necessarily bound by them.[47]

One might doubt, as I do, whether it is the party that interprets doctrine. It is also likely that, up until the 1940s, political action had a more ideological flavor than in recent decades. But as Cline observed, the contemporary scene is marked by pragmatism: at most, in Linz's sense, a mentality, certainly not an ideology.

APATHY VERSUS MOBILIZATION

Like the prototypical authoritarian regime, Mexico exhibits a relatively low degree of political mobilization. To be sure, there have been moments of intense, profound, and widespread mass mobilization. One such era was the decade of the Revolution, 1910-20; another was the popular fervor surrounding Cárdenas' expropriation of oil companies in 1938; there have been other, less spectacular occasions in the interim. But as Linz suggests, the most important phases of mobilization came during the formative stages of the Mexican regime. Since the mid-1940s, when the contemporary system put down institutional roots, the populace has provided the polity with passive acceptance rather than active, enthusiastic support.

Various factors underlie this situation. One is the size of what González Casanova calls the "marginal" population, perhaps 50 to 70 percent of the total, including many Indians, a stratum which has virtually no direct contact with the national political arena.[48] The deduction is simple enough: this is the most socially and economically deprived portion of Mexican society, it cannot mount effective demands on the system, *ergo* the system does not have to confront any basic challenges from those who have the most to gain from structural change.[49]

Apart from the data on literacy, schooling, and income distribution, which document the case for deprivation, two indicators illustrate the instruments of social control. One is the extent, or lack of extent, of unionization: in 1940 only 9.2 percent of Mexico's working class (including peasants and laborers) belonged to syndicates, and by 1960 the figure had barely risen to 11.8 percent.[50] The vast majority of lower-

[47] Quoted in Stanley R. Ross, ed., *Is the Mexican Revolution Dead?* (New York: Alfred A. Knopf, 1966). p. 66.

[48] *Democracy*, esp. ch. 5.

[49] Note how this relates to the notion of the "two faces of power" developed by Peter Bachrach in *The Theory of Democratic Elitism: A Critique* (Boston: Little, Brown, 1967), and in his other writings.

[50] González Casanova, *Democracy*, p. 230.

class citizens, especially the *campesinos*, have therefore had no organized means of protecting or promoting their own interests. But by the
same token, the unions that do exist, such as the Confederación de
Trabajadores Mexicanos (CTM) and the Confederación Nacional
Campesina (CNC), tend to be dependent upon the regime, function-
ing as part and parcel of the system. And when the rank and file gets
out of line, as in the strikes of 1958, the government's reaction can be
swift and brutal.[51]

A second indicator, more a result than a cause of low mobilization,
is the form and rate of participation in presidential elections. Since the
victory of the government candidate is a foregone conclusion, I am inclined to regard these elections as plebiscites, as demonstrations of
support for the regime, rather than as occasions for the popular selection of national leadership. Cast in this light, the data in Table 2-7
are richly suggestive. While they indicate that voters have sided heavily
with the official candidate, the figures also reveal that voter turnout
has been usually low, ranging from 43 to 69 percent, and that the system has never received expressions of positive support (displayed in
column 3) from much more than one-half the eligible adult population in any election year since 1946 (with the exception of 1976, to be
discussed in Chapter 10). Since the campaigns amount to sexennial
mobilization efforts, and since abstainers run risks of legal and non-
legal reprisal, this rate of support is remarkably low. Of course, some
nonvoting represents active opposition to the regime, and a very high
level of political consciousness; and much if not most of the voting
reflects passive obedience.[52] But even allowing for these effects, Table
2-7 reveals a low degree of mobilization, and it underscores a central
point: the Mexican regime draws its sustenance from a relatively small
segment of the population.

Survey research has reinforced this theme in other ways. According
to one well-known study, two-thirds of the Mexican respondents indicated that the national government had "no effect" on daily life, and

[51] See, for example, Susan Kaufman Purcell, *The Mexican Profit-Sharing Decision: Politics in an Authoritarian Regime* (Berkeley and Los Angeles: University of
California Press, 1975), pp. 18-26; and Rosa Elena Montes de Oca, "The State and
the Peasants," in *Authoritarianism in Mexico*, ed. José Luis Reyna and Richard S.
Weinert (Philadelphia: ISHI, 1977), pp. 47-63.

[52] As Susan Eckstein has observed, for example, Mexico's urban poor often take
part in elections but they basically regard voting "more as a duty than a right."
Eckstein, *The Poverty of Revolution: The State and the Urban Poor in Mexico*
(Princeton: Princeton University Press, 1977), p. 129. See also the extensive analysis
of political participation in Wayne A. Cornelius, *Politics and the Migrant Poor in
Mexico City* (Stanford: Stanford University Press, 1975), esp. chs. 3 and 4.

SOCIETY AND POLITICS

TABLE 2-7

Voting in Presidential Elections, 1934-76

Year	(1) Turnout (% Voters among Adults)[a]	(2) % Votes for Government Candidate	(3) Rate of Active Support (1 x 2)
1934	53.6	98.2	52.6
1940	57.5	93.9	54.0
1946	42.6	77.9	33.2
1952	57.9	74.3	43.0
1958[b]	49.4	90.4	44.7
1964	54.1	88.8	48.0
1970	63.9[c]	86.0	55.0
1976	69.1	93.6	64.7

SOURCES for data in columns 1 and 2: Pablo González Casanova, *Democracy in Mexico*, trans. Danielle Salti (New York: Oxford University Press, 1970), pp. 199-200 and 221; James W. Wilkie, *Statistics and National Policy*, Supplement 3 (1974) of *Statistical Abstract of Latin America* (Los Angeles: UCLA Latin American Center, 1974), p. 28; *Facts on File 1970* (New York: Facts on File, 1970), p. 544; and a personal communication from Rafael Segovia.

[a] Among adult population age 20 or over; the legal voting age prior to 1970 was 21.
[b] Women joined the presidential electorate in 1958; they are excluded from the computations for prior years.
[c] With legal voting age lowered to 18.

19 percent said they would be better off without governmental action: these levels of apathy and disaffection were much higher than those in the United Kingdom, the United States, Germany, and Italy.[53] With a much more refined survey instrument, Richard Fagen and William Tuohy have further explored the attitudinal components of passive nonresistance. Their findings emerge only from the city of Jalapa, but they almost certainly apply to broader segments of the national population:

Jalapa is a community appreciated by most of its citizens, but one where a large majority is deeply distrustful of politics and politicians. It is a city in which most citizens view themselves as powerless to affect local decisions but think that they will be treated as well as (or no worse than) others in encounters with police and bureaucrats. It is a city in which contact with the existing political system tends

[53] Gabriel A. Almond and Sidney Verba, *The Civic Culture: Political Attitudes and Democracy in Five Nations* (Princeton: Princeton University Press, 1963), pp. 79-85.

to increase negativism toward that system, but in which no opposition or reform movement exists to capitalize on the negativism. Withdrawal, apathy, feelings of powerlessness, and indifference to democratic practices form the dominant textures of citizen orientations, interlaced with individual threads of self-esteem and hope, feelings that one can and somehow will manage.

Thus, there are no masses struggling to free themselves in Jalapa; there is no widespread sense of oppression or repression. Those who are most deprived both economically and politically are least involved in the political life of the community, organizationally, ideologically, and psychologically. Those who are more advantaged are most active, allegiant, and satisfied. A long learning process, reinforced by the elitist and bureaucratic nature of politics, has created a public that is on the one hand negative toward politics and on the other hand uninvolved.[54]

The Revolution and its legacy thus provide the system with the mantle of legitimacy, and social institutions—particularly schools—constantly reinforce the message. In large part, Mexicans tolerate the system, albeit passively, because they are taught and trained to do so.[55]

Perhaps in recognition of public apathy and the regime's narrow social base, Mexican political leaders have, through periodic mobilization efforts and organizational campaigns, frequently attempted to broaden the system's constituency. It is, as Susan Kaufman Purcell has remarked, an "inclusionary" regime, one that is publicly committed to the broad incorporation of large blocs of the population.[56] Admittedly, the ulterior goal is manipulative: the purpose is to limit and control demands upon the system, to deradicalize popular pressures, not to stimulate grass-roots support for redistributive initiatives.[57] Yet in this sense Mexico still stands in stark contrast to the overtly repressive regimes of Argentina, Brazil, and Chile, where "bureaucratic-authoritarian" governments have attempted to exclude already mobilized sectors of the population (principally the working class) from political participation. Part of the difference no doubt stems from variations in historical sequence and timing: the Mexican state began to control working-class organizations *before* embarking on the road to intensive

---

[54] Richard R. Fagen and William S. Tuohy, *Politics in a Mexican City* (Stanford: Stanford University Press, 1970), pp. 129-130.

[55] On the political function of schools see Rafael Segovia, *La politicización del niño mexicano* (Mexico: El Colegio de México, 1975).

[56] Purcell, *Profit-Sharing*, pp. 3, 8.

[57] José Luis Reyna, "Redefining the Authoritarian Regime," in *Authoritarianism in Mexico*, ed. Reyna and Weinert, esp. p. 161.

industrialization, whereas the southern-cone states tried to move in afterward.[58] If the Mexican regime employs intermittent repression, and often intimidates opponents, it nonetheless relies primarily on inclusion and cooptation. An observer, in casual conversation, once summed up the government's approach: two carrots, then a stick.

ARMY AND PARTY

By all these criteria Mexico plainly qualifies as an authoritarian regime: a system of limited pluralism, with leaders guided by mentalities (not ideologies) and the masses held at low (or uneven) levels of mobilization. While Mexico complies with these defining characteristics, though, it does not share some of the accompanying characteristics which Linz found in Franco's Spain. It is important to understand these deviations from the basic model since they offer clues about the forms and special qualities of authoritarian politics in Mexico.

First, Linz extrapolates from the Spanish experience to suggest that the army occupies an ambiguous place in authoritarian regimes. Leaders often come from the military, they depend on the military, and yet they try to contain its influence. The picture is one of tension, balance, uncertainty. This ambivalence does not exist in Mexico, where the army is clearly subordinate to the state. It might be argued that Mexico passed through its phase of tension in the 1920s and 1930s, and in this sense is a more "finished" authoritarian regime than was Franco's Spain. But this is still a difference.

Second, Linz states that the authoritarian party is neither well-organized nor monopolistic, essentially a secondary institution. The PRI in Mexico is obviously a primary institution. It is visible and valuable, both as a means for claiming legitimacy and, especially, as an instrument of cooptation and control. It possesses considerable economic resources, often in the form of government subsidies, and it claims literally millions of members. It is not an arena of key decisionmaking; nor is it a pathway to power. As shown by Figure 2-2, in fact, no more than 14 percent of the cabinet members in any presidential administration since 1928 had ever served on the party's National Executive Committee; no more than 26 percent had ever held any significant party post of any kind. It would be incorrect, I think, to assert that the party runs the government in Mexico, and the reverse is probably closer to the truth. (For this reason I shall usually refer to the regime as "tutelary" or "authoritarian," not as a "single-party" or "dominant-party" one.)

[58] See Robert R. Kaufman, "Mexico and Latin American Authoritarianism," in *Authoritarianism in Mexico*, ed. Reyna and Weinert, pp. 193-232.

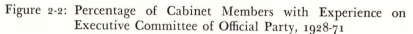

Figure 2-2: Percentage of Cabinet Members with Experience on Executive Committee of Official Party, 1928-71

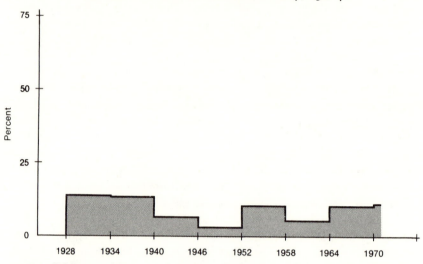

NOTE: Cabinet positions are defined as those with scale values of 8 for the HIGHEST OFFICE variable (see Appendix A, Table A-3).

On the other hand, the party is a major component of the political system.[59]

STATE AND ECONOMY

One of the implicit characteristics of an authoritarian regime concerns its role in economic affairs. A totalitarian state, by most definitions, completely controls the economic system, while a democratic polity tends to regulate the operation of an otherwise unfettered market system. An authoritarian regime, by contrast, plays an active economic role: it intervenes in, and to some extent controls, the economy, without fully dominating it.

Mexico fits this pattern in paradoxical ways. A central function of the state, especially since the 1950s, has been to serve as an employment center. According to one recent analysis, the absolute number of upper-level bureaucratic positions in the national government nearly doubled during the 16-year period between 1956 and 1972, growing from about 1,200 posts to 2,200[60]—not to mention clerical and other jobs. (Even in 1960, according to Table 2-2, the government provided jobs for nearly

[59] On the role of the party see also Purcell, *Profit-Sharing*, pp. 41-46.
[60] Rainer Horst Godau, "Mexico: A Bureaucratic Polity" (M.A. thesis, University of Texas at Austin, 1975), p. 134. For additional data see Merilee Serrill Grindle, *Bureaucrats, Politicians, and Peasants in Mexico* (Berkeley and Los Angeles: University of California Press, 1977), pp. 188-189.

4 percent of the work force, a figure that has surely risen in the mean-time.) Much of this bureaucratic expansion has merely created oppor-tunities for sinecure and patronage, in keeping with the premises of *camarilla* politics, but it has also augmented the state's role as an em-ployer.

The Mexican government has played a major part in national in-vestment. In addition to direct spending through federal departments and ministries, the state allocates a large share of the budget—well over half in recent years—to dozens of special agencies and state-sup-ported companies. The leading lending institutions, most conspicu-ously the Nacional Financiera, are operated by the government, and the manipulation of credit regulations endows the state with consider-able influence over the economy. As shown in Table 2-8, the govern-ment as of 1970 controlled principal shares in 9 of the country's top 10 firms, in 13 out of the top 25, and in 16 out of the top 50.[61] Most of the leading state-dominated firms have been involved in credit bank-ing, public services (telephones and electricity), or in high-cost infra-structural activities (such as steel production), so they do not always compete directly with the private sector. Nonetheless, the state contin-ues to be a major investor in Mexico's capitalist society.

TABLE 2-8

Principal Shareholders in 50 Largest Companies, 1970

Principal Shareholder	Top 10 Companies	Top 25 Companies	Top 50 Companies
Mexican government	9	13	16
Mexican private	1	9	14
Foreign private	—	1	14
Mixed	—	2	3
Unknown	—	—	3
Totals	10	25	50

SOURCE: Adapted from David Barkin, "Mexico's Albatross: The U.S. Economy," *Latin American Perspectives* 2, no. 2 (Summer 1975): 68.

But it does not completely dominate the national economy. For one thing, Mexico's pattern of growth has led to the formation of a fairly powerful and concentrated domestic private sector—landowners, mer-

61 See also the data in Frank Brandenburg, "The Relevance of Mexican Experi-ence to Latin American Development," *Orbis* 9, no. 1 (Spring 1965): 196.

chants, financiers, industrialists. The most visible expression of this situation is the preeminence of about a dozen investment groups, generally known by the names of their leaders or dominant families (Luis G. Legorreta, Raúl Baillerés, Carlos Trouyet, Bruno Pagliai, Luis Águilar, the Garza Sada clan, and so on). Instead of specializing within limited fields, these groups typically have complex webs of interest in finance, industry, commerce, and real estate. Organizations within a group work closely together, and there have also been alliances between different groups as well.[62] Through arrangements of this sort, as revealed in Table 2-8, Mexican investors controlled 9 of the country's top 25 companies in 1970, taking second place only to the state, and they held principal shares in 14 out of the top 50, keeping an even pace with foreigners. The national private sector is far from monolithic, but horizontal linkages and alliances tend to blur distinctions between its component segments, and, united or not, it exerts considerable impact on the Mexican economy.

Nor does the state command an overwhelming share of national income. According to the data in Table 2-9, for instance, Mexican central government expenditures in 1973 amounted to only 7.2 percent of the gross domestic product, a genuinely modest rate by international standards—much lower than the corresponding figures for such Latin American nations as Peru (18.6 percent), Uruguay (12.8 percent), and Venezuela (12.7 percent), not to mention Algeria or the United Kingdom (20.2 percent each), and substantially lower than the figures for such countries as Argentina (9.5 percent), France (14.7 percent), or the United States (11.7 percent), where the central government controlled much smaller shares of total public spending than in Mexico.[63] Despite the evident power of the Mexican government, and notwithstanding the overbearing prestige of the president, the state does not control the society in anywhere near totalitarian fashion. It is an active, strong, and influential regime, a position thoroughly in keeping with its authoritarian character.

In conclusion, Mexico has developed an authoritarian regime, one with considerable power, though somewhat less legitimacy. Public office, in this system, can furthermore provide incumbents with access to

[62] See Robert T. Aubey, *Nacional Financiera and Mexican Industry: A Study of the Financial Relationships between the Government and the Private Sector of Mexico* (Los Angeles: UCLA Latin American Center, Latin American Studies, Vol. 3, 1966), pp. 76-78.

[63] See also the treatment in Hansen, *Politics*, p. 84. For additional data on the relative size of Mexico's government budget see Morris Singer, *Growth, Equality, and the Mexican Experience* (Austin: University of Texas Press, 1969), p. 211; and Reynolds, *Mexican Economy*, p. 269.

TABLE 2-9

Government Expenditures as Percent of GDP,
Selected Countries, 1973

Country	Total Current Government Expenditure as % of GDP	Central Government Expenditure as % of GDP
Argentina	11.2	9.5
Brazil	25.4	n.a.
Colombia	10.4	4.1
Mexico	n.a.	7.2
Peru	19.3	18.6
Uruguay	27.4	12.8
Venezuela	14.6	12.7
Algeria	n.a.	20.2
France	32.3	14.7
United Kingdom	35.9	20.2
United States	30.6	11.7

SOURCE: Adapted from World Bank, *World Tables 1976* (Baltimore: Johns Hopkins University Press, 1976), Table 7.

substantial economic gain (a topic to be dealt with in more detail below). Because of these rewards, political office is a highly prized commodity: in the words of Fagen and Tuohy, "there exists a complex and meaningful struggle for position and advantage, as well as for the symbolic and material rewards of office."[64] It is the object of this inquiry, of course, to find out who competes, who wins, and how. The result, I hope, can provide an empirical foundation for understanding the *kind* of authoritarian regime that prevails in modern Mexico. To repeat a statement made in Chapter 1: if authoritarianism consists of "limited pluralism," it makes sense to determine who falls on which side of the limits—who does (and does not) have the functional right to organize and compete for power. As Linz himself has indicated, the composition of elites must necessarily comprise a central dimension of any eventual classification or typology of authoritarian regimes.[65]

And changes in elite composition, in turn, can presumably result from variations in either socioeconomic or political factors. As outlined in this chapter, economic change in twentieth-century Mexico

[64] Fagen and Tuohy, *Politics*, p. 23.
[65] On this point see Juan J. Linz, "Notes toward a Typology of Authoritarian Regimes" (paper presented at the annual meeting of the American Political Science Association, Washington, D.C., 1972), p. 27.

has entailed, primarily, growth, industrialization (of the capital-intensive variety), concentration of wealth, reliance on foreign capital, and state intervention. Social concomitants of these processes have included urbanization, the appearance of an industrial bourgeoisie, expansion of the middle class, the emergence of an urban proletariat, and the maintenance of class distinctions. The key political events are plain to see: the Revolution, with all its contradictions and complexities, such as the principle of "no-reelection," and the formation of a stable authoritarian regime. It is the guiding purpose of this book to determine which of these sets of factors—economic, social, or political—have had *what kind* and *how much* impact on the transformation of elites over time.

Part II

THE RESULTS OF REVOLUTION

· 3 ·

THE SOCIAL CONDITIONS
OF RULE

One of the central concerns of this study focuses upon the social conditions of rule in twentieth-century Mexico. In virtually all societies, no matter what the system of stratification, people from specific social backgrounds acquire a greater share of political power than do others. That is, the possession of certain attributes can yield decisive advantage (or disadvantage) in the pursuit of power. Some political systems have relied on racial segregation, for example, with blacks excluded from participation; in such an instance, white skin would be a social "condition" of rule. Other systems have furnished disproportionate amounts of power to the well-born at the expense of the poor, to university graduates instead of the less educated, to city dwellers rather than country people, to lawyers or soldiers instead of teachers or laborers.

This subject acquires special salience because Mexico has undergone a popular revolution. One of the most persistent ideas in contemporary political literature is that—whatever else it might have done—the Revolution sharply expanded the range and frequency of social mobility. In particular, it is argued, the political system became open to people of talent, at least on a relative scale, and an ever-larger share of the population has been able to aspire to (if not attain) political office. In other words, the social conditions of rule have been relaxed; the passports to power have become less restrictive than before. It is the purpose of this chapter, and the other sections of Part II, to find out whether this is true. What have been the social characteristics of political leadership in Mexico, and how they have changed over time?

To begin exploring these issues I shall trace the quantitative incidence of specific social background attributes within Mexico's national political elite from 1900 to 1971. As explained in Chapter 1, and also in Appendix A, I have operationally defined the elite as those people holding major national office, from seats in the legislature to governorships to cabinet portfolios and so on, for a total of 6,302 individuals. Partly because of my decision to work with such large pools of officeholders, several key indicators of social background have proved impossible to get, at least in any meaningful amount: family wealth, income level, social class (however defined), skin color. I particularly regret my inability to find solid or extensive data on kinship and family connections, though I touch on this theme in Chapters 9 and 10. As a result, information is restricted to:

  a. place of birth, which can reveal regional dimensions in political recruitment and also shed light on the importance of urban-rural distinctions;

  b. father's occupation, normally a useful (though problematic) indicator of socioeconomic origin, but available for so few individuals as to be of somewhat dubious significance;

  c. level of education, obviously a crucial determinant of "life chances" in a stratified society, perhaps my best proxy measure of socioeconomic status (as distinct from origin);

  d. place of education, which can reveal opportunities for the formation of friendships, contacts, and incipient alliances;

  e. occupation, a valuable but often deceptive indicator of socioeconomic status;[1]

  f. date of birth, which yields information on career patterns and on the age structure of political elites.

In order to locate patterns of change over time, I focus on two kinds of chronological unit: one refers to individual presidential regimes, the other consists of officeholding cohorts. For both analyses I separate an upper-level elite from the total elite and, where possible, I compare the composition of elites to the national population at large. To gain additional perspective, I also compare some of the findings on Mexico to situations in some other polities.

REGIONAL ORIGIN

Regionalism has long been a major force in Mexican politics. The country's natural terrain has presented formidable obstacles to integration and communication, and prevailing political styles—with their stress on personal, face-to-face contact—have tended to dwell on local loyalties. Many Mexicans thus have come to see their region—village, city, state, or area—as the primary arena for political action. This phenomenon was particularly apparent in the nineteenth century, when large landowners and regional bosses (*caudillos*) built their strength around locally based, usually multiclass coalitions. To some extent these patterns had an economic foundation, too, as the port area of

[1] On the difficulty of equating occupation with socioeconomic status see the items in note 29 of Chapter 2.

Veracruz and the bureaucratic-industrial center in Mexico City gained supremacy and came to constitute a dominating axis that was both recognized and resented by people from other areas.[2] According to most interpretations, the *Porfiriato* (1876-1911) led to consolidation and centralization of power, and the Revolution, notwithstanding its vicissitudes, further promoted the cause of national integration. If these views are correct, the regional location of one's birthplace should have had a small, and declining, impact on one's chances of gaining access to the national political elite since the turn of this century.

To examine this hypothesis I shall classify birthplaces by states and also by official census regions. As shown by the map in Figure 3-1, the *Pacific North* includes the states and federal territories of Baja California (Norte and Sur), Nayarit (formerly Tepic), Sinaloa, and Sonora. The *North* contains Chihuahua, Coahuila, Durango, Nuevo León, San Luis Potosí, Tamaulipas, and Zacatecas. The *Center* consists of Aguascalientes, Guanajuato, Hidalgo, Jalisco, México, Michoacán, Morelos, Puebla, Querétaro, and Tlaxcala. Because of its special importance the *Federal District*, with Mexico City and its environs, is here considered as a separate region, though the census includes it as part of the Center. The *Gulf* comprises Campeche, Quintana Roo, Tabasco, Veracruz, and Yucatán. The *Pacific South* contains Chiapas, Colima, Guerrero, and Oaxaca.

Illustrating regional representation within the national political elite, Table 3-1 presents data on the proportional composition of the total elites and upper-level elites, by cohort, plus the general population in pertinent census years.[3] Since the total elites include allegedly elective positions (governorships and seats in the national legislature) they tend to match the general population more closely than do the upper elites—suggesting, in fact, that one primary function of electoral office has been to assure a relative balance of regional interests. Even then, the patterns are revealing.

Under Díaz, the prerevolutionary cohort presented an ambiguous

[2] See Harry Bernstein, "Regionalism in the National History of Mexico," in *Latin American History: Essays on Its Teaching and Interpretation,* ed. Howard Cline (Austin: University of Texas Press, 1967), I, 389-394; and Bernstein's extraordinarily perceptive treatment of Mexico in *Modern and Contemporary Latin America* (Chicago, Philadelphia, New York: J. B. Lippincott, 1952), chs. 3-9.

[3] The handful of officeholders born in other countries has been excluded from the computations. Ideally, it would have been desirable to depict the geographical distribution of the total population for years closest to the median date of birth for each cohort, but there were no national censuses taken before 1895. In order to make the data comparable for all the cohorts, I therefore decided to use data from censuses taken near the midpoint of their officeholding periods and at equal (30-year) intervals.

Figure 3-1: Map of States and Regions of Mexico

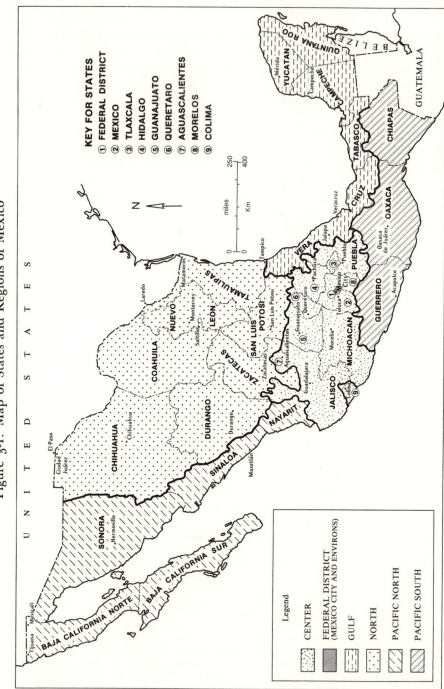

KEY FOR STATES
① FEDERAL DISTRICT
② MEXICO
③ TLAXCALA
④ HIDALGO
⑤ GUANAJUATO
⑥ QUERETARO
⑦ AGUASCALIENTES
⑧ MORELOS
⑨ COLIMA

Legend
CENTER
FEDERAL DISTRICT
(MEXICO CITY AND ENVIRONS)
GULF
NORTH
PACIFIC NORTH
PACIFIC SOUTH

TABLE 3-1

Regional Origins of Total Elite, Upper-Level Elite, and General Populations, by Cohort

Region[a]	Prerevolutionary Cohort, 1900-1911 % among Total Elite (N = 185)	% among Upper Elite (N = 23)	% among General Population, 1900[b]
Pacific North	5.4	4.2	5.3
North	24.9	20.8	19.0
Center	26.5	16.7	46.9
Federal District	13.5	20.8	4.0
Gulf	18.9	20.8	11.3
Pacific South	10.8	12.5	13.6

Region	Revolutionary Cohort, 1917-40 % among Total Elite (N = 745)	% among Upper Elite (N = 151)	% among General Population, 1930[c]
Pacific North	11.4	15.9	5.9
North	27.7	28.5	18.9
Center	32.3	32.5	41.2
Federal District	5.4	7.3	7.4
Gulf	11.4	7.3	12.6
Pacific South	11.8	8.6	14.0

Region	Postrevolutionary Cohort, 1946-71 % among Total Elite (N = 1,205)	% among Upper Elite (N = 135)	% among General Population, 1960[d]
Pacific North	8.5	5.2	8.0
North	21.4	19.3	23.9
Center	33.5	24.4	30.3
Federal District	10.1	20.0	18.3
Gulf	13.5	20.7	11.0
Pacific South	12.9	10.4	8.5

[a] On the composition of the regions, see map in Figure 3-1.

[b] Regional distribution of total population as of 1900; the geographical origins of the birthplaces of the native-born population (as of the same year) is virtually identical. Source: Secretaría de Economía, Dirección General de Estadística, *Estadísticas sociales del porfiriato 1877-1910* (Mexico: Talleres Gráficos de la Nación, 1956), Cuadros 1 and 5, pp. 8, 12.

[c] Regional distribution of total population as of 1930. Source: Secretaría de la Economía Nacional, Dirección General de Estadística, *Anuario estadístico de los Estados Unidos Mexicanos 1939* (Mexico: Talleres Gráficos de la Nación, 1941), p. 29.

[d] Regional distribution of literate adult male population as of 1960. SOURCE: Secretaría de Industria y Comercio, Dirección General de Estadística, *VIII censo general de la población 1960. Resumen general* (Mexico: Talleres Gráficos de la Nación, 1962), pp. 290-307.

picture. All regions found fairly substantial representation, even among the upper-level elite, where the smallest delegation, that of the Pacific North (4.2 percent) was just barely under the area's share of the general population (5.3 percent). This broad distribution of offices appears to be entirely consistent with Díaz's political style. As a master compromiser and consummate coalition-builder, he was extraordinarily adept at playing competing interests off against each other in order to maintain his own supremacy—and it can be safely assumed that regions figured in his calculus.[4]

But there were also some imbalances. A native of Oaxaca, he drew a disproportionate share of top-level leaders from his home state (which accounts for the entire 12.5 percent from the Pacific South), thus continuing the nineteenth-century pattern of presidential prerogative. Equally striking is the ascendancy of the Federal District, with 20.8 percent of upper-level positions (contrasting to only 4 percent of the population), and the Gulf, mainly Veracruz, with nearly double its expected share of top positions. Clearly, Díaz built his coalition around the power of the traditional Mexico-Veracruz axis, the commercial network that provided the necessary linkage to the international economic system. To this alliance he added the economically powerful North when, in 1904, he chose Ramón Corral of Sonora to be vice-president. These preferences came at the explicit expense of the Center, which was severely underrepresented among both total and upper-level elites.

The Revolution disrupted the Porfirian equilibrium and, if anything, accentuated the pattern of interregional struggle. Francisco Madero embodied a challenge from the North; himself from Coahuila, he recruited nearly one-third of his cabinet from his native state alone. The Center, so neglected under Díaz, found fleeting moments of preeminence under two successive regimes—first under Victoriano Huerta (1913-14), from Jalisco, then under the Convention of 1914-15. But the triumph went to the North, with the victory of Carranza, a native of Coahuila, and then it passed to the Pacific North—and, more particularly, to the state of Sonora, which produced four of the country's six presidents between 1920 and 1934 (de la Huerta, Obregón, Calles, and Rodríguez).

---

[4] For a detailed description of the Díaz cabinets see Daniel Cosío Villegas, *Historia moderna de México. El porfiriato: La vida política interior, segunda parte* (Mexico: Editorial Hermes, 1972), pp. 11-23 and 393-401. Cosío Villegas does not discuss the regional or social composition of the cabinets (nor, for that matter, does Bernstein); my point is that, from the description given by Cosío, it would have been entirely consistent for Díaz to recruit his cabinet according to regional as well as other political considerations.

As a result, Table 3-1 reveals that the North had well over its share of representatives in the revolutionary cohort, and the Pacific North had nearly three times its expected proportion of upper-level leaders (15.9 percent compared to 5.9 percent for the general population). The Center remained underrepresented, though less so than under Díaz (two presidents of the 1917-40 era, Pascual Ortiz Rubio and Lázaro Cárdenas, were from the central state of Michoacán). For these rearrangements, there can be no doubting who paid the price: the Federal District, which lost its prerevolutionary advantage, and the Gulf, which slipped down to a position of relative disadvantage. The Revolution by no means eliminated the nineteenth-century game of regional politicking. On the contrary, the movement clearly had a regional foundation, representing a challenge of the country's northern tier against the Mexico City-Veracruz axis. And it was by playing the regional game, in fact, that leaders of the revolutionary cohort broke the pattern of the Mexico City-Veracruz hegemony.

It remained for the postrevolutionary cohort to create an equilibrium. To be sure, individual presidents have generally continued to favor sons of their native states; Alemán and Ruiz Cortines did so with Veracruz, López Mateos did the same with México, and Echeverría did so with the Federal District. This process no doubt reflects the continuing importance of personal contacts and friendship, a point to be taken up in some detail in Chapters 9 and 10, and it also means that the location of one's birthplace can seriously affect one's chances of reaching high national office under any single president. But the crucial point is that since 1946 the presidency has been passed around among states and regions, and the *cumulative* effect of this process has been to create regional equilibrium in elite recruitment—as reflected, for the most part, in the postrevolutionary cohort data in Table 3-1. Thus there has been a regional balance, but it is due partly to an adaptation of traditional practices of local loyalty as well as to a broad-based process of national recruitment.[5]

URBAN-RURAL BACKGROUNDS

Aside from variation in region and state of origin, twentieth-century Mexican elites have undergone significant change along urban-rural dimensions. It is common, in most societies, for political leadership to come from relatively urbanized communities, since educational facili-

[5] On this point see also Paul W. Drake, "Mexican Regionalism Reconsidered," *Journal of Interamerican Studies and World Affairs* 12, no. 3 (July 1970): 401-415, esp. 410.

ties, diverse occupational opportunities, and governmental institutions tend to cluster in cities. As Robert Putnam has reported, many elites around the world "are drawn disproportionately from cities, especially metropolitan areas. The underrepresentation of farm, village and small town characterizes both developed and underdeveloped countries, both capitalist and communist systems."[6] But in Mexico a recruitment bias in favor of urban residents would be especially discriminatory, given the historically rural character of the population: in 1910 around 71.3 percent of the people lived in the countryside, in 1930 about 66.5 percent did so, and by 1960 approximately 49.3 percent still remained outside the cities.[7] Where did the elites come from?

A partial answer to this question appears in Figure 3-2, which plots the proportion of upper-level officeholders in successive presidential regimes that are known to have come from three types of communities: a *metropolis*, or major city, defined as one with 50,000 or more inhabitants as of 1921; a medium-sized *city or town*, with 10,000 to 49,999 inhabitants; and a *village or the country*, that is, a relatively rural community, one with less than 10,000 inhabitants. (One problem with this categorization is that it refers to community size only in 1921, the first year that the census provided a complete list of cities by population size, and Mexican cities have undergone dramatic growth in the past 100 years or so. The rank order of cities by population size has held fairly constant, however, so the scheme presents a reasonably accurate picture of the relative importance of the major urban areas.)

Despite uncertainties of measurement, the overall pattern is strikingly clear. The Porfirian elite was an urban elite. In the 1904-10 administration, for instance, one-third of the upper-level officeholders came from metropolitan communities; 40 percent came from medium-sized cities; despite the overwhelmingly rural character of the national population at the time, barely one-quarter came from villages, and hardly anyone was from the "countryside" as such. While Díaz made some effort to strike a balance among the regions, that is, he distinctly favored people from the urbanized communities.

The Revolution broke this pattern. Starting with the Madero regime, Figure 3-2 reveals a sharp and upward shift in the proportion of leaders from rural villages, which roughly doubled from around 25 percent to 50 percent. Intermediate cities continued to hold their own,

[6] Robert D. Putnam, *The Comparative Study of Political Elites* (Englewood Cliffs, N.J.: Prentice-Hall, 1976), p. 32.

[7] James W. Wilkie, *The Mexican Revolution: Federal Expenditure and Social Change since 1910* (Berkeley and Los Angeles: University of California Press, 1967), pp. 218-219. Rural communities are here defined as those with less than 2,500 inhabitants.

Figure 3-2: Size of Birthplace for Upper-Level Elites, 1900-1971 (By N inhabitants as of 1921)

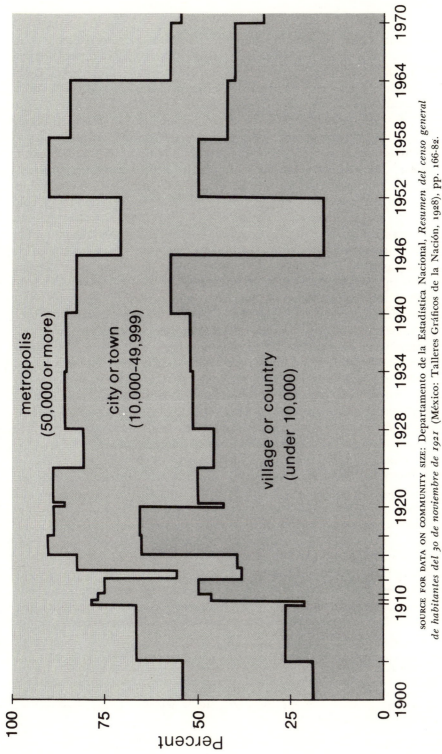

SOURCE FOR DATA ON COMMUNITY SIZE: Departamento de la Estadística Nacional, *Resumen del censo general de habitantes del 30 de noviembre de 1921* (México: Talleres Gráficos de la Nación, 1928), pp. 166-82.

while the metropolitan communities had their share reduced to 20 percent or so—a pattern that stabilized around 1920 and persisted until the early 1940s. In part, then, the Revolution represented a movement of the countryside against the city, and specifically of small-town people against sons of the metropolis.

Then a reversal took place. Beginning in 1946, as shown in Figure 3-2, the Alemán regime reduced the recruitment of village-or-country elites and increased the share for metropolitan locations and, particularly, for medium-sized cities. After Ruiz Cortines temporarily reestablished the post-1920 pattern of rural hegemony, a secular trend then emerged: increasing proportions of upper-level positions for people from major cities at the expense of *both* the intermediate communities and rural areas. Since the consolidation of the tutelary regime in the late 1930s and early 1940s, the upper echelons of power have been recaptured by the cities—most notably by big cities and, in particular, by the Federal District (see also Table 3-1).

A full interpretation of these changes must account for rising levels of urbanization in the general population, however, and for this reason Table 3-2 offers data on the cohorts—and contrasts them with corresponding figures for the nation as a whole.[8] As suggested by Figure 3-2, the Díaz elite was much more urban than the population at large. No matter what the definition of urbanization—as a state capital, as a modern city or a state capital, or as a metropolitan community— people from urban areas had five or six times their expected share of leaders in the political elite. For the prerevolutionary cohort, cities provided an important pathway to national office.

Data on the revolutionary cohort sharply modify the implications of the time-series trends. While Figure 3-2 clearly demonstrates that the 1917-40 leadership was decidedly more rural than preceding and succeeding elites, Table 3-2 reveals that it was not more rural than the population as a whole: *in most respects it was more urban.* Among the upper-level officeholders, for example, 34.7 percent came from state capitals, where only 13.7 percent of the population lived in 1930; a similar imbalance holds for the city-or-capital category (41.9 percent against 16.8 percent). For the large, metropolitan communities, however, the percentages came out about even, 13.5 for the top elite and 11.6 for the population, which means that people from the major cities

[8] Note that figures for the general population refer to place of *residence* in the given census year, rather than the size of the community at birth (or in 1921), and this tends to inflate the nationwide figures for urbanization of birthplace. On the other hand, the literate adult male population—with which I would have liked to compare the elites—was undoubtedly more urban in origin than the population at large, so this bias in the data might actually improve the accuracy of the estimate. See also note 3 above.

TABLE 3-2

Urban Origins of Total Elite, Upper-Level Elite,
and General Populations, by Cohort

Type of Birthplace	Prerevolutionary Cohort, 1900-1911		
	% among Total Elite (N = 178)	% among Upper Elite (N = 22)	% among General Population, 1900[d]
Capital of state or territory[a]	57.3	66.7	9.0
City or capital[b]	65.2	77.3	12.7
Metropolis[c]	30.3	36.4	6.2
Type of Birthplace	Revolutionary Cohort, 1917-40		
	% among Total Elite (N = 694)	% among Upper Elite (N = 148)	% among General Population, 1930[e]
Capital of state or territory	34.8	34.7	13.7
City or capital	38.0	41.9	16.8
Metropolis	15.7	13.5	11.6
Type of Birthplace	Postrevolutionary Cohort, 1946-71		
	% among Total Elite (N = 1,158)	% among Upper Elite (N = 135)	% among General Population, 1960[f]
Capital of state or territory	40.5	51.1	20.4
City or capital	45.8	60.0	23.9
Metropolis	23.4	31.9	15.0

[a] Mexico City is counted as the capital of the Federal District.

[b] Either a capital or a city with 20,000 or more inhabitants as of 1921. See Departamento de la Estadística Nacional, *Resumen del censo general de habitantes del 30 de noviembre de 1921* (Mexico: Talleres Gráficos de la Nación, 1928), pp. 166-182.

[c] Cities with 50,000 or more inhabitants as of 1921.

[d] Estimated residential distribution for total population as of 1900, based on data in Secretaría de Economía, Dirección General de Estadística, *Estadísticas sociales del porfiriato 1877-1910* (Mexico: Talleres Gráficos de la Nación, 1956), p. 9; and Secretaría de la Economía Nacional, Dirección General de Estadística, *Anuario estadístico de los Estados Unidos Mexicanos 1939* (Mexico: Talleres Gráficos de la Nación, 1941), pp. 43, 48; with some extrapolation drawn from relative sizes of cities according to source cited in note b.

[e] Estimated residential distribution for total population as of 1930, based on data in Secretaría de la Economía Nacional, Dirección General de Estadística, *Quinto censo de población, 15 de mayo de 1930. Resumen general* (Mexico: Talleres Gráficos de la Nación, 1934), pp. 35-37, 151-152; and Secretaría de la Economía Nacional, Dirección General de Estadística, *Anuario estadístico . . . 1939*, pp. 43, 48; with some extrapolation drawn from relative sizes of cities according to source cited in note b.

[f] Residential distribution for total male population as of 1960, based on data in Secretaría de Industria y Comercio, Dirección General de Estadística, *VIII censo general de la población, 1960. Resumen general* (Mexico: Talleres Gráficos de la Nación, 1962), pp. 11-51.

were getting just about their fair share of upper-level positions—no more and no less. It would be inappropriate, in other words, to speak of the revolutionary cohort as a genuinely rural elite; at no time did the rural population possess more than its expected share of offices. But it is equally true that the Revolution reduced the relative advantage of being from a state capital and actually eliminated the advantage of being from a major city. In other words, it tended to elevate people from relatively small and medium-sized communities to power. Just as the Revolution meant a regional challenge of the North against the Mexico-Veracruz axis, it also entailed a movement of town against metropolis.

The post-1946 adjustment then reurbanized the national elite, as illustrated in Figure 3-2, but, since the general population was also becoming more urban, the inequalities were not nearly so glaring as under the *Porfiriato*. In general, people from cities (however defined) acquired two to three times their expected share of national offices, either in the total elite or the upper elite. City life again provided a head start, but a smaller one than in prerevolutionary years.

The reasons for this semicyclical pattern in elite composition (extremely urban, not so urban, highly but not extremely urban) are less apparent than the fact of its existence. Throughout this century, city dwellers in Mexico have possessed relative advantage in the pursuit of political careers—perhaps because of exposure to educational systems, governmental institutions, and personal networks. This was particularly true during periods of relative stability: the late *Porfiriato* and unchallenged tutelary rule since 1946. By contrast, the military campaigns of the Revolution mobilized the rural population, made it an active participant in politics, and elevated numerous sons of rural and small-town families to positions of national prominence.[9] When things later quieted down, the big-city types took over once again.

---

[9] This same pattern appeared in the revolutionary movements of Algeria and Yugoslavia, but not in the case of Kemalist Turkey, where the revolutionary cadre tended to be more urban than its rivals. On the basis of this fragmentary evidence, it appears that revolutionary movements that endured long periods of sustained, physical violence tended to incorporate rural elements into leadership positions; those which took power with relative speed, and less violence, remained more urban in origin. For the data behind this generalization see William B. Quandt, *Revolution and Political Leadership: Algeria, 1954-1968* (Cambridge: M.I.T. Press, 1969), pp. 72-73; Lenard Cohen, "The Social Background and the Recruitment of Yugoslav Political Elites, 1918-48," in *Opinion-Making Elites in Yugoslavia*, ed. Allen H. Barton, Bogdan Denitch, and Charles Kadushin (New York: Praeger, 1973), pp. 54-55; and Frederick W. Frey, *The Turkish Political Elite* (Cambridge: M.I.T. Press, 1965), pp. 186-187.

FATHER'S OCCUPATION

Despite its intrinsic significance, the discovery that leaders came from cities merely begs another set of questions. What was their class origin? Did they come from the upper strata of society? Has it ever been possible for people from humble backgrounds to have substantial access to positions of power? Has politics in Mexico offered much chance for upward social mobility?

As an extremely tentative effort to start coping with such issues, Table 3-3 offers data on the distribution of known occupations for fathers of members of the three officeholding cohorts. The table suffers from serious limitations. First, the information pertains to less than one-tenth of the respective cohorts, and there is no reason to be-

TABLE 3-3

Fathers' Occupations for Political Elites, by Cohort

Class and Occupation	% among Prerevolutionary Cohort, 1900-1911 (N known = 35)	% among Revolutionary Cohort, 1917-40 (N known = 101)	% among Postrevolutionary Cohort, 1946-71 (N known = 192)
Upper class:			
Businessman	0.0	1.0	1.6
Landowner	5.7	8.9	3.1
Unspecified	28.6	5.0	1.0
Subtotals	34.3	14.9	5.7
Middle class:			
Lawyer	5.7	7.9	7.8
Military	0.0	6.9	8.3
Other professional	14.3	13.9	16.7
Politician	17.1	9.9	13.0
Merchant	5.7	5.0	4.2
Farmer	0.0	5.9	6.3
Civil servant	0.0	4.0	2.6
Employee	0.0	0.0	2.6
Unspecified	11.4	14.9	8.9
Subtotals	54.3	68.3	70.3
Lower class:			
Worker	0.0	0.0	3.6
Peasant	5.7	5.0	11.5
Unspecified	5.7	11.9	8.9
Subtotals	11.4	16.8	24.0
Totals	100.0	100.0	100.0

77

lieve that the present observations necessarily constitute random samples of the cohort populations. Second, the names of occupations furnish no direct guide to income levels or social status. Third, despite the problem of occupational categorization, I have grouped the father's positions according to a wholly impressionistic set of socioeconomic classes, partly in order to take advantage of some judgmental data (so-and-so came "from a wealthy family," or was "of humble circumstance") and partly in order to stress the separation of manual laborers from white-collar types. The distinction between the upper and middle classes is, as I have said in Chapter 2, a largely arbitrary one.[10] The gap between the upper-middle groups and the lower class is more significant.

Notwithstanding all these limitations, Table 3-3 conveys some strong impressions. The most compelling suggestion is that *Mexico's national political elites have consistently come from "middle-class" origins.* During the prerevolutionary era, when this stratum contained only 8 or 9 percent of the population at large, as shown in Chapter 2 (Table 2-4), over 50 percent of the cohort members had fathers in the middle class. The figure climbed to nearly 70 percent for the revolutionary cohort, and stayed at that same level for the postrevolutionary generation, by whose time the middle class still accounted for less than 20 percent of the national population. Throughout, most of these fathers have been engaged in the professions—law, the military, or "other" professions such as medicine, teaching, journalism, and so forth—and quite a few had taken active part in public life.

Just as people of middle-class origin have steadily dominated the ranks of the elite, those from lower-class background have never (except, perhaps, for 1914-15) occupied a conspicuous place among the country's national leaders. Under Díaz, approximately 11.4 percent of all known officeholders are thought to have come from the lower strata, which contained about 90 percent of the Mexican population. Though the Revolution is often believed to have greatly expanded the rates of social mobility, the figure moved up to only 16.8 percent for the 1917-40 cohort. For the postrevolutionary cohort the proportion crept up again, to 24 percent, but it was still far below the corresponding share (about 80 percent) for the society at large.

The data also point to a gradual erosion in the political role of the Mexican upper class. Over one-third of the prerevolutionary cohort is

---

[10] But not entirely, at least on the conceptual level. The "upper" class, in this scheme, is meant to correspond to the social stratum which, in a capitalist society, possesses direct ownership and control over the means of production. The "middle" class, though often amply rewarded, performs its functions largely in the service of the upper class.

thought to have come from the country's top socioeconomic stratum. The Revolution cut this percentage in half (to 14.9 percent), and the figure has since continued its decline (reaching 5.7 percent for the postrevolutionary cohort). Though these figures may well understate the political salience of the upper class, the trend suggests an identifiable, and growing, separation between the country's economic and political elites. (I shall return to this point in Chapter 7.)

Despite the weakness of the data base, these findings have momentous implications. First, and most obviously, they lend empirical support to the notion that the Mexican Revolution, at least regarding leadership, was a bourgeois movement that sought to modernize, not overthrow, the country's capitalist system. Of course it is possible for leaders to betray their class, and, as mentioned in Chapter 1, social origin is a deceptive guide to social purpose (witness Fidel Castro). On the other hand, most socialist movements—from the early British Labour Party[11] to the Yugoslav Communist Party[12] to the central committees of China[13] and the Soviet Union[14]—have recruited substantial numbers of leaders from the lower classes, usually in collaboration with some intellectuals, especially in the initial stages of the movements. Mexico, by contrast, *never* went through a period of proletarian or peasant preeminence, a point I shall reiterate below. And though this factor is far from unicausal, it at least provides a social basis for interpreting the direction of national policy.

Second, the transformations in Mexico comply closely with trends in other Western, or capitalist, societies. From the mid-nineteenth century to the contemporary era, data on the social origins of political elites in Britain, France, Germany, and the United States all reveal three basic trends: a decline in the political role of the upper class, an expansion in the importance of the middle class, and, later, the rise (within limits) of the lower class. Since these patterns have taken hold despite great differences in political organization, they appear to reflect, and result from, the socioeconomic consequences of the Industrial

[11] W. L. Guttsman, "Changes in British Labour Leadership," in *Political Decision-Makers*, ed. Dwaine Marvick (Glencoe, Ill.: Free Press, 1961), pp. 91-137 and esp. pp. 99-107.

[12] Cohen, "Social Background," pp. 43-44.

[13] Derek J. Waller, "The Chinese Communist Political Elite: Continuity and Innovation," in Carl Beck et al., *Comparative Communist Political Leadership* (New York: David McKay, 1973), p. 162.

[14] John D. Nagle, "The Soviet Political Elite, 1917-1971: Application of a Generational Model of Social Change" (paper presented at the annual meeting of the American Political Science Association, New Orleans, 1973), Table v; and Nagle, *System and Succession: The Social Bases of Political Elite Recruitment* (Austin: University of Texas Press, 1977), Tables 8, 44, and passim.

Revolution.[15] As for Mexico, I suspect that the expulsion of the upper class from the elite positions was hastened, and to some extent caused, by the political revolution, which possessed a decided antioligarchic bias. But the timing, the slowness, and the steadiness of changes in elite origins—especially the partial incorporation of the lower class— suggest that they may have been determined more by alterations in economic and social structures than by the Revolution of 1910-20. As Mexico's class structure changed, expanding the middle class and mobilizing portions of the lower class, the patterns of elite recruitment have increasingly relied upon, and coopted, people from these crucial strata.

EDUCATION

One of the most precious commodities in twentieth-century Mexico has been education. In 1900 around 74 percent of the population could neither read nor write, in 1930 about 59 percent could neither read nor write, and by 1960 the figure remained as high as 32 percent.[16] University training, in particular, has been restricted to a tiny fraction of the population. In Mexico, as elsewhere, education thus functions as a critical determinant of career opportunity—what Max Weber has called "life chances"—and educational attainment becomes a valuable indicator for assessing the social requisites of rule.

As rough approximations of educational backgrounds of the upper-level elites, by regime, Figure 3-3 provides two separate measurements. One, depicted by a solid line, traces the percentage of top-level office-holders who are believed to have attended a university. For several reasons the figures might be slightly inflated: (1) the numerator includes people who attended university but did not receive degrees; (2) it also includes those who attended degree-granting "institutes" during the nineteenth century, when universities hardly existed as such; (3) the denominator for each calculation includes only those of known educational levels, while their more obscure colleagues—who may have been less likely to attend a university—are excluded from the count. To control for such biases the second indicator, depicted by a broken line, traces the number of people possessing professional

---

[15] See Putnam, *Comparative Study*, pp. 176-177, 184-189.

[16] Secretaría de la Economía Nacional, Dirección General de Estadística, *Quinto censo de población, 15 de mayo de 1930. Resumen general* (Mexico: Talleres Gráficos de la Nación, 1934), p. 55; and Dirección General de Estadística, Secretaría de Industria y Comercio, *VIII censo general de población, 1960. Resumen general* (Mexico: Talleres Gráficos de la Nación, 1962), pp. 290-307.

Figure 3-3. University Training among Upper-Level Elites 1900-1971

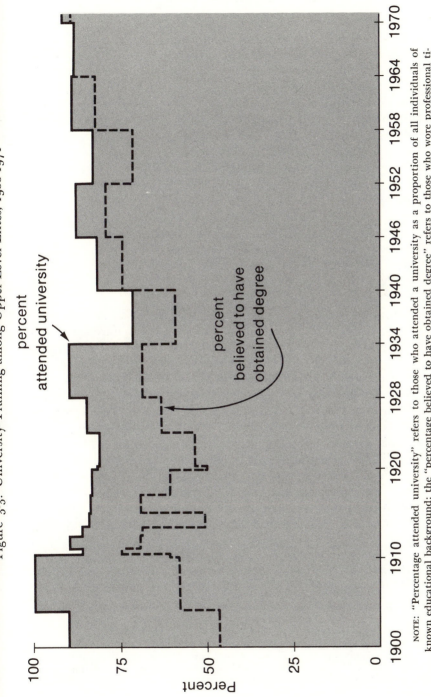

percent
attended university

percent
believed to have
obtained degree

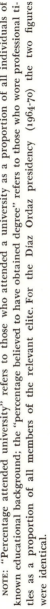

NOTE: "Percentage attended university" refers to those who attended a university as a proportion of all individuals of known educational background; the "percentage believed to have obtained degree" refers to those who wore professional titles as a proportion of all members of the relevant elite. For the Díaz Ordaz presidency (1964-70) the two figures were identical.

titles (and therefore presumed to have obtained degrees)[17] as a percentage of *all* upper-level officeholders. Largely because of imperfections in the data, the distance between the two lines is greatest in the early part of the century; as time goes on, and data improve, the gap narrows and finally disappears.

Notwithstanding all these caveats, Figure 3-3 conveys a simple message: university training has always been a virtual requirement for admission to Mexico's upper-level elites. At least 80 percent, and often over 90 percent, of top-echelon officeholders are believed to have attended a university. Sizable and growing shares are also believed to have obtained degrees. The proportion of university graduates has shown some fluctuation around the norm—with the Díaz regime,[18] the Convention government (1914-15), the Obregón presidency (1920-24), and the populist Cárdenas administration (1936-40) exhibiting somewhat less academic accomplishment than most other groups. Even so, Mexico's *universitarios* have maintained a steady grip on upper-level offices, regardless of the Revolution, regardless of the PRI, regardless of the era or the president.

This finding might seem insignificant because it belabors the obvious. Political leadership requires knowledge and skill, universities provide knowledge and skill, *ergo* political leaders come from universities. Fair enough. But the *extent* to which university education has remained a prerequisite for higher office still seems remarkable. It should be noted, in the first place, that only about 2.7 percent of literate adult males in Mexico had attended (or were attending) a university in 1960,[19] and in previous years this proportion would certainly have been smaller than that. This means, as a result, that the bulk of Mexico's political leadership has come from a tiny, and highly privileged, socioeconomic stratum.[20] Second, this has *always* been the case, even through the chaotic years of violence (1910-20). Though the Revolution de-urbanized the national elite, it did not de-educate the elite. No matter what their practical experience, in politics or on the battlefield,

[17] Occasionally, however, especially in rural areas, the title of *licenciado* has been granted to local "intellectuals" regardless of actual academic accomplishment.

[18] Though Díaz is sometimes pictured in the historical literature as a semiliterate brute, it should be noted that he himself attended a religious seminary for five years and later studied law at the prestigious Instituto de Ciencias y Artes de Oaxaca. Apparently he finished all his course work in law but never took the final exams.

[19] See note *f* of Table 3-5.

[20] This is, of course, a nearly universal phenomenon. See, for instance, Putnam, *Comparative Study*, pp. 26-32; Donald R. Matthews, *U.S. Senators and Their World* (Chapel Hill: University of North Carolina Press, 1960), p. 26; and, for an extremely close resemblance to the Mexican case, Frey, *Turkish Political Elite*, pp. 43-46.

country people and those of modest background had little chance of reaching the top echelons of office—unless they had received some higher learning.

To emphasize this point, Table 3-4 presents, for each of the cohorts, the relationship between fathers' occupational class and educational attainment. The small number of observations makes the results suggestive, by no means definitive, especially for the prerevolutionary group, but two basic patterns still seem to emerge. First, the correlation between social origin and educational achievement was clearly and consistently positive: the higher the social origin, the higher the level of education. But second, there were variations on this theme. The late Díaz elite, class-based as it was, drew the bulk of its membership from

TABLE 3-4

Relationship between Father's Occupational Class and Level of Education, by Cohort

Level of Education[b]	Prerevolutionary Cohort, 1900-1911 Father's Occupational Class[a]			Totals
	Lower	Middle	Upper	
Lower	0	1	0	1
Middle	0	1	0	1
Higher	1	10	9	20
Totals	1	12	9	22

Level of Education[b]	Revolutionary Cohort, 1917-40 Father's Occupational Class[a]			Totals
	Lower	Middle	Upper	
Lower	5	5	2	12
Middle	1	11	2	14
Higher	6	42	10	58
Totals	12	58	14	84

Level of Education[b]	Postrevolutionary Cohort, 1946-71 Father's Occupational Class[a]			Totals
	Lower	Middle	Upper	
Lower	14	10	1	25
Middle	10	21	1	32
Higher	12	98	8	118
Totals	36	129	10	175

[a] As categorized in Table 3-4.

[b] Lower = none, primary, or secondary;
Middle = preparatory, vocational, or special academy;
Higher = university, with or without degree.

university-trained elements of the upper and middle classes, most conspicuously the *científicos*.[21] Similarly, the revolutionary cohort drew a large proportion (approximately 60 percent) of its leaders from highly educated strata of the middle class, but it also contained some lower-class people who went to university. In this incorporation of high-education, low-status elements the Mexican Revolution was similar to many other revolutionary movements, from Vietnam to India to Algeria,[22] and it confirms Pareto's notion about status discrepancy and the circulation of elites: when political skill accumulates among the underprivileged, instability occurs. As if in recognition of this proposition, Mexico's established tutelary system has continued to maintain stability, in part, by coopting some highly educated individuals (12 out of 175) from the lower class—along with the preponderant number (98) of university-trained types of middle-class background.

For people from all social classes, then, a university education has consistently improved the chances of entering the political elite—but not any university would do, especially not in recent years. For it has been the national university located in the Federal District, since 1929 known as UNAM, which has furnished the principal training ground for the country's political leaders. In support of this assertion Table 3-5 offers data on educational backgrounds of the prerevolutionary, revolutionary, and postrevolutionary officeholding cohorts. For the total elites and the upper-level elites, the proportion who attended UNAM (or its functional predecessors, including the Escuela Nacional de Jurisprudencia) is computed in two ways: as a percentage of all those individuals of known educational level; and as a percentage of all those with known educational level and whose university, if applicable, can also be positively identified.

For the total elites, the figures show a fairly strong concentration of UNAM (or pre-UNAM) students among the prerevolutionary cohort, between about one-quarter and one-half, followed by a decrease for the revolutionary cohort and then by a return to 1900-1911 levels for the postrevolutionary cohort. For the upper-level elites, the percentages for the prerevolutionary and revolutionary cohorts are virtually identical (20 to 50 percent, depending upon the computation), and the postrevolutionary group displays a marked increase in the share of UNAM graduates (between about 50 and 70 percent).[23] As of 1960, when UNAM could count so many political leaders among its graduates, it

---

21 See Cosío Villegas, *Historia moderna*, p. 850.

22 Putnam, *Comparative Study*, pp. 191-193.

23 My figures are very close to those of Roderic Ai Camp, who counts the proportion of UNAM graduates among top-level Mexican politicians with university backgrounds as 64.6 percent. Camp, *The Education of Mexico's Revolutionary Family* (forthcoming), Table III-G.

TABLE 3-5

Educational Background of Total Elite, Upper-Level Elite, and General Populations, by Cohort

Education	Prerevolutionary Cohort, 1900-1911		
	% among Total Elite (N = 171)[a]	% among Upper Elite (N = 25)[a]	% among General Population, 1900
Attended a university	87.7	96.0	1.7[b]
Attended UNAM[c]	22.6, 48.7[d]	20.0, 50.0[d]	—[e]
Education	Revolutionary Cohort, 1917-40		
	% among Total Elite (N = 657)[a]	% among Upper Elite (N = 139)[a]	% among General Population, 1930
Attended a university	76.1	83.5	—[e]
Attended UNAM[c]	12.7, 29.1[d]	22.3, 49.2[d]	—[e]
Education	Postrevolutionary Cohort, 1946-71		
	% among Total Elite (N = 1,371)[a]	% among Upper Elite (N = 151)[a]	% among General Population, 1960
Attended a university	73.5	86.8	2.7[f]
Attended UNAM[c]	27.8, 46.8[d]	50.3, 69.7[d]	1.8[g]

[a] Ns refer to the number of individuals with known educational level.

[b] Estimated number of university graduates, based on extrapolations from data on *universitarios*, as percent of estimated literate adult male population. Source: Secretaría de Economía, Dirección General de Estadística, *Estadísticas sociales del porfiriato 1877-1911* (Mexico: Talleres Gráficos de la Nación, 1956), pp. 52-53.

[c] That is, either the UNAM or its predecessor.

[d] The first figure refers to the number of former UNAM students as percent of all those with known educational level; the second figure refers to former UNAM students as percent of all those with known educational level and whose university, if applicable, can also be identified.

[e] No data available.

[f] Number of males age 15 or over with more than 12 years of schooling as percent of all literate males age 15 or over, as of 1960. Source: Dirección General de Estadística, Secretaría de Industria y Comercio, *VIII censo general de población, 9160. Resumen general* (Mexico: Talleres Gráficos de la Nación, 1962), pp. 308-340.

[g] Percentage based on literate adult male population age 15 or over. To estimate a numerator, I added up the annual number of male students at the UNAM between 1929 and 1960 and divided the total by 5 (five years being the approximate average length of a university career); the figure is rough and may well be too high, since it makes no allowance for mortality. See the data in Arturo González Cosío, *Historia estadística de la Universidad 1910-1967* (Mexico: UNAM, Instituto de Investigaciones Sociales, 1968), p. 75.

could claim only about 1.8 percent of literate adult males as its alumni.[24] Clearly, Mexico's national university has been filtering a remarkable number of its students into public life.[25]

Why? According to Chapter 2, especially Table 2-6, UNAM has drawn most of its students from the middle class, so it does not appear that the university has tended to level social differences and create an aristocracy of talent. Rather, it has operated as a kind of gateway into politics for children of the bourgeoisie.

The explanation, I think, lies in the institution's geographic and political location. Being near the seat of the national government, and near the center of the decisionmaking apparatus, UNAM has provided its students with opportunities to observe and meet national leaders (and vice versa). It has been a place where students have developed their political sensitivities, where they have formed crucial friendships and alliances, and where they have taken part in overt action (most notably through strikes). Frequently, too, political leaders have held part-time positions on the UNAM faculty, and used the opportunity to recruit students to their teams, machines, or *camarillas*.[26] In general, though, contacts from the university do not result in the formation of solid groups which move into the political system as coherent, committed, and disciplined groups. Rather, students have tended to embark upon their own careers as individuals, and then activate the UNAM contacts at the necessary moments. Friendships from the UNAM have thus functioned mainly as resources for the future, rather than as the instruments for immediate action.

In such ways the pool of potential talent at the UNAM has enabled reigning political elites to select and train new prospects in a closed and concentrated fashion, assuring centralized control of the recruitment process. In this sense it is no accident that, according to Table 3-5, UNAM became more important as a training ground for the post-

[24] See note g of Table 3-5.

[25] The same is true of the Escuela Nacional Preparatoria, though data on this point are less reliable. Camp calculates that of political leaders since 1934 *who are known to have attended preparatory school, and whose preparatory school can be identified*, about 77.3 percent attended the ENP: *Education*, Table III-F. No doubt the percentage of ENP alumni in the overall elite was smaller—but by how much, we do not know. My own information on this point is extremely crude, and probably underestimates the incidence of ENP alumni, but indicates a chronological trend within the total elites: 19.4 percent for the prerevolutionary cohort, 17.2 percent for the revolutionary cohort, then up to 29.7 percent for the postrevolutionary group. It also appears that the proportion of ENP graduates among upper-level elites is consistently higher than among the total elites.

[26] See Camp, *Education*; and the perceptive essay by Larissa Lomnitz, "Carreras de vida en la UNAM," *Plural* 54 (March 1976): 18-22.

revolutionary cohort than for the revolutionary group; as I shall argue later on, this has been part of an overall trend in elite centralization.

OCCUPATION

One of the most direct ways to evaluate the combined influence of birthplace, family background, and educational attainment is through an examination of occupation. Despite the difficulties connected with studies of occupational status, the special virtue of this approach, at least for this analysis, is that data on jobs usually offer a glimpse (however murky) of a person's socioeconomic position *at the moment* of initiating a political career.[27] One's occupation sketches, as it were, a picture of the final social stepping-stone to public life. What were the principal occupations of political elites in twentieth-century Mexico, and how did they change over time?

Table 3-6 deals with this question by presenting data on the occupational background of total elites and upper-level elites, by cohort. Somewhat hesitantly, I have grouped the jobs into various class categories, as with father's occupation (Table 3-3), though I have here added an extra distinction between the "professional" and "employee" components of the middle class. Because some individuals are known to have engaged in more than one occupation, the percentage totals substantially exceed 100 (university professorships, in particular, were almost always part-time positions, and they thus contribute to inflation of the sums).

In broad outline, the results bear substantial resemblance to the profiles for the fathers' occupations. For all three cohorts, the great majority of national leaders held middle-class occupations. The proportion of people in upper-class jobs—that is, people who are known to have controlled substantial amounts of capital, either as landowners or as businessmen—has been always rather low. Quite frankly, I suspect that the share of people in the upper class has been underenumerated by the sources available to me: it is very likely that many men in middle-class positions acquired upper-class quantities of wealth. But if the rate of underestimation is assumed to be approximately constant across cohorts, the data can be interpreted to reveal a clear and secular *decline* in the political participation of the upper class. Conspicuously, too, this decline has affected businessmen as well as landowners, notwithstanding the fact that Mexico has undergone a steady and accelerating

---

[27] This is *generally* true for the data at my disposal, though it has often been difficult to ascertain whether the available information has referred to occupations pursued before, during, or after political careers.

Table 3-6
Occupations of Total and Upper-Level Elites, by Cohort

Class and Occupation	Prerevolutionary Cohort, 1900-1911		Revolutionary Cohort, 1917-40		Postrevolutionary Cohort, 1946-71	
	% among Total Elite (N = 215)	% among Upper-level Elite (N = 27)	% among Total Elite (N = 907)	% among Upper-level Elite (N = 164)	% among Total Elite (N = 1,429)	% among Upper-level Elite (N = 153)
Upper:						
Businessman	6.0	11.1	4.5	7.9	4.8	6.5
Landowner	3.7	0.0	2.1	3.0	2.3	2.0
Middle/professional:						
Lawyer	45.1	44.4	31.4	37.8	39.4	47.1
Doctor	7.9	0.0	8.0	10.4	10.0	7.8
Engineer	9.3	22.2	9.0	15.9	9.2	18.3
Schoolteacher	23.7	37.0	15.3	22.0	25.0	37.3
University professor	19.7	37.0	8.5	18.9	19.2	38.6
Journalist	19.1	11.1	11.5	14.0	6.0	5.2
Military	25.1	14.8	35.9	29.3	12.2	12.4
Other professional	7.4	7.4	3.2	5.5	7.8	11.1
Middle/employee:						
Employee	3.7	3.7	5.3	9.8	6.8	7.2
Lower:						
Worker	0.0	0.0	2.1	3.0	2.6	0.7
Peasant	0.0	0.0	1.0	0.6	0.6	0.7
Labor leader[a]	0.0	0.0	1.5	1.8	9.0	3.9
Totals[b]	170.7	188.7	139.3	179.9	154.9	198.8

[a] Refers to activists in peasant organizations as well as in industrial unions.
[b] Totals exceed 100 because some people are known to have held more than one occupation.

pattern of industrial growth, especially since 1940. As with the information on fathers' occupations, the trend implies that the economic elite has, over time, become disengaged from the political elite.

Particularly striking, within this context, is the persistent predominance of the legal profession. Among the prerevolutionary upper-level elite, for instance, 44.4 percent are believed to have practiced (or at least had training in) the field of law; for the revolutionary cohort the figure declined a bit, to 37.8 percent, and for the postrevolutionary group it went back up to 47.1 percent. The proportions for the total elites are similar in magnitude and trend (45.1 percent, 31.4 percent, and 39.4 percent). Before, during, and since the Revolution, the legal profession has consistently operated as a direct channel into Mexican politics.

This pattern matches the experience of many other countries, particularly in the Western world.[28] In the United States, 70 percent of the presidents, vice-presidents, and cabinet members between 1877 and 1934 were lawyers. Of a total of 995 elected governors in all American states between 1870 and 1950, 46 percent were practicing lawyers,[29] as were just about half of all the senators from 1947 to 1957.[30] Slightly lower but comparable proportions of parliamentary bodies in France, Italy, and (to a lesser extent) Britain have come from the ranks of lawyers.[31] And in Colombia, a competitive but oligarchical system, more than 50 percent of the 468 cabinet ministers from 1900 to 1975 were men with legal training.[32]

Why should this be so? In his well-known study of Turkey, Frederick Frey has noted that the proportion of lawyers among the political elite was lowest at the apex of the one-party Kemalist period (around 12 or 13 percent) and highest during the periods of multiparty competition (26 or 27 percent)—and from this he speculates that multiparty systems tend to rely on lawyers because, by training and outlook, they are specialists in the art of persuasion, a skill that becomes most useful and effective in a competitive context.[33] But this alone cannot explain the case in Mexico, where the government party has ruled without any serious challenge and where the incidence of lawyers, no

28 Putnam, *Comparative Study*, p. 59.

29 Heinz Eulau and John D. Sprague, *Lawyers in Politics: A Study in Professional Convergence* (Indianapolis: Bobbs-Merrill, 1964), pp. 11-12.

30 Matthews, *U.S. Senators*, pp. 33-36.

31 Mattei Dogan, "Political Ascent in a Class Society: French Deputies, 1870-1958," in *Political Decision-Makers*, ed. Marvick, pp. 69-70 and 78.

32 John I. Laun, "El reclutamiento político en Colombia: Los ministros de estado, 1900-1975" (Bogota: Universidad Nacional de los Andes, 1976), p. 10.

33 Frey, *Turkish Political Elite*, pp. 181-182 and 395-396.

matter what the measure, has been higher than that in Turkey and similar to that of Western-style democracies.

As a matter of fact Juan Linz has argued, contrary to Frey, that lawyers frequently play major roles in authoritarian regimes, just as in democratic polities, whereas totalitarian systems do not draw many leaders from the legal profession.[34] In Spain, for instance, about 42 percent of the prototypically authoritarian Franco cabinet consisted of lawyers—a figure very close to the Mexican data, and not too far below the 56 percent level that obtained under the Republic. Reasons for this may vary. First, "limited pluralism" relies on cooptation as well as on force, and skill in persuasion, as in open systems, becomes a valuable attribute. Second, authoritarian regimes often rely on discretionary procedures, where the final impact of a law comes at the point of implementation, and lawyers are trained to maximize the limits of discretion: hence, in Linz's words, "the strange combination of Rechstaat and arbitrary power, of slow legalistic procedure and military command style, that characterizes some of these regimes."[35] Third, as often pointed out in other contexts, lawyers can afford to enter politics: governmental experience usually enhances their private practice, and after their terms in office they can move back easily into their firms or corporations.[36] This may be particularly true in a country such as Mexico, where the state plays an active role in the economy: as I shall suggest below, especially in Chapters 7 and 9, ex-officeholding lawyers may be in a particularly useful (and profitable) position to serve as intermediaries between the public and private sectors.

Another suggestive finding from Table 3-6 concerns the incidence of teachers and professors (each around 37 percent, 20 percent, and 38 percent for the upper-level officeholders in the respective cohorts). However, these were rarely full-time careers. Young people, in their late teens or early twenties, often did a stint of teaching, sometimes as schoolmasters in the countryside.[37] And as indicated above, professorships were generally part-time, honorific posts. It is my interpretation

[34] The relatively low number of lawyers in Communist elites is shown for Yugoslavia in Cohen, "Social Background," p. 45 (16 percent); for the USSR in George K. Schueller, "The Politburo," in *World Revolutionary Elites: Studies in Coercive Ideological Movements*, ed. Harold D. Lasswell and Daniel Lerner (Cambridge: M.I.T. Press, 1966), p. 121 (2 out of 27); and for China in Waller, "Chinese Communist Political Elite," p. 165 (30.3 percent from education, journalism, *and* law).

[35] Linz, "An Authoritarian Regime: Spain," in *Mass Politics: Studies in Political Sociology*, ed. Erik Allardt and Stein Rokkan (New York: The Free Press, 1970), pp. 273, 278.

[36] See also Dankwart A. Rustow, "The Study of Elites: Who's Who, When, and How," *World Politics* 18, no. 3 (July 1966): 705-707.

[37] See James D. Cockcroft, "El maestro de primaria en la Revolución Mexicana," *Historia Mexicana* 16, no. 4 (April-June 1967): 565-587.

that these occupations reveal less about the socioeconomic status of elites than they show about the social mechanisms of the recruitment process. As teachers or professors, would-be politicians could develop their senses of leadership, cultivate their skills in interpersonal relations, and—perhaps most important—begin to build up followings. *Camarillas* were frequently formed in schools and universities, and teaching positions have thus offered valuable political resources to ambitious Mexicans.

An additional consistent entrée to officeholding in Mexico has been through technical professions. Engineers, from cohort to cohort, have usually held around 10 percent of the positions in the total national elite, and 20 percent of the upper-level posts. Trained in such diverse fields as agriculture, hydraulics, and construction, engineers have represented a cadre of technically qualified (though often politically motivated) personnel. To an extent their continuing presence reflects persisting recognition of the need for effective and practical action in coping with the country's awesome economic problems—or, at least, it constitutes a symbolic (not to say empty) gesture toward the cause of economic development. This latter point is more clear-cut in the case of economic specialists, the *licenciados en economía*, who made their first appearance in the 1920s and who have made spectacular advances in recent years—from 2.5 percent of the upper-level elite under López Mateos (1958-64) to nearly 10 percent under Díaz Ordaz (1964-70) to almost 20 percent at the beginning of the Echeverría regime (1970-71). In the early Echeverría administration, in fact, the number of engineers plus economists was just about equal to the number of lawyers. Unquestionably, these technicians had come to form a functional elite, as they possessed the credentials (if not always the ability) to guide the processes of economic growth. As the Mexican government maintained its commitment to development, and as the state increased its role in the economy, the *técnicos* became crucial personnel.[38] One almost senses, from Table 3-6, a pattern of displacement: people with literary skills (such as journalists) were becoming gradually less valuable to the regime, and those with technical skills were on the rise.

Shuffles of this kind took place within the middle class. People from lower-class occupations, by contrast, have never formed substantial portions of the national political elite. It comes as no surprise to learn that *campesinos* and industrial workers were totally excluded from the Díaz group. What is surprising is the fact that they have been almost as totally excluded from the revolutionary and postrevolutionary co-

[38] Consult Roderic Ai Camp, "The Cabinet and the *Técnico* in Mexico and the United States," *Journal of Comparative Administration* 3, no. 2 (August 1971): 188-214.

horts. It is likely that my data suffer from undercounting, especially in the case of labor leaders (who were often lawyers anyway), but the inference is unambiguous. The two major groups in whose name the Mexican Revolution presumably took place, peasants and workers, have had very few agents from their own ranks in decisionmaking centers of the government. To an extent this situation might reflect the need for political skills that are more easily acquired by high-status people than by low-status people, and it is perfectly possible for the working class to have found adequate representation of its interests in other ways, either through capable middle-class spokesmen or through parapolitical unions and *sindicatos* (although, as explained in Chapter 1, circumstantial evidence suggests that unions have been captives of the government). At a bare minimum, the data reveal that neither the Revolution nor the tutelary system has managed to open the recruitment process to the country's popular masses. To be sure, the data in Table 3-6 show a modest increase in officeholders from the employee stratum (from 3.7 percent under Díaz to 5.3–9.8 percent in 1917-40), perhaps suggesting that the Revolution increased mobility for members of the lower middle class. But by and large, government has been the province of educated civilian professionals.

In extension of this point, Table 3-7 displays the relationships between fathers' occupational class and professional title, by cohort. The data are fragmentary but some of the patterns are clear. Throughout the twentieth century, politicians from upper-class backgrounds have either not obtained degrees, presumably because university careers were not perceived as necessary, or they have tended to study law. People from the middle class have more often been to university and, particularly for them, the primary channel to political office has been through the legal profession. This was true for about one-third of the middle-class officeholders in the prerevolutionary and revolutionary cohorts, and for nearly one-half of such people in the postrevolutionary group: thus the modal type of officeholder changed from a person of middle-class origin with no professional title in 1917-40 (27 out of 100) to a middle-class lawyer in 1946-71 (65 out of 192). For people of lower-class origin, as already shown in Table 3-4, education has been difficult to get. But when such people have received degrees, they have usually done so in fields other than law—sometimes in technical disciplines, such as engineering, but most often in education. Among the civilian professions it has been teaching, not law, which has furnished a pathway to politics for Mexicans of humble origin.[39]

[39] In the United States, by contrast, sons of modest farmers have traditionally gained upward mobility into the political elite through the legal profession. Putnam, *Comparative Study*, p. 188.

TABLE 3-7

*Relationship between Father's Occupational Class
and Professional Title, by Cohort*

Professional Title	Prerevolutionary Cohort, 1900-1911 Father's Occupational Class[a]			Totals
	Lower	Middle	Upper	
None	3	9	6	18
Lawyer[b]	0	6	6	12
Other	1	4	0	5
Totals	4	19	12	35

Professional Title	Revolutionary Cohort, 1917-40 Father's Occupational Class[a]			Totals
	Lower	Middle	Upper	
None	12	27	7	46
Lawyer[b]	2	23	5	30
Other	3	18	3	24
Totals	17	68	15	100

Professional Title	Postrevolutionary Cohort, 1946-71 Father's Occupational Class[a]			Totals
	Lower	Middle	Upper	
None	28	33	4	65
Lawyer[b]	6	65	4	75
Other	12	37	3	52
Totals	46	135	11	192

[a] As categorized in Table 3-4.
[b] Includes some *licenciados* who are not specified as being *licenciados en derecho.*

The military, too, has often been viewed as an avenue of upward social mobility. Especially during wartime, it is thought, men have an opportunity to demonstrate their strength and leadership, and, on the basis of their merit, they can overcome the barriers of social class. Certainly the Mexican military was long a potent and often a dominating factor on the political scene. According to Table 3-6 the proportion of military men in national office underwent a cycle of surge and decline —up from 25.1 percent for total membership of the prerevolutionary cohort to 35.9 percent for the revolutionary cohort, then down to only 12.2 percent for the 1946-71 group. To pinpoint this pattern with extra precision, Figure 3-4 plots the regime-by-regime percentages of upper-level positions held by military men.

The curve depicts three separate epochs. The prerevolutionary regime, moderately militarized, drew a fair share of leaders from the

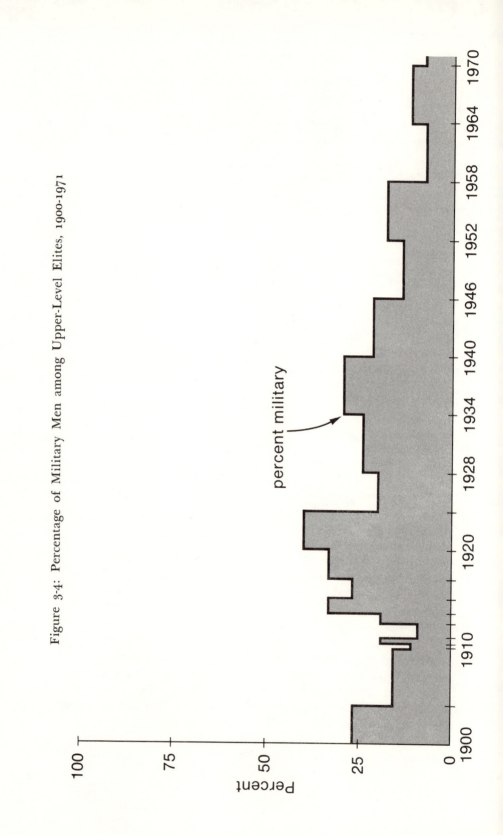

Figure 3-4: Percentage of Military Men among Upper-Level Elites, 1900-1971

officer ranks of the *Reforma* movement, where Díaz started his own career, and also from the Porfirian army itself. After the heavy fighting broke out in 1913, leaders of the revolutionary armies moved into positions of political command: the proportion climbed to 34 percent during the era of the Convention (1914-15), went down a bit under Carranza (1915-20), moved up to 40 percent under Obregón (1920-24), slipped down under Calles and the *Maximato* (1924-34), drew back near 30 percent under Cárdenas (1934-40)—and then began a long and steady decline. During the third era, from Alemán to Echeverría, military men came to play an ever less conspicuous role among the upper elites. The timing of this later transition was apparently the product of two factors. One was simply the aging, retirement, and death of those who fought the Revolution.[40] Second was the formation of the PRM and later the PRI, which institutionalized procedures for political succession. By the 1940s, Mexico was on the road to creating its *rara avis*: an authoritarian regime throughly dominated, at its upper levels, by people of civilian background.[41]

What kind of people went into politics through the military? For this question Table 3-8 presents data on the relationship between military status and level of education, by cohort (education is here used as a proxy for socioeconomic status because the number of observations for father's occupation becomes too small for cross-tabulations with military status).

Results for the prerevolutionary cohort are difficult to interpret, given the scarcity of people with less than high education, though it appears that those with middling education showed the greatest propensity to enter military careers. For the revolutionary cohort, it was men of low educational (and presumably social) status who were most inclined to make it through the army, as 33 out of 69 individuals in this category (47.8 percent) followed this route; nearly the same proportion of those with middle-level education (38 out of 87, or 43.7 percent) did the same. An additional breakdown, not reported here, shows a further effect: for the 1917-40 cohort men of low educational attainment *and from rural backgrounds*[42] revealed a special inclina-

40 On the disappearance of the active revolutionaries see Table 1-2.

41 On the political relocation of the military see Edwin Lieuwen, *Mexican Militarism: The Political Rise and Fall of the Revolutionary Army, 1910-1940* (Albuquerque: University of New Mexico Press, 1968); and on the army's continuing roles see David F. Ronfeldt, "The Mexican Army and Political Order since 1940," in *Contemporary Mexico: Papers of the IV International Congress of Mexican History*, ed. James W. Wilkie, Michael C. Meyer, and Edna Monzón de Wilkie (Berkeley and Los Angeles: University of California Press, 1976), pp. 317-336.

42 That is, they were born neither in state capitals nor in cities with 20,000 inhabitants as of 1921. (See Table 3-3, note b.)

tion for military careers, as more than 60 percent of the people in this category (30 out of 52) entered the elite via the army; for all those of higher educational attainment, no matter what the urban-rural background, and for all those of urban background, no matter what the level of education, civilian careers predominated. At this specific historical juncture, then, the military appears to have provided routes of access for socially deprived *campesinos*. From the 1940s onward, as

TABLE 3-8

Relationship between Level of Education
and Military Status, by Cohort

Military Status	Prerevolutionary Cohort, 1900-1911 Level of Education[a]			
	Lower	Middle	Higher	Totals
Civilian[b]	3	7	113	123
Officer	1	8	8	17
Totals	4	15	121	140
Military Status	Revolutionary Cohort, 1917-40 Level of Education[a]			
	Lower	Middle	Higher	Totals
Civilian[b]	36	49	278	363
Officer	33	38	47	118
Totals	69	87	325	481
Military Status	Postrevolutionary Cohort, 1946-71 Level of Education[a]			
	Lower	Middle	Higher	Totals
Civilian[b]	106	174	681	961
Officer	13	48	29	90
Totals	119	222	710	1,051

[a] Lower = none, primary, or secondary;
  Middle = preparatory, vocational, or special academy;
  Higher = university, with or without degree.
[b] Or not known to have been a military officer.

shown by the data for the postrevolutionary cohort, men of middling educational achievement—from the cities as well as from the country— showed the greatest likelihood of entering the elite by means of a military career.[43]

[43] Note that military academies are counted as middle-level institutions, principally because they have not enjoyed the same prestige as universities.

AGE

From these diverging and converging social backgrounds, elites gained access to office at different times of life. Since everyone grows old, age at taking office reveals less about social prerequisites for entering the system than about the mechanisms of political ascent (which will form the subject of Chapters 5 and 6). The age factor can also illuminate generational dimensions of conflict and change.

To capture such trends, Figure 3-5 traces the proportion of upper-level officeholders in each presidential regime who fell into each of three brackets: under 40, 40 to 59, 60 and over. It should be understood that the data depict the age structure of presidential regimes, which is somewhat distinct from age of individual access to top-echelon posts (since some people served in more than one regime); and for the sake of simplicity and comparability, age is computed from the start of the administration for all officeholders, including those who may have taken up their posts sometime after the first year of the regime.

The trends come forth with startling clarity. As all other evidence suggests, the late Díaz regime was old: none of the top-level elite fell in the under 40 bracket, and nearly half were 60 or more. Partly in reaction to this situation, the Revolution was a revolt of the young. Precisely 50 percent of those of known age in the Madero group were in their thirties; more than 40 percent were between 40 and 59; less than 10 percent were 60 or more. After Huerta's downfall the surge of youth is even more impressive, as the under-40 age group accounted for more than 75 percent of top officeholders during the Convention era, for 64 percent during Carranza's constitutional presidency, for 70 percent during the Calles regime and nearly 60 percent in the *Maximato*. Unmistakably, a new generation had taken hold of politics.

In the late 1920s and through the '30s, however, the middle age bracket (40 to 59) began to assert itself. In part this represents the natural aging of the generational cohort which fought and won the Revolution, and which moved from the youngest to the intermediate age category before or during their tenure in office. More remarkable is the expansion of the 40-59 bracket since the early 1940s, when most members of the revolutionary generation had passed from the political scene. Miguel Alemán, for instance, drew 80 percent of his top-level officeholders from the middle bracket, some from the under-40 set, hardly any from the 60-plus generation. This overwhelming predominance of the 40-59 bracket has continued ever since, holding around 70 percent in the most recent administrations, with one other subtle

97

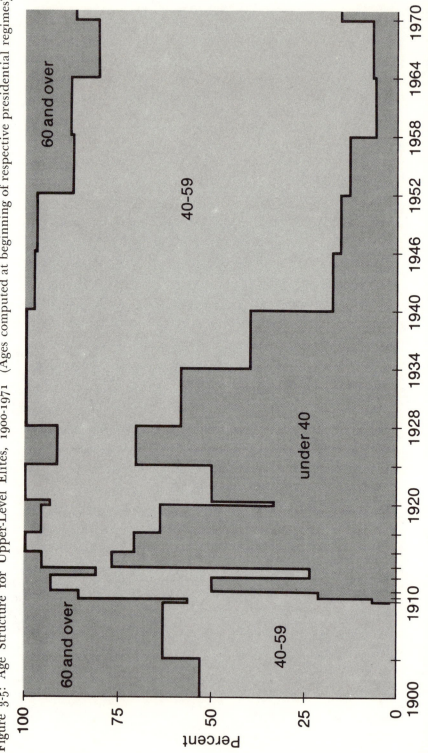

Figure 3·5: Age Structure for Upper-Level Elites, 1900-1971 (Ages computed at beginning of respective presidential regimes)

shift: a gradual eclipse of the under-40 group (up to the Echeverría inauguration) and a mild expansion in the presence of the 60-plus group. It would seem that another political generation, one that came to the fore with Alemán, was showing its determination to stay in office—and, inexorably, its advancing age as well.

The patterns of generational displacement find direct expression in Table 3-9, which displays the percentages of upper-level officeholders born within successive 20-year intervals, by presidential regime. The upper echelons of the Díaz elite came, quite clearly, from the 1840-59 birth cohort: 62.5 percent of the men in the 1904-10 administration were in this bracket, and another 25 percent were born even earlier than that.[44] Equally clearly, the Madero movement represented a challenge from the 1860-79 cohort, as 83.3 percent of this elite was born within this interval; a full 50 percent, in fact, was born in the single decade of 1870-79. By the end of the Revolution, in 1917, preeminence had passed to the 1880-99 generation, a group that reached its apogee of influence under the *Maximato* (1928-34), when 81.1 percent of the upper-level leaders came from this cohort. With the Alemán administration (1946-52) a new generation took hold, as the 1900-1919 birth cohort moved into top positions and remained preeminent till 1970. Then, under Echeverría, still another group came into power, the cohort of 1920-39.

Within these patterns of generational takeover there has also been, since the Revolution, a good deal of fluidity. Undoubtedly the *maderista* movement had a strong and probably self-conscious generational aspect; so too the Alemán elite, 70 percent of whose members were born in the 1900-1909 decade. Such moments aside, though, men of rising generations have had fairly steady access to high office. Unlike most revolutionary leadership groups, which show a generalized tendency toward aging (as in Communist China and the Soviet Union),[45] the Mexican political elite has constantly managed to rejuvenate itself.[46]

---

[44] The data for Díaz's 1910-1911 administration are clouded by the fact that he appointed a compromise cabinet just before his exit from office.

[45] Putnam, *Comparative Study*, pp. 196-197; and John D. Nagle, "A New Look at the Soviet Elite: A Generational Model of the Soviet System," *Journal of Political and Military Sociology* 3 (Spring 1975): 1-13, esp. 8.

[46] In a fascinating comparative study, John D. Nagle has shown that Mexican political elites since 1946 have had consistently lower levels of generational concentration—and higher levels of generational diffusion, or "fractionalization"—than comparable leadership groups in West Germany, the United States, and the USSR. Nagle, "System and Succession: A Generational Analysis of Elite Turnover in Four Nations" (paper presented at the annual meeting of the Southern Political Science Association, Atlanta, November 1973), pp. 31-32.

TABLE 3-9

Dates of Birth for Upper-Level Elites, 1900-1971
(by Presidential Regime)

Regime		Percentages by Periods						
		1820-39	1840-59	1860-79	1880-99	1900-1919	1920-39	1940-plus
Díaz, 1900-1904	(N = 13)	38.5	61.5	—	—	—	—	—
Díaz, 1904-10	(N = 16)	25.0	62.5	12.5	—	—	—	—
Díaz, 1910-11	(N = 16)	18.8	50.0	31.3	—	—	—	—
De la Barra, 1911	(N = 14)	—	28.6	71.4	—	—	—	—
Madero, 1911-13	(N = 18)	—	16.7	83.3	—	—	—	—
Huerta, 1913-14	(N = 30)	—	26.7	63.3	10.0	—	—	—
Convention, 1914-15	(N = 22)	—	4.6	50.0	45.5	—	—	—
Carranza as First Chief, 1915-17	(N = 16)	—	6.3	31.3	62.5	—	—	—
Carranza as President, 1917-20	(N = 24)	—	8.3	33.3	58.3	—	—	—
De la Huerta, 1920	(N = 14)	—	7.1	57.1	35.7	—	—	—
Obregón, 1920-24	(N = 24)	—	—	45.8	54.2	—	—	—
Calles, 1924-28	(N = 24)	—	—	20.8	79.2	—	—	—
Maximato, 1928-34	(N = 53)	—	—	15.1	81.1	3.8	—	—
Cárdenas, 1934-40	(N = 48)	—	—	6.3	77.1	16.7	—	—
Ávila Camacho, 1940-46	(N = 40)	—	—	2.5	72.5	22.5	2.5	—
Alemán, 1946-52	(N = 39)	—	—	—	28.2	71.8	—	—
Ruiz Cortines, 1952-58	(N = 31)	—	—	—	41.9	58.1	—	—
López Mateos, 1958-64	(N = 33)	—	—	—	12.1	81.8	6.1	—
Díaz Ordaz, 1964-70	(N = 41)	—	—	—	7.3	63.4	29.3	—
Echeverría, 1970-76 (as of 1971)	(N = 37)	—	—	—	—	40.5	56.8	2.7

To be more precise, going back to Figure 3-5, the consolidation of Mexico's tutelary regime in the 1930s and '40s brought with it the hegemony of the 40-to-59 age group. With the advent of stability, political careers took on more shape and structure (a point to be explored in Chapter 5). Young men could no longer burst onto the scene, as in the revolutionary era; they had to undergo intensive processes of preparation and probation. And as will be emphasized in Chapter 6, politics in Mexico had not become an old man's game; the national regime is not gerontocratic. At its upper reaches, it is the domain of the middle-aged.

Summary

In this chapter I have attempted to trace transformations in the social backgrounds of political elites in twentieth-century Mexico, with special reference to the distribution of social requirements for access to national office. The data have been crude and evidence uncertain, but patterns have nonetheless emerged. Here I shall recapitulate some of the most important findings and, in doing so, focus upon the question of causality. Did the Revolution lead to basic changes in the social requisites of rule? What was the impact of regime consolidation? Or did the trends result from socioeconomic factors instead of political ones?

The central discovery of this investigation is that, from the beginning of this century, Mexico's political elites have come mainly from the middle class—before, during, and since the Revolution. Admittedly, each of my indicators of class origin or status is rather imprecise: father's occupation is available for only a small percentage of incumbents; the occupation of the officeholders offers a dubious guide to social position, and level of education can be equally misleading. But all three indicators point in the same direction, and the cumulative weight of the evidence thus becomes impressive. The middle class, itself a privileged stratum, has constantly dominated the upper reaches of political power in Mexico, and, if anything, its hegemony has been increasing over time.

Obviously, then, the Revolution did not lead to any major change in the class basis of political leadership. As in other countries (Britain, France, and the United States) the fundamental determinants of elite composition appear to have derived from socioeconomic, not political, factors. As a developing capitalist society, Mexico has had a growing middle class, and the stability and authority of the tutelary regime has been dependent upon its incorporation and support. Industrialization, too, has spawned a sizable urban working class, while there remains a rural peasantry, and leaders of both of these lower-class groups have been constantly coopted by the nation's rulers. Hence, in part, the changing structure of elites: growing dominance of the middle class, increasingly in alliance with people from the lower class instead of from the upper class.

Which is not to say that the Revolution was inconsequential. Quite the contrary. First, I suspect that the Mexican Revolution, as a political movement, hastened the removal of upper-class elements from high governmental office, and, as I shall argue in Chapter 7, the consequent separation of political and economic elites has substantial implications for our understanding of the Mexican system. Second, and more pervasively, *the Revolution redistributed political power among relatively dispossessed segments of the nation's middle class.*

As the biographical data have shown, the revolutionary group (or cohort) differed from the prerevolutionary elite in several discernible ways. The post-1917 leaders came disproportionately from the northern tier, especially the state of Sonora, thus presenting a regional challenge to the Mexico City-Veracruz axis. They came from small towns and cities, more so than the population as a whole, in contrast to the metropolitan makeup of the late Porfirian elite. And, of course, they were young, especially in comparison to the aged Díaz group. The Mexican Revolution captured a sharp generational cleavage in Mexican society, with the year 1860 separating the birthdates of prerevolutionary and revolutionary elites.

In other words, the Revolution marked a struggle between two elements of Mexico's middle class: the ins and the outs. The outs, as might be expected, were just as highly educated as the ins, often trained in law, and they presumably believed themselves to be ready and prepared for leadership. As with many revolutionary movements, then, leadership in Mexico came from well-educated segments of the dispossessed—that is, a dispossessed fragment of the middle class, not so much the lower class, and a fragment that, being young, may well have resented perceived barriers to future mobility more than their objective or existing deprivation. In time this group found allies, most conspicuously among relatively well-educated people of lower-class origin. But in general, the Mexican Revolution took its direction from the middle class.

The data on elite background also reflect, though somewhat dimly, the social dimensions of conflict within the Revolution. By most available indicators, the government of the Convention (1914-15), supported by Emiliano Zapata and Pancho Villa, was the most popular (or the least elitist) in origin. It was among the most rural and least educated, and it offered the greatest share of upper-level posts to military men—soldiers whose principal claim to authority rested upon the force of their armies, rather than upon their social status or academic training.[47] When Venustiano Carranza won his victory over Villa and Zapata, the portals to power were closed once again.

After the crises of the 1920s and '30s, the consolidation of Mexico's tutelary system ushered in a series of further changes. From the 1940s onward, top-echelon officeholders were drawn less from the ranks of the military and more from university-trained professionals, especially middle-class lawyers and, more recently, economists. In this, the rise of the *técnico*, the impact of socioeconomic change is clearly evident. Economic technicians comprise a strategic elite in a managed economy like Mexico's, and because of their expertise they have accumulated considerable shares of influence.

The consolidated regime has been highly centralized, and this quality, essentially political in character, may well account for other aspects of recruitment. The National University, UNAM, became the prime training ground for aspiring *políticos*; itself a middle-class institution, UNAM provided a secure and centralized arena for elite recruitment. Perhaps in further reflection of the centralizing trend, a large percentage of the post-1940s elite came from urban centers, most notably the Federal District; under the stabilized system, the city recaptured control of the system from the small towns and countryside. Additional results of institutionalization were bureaucratization and the establishment of rituals and procedures for political apprenticeship, as reflected in the fact that men took high office most typically while in their middle years, somewhere between 40 and 59; recent top-level elites have been neither as old as the Díaz clique nor as young as the revolutionaries.

In many ways, the elites which took over from the revolutionary cohort in the 1940s bore a striking resemblance to the late Díaz group. Admittedly, the age structure was different, the role of the military changed, and the upper class was less apparent. But like their prerevolutionary counterparts, recent (postrevolutionary) leaders have been of urban origin; they have been highly educated; many have been lawyers or professors; like the *científicos*, many have been trained as *técnicos* to deal with problems of development. It might not be going too far to conclude, or at least hypothesize, that institutionalization of the Mexican regime has reinstated the social requisites for rule that prevailed under the late *Porfiriato*.

---

[47] I base this statement in part on a seminar paper by Frances Armstrong, "The Sovereign Revolutionary Convention in Mexico: Patterns in Leadership" (University of Wisconsin, January 1972).

· 4 ·

SOCIAL BACKGROUND AND
POLITICAL SUCCESS

Chapter 3 has revealed the existence of relatively clear social prerequisites for political rule in twentieth-century Mexico. Location of birthplace, level of education, university affiliation, and occupation—indirect but nevertheless usable indicators of ascriptive advantage—have to varying extent served as filters for the recruitment and selection of national leaders. Moreover, those who made it to the top echelons of the system, the so-called upper-level elite, possessed these attributes in greater degrees than did the political elites as a whole. It therefore seems reasonable to suppose that, for those who reached office in the national arena, there might have been a systematic connection between social background and the level of office acquired. In the form of a hypothesis, the idea would be: the greater the fulfillment of social prerequisites for entrance into the elite, the higher the ranking within the elite. Or, in somewhat different form: the higher the level of socio-economic advantage, the higher the level of office attained.

This relationship appears to be so universal that it has come to be known, in the phrase of one authority, as "the law of increasing disproportion." In political systems as diverse as those of the United States, Britain, the Soviet Union, Turkey, and Tunisia, the same association has been found: the higher the status the higher the office, and the less representative are the incumbents.[1] There is no compelling reason to believe that Mexico should be an exception to the general rule, so the task of this chapter is not so much to find out whether this connection has existed. Rather, it is to ascertain the strength of this association, and to see how that has varied over time.

Variations in the degree of "increasing disproportion" could conceivably be due to many things, and I shall here concentrate on two distinct (but not necessarily inconsistent) sets of causal factors. One concerns the quality and extent of social stratification. Where class cleavages are deep and mobility is scarce within society at large, it

---

[1] On the "law of increasing disproportion" see Robert D. Putnam, *The Comparative Study of Political Elites* (Englewood Cliffs, N.J.: Prentice-Hall, 1976), pp. 33-36; also Donald R. Matthews, *The Social Background of Political Decision-Makers* (New York: Random House, 1954), pp. 30, 32; and Frederick W. Frey, *The Turkish Political Elite* (Cambridge: M.I.T. Press, 1965), esp. pp. 400-406.

might be expected that the relationship between status and authority within the political elite would be correspondingly strong: those with privileged backgrounds would have disproportionate advantages in acquiring the skills and social contacts required for high office, they would demand (and receive) social deference, and so on. As class differences become less pronounced over time, and if opportunities for upward mobility expand, one might anticipate that the association between the two variables would weaken and decline. Needless to say, the hypothesis relates only to a political elite whose members are drawn from more than one stratum or class, and in the previous chapter we have already seen the predominantly middle-class composition of political leadership in twentieth-century Mexico. Obviously, this proposition has limited application to the material at hand, but it still deserves consideration.

Patterns of Mexican history provide the basis for speculating about a second set of causal factors, those deriving from political conditions. In the late Porfirian era, after the political elite had allegedly undergone a process of "aristocratization," as Francisco Bulnes put it,[2] one might expect a close association between background and level of office: in a centralized system, people of privilege could move directly into uppermost positions without undergoing any political apprenticeship. By contrast the Revolution is often thought to have opened up the political structures and made it possible for people of humble origin to reach the pinnacles of power. Though evidence in Chapter 3 has cast much doubt on this assertion, at least insofar as *access* to the elite is concerned, it is still conceivable that ascriptive characteristics would have less influence on political attainment than in the prerevolutionary years. After all, the system was undergoing a prolonged state of crisis, and political success—and survival—were likely to depend much more on skill, tactics, and luck than on social background. After the institutionalization of the system in the 1930s and '40s, however, the connection between social origin and relative political success might well have regained its former strength. Having secured control of the system, the nation's leadership could afford to reestablish elitist recruitment processes—and reserve the uppermost positions for people of uppermost privilege. I am suggesting, in other words, a pervasive relationship between the conditions for elite attainment and the existence of political stability: where there is relative stability (as in the late Díaz and post-1940 eras), social origin exerts a major influence on the level of office attained; where there is relative instability (as in the

---

[2] Francisco Bulnes, *El verdadero Díaz y la Revolución* (Mexico: Editora Nacional, 1967), esp. pp. 171-190, 197-205, and 356-370.

1917-40 era), social origin exerts a minor influence on the level of office attained.

Unfortunately, the instruments for exploring these propositions are extremely crude. As a measure of political attainment, or relative "success," I have devised a variable that reflects, for every officeholder under study, the highest level of office attained throughout the course of an entire political career. Known here as the HIGHEST OFFICE variable, it contains an 8-point scale, ranging from 1 (the lowest office-holding stratum) up to 8 (the highest), as shown below.

1 = National deputy
2 = Governor of a relatively minor state
3 = Senator
4 = Member of subcabinet
5 = Member of national committee of government party
6 = Governor of a major state
7 = Party president, or director of a major decentralized agency or state-supported company
8 = President, vicepresident (when relevant), or member of cabinet

The scheme is exceedingly rough, as any attempt to operationalize political attainment would have to be, and even in the best of all methodological worlds it is somewhat questionable to equate levels of office with political success (which depends on personal aspirations). In sum, the use of this index rests upon a series of assumptions, each defensible but none airtight: that political offices can be ranked according to importance and prestige, that the HIGHEST OFFICE scale reflects that ranking, that Mexican politicians perceived the same ranking, and that they wanted to move up the ladder to the top. (For further discussion of the index see Appendix A, and especially Table A-3.)

As in the previous chapter, the data on social background are fragmentary, and they provide only indirect guides to social position—or "origin" or "status" or "class" or "advantage." There is some information on, for example, father's occupation. Categorized by social class, these data could in principle provide a fairly direct test of the relationship between social origin and political attainment; in practice, however, the number of observations is too small for the results to be significant. Data on region of birthplace are more complete. In Chapter 3 we have seen that at different times different regions were favored in the recruitment of elites; the task here would be to see if the biases were systematic, and if people from certain regions had disproportionate access to higher (or lower) positions on the ladder of political success. Urbanization of birthplace is another key attribute, and it could be supposed that, primarily because of access to political and governmental institutions, people from cities would get higher on the officeholding ladder than would people from the countryside. Educational attainment would presumably exert a crucial impact on political careers, especially in view of the demonstrated importance of university training: the higher the level of education, one might guess, the higher the level of office attained. Attendance at the national university, where so many national politicians pursued advanced degrees, would hypothetically yield a further advantage; according to this logic, those who went to UNAM would get higher on the officeholding ladder than those who did not. Finally, there are reasonably solid data on occupations, thus making it possible to test the idea that certain kinds of skills and pursuits—such as law or the military—were more conducive to political success than others.

For most variables the possession or nonpossession of an attribute has been coded in a dichotomous (no-yes) way. Take an occupational variable, for instance, such as whether or not a person practiced law: those who had not practiced law would receive a "low" score on this dimension, those who did would get a "high" score, and those with unknown occupations would be removed from that part of the analysis. The same would hold true for regional attributes, such as whether a person came from the Pacific North, as well as for most of the other social-background characteristics. Because the indicators are so crude I shall generally treat them as ranked categories, which is what they really are. But at a later stage of the analysis, I shall take the liberty of assigning numerical values to the categories, with individuals getting a 1 if they possessed the attribute in question and a 0 if they did not. In a way this scoring procedure violates the qualities of the data, but one virtue of the resulting variables (often known as "dummy" variables) is that they permit the use of rather sophisticated statistical techniques, and for this reason they can express a good deal of information in compact form.

To examine basic relationships between political success (that is, the HIGHEST OFFICE variable) and various social-background attributes, I shall in the section that follows rely on *gamma coefficients*. Ranging from +1 to −1, these coefficients provide information on both the *strength* and the *direction* of statistical associations, and they are especially appropriate for the situation at hand (where, in technical terms, both variables consist of ordered nominal scales).[3] The func-

---

[3] For a good discussion of gamma see John H. Mueller, Karl F. Schuessler, and Herbert L. Costner, *Statistical Reasoning in Sociology*, 2nd ed. (Boston: Houghton Mifflin, 1970), pp. 279-292.

tion of these coefficients is to summarize the main characteristics of bivariate tables, or cross-tabulations, and it should be understood that behind each coefficient there is a table (in most cases, one with two columns and eight rows); where notable correlations exist, I shall present the tables themselves.[4] If a relationship between two variables in a table (let us say, HIGHEST OFFICE and level of education) is strong, the gamma coefficient approaches an absolute value of 1, suggesting a very close fit between educational background and the distribution of political office. With a weak relationship the coefficient approaches zero. If a relationship is positive—that is, if HIGHEST OFFICE is high when education is high—the coefficient has a plus (+) sign, suggesting that higher education yields some sort of advantage in the pursuit of higher political office. If the relationship is negative the coefficient carries a minus (−) sign, indicating that people of lesser educational attainment have disproportionately favorable access to top-level offices.

As elsewhere, I shall separate Mexican officeholders into three chronological cohorts, the officeholding groups for 1900-1911, 1917-40, and 1946-71. With separate sets of coefficients for each officeholding cohort, it is possible to compare the results over time and thus detect changes in both the form and strength of the associations.[5]

SIMPLE RELATIONSHIPS

Data on father's occupation offer a reasonable guide to social origin, and they furnish a suggestive starting point for the analysis. As in Table 3-4 of Chapter 3, I have grouped the data into three "class"

[4] As hinted in Appendix A, missing data for the social-background variables have led to systematic underrepresentation of less eminent public figures in this phase of the analysis; this is particularly true for people who never got beyond the Chamber of Deputies (scale value 1). Because we have complete information on the distribution of HIGHEST OFFICE for all members of the cohorts, it would have been possible to adjust for the elitist bias of data availability through a weighting scheme, but after extensive consideration (and some experimentation) I decided not to do so. In the first place, weighted data would reduce the variance in HIGHEST OFFICE, and give undue importance to being in or beyond the Chamber of Deputies (for reasons illustrated in Table A-3 of Appendix A). Second, I have found it more useful, in cases where correlations appear, to recompute gamma for people with scale values of 2 through 8, since the marginal distribution of known data for these categories does not differ too much from the distribution for the entire cohorts.

[5] In all computations I have deleted officeholders who either (a) first gained access to the national political elite during the Díaz Ordaz administration (1964-70), or (b) held any national office under Echeverría (1970-1976), the purpose being to make sure that all individuals in the calculations had a reasonable chance of reaching the pinnacles of their careers. Needless to say, the practical effect of this restriction applies almost exclusively to the postrevolutionary cohort.

categories: lower, middle, and upper. Correlated with the HIGHEST OFFICE variable, the data yield, for the prerevolutionary cohort, a gamma coefficient of +.028 (N = 35), indicating that there was virtually no relationship at all between social background and political attainment with the Porfiian elite. For the revolutionary cohort of 1917-40 the gamma is almost identical, +.062 (N = 100). But then there is a startling shift. For the 1946-71 group the gamma comes out to +.654 (N = 96), implying that, in postrevolutionary Mexico, the law of increasing disproportion has indeed come to assert itself.

Because the data are so sparse, as stated above, these findings could well be spurious.[6] On the other hand they are provocative, and they provide the basis for advancing three propositions. First, the association between status and success may have been weak in the prerevolutionary period, despite the existence of stability, because of the highly personalized nature of recruitment under Díaz: the whim, caprice, and studied calculations of the dictator might have gone against the "normal" workings of increasing disproportion. (Note also that many Porfirian collaborators had reached adulthood during the strife-ridden years of the *Reforma*, and the instability of this period may have further reduced the effects of social background.) Second, as already hypothesized, the transition from the revolutionary to the postrevolutionary cohort, from a period of tumult to a period of calm, led to an accentuation of the status-authority relationship. Third, within the 1946-71 cohort, much of the association derives from the fact that the national legislature, in particular the Chamber of Deputies (scale position = 1), has tended to serve as a receptacle for people of lower-class origin: out of 28 politicians from the lower class, 20 never got beyond the Chamber, and 5 more made it only to the Senate (scale position = 3). When the Chamber of Deputies is omitted from the calculation, the gamma coefficient drops to +.348, showing that the law of increasing disproportion applies less strongly to offices above the lower house. These notions must remain tentative because of weaknesses in data, as I have said, but they help to sharpen the focus of this inquiry.

A set of reasonably reliable coefficients, concerning the regional location of birthplace, appears in Table 4-1. The data on region have been broken down into five separate variables. Someone born in the Gulf area, for example, would get a "yes" for the GULF variable, and "no" for the other four (the corresponding numerical values being 1 and 0). By correlating each variable with HIGHEST OFFICE I have

[6] That is, the results are not "significant" in the statistical sense of the term, and they cannot be extended with much confidence to the entire populations in the officeholding cohorts.

TABLE 4-1

Correlations between Regional Variables and HIGHEST OFFICE,
by Cohort (Gamma Coefficients)

		Correlations with HIGHEST OFFICE Variable		
Variable Name	Definition and Code[a]	Prerevolutionary Cohort, 1900-1911 (N = 183)	Revolutionary Cohort, 1917-40 (N = 743)	Postrevolutionary Cohort, 1946-71 (N = 557)
PACIFIC NORTH	Born in the Pacific North? (o = no, 1 = yes)	-.112	+.188	+.015
NORTH	Born in the North? (o = no, 1 = yes)	+.191	+.044	-.052
CENTER	Born in the Center? (o = no, 1 = yes)	-.067	+.236	-.023
FEDERAL DISTRICT	Born in the Federal District? (o = no, 1 = yes)	-.032	-.060	+.236
GULF	Born in the Gulf? (o = no, 1 = yes)	+.014	-.098	+.080
PACIFIC SOUTH	Born in the Pacific South? (o = no, 1 = yes)	-.155	-.162	-.108

[a] Pacific North = Baja California Norte, Baja California Sur, Nayarit, Sinaloa, Sonora
North = Chihuahua, Coahuila, Durango, Nuevo León, San Luis Potosí, Tamaulipas, Zacatecas
Center = Aguascalientes, Guanajuato, Hidalgo, Jalisco, Mexico, Michoacán, Morelos, Puebla, Querétaro, Tlaxcala
Federal District = Distrito Federal
Gulf = Campeche, Quintana Roo, Tabasco, Veracruz, Yucatán
Pacific South = Chiapas, Colima, Guerrero, Oaxaca (See also Figure 3-1 in Chapter 3.)

obtained five different coefficients for each of the three officeholding cohorts.

Even allowing for problems of measurement the resulting correlations are low, surpassing .20 in only 2 out of the 15 instances and clearly implying that regional origin made very little difference in efforts to climb the ladder of political prestige. The change in sign for the PACIFIC NORTH, negative in the prerevolutionary era and positive in the revolutionary years, yields a faint glimpse of the rise and dominance of the Sonoran dynasty. As a reflection of regional rivalry, indeed, it is striking that the correlations for the 1917-40 cohort are positive for the northern areas and the CENTER, and negative for all the other areas. For the subsequent generation of 1946-71, the correlations do not show any clear characteristic—except for the positive association (+.236) for the FEDERAL DISTRICT, a rather mild relationship suggesting that people from the District have in recent years enjoyed a slight advantage in the race for higher office. Born and bred in Mexico City, they can apparently become familiar with the workings of the governmental bureaucracy and, perhaps more important, they have the opportunity to make friendships and alliances in a way that people from the provinces cannot. This is consistent with the process of centralization that has taken place under the PRI, and it pertains only to the post-1946 generation (note, parenthetically, that the coefficients for FEDERAL DISTRICT were actually somewhat *negative* for the two prior cohorts).

But these are only nuances. The correlations remain undeniably weak. At all times, that is, politicians from all regions found themselves more or less evenly distributed according to level of office. In part this reflects the influence of some institutions, such as the national congress and the governorships, which have implicit or de facto regional quotas.[7] More crucial is the fact that Mexico's national elites have generally recognized the need to provide ample representation for all regions at all levels of government, within generations if not within individual presidential regimes, and thus forestall resentments and rivalries. This was less true of the revolutionary cohort (1917-40) than of the other groups, as shown in Table 3-1 of Chapter 3, but it still seems to have been a guiding principle.

Table 4-2 presents the correlations between HIGHEST OFFICE and four variables relating to urban origin, that is, the size and type of communities in which people were born. Chapter 3 has already revealed sharp discontinuities in the incidence of urban origin—which

---

[7] This is not necessarily so, since congressmen and most governors do not have to be natives of the states they serve, but in recent decades most have been so.

TABLE 4-2

Correlations between Urbanization Variables and HIGHEST OFFICE, by Cohort (Gamma Coefficients)

Variable Name	Definition and Code	Correlations with HIGHEST OFFICE Variable		
		Prerevolutionary Cohort, 1900-1911 (N = 176)	Revolutionary Cohort, 1917-40 (N = 691)	Postrevolutionary Cohort, 1946-71 (N = 524)
CAPITAL	Born in capital of a state or territory? (0 = no, 1 = yes)	+.085	-.015	+.136
URBANISM	Urbanization of birthplace as of 1921 (1 = population under 10,000; 2 = 10-20,000; 3 = 20-50,000; 4 = 50-500,000; 5 = over 500,000)[a]	-.016	-.022	+.087
METROPOLIS	Born in a city with 50,000 or more inhabitants as of 1921? (0 = no, 1 = yes)	-.070	-.198	+.048
CITY/CAPITAL	Born in a state/territory capital or in a city with 20,000 or more inhabitants as of 1921?[a] (0 = no, 1 = yes)	-.024	+.003	+.132

[a] See Departamento de la Estadística Nacional, *Resumen del censo general de habitantes de 30 de noviembre de 1921* (Mexico: Talleres Gráficos de la Nación, 1928), pp. 166-182.

turned out to be high in the prerevolutionary era, relatively low just after the Revolution, and high again for the post-1946 cohort. Given this variation, Table 4-2 confronts a different question: for people who gain access to the system, has urban origin affected their chances of moving upward within the elite? Have the opportunities and lifestyles of growing up in cities provided advantage in the quest for political success?

Apparently not much. The coefficients are uniformly low, with none of them reaching plus-or-minus .20. No matter what the index of urbanization, type of birthplace has exerted no strong impact on the outcome of political careers. There does exist a hint, ever so mild, that the association, such as it is, may have changed direction. For both the prerevolutionary and revolutionary cohorts, three out of the four coefficients are negative, including the strongest single association in the entire table ($-.198$ for the METROPOLIS variable in 1917-40); for the postrevolutionary group (1946-71) the correlations are all positive, even though they are weak. It is tempting to infer, from this pattern, that the qualities of urban life have become somewhat more conducive to the accumulation of political skills in recent eras than in former years, a trend in keeping with the steady urbanization of Mexican society as a whole. But in view of the low numbers, this remains nothing more than a temptation. The main message to be gleaned from Table 4-2 is that urbanization of birthplace has exerted very little direct influence on chances for climbing the political ladder, a fact which may well have a simple explanation: that rural-born politicians have moved to urban or at least semiurban areas at fairly early ages, while they could still reap the benefits of urban environments.

One of these benefits would have been the opportunity for education—as shown in Chapter 3, a prime prerequisite for gaining entrance into the national political elite. Since education provides people with knowledge, skill, and social contacts, it would seem reasonable to suppose that level of education would show a strong and positive influence on the level of office attained.

The correlations in Table 4-3 provide a means of testing this idea, and they offer partial confirmation of it. All of the first three variables, which measure educational accomplishment in different ways—LEVEL OF EDUCATION, EDUCATIONAL ATTAINMENT, and UNIVERSITY—show positive correlations with HIGHEST OFFICE. Moreover, each of the three sets of statistics reveals a slight decline in strength between the prerevolutionary and revolutionary cohorts, followed by fairly strong associations for the postrevolutionary group. To take only one example, and perhaps the most meaningful one, UNI-

TABLE 4-3

Correlations between Educational Variables and *HIGHEST OFFICE*,
by Cohort (*Gamma Coefficients*)

		Correlations with HIGHEST OFFICE Variable		
Variable Name	Definition and Code	Prevolutionary Cohort, 1900-1911 (N = 165)	Revolutionary Cohort, 1917-40 (N = 649)	Postrevolutionary Cohort, 1946-71 (N = 688)
LEVEL OF EDUCATION	Code: 1 = no primary school, 2 = primary, 3 = secondary, 4 = preparatory, 5 = commercial or special academy, 6 = university	+.167	+.140	+.202
EDUCATIONAL ATTAINMENT	Code: 1 = none, primary, or secondary; 2 = preparatory, vocational, or special academy; 3 = university	+.151	+.129	+.218
UNIVERSITY	Ever attend a university? (0 = no, 1 = yes)	+.183	+.136	+.273
UNAM	Ever attend UNAM?[a] (0 = no, 1 = yes)	−.088	+.245	+.494
NATIONAL UNIVERSITY	Ever go to National[b] University (UNAM)? (0 = no, 1 = yes)	−.014	+.412	+.486

[a] Among all those people whose level of education is known, though the precise identification of the university (if applicable) may be unknown.

[b] Among all those people whose level of education is known *and* whose university, if applicable, can also be identified. This restriction means that the populations for the NATIONAL UNIVERSITY calculations are smaller than those for UNAM.

VERSITY, the coefficients slip from +.183 to +.136 between the pre-revolutionary and revolutionary cohorts, and then the figure rises to +.273 for the postrevolutionary generation. The inferences are fairly clear. The Revolution did not eliminate the political advantages of educational attainment; it only reduced them, and temporarily at that. With the subsequent institutionalization of the dominant-party system, education has assumed increasing relevance to the chances for political success.

Yet as demonstrated in Chapter 3, it has been not only the level of education, usually university training, which has influenced access to the elite. It has also been the place of education, the most prominent institution being the UNAM. For members of the elite, however, the role of the national university appears to have undergone a change. This transition finds remarkably pure expression in the coefficients relating attendance at the national university to political attainment in Table 4-3. During the Porfirian era, attendance at the national school actually exerted a slightly negative influence on the odds for political success (the UNAM gamma being −.088), as Díaz recruited a substantial number of cabinet members and important governors from the ranks of provincial university graduates. For the revolutionary generation the coefficient turned positive (+.245), and for the postrevolutionary cohort it became positive and moderately powerful (+.494). Since the 1930s, again, UNAM has functioned as a crucial training ground and meeting place for future political leaders, and those who went there have had a better chance for attaining ultimate political success than those who did not.[8]

To illustrate the situation for the postrevolutionary generation, Table 4-4 displays the data relating university experience to political achievement. Of the 688 individuals whose educational attainment is known, only 154 had not gone to a university—and of that group 81 never moved up beyond the Chamber of Deputies, and only 18 (11.7 percent) made it into what I have defined as the "upper-level" elite (consisting of scale positions 7 and 8 for the HIGHEST OFFICE variable). Similarly, graduates of schools other than UNAM tended to cluster near the bottom of the ladder: 38 of the 63 people in this cate-

---

[8] A similar pattern emerges from data on preuniversity training. With preparatory-school backgrounds divided into three categories (none, other than Escuela Nacional Preparatoria, and Escuela Nacional Preparatoria) and treated as an ordered nominal variable, the gamma coefficients come out as follows: prerevolutionary cohort, +.075 (N = 36); revolutionary cohort, +.147 (N = 144); postrevolutionary cohort, +.409 (N = 173). Like UNAM, the ENP appears to have been gaining importance as a training ground for members of upper-level elites.

gory never got beyond the Senate, and only 11 (17.5 percent) reached the upper-level ranks. By contrast, the 162 individuals from UNAM moved up the ladder fairly easily: more than half (52.5 percent) went beyond the Senate, and fully one-third of the group (a total of 54) made it into the upper-level elite. Painly, UNAM has given its graduates some special resources in the struggle for political prestige.

TABLE 4-4

Relationship between University Experience and HIGHEST OFFICE: Postrevolutionary Cohort, 1946-71

			University Experience			
HIGHEST OFFICE (scale value in parentheses)		None	Attended UNAM[a]	Attended Other than UNAM	Attended University, Institution Unknown	Totals
Deputy	(1)	81	38	21	148	288
Governor of lesser state	(2)	4	8	3	18	33
Senator	(3)	30	31	14	29	104
Subcabinet	(4)	7	19	6	53	85
Party executive commiteee	(5)	9	7	2	11	29
Governor of major state	(6)	5	5	5	10	25
Party president, leader in semipublic sector	(7)	3	8	3	14	28
Cabinet, president	(8)	15	46	9	26	96
Totals		154	162	63	309	688

[a] Or its predecessors, including the Escuela Nacional de Jurisprudencia.

After education came one or more jobs, at least in most cases, and Table 4-5 sets forth correlation coefficients for relationships between selected occupational variables and ultimate political accomplishment. Computations for the first three variables, PROFESSIONAL TITLE through MILITARY OFFICER, consider total membership in each cohort as the base populations (since titles and military ranks could be determined for virtually everyone). Calculations for the others, PROFESSOR through OCCUPATIONAL CLASS, count only those with known occupations within each cohort as the base population. It

TABLE 4-5

Correlations between Occupational Variables and HIGHEST OFFICE, by Cohort (Gamma Coefficients)

Variable Name	Definition and Code	Correlations with HIGHEST OFFICE Variable		
		Prerevolutionary Cohort, 1900-1911 (N = 600; 209)[a]	Revolutionary Cohort, 1917-40 (N = 2,278; 898)[a]	Postrevolutionary Cohort, 1946-71 (N = 1,225; 740)[a]
PROFESSIONAL TITLE	Have a professional title?[b] (0 = no, 1 = yes)	+.655	+.692	+.542
LICENCIADO	Have title of *licenciado*? (0 = no, 1 = yes)	+.717	+.606	+.578
MILITARY OFFICER	Have rank as military officer? (0 = no, 1 = yes)	+.522	+.544	+.416
PROFESSOR	Ever a university professor? (0 = no, 1 = yes)	+.079	+.286	+.484
LAWYER	Ever a lawyer? (0 = no, 1 = yes)	+.204	+.141	+.341
DOCTOR	Ever a doctor? (0 = no, 1 = yes)	-.627	+.111	-.095
ENGINEER	Ever an engineer? (0 = no, 1 = yes)	+.233	+.348	+.120
TEACHER	Ever a school teacher? (0 = no, 1 = yes)	+.030	+.110	+.202
JOURNALIST	Ever a journalist? (0 = no, 1 = yes)	-.142	-.192	+.190
LIBERAL PROFESSION	Practice a liberal profession?[c] (0 = no, 1 = yes)	-.009	+.148	+.165
OCCUPATIONAL CLASS	Highest occupational status attained (1 = worker or peasant, 2 = employee, 3 = professional, 4 = owner [businessman, landowner, etc.])	+.041	+.186	+.324

[a] First N refers to correlations involving first three variables (PROFESSIONAL TITLE through MILITARY OFFICER); second N refers to correlations for all others.

[b] Titles include: *Licenciado, Doctor, Profesor, Ingeniero, Arquitecto, Contador, Químico.*

[c] The liberal professions, as here defined: lawyer, doctor, engineer, economist, teacher, professor, journalist, and other miscellaneous professions.

should also be noted that quite a few individuals had more than one of the occupations listed in the table.[9]

Some of the coefficients are striking. PROFESSIONAL TITLE, particularly, has one of the strongest sets of correlations among all social. background variables, and the signs are uniformly positive: +.655 for the 1900-1911 generation, +.692 for the 1917-40 group, and +.522 for the 1946-71 cohort. A nearly identical pattern holds for the possession of the title of *licenciado*, which has usually meant that the person was a lawyer (+.717, +.606, and +.578, respectively). The coefficients for the LAWYER variable are also positive though not so powerful (+.204, +.141, +.341). A solid implication of these figures is that the exercise of a liberal profession has substantially improved the chances for attaining relative success within the national political elite. In addition, the greatest advantage has accrued from broadly defined professions, particularly law, fields in which people would be more likely to develop social skills and contacts than specialized expertise. Engineering, to be sure, has positive coefficients, the strongest pertaining to the 1917-40 cohort (+.348). But these are not nearly as strong as the LICENCIADO correlations, for instance, and the other technical occupation, DOCTOR, carries negative signs in two out of the three instances. The rule appears to hold: almost any profession would increase the likelihood of political success, as indicated by the PROFESSIONAL TITLE correlations, and socially oriented professions (such as law) have been more useful than technical ones (with the notable exception of economics).[10]

In elaboration of this point, Table 4-6 offers data on the relationship between professional title and political attainment for the revolutionary generation (1917-40). One sees, at a glance, that the possession of a professional title was nearly a prerequisite for moving up from the Chamber of Deputies: of the 1,791 individuals without any title just 542 (30.3 percent) reached any position above the deputy level, while the vast majority (1,249 = 69.7 percent) did not. Among the 487 people holding professional titles, however, a total of 380 (78 percent) attained posts above the Chamber, and 156 (32 percent) entered the upper-level elite; only 107 (22 percent) had to rest content

[9] Most of the recorded occupations seem to have been held prior to entering politics, though some were held during and even after the course of political careers. Unfortunately my data do not permit consistent distinctions on this point.

[10] In very recent years economists have gained important positions in the upper circles of power, but this does not show up very clearly in the data for the 1946-1971 group (partly because of the removal of younger people from the analysis, as explained in note 5).

with deputyships. The connection was not overwhelmingly powerful, but it was persistent and pervasive: at all levels of political attainment, the possession of a professional title improved the chances for moving up within the hierarchy.[11]

TABLE 4-6

Relationship between Professional Title and HIGHEST OFFICE: Revolutionary Cohort, 1917-40

HIGHEST OFFICE (scale value in parentheses)		None	Licenciado en derecho[a]	Licenciado (unspecified)	Other	Totals
			Professional Title			
Deputy	(1)	1,249	52	13	42	1,356
Governor of lesser state	(2)	137	10	14	17	178
Senator	(3)	170	32	19	33	254
Subcabinet	(4)	48	6	4	20	78
Party executive committee	(5)	21	4	4	10	39
Governor of major state	(6)	82	12	17	22	133
Party president, leader in semipublic sector	(7)	10	4	0	7	21
Cabinet, president	(8)	74	67	20	58	219
Totals		1,791	187	91	209	2,278

[a] Includes one *doctor en derecho.*

Further, Table 4-6 furnishes evidence on the particular advantages enjoyed by lawyers. Of the 187 individuals in the revolutionary cohort known to have been *licenciados en derecho*—and therefore trained in law, though they might not have practiced it—a notable number reached positions in the upper-level elite: 71, or 37.9 percent. (For the prerevolutionary group, the corresponding figure was 36.6 percent; for the postrevolutionary cohort it was 47.2 percent.) These are provocative proportions. On the average, and in rough terms, they mean that out of every five lawyers who entered the national political elite, about two could expect to reach the upper pinnacles of prominence—only

[11] When people at scale position 1 are removed from consideration, the coefficient for the distribution between scale positions 2 and 8 remains fairly high (+.409).

one would have to settle for a deputyship, and the other two would wind up somewhere in between. To put it mildly, training in law has been a help.

By their nature the data on professional titles combine information on two distinct dimensions, education and occupation, and to this extent they provide a proxy indicator of social position. Interpreted in this regard, the information in Tables 4-5 and 4-6 conveys a clear suggestion: the higher the class, the higher the level of office attained. In an effort to obtain a reasonably direct measure of this association I have constructed a four-point scale for OCCUPATIONAL CLASS and computed the correlations with HIGHEST OFFICE. As shown in Table 4-5, the social-class variable has consistently positive—and increasing—associations with political attainment: +.041 for the prerevolutionary cohort, +.186 for the revolutionary cohort, and +.324 for the postrevolutionary group. So the *form* of the relationships is consistent with the hypothesis, although they are lacking in strength. The reason for the weakness of the association is straightforward enough. Mexican politicians have tended to be socially homogenous, at all times throughout the twentieth century, largely consisting of people from the professional stratum (a point made earlier in Chapter 3, and documented in Table 3-7). Accordingly there has not been much variance in social class; to the degree that variance has existed, however, it shows a linkage with political achievement. Notwithstanding the Revolution, too, that linkage has been gaining strength over time.

Two other occupational variables in Table 4-5 also merit consideration, not because they reflect the social status of officeholders but because they yield some implications about the operation of the recruitment system. Indicators relating to teaching careers both show positive and steadily increasing associations with HIGHEST OFFICE: TEACHER has correlations of +.030, +.110, and +.202 for the respective cohorts; PROFESSOR has coefficients of +.079, +.286, and +.484. Since teaching positions have usually been temporary or part-time, I would not interpret these results as demonstrations of class position. Rather, I suspect that they reflect the growing utility of teaching, especially on the university level, as a means of developing leadership skills and, more important, political and social contacts. In this connection it is especially revealing that the strongest correlation in this series belongs to the PROFESSOR variable for the 1946-71 cohort. As suggested more than once above, the universities in recent years—most notably UNAM—have functioned as training grounds and recruitment centers for political elites. Professors have often drawn students into their *camarillas*, and vice versa; on frequent occasions, ex-students have rewarded their former professors with political appointments.[12] Since the 1940s the professors have been doing rather well.

Last, but by no means least, Table 4-5 reveals a relatively strong set of coefficients for relationships between military status and political achievement. The associations between MILITARY OFFICER and HIGHEST OFFICE are uniformly positive and fairly powerful: +.522 for the prerevolutionary group, +.544 for the revolutionary group, and +.416 for the postrevolutionary cohort. The findings for the first two groups come as no surprise. Himself a general, Porfirio Díaz rewarded fellow soldiers with political positions, frequently as governors of major states (scale position 6). Likewise, it seems only natural that officers from the revolutionary armies should take command of political office: within the 1917-40 cohort they utterly dominated the presidency, they drew about 18 percent of all soldiers in the elite into cabinet-level posts, and they elevated about 17 percent to governorships of major states. But with Miguel Alemán's inauguration in 1946, civilians gained control of the bureaucratic apparatus—and old soldiers, it is sometimes thought, just faded away. Then how come the correlation?

The answer lies in Table 4-7, which displays the relationship between military status and political success for the 1946-71 cohort. As expected, the data indicate that a rather small share of all officeholders consisted of military personnel, not much more than 10 percent. But when Mexican civilian elites have rewarded and coopted military officers with political positions, they have done so by dispensing middle and upper-middle posts. Of the 128 officers in the group, only 37 (28.9 percent) had to settle for deputyships. Frequent levels of attainment have been the Senate (22.6 percent), the subcabinet (16.4 percent), and the cabinet itself (13.3 percent). Some of those who made it to the cabinet, too, had also served as presidents of the PRI: Agustín Olachea Avilés, for instance, and Alfonso Corona del Rosal (who also has a degree in law). In sum, military officers have moved into the political elite less frequently than in previous generations. But when they've entered the elite, they have come in at levels of substantial prestige and prominence.

Generally speaking, then, social-background characteristics have exercised discernible but modest influence on the likelihood of political attainment, as measured by HIGHEST OFFICE. Variables relating to social origin, such as father's occupation, urbanization of birthplace,

12 See Roderic Ai Camp, *The Education of Mexico's Revolutionary Family* (forthcoming).

TABLE 4-7

Relationship between Military Status
and HIGHEST OFFICE: Postrevolutionary Cohort, 1946-71

HIGHEST OFFICE (scale value in parentheses)		Military Status[a]		
		Civilian	Officer	Totals
Deputy	(1)	685	37	722
Governor of lesser state	(2)	38	8	46
Senator	(3)	116	29	145
Subcabinet	(4)	83	21	104
Party executive committee	(5)	29	7	36
Governor of major state	(6)	29	9	38
Party president, leader in semipublic sector	(7)	29	0	29
Cabinet, president	(8)	88	17	105
Totals		1,097	128	1,225

[a] As reflected in the wearing of military titles.

and education, have shown their strongest relationships in the post-revolutionary cohort; variables relating to occupational status have shown fairly constant associations over time. But what about the impact of education on occupation? Might not urbanization have affected opportunities for education? What were the cumulative effects of various social-background characteristics, in combination, upon the relative prospects for political achievement? To deal with questions of this kind, it is necessary to explore complex associations.

MULTIVARIATE RELATIONSHIPS

Among the techniques available for dealing with multivariate situations, where more than two variables are involved, I have selected *path analysis*. A central characteristic of this method is that it requires the formulation of a causal model (or theoretical scheme) that, as shown below, can be depicted in a diagram. Presumed patterns of causality take the form of "paths," the strength and sign of which are given by "path coefficients." Thus path-analytic models not only measure the combined impact of selected independent variables upon a single dependent variable, in this case HIGHEST OFFICE. Equally important, they provide a means of evaluating the impact of each of the independent variables upon HIGHEST OFFICE while controlling for the cumulative effects of all the other independent variables, something that the gamma coefficients in the prior section have not done. Moreover, path analysis makes it possible to analyze the impact of the independent variables upon each other.[13]

After extensive experimentation I have constructed models involving similar variables for each of the three generational cohorts. There are, in this scheme, two thoroughly independent or "exogenous" variables that are presumably caused by nothing else within the model. (Since they both deal with conditions at birth, they are unlikely to have been influenced by developments at later stages in life.) One of these variables is the CITY/CAPITAL dichotomy, with individuals receiving a score of 1 if they were born in a state capital or a substantial city[14] and a 0 if they were not. Though this variable seems to have had a very weak direct association with HIGHEST OFFICE (see Table 4-2), it is included in the model because of the manifold ways that urbanization (or the existence of state capitals, regardless of population size) might have affected access to education, occupational pursuits, and social contacts.

The second exogenous variable, not yet brought into this chapter, is YEAR OF BIRTH, a self-explanatory four-digit figure. My assumption here is that the later a person was born, the greater the opportunity for education, in view of the steady expansion of the Mexican educational apparatus over time. Similarly, I would suppose that, as a result of changes in the country's economic structure, described in Chapter 2, later generations would have greater chances for engaging in liberal professional occupations. The type of direct influence that birthdates might have on HIGHEST OFFICE would probably vary according to cohort: for the thoroughly gerontocratic Díaz regime, one would expect the impact to be strongly negative; this might be less true for the youthful revolutionary generation of 1917-40; for the post-revolutionary group, the a priori relationship remains uncertain.

The model then includes three "endogenous" variables, ones that are presumably affected by the exogenous factors but which would also have an independent impact on political attainment. The first of these

[13] On path analysis see Otis Dudley Duncan, "Path Analysis: Sociological Examples," *American Journal of Sociology* 72, no. 1 (July 1966): 1-16; and Kenneth C. Land, "Principles of Path Analysis," in *Sociological Methodology 1969*, ed. Edgar F. Borgatta (San Francisco: Jossey-Bass, 1969), pp. 3-37.

[14] That is, one with over 20,000 inhabitants as of 1921. (See Table 4-2, note *e*.)

is NATIONAL UNIVERSITY, with individuals scored with 1 if they attended UNAM and 0 if they did not. This variable serves as a surrogate index for level of education, since many politicians went to a university, but it also touches on an equally critical point—the role of UNAM, a theme that has already come up more than once. Given the central location and multiple functions of this institution, I would expect this variable to have a positive impact on HIGHEST OFFICE, perhaps, as suggested by Table 4-3, increasing its relative strength vis-à-vis other variables over time.[15] I would also anticipate a uniformly positive impact on the likelihood of entering a liberal profession, since UNAM graduates have typically gone into such occupations, and a uniformly negative impact on the likelihood of taking up a military career.

The other endogenous independent variables deal with occupations. One, LAWYER, shows whether or not a person is known to have practiced law (0 = no, 1 = yes).[16] The other, MILITARY OFFICER, shows whether or not a person wore a military rank (0 = no, 1 = yes). For reasons already described in connection with Table 4-5, my anticipation is that both of these would at all times have positive relationships to the final dependent variable, HIGHEST OFFICE, but I would also guess that the influence of the LAWYER variable would tend to strengthen its relative position from cohort to cohort, especially after the onset of civilian domination in the 1940s, while the relative effect of MILITARY OFFICER would show a slight decline.

Conceptualized in this fashion, the empirical models—one for each officeholding cohort[17]—are set forth in Figures 4-1, 4-2, and 4-3. The straight, single-headed arrows represent causal paths, and the accompanying numbers are the corresponding coefficients for each path (in technical terms, these are standardized regression coefficients, also

[15] For technical reasons I consider it inappropriate to compare the absolute strength of beta coefficients between separate path models, and I shall refrain from doing so in this analysis. But I think it is appropriate to compare the relative position (or rank order) of the beta weights, in relation to other variables within the same model, and it is also legitimate to compare the signs of beta weights in different models.

[16] I have decided to utilize the LAWYER variable instead of PROFESSIONAL TITLE or LICENCIADO, both of which had stronger correlations with HIGHEST OFFICE (Table 4-5) in order to maximize substantive precision. It should be noted, however, that individuals have been coded as "lawyers" if they possessed degrees in law, so the LAWYER variable is practically identical to LICENCIADO.

[17] The number of observations for each path model is much smaller than the number of individuals in each cohort because it was necessary to restrict the path analysis to those individuals with complete information on all variables concerned —including the precise identification of university attended, if applicable. It is unlikely that the resulting groups constitute valid "random" samples of their cohorts, so the results of this analysis should be interpreted with caution.

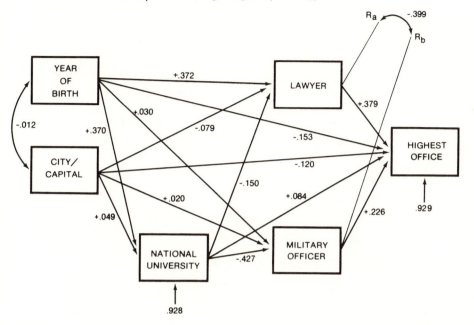

Figure 4-1: Social Determinants of Highest Political Office: Prerevolutionary Cohort, 1900-1911 (N = 63)

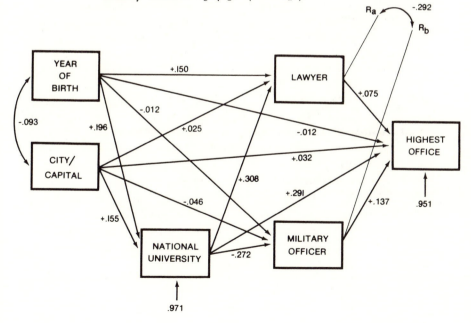

Figure 4-2: Social Determinants of Highest Political Office: Revolutionary Cohort, 1917-40 (N = 246)

Figure 4-3: Social Determinants of Highest Political Office: Postrevolutionary Cohort, 1946-71 (N = 280)

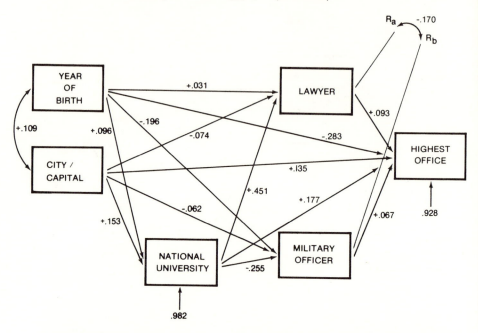

known as beta weights). The curved, double-headed arrows refer to relationships between pairs of independent variables which are thought to operate simultaneously on other variables (the numbers are zero-order correlation coefficients for the exogenous variables, and partial correlations for the endogenous ones). Finally, the figures underneath the vertical arrows pointing up to **NATIONAL UNIVERSITY** and **HIGHEST OFFICE** estimate the relative inputs of outside, unmeasured forces on each of the two variables; ranging from 0 to 1, these "coefficients of alienation" are functions of what is "unexplained" by variables already in the model.[18]

Perhaps the most striking single aspect of the models is that, even in combination, the five independent variables explain relatively small portions of the variance in **HIGHEST OFFICE**: respectively, 13.6 percent, 9.6 percent, and 13.8 percent. In part this results from a measurement problem since, unlike the gamma coefficients, the computational procedures behind the equations treat the points on the **HIGHEST OFFICE** scale as *numbers* and not as *categories*, and it is difficult for

[18] The coefficient of alienation equals $\sqrt{1 - R^2}$ where R^2 is the proportion of variance explained in the variable under consideration.

the models to attain a great deal of explanatory power.[19] But even so, the coefficients of alienation all exceed .90: for the prerevolutionary cohort it is .929, for the revolutionary cohort it is .951 and for the post-revolutionary group it stands at .928. It is to some extent revealing that the coefficient is highest for the 1917-40 era, suggesting that social-background characteristics may have had less to do with political attainment in those years than either before or after—implying, as hypothesized above, that the Revolution opened up the channels to success for a temporary period. But the differences are very slight.[20] According to these models, chances for climbing the political ladder have been to a substantial degree independent of social origins throughout the twentieth century.

To the extent that background has determined achievement, the diagrams reveal suggestive patterns. As hypothesized, occupational variables LAWYER and MILITARY OFFICER have consistently positive paths toward HIGHEST OFFICE, controlling for the effects of all the other variables. The strength of the MILITARY OFFICER path undergoes the predicted decline, slipping from second place in the prerevolutionary and revolutionary models to last place in the post-revolutionary one. Contrary to expectation, so does the LAWYER path, whose relative standing drops from first to third to fourth. What the data appear to reveal, in short, is a secular decline in the cumulative impact of occupational variables on political attainment.

As a matter of fact, the occupational characteristics appear to be displaced, as explanatory variables, by the influence of NATIONAL UNIVERSITY, whose consistently positive path coefficients rise from +.084 in 1900-1911 (when it was the weakest of all) to +.286 in 1917-40 (when it was the strongest) with a slight dip back to +.177 in 1946-71 (when it was in second place). This confirms a pattern that we have seen before, specifically in Tables 4-3 and 4-4: right after the Revolution, UNAM established itself as a relatively meaningful determinant in the outcome of political careers. Parenthetically, it also had clear relationships to occupation, with generally positive coefficients toward LAWYER (except for the 1900-1911 period, when provincial

[19] That is, the data are assumed to have the properties of interval scales. The use of dummy variables thus presents an instance of analysis of variance, the distinctive condition of this situation being that (given the existence of an 8-point scale for HIGHEST OFFICE) there must always be considerable variance within as well as between the categories of the independent variable. Consequently, the proportion of variance explained cannot get very high.

[20] Even at that, the results are still elusive. When the R^2 values are adjusted to account for degrees of freedom, they show a slight but steady increase over time: .061, .081, .123.

lawyers seem to have prevailed) and consistently strong negative co-efficients in the direction of MILITARY OFFICER.

The YEAR OF BIRTH variable exhibits some provocative alterations. As predicted, the path to HIGHEST OFFICE is negative for the prerevolutionary cohort, meaning that older people tended to possess the higher offices. The coefficient is ever so slightly negative for 1917-40, indicating that youth was not a serious disadvantage in the revolutionary era. For 1946-71, however, the coefficient gains strength again (−.283) and becomes the strongest of the five. With the institutionalization of the political system and the establishment of stable careers, power (or at least office) tended to remain in the hands of the elders. It is apparent, in fact, that with the leadership change in the 1940s a generation took over the system—and stayed in control of the upper echelons through the decade of the 1960s (a point foreshadowed by the endurance of the 1900-1919 birth cohort, as shown in Table 3-10).

The CITY/CAPITAL variable shows additional changes. Despite the overwhelmingly urban quality of the late Díaz elite, already seen in Chapter 3, being from a city or state capital actually had a negative impact on chances for climbing the ladder of prestige, as also implied by the gamma coefficient in Table 4-2. For subsequent generations the path turns out to be positive, as predicted: +.032 for the revolutionary cohort and +.135 for the postrevolutionary group. In time, but only in time, the amenities of urban life came to furnish slight advantages in the quest for political success.

Other paths merit less attention. In accordance with my hypothesis, the CITY/CAPITAL variable shows consistently positive relationships to NATIONAL UNIVERSITY, implying that urban origin has enhanced access to higher education—and entrance to the UNAM. Positive coefficients from YEAR OF BIRTH to NATIONAL UNIVERSITY suggest, too, that younger members of each cohort had better chances of going to UNAM than did their elders (although the coefficient of alienation for the university variable remained constantly high). YEAR OF BIRTH also has a strong coefficient (+.372) for the path toward LAWYER in the 1900-1911 model, indicating that lawyers in the Díaz elite tended to be relatively young, but this coefficient loses strength in models for the other cohorts. By contrast, soldiers in the 1946-71 elite have tended to be older than their officeholding colleagues, the path coefficient from YEAR OF BIRTH to MILITARY OFFICER coming out to −.196.

Perhaps the main contribution of these path models has been to confirm, and to some extent modify, the impressions derived from the cross-tabulations and the gamma coefficients in the preceding section. After controlling for the effects of all other independent variables, the paths from each independent variable to HIGHEST OFFICE are very similar to the patterns in the gamma coefficients. The models reflect once more the growing importance of UNAM, as the relative contribution of paths from NATIONAL UNIVERSITY was stronger in both 1917-40 and 1946-71 than were the contributions from LAWYER and MILITARY OFFICER. They shed some light on interconnections among the independent variables, particularly in the positive relationships between CITY/CAPITAL and NATIONAL UNIVERSITY. And finally, through the coefficients of alienation, they show that the cumulative effect of all the social-background variables had fairly little influence on political attainment; this was especially true for the revolutionary cohort, but it applied to the others as well.

Conclusions

In this chapter I have attempted to furnish empirical tests for the proposition that social background has exercised a determining influence on political success in Mexico. Operationalizing the concept of political achievement with a variable called HIGHEST OFFICE, I have employed two methods, bivariate cross-tabulation (with corresponding gamma coefficients) and multivariate path analysis, in search for clues about the form and strength of statistical associations between social status and career accomplishment.

One basic thrust of the findings is that, among Mexican politicians, social-background attributes have never provided ironclad indicators (or prerequisites) of relative success. Most of the gamma coefficients were below .50 and almost all were less than .60. Similarly, each of the multivariate path models explained less than 15 percent of the variance in HIGHEST OFFICE. Notwithstanding formidable problems of measurement, the influence of social background on political attainment appears to have been: some, but not too much.

But there are patterns within these limitations. It is fairly clear, for instance, that the status-authority relationship has been more pronounced for the postrevolutionary cohort than for the previous two groups. In my view this trend results from two political factors, system stability and institutionalization, which permitted the law of increasing disproportion to operate without undue distortion. The Porfirian period was stable but recruitment was personalized rather than institutionalized. The 1917-40 era was neither stable nor institutionalized. Only the 1946-71 years were *both* stable and institutionalized, at least in comparison to prior times,[21] so it showed the strongest correlations.

In determining the shape of the postrevolutionary relationships, patterns of stratification within Mexican society at large have exerted influence at a very specific location within the political system. National officeholders of lower-class origin often made it only to the Chamber of Deputies, the lowest position on the HIGHEST OFFICE scale, and the likelihood of getting beyond the Chamber has borne quite a strong relationship to social origin. Offices above the Chamber have been practically monopolized by people of middle- and upper-class origin, and—within these levels of authority, within these social strata—the linkage between relative status and relative attainment has been weak.

But what is strong and what is weak? How does Mexico compare with other places? Table 4-8 presents some data on educational attainments of elites, by level, in three countries: postwar Britain, one of the most stable polities in the world; contemporary Tunisia, one of the most highly stratified societies in the world; and Mexico, represented by data on the 1946-71 cohort. The figures defy straightforward comparison, since the social meaning of education varies from country to country, and the different levels of office perform different political functions, but they provide at least a benchmark for evaluating the Mexican situation.

In my opinion the table implies that the law of increasing disproportion has been no more inexorable in Mexico than elsewhere, and it might even have been less so. About 65 percent of Mexican cabinet ministers attended UNAM, slightly less than the 72 percent of British counterparts who came from Oxford or Cambridge. Also, the gap between the Mexican cabinet and Senate (65-41 percent) is smaller than the one between the British cabinet and Parliament (72-37 percent) although, for reasons mentioned above, the Mexican Chamber of Deputies falls rather far behind (27 percent). Similarly, a university education is less necessary for entrance to the cabinet in Mexico, where 83 percent of the ministers have had higher education, than in Tunisia, where the rate is 100 percent.[22] The educational levels of the Tunisian assembly and the Mexican legislature are practically identical. The figure for Tunisian governors slips to 50 percent, however, while for Mexican governors—whose political role is more important than that

[21] Note that this is a *relative* statement. As will be made clear in Chapter 9, I believe that many aspects of the recruitment and selection process are still highly personalized.

[22] Lately, however, the Mexican figure has been close to the 100 percent level.

TABLE 4-8

Educational Attainments of Political Elites by Levels of Office: Britain, Tunisia, and Mexico

Britain		Tunisia		Mexico		
Level	% Oxford or Cambridge	Level	% University	Level	% University[a]	% UNAM[b]
Cabinet	72	Cabinet	100	Cabinet	83	65
Parliament	37	Assembly	70	Senate	71	41
		Governors	50	Deputies	72	27

SOURCES: Britain: Robert D. Putnam, *The Comparative Study of Political Elites* (Englewood Cliffs, N.J.: Prentice-Hall, 1976), p. 35. Tunisia: William B. Quandt, "The Comparative Study of Political Elites," *Sage Professional Papers in Comparative Politics*, 01-004 (Beverly Hills, Cal.: Sage Publications, 1970), p. 186; also in Putnam, *Comparative Study*, p. 36.

[a] Among those whose level of education is known.

[b] Among those whose level of education is known and whose university, if applicable, can also be identified.

of most legislators—the proportion is greater than 80 percent. Social inequalities thus exist within the Mexican political elite, but, partly because the elite is so homogenous, the inequalities are no more glaring than they are in other countries.

In general, throughout the twentieth century, and with some variation over time, social origin has therefore exerted a *differential impact* on political recruitment in Mexico. Through education, occupation, father's occupation, and to some degree birthplace, as shown in Chapter 3, social background has played a critical role in determining the likelihood of gaining access to the national political elite. But once a person has joined the elite, social-background attributes have played a discernible but relatively minor role in determining how high one could climb on the ladder. Background could help you get in, but it could not do too much to help you get up. A university education, for example, has in recent years become almost a *necessary* condition for reaching the presidential cabinet, but, among aspiring politicians, it has by no means been *sufficient*. Entrance to the elite has been based largely on ascription; upward mobility within the elite may have been based on achievement (of one sort or another). At any rate, the situation calls for new hypotheses.

· 5 ·

THE STRUCTURES OF
POLITICAL CAREERS

The relatively weak correlations in the previous chapter give rise to the proposition that, in twentieth-century Mexico, political attainment might have had more to do with institutional location than with social background. That is, movement within the system may have depended on the possession of a given office rather than ascriptive personal attributes. Incumbency in office A might have led to office B, and office B might have led to office C; a similar and separate network might have involved offices X, Y, and Z. High office might thus be acquired only through specific routes, according to this view, and the likelihood of reaching top-level posts would be determined by one's position in (or proximity to) these particular routes.

A key assumption behind this proposition is that, in Mexico as well as elsewhere, politicians are ambitious—that is, they seek high office— and that they tend to calculate the possibilities of success on the basis of their present position. Who they were and where they came from is less important, in this sense, than where they stand and where they can expect to go from there. As Joseph A. Schlesinger has put it in reference to the contemporary United States:

> A man in an office which may lead somewhere is more likely to have office ambitions than a man in an office which leads nowhere. This assumption has virtue because it is part of the relevant situation: it is one commonly made by most observers; therefore the assumption creates the opinion to reinforce itself. The small band of governors in sizeable and competitive states and the conspicuous members of the Senate who together compose the presidential "hopefuls" are hopeful as much because of the expectations of others as because of their own. Each lesser office has its own band of hopefuls which exists in the mind of the observant public; and public opinion affects the politician because it defines his success or failure. A New York governor who does not make the presidency has failed in a sense in which his counterpart in Mississippi or South Dakota cannot fail. Politics is, after all, a game of advancement, and a man succeeds only if he advances as far as his situation will permit.[1]

[1] Joseph A. Schlesinger, *Ambition and Politics: Political Careers in the United States* (Chicago: Rand-McNally, 1966), pp. 8-9. See also Gordon S. Black, "A Theory

Limitations on the size of the relevant political audience (as described in Chapter 2) and the generally hierarchical, appointive method of political recruitment obviously suggest that the role of "public opinion" might have been less significant in Mexico than in the United States, but the fundamental proposition holds: chances for success might depend on strategic location, not personal background.

In this chapter I shall attempt to explore underlying regularities or patterns in political careers in Mexico. I shall make no extended effort to develop concomitant theories of political ambition, as Schlesinger does, reserving treatment of some of the optimal officeholding and office-getting strategies for a later point in the book (see Chapter 9). Nor shall I concern myself with the likelihood of political "failure"—that is, the loss of political office—since that constitutes the subject of Chapter 6. My purpose here is to analyze the structures of political success and the ways in which they may or may not have changed over time.

It is my general hypothesis that career patterns varied according to political factors, rather than socioeconomic ones. Virtually all the literature on Mexico implies that political careers had congealed, and taken static form, under the prerevolutionary Díaz regime. A small band of men, old ones at that, had taken hold of the national apparatus, and there they sat, immobile—the same people in the same places, with change occurring more often through mortality than any other factor. The Revolution, with its slogan of "effective suffrage—no reelection," is thought to have broken this pattern, introducing an era of fluid interpositional mobility. At this point the literature usually stops—and it is precisely here that I hope to make an original contribution. For my own suspicion is that the disorder that came in the wake of the Revolution, and the dispersion of political resources, brought in an era of great instability for officeholding aspirants. That is, the Revolution removed the element of predictability from political careers and inaugurated a kind of open-ended game in which people moved from office to office in a near-random pattern, and in which they could utilize almost any available means to seek almost any office in the system—thus engaging in constant rivalry, backbiting, and factionalism. I would further guess that institutionalization of the regime in the 1930s and '40s reintroduced predictability into political careers, as the founders of the party may have hoped: not as much regularity as under Díaz, of course, but enough to impose some order, delimit expectations, and put a damper on uncontrolled ambition.

of Political Ambition: Career Choices and the Role of Structural Incentives," *American Political Science Review* 66, no. 1 (March 1972): 144-159.

In order to examine these propositions I shall, as in previous chapters, build the analysis around comparisons for three separate cohorts —consisting of national officeholders in 1900-1910, 1917-40, and 1946-71. For each cohort I shall focus on the frequency of movement from one kind of office to another. In technical terms the unit of analysis will be the *transition*, rather than the individual officeholder. A single politician could, for instance, make one move from the Chamber of Deputies to the Senate, another from the Senate to a governorship, another from the governorship to a subcabinet post, and yet another from there to the cabinet itself: my concern in this chapter lies with the regularity and relative occurrence of those four transitions, rather than with the fact that they were made by one individual. I am concentrating on the moves instead of the movers themselves.

For the sake of simplicity I have found it necessary to collapse the multitudinous positions of Mexico's political hierarchy into 15 separate categories:

1. the cabinet, including the president—at the top of the ladder of power and prestige (as shown in Appendix A, Table A-3, these are positions with the maximum scale value of 8 in the HIGHEST OFFICE variable);

2. the subcabinet—mainly subsecretaries and *oficiales mayores* in the national secretariats (these correspond to scale position 4 for HIGHEST OFFICE);

3. other federal posts—including any other appointment in the federal bureaucracy;

4. the National Executive Committee of the government party, founded in 1928-29;

5. other positions in the party hierarchy;

6. directorships of semipublic agencies, starting with the creation of the Banco de México in 1925;

7. other positions in the semipublic sector;

8. Senate seats;

9. seats in the Chamber of Deputies;

10. governorships;

11. other positions in state-level governments, ranging from seats in state assemblies to the functional equivalents of lieutenant governorships;

12. any position in any municipal government;

13. any position in a "functional organization," such as a labor union or a peasant organization;

14. any military assignment, though these are severely underreported in my sources, which would often describe someone as an army

general but *not* furnish information on his step-by-step ascent
within the military hierarchy;

15. other, an eclectic blend of miscellaneous offices, ranging from
membership on labor arbitration boards to ambassadorships.

Of course the observation and comprehension of any office-to-office
transition depend on the categorization of the offices, and in adopting
this particular scheme I have given considerable weight to the question
of institutional coherence and autonomy. In other words, I have not
distinguished between leading members of the Senate and backbench-
ers, nor have I separated governors of major states from minor ones.
By treating the Senate, governorships, and other institutions as identifiable and meaningful units, I am focusing in large part on patterns
of *interinstitutional* mobility. Instead of ranking offices along horizontal strata from "low" to "high," as in Chapter 4, I now deal with
movement from one functional type of office to another, with access to
the cabinet still representing the pinnacle of political achievement.

In the interest of accuracy I shall construct the analysis from career
data that seem to be both thorough and reliable.[2] Because so much of
the evidence is so fragmentary for so many people, this restraint leads
to a severe reduction in the numbers of individuals involved. The
prerevolutionary cohort of 1900-1911, for example, consists of 610
politicians in all; only 96 are included in this analysis. Similarly, the N
for the revolutionary cohort of 1917-40 drops from 2,289 to 472; for
the 1946-71 group it declines from 2,008 to 708. Because information
on careers (as well as social background) tends to be most accessible
for the most prominent figures, I would guess that officeholders who
meet the criteria for data quality have been more successful than their
less renowned colleagues. Consequently, there is some bias in the following analysis, which probably exaggerates the likelihood of interpositional mobility for the entire cohorts, though I have no way of
estimating the amount of distortion in the results. But if the degree
of bias is approximately constant from cohort to cohort, as it may or
may not be,[3] the data can still yield an accurate picture of change over
time.

2 To be included in the analysis, individuals had to meet two conditions: (1) they
must have been located in at least one source (such as a biographical dictionary)
other than official directories of officeholders; and (2) in coding the data, my assistants and I must have judged the sequential ordering of positions held to be at
least "fairly reliable."

3 The populations under study from the first two cohorts represent very similar
proportions of their entire groups (15.7 percent and 20.6 percent). For 1946-1971
the proportion rises to 35.3 percent, implying that the data for this cohort might
include more information on lower-level officeholders. (On the differential availability of data see also Figure A-1 of Appendix A.)

Partly because of the reduced number of individuals under study, many of whom disappeared after brief periods in office, I have for each cohort cumulated the data for 11 separate transitions (first office to second office, second office to third office, third to fourth, . . . up to eleventh to twelfth). Most, but not all, of the transitions were immediate; in some cases the time lag between leaving office A and assuming office B may have been considerable.[4] The aggregation procedure makes it possible to analyze large numbers of transitions at once, as we shall see below. But it tends to give further weight to the most successful politicians—those with long and varied careers—and it moreover entails a critical assumption: that the probability for any given transition (for instance, fourth office to fifth) is independent of the outcomes from previous transitions (first to second, second to third, third to fourth). In dealing with careers, that is, I have assumed that the likelihood of going from office A to office B is unrelated to the office (or chain of offices) held prior to office A.[5] The emphasis, again, is not on where people have been; it is on where they are at any given moment, and on where they might hope to go from there.

PREREVOLUTIONARY PATTERNS, 1900-1911

Notwithstanding these conceptual constraints and empirical limitations, Table 5-1 presents data on 674 office-to-office moves by 96 members of the 1900-1911 elite.[6] As the table is arranged, in the form of a *transition matrix*, entries in the individual cells represent the probability of moving from one position (the row variable) to another (the column variable). The sum of all the probabilities, reading from left to right, comes to 1.0, with allowance made for rounding. To take an example: a person moving out of a cabinet post, if he got another position at all, had a .617 chance of gaining another cabinet spot, a zero (.000) chance of moving to the subcabinet, a .133 chance of going to another federal post, a .067 chance of moving to the Senate, and so on. The "total" figures in the extreme right-hand column give the total number of moves made *from* the position in question (60 in the case of the cabinet). The "total" figures at the bottom indicate the total number of moves made *into* the position (72 for the cabinet), and the "overall distribution" entries below that express the propor-

---

[4] Some of the transitions also took place before or after the time boundaries for defining each cohort.

[5] These probabilities are presented as *descriptive* statements, not as a predictive model.

[6] The table contains no entries for the semipublic sector, the party hierarchy, or functional organizations, because they did not exist in the prerevolutionary period.

tion of all transitions that were made into the position (.107) for the cabinet. Since these overall proportion figures reflect the structure of political opportunity, by showing the relative availability of political positions for this group of officeholders, we can also compute a "probability ratio" in order to see if people leaving office A were making more or less than their randomly expected number of moves into office B. (A ratio of 1.0 would reveal exact compliance between the actual number of moves and the expected number of such moves.) For cabinet members, for instance, the actual proportion of moves back into the cabinet was .617; the randomly expected proportion was .107, so the probability ratio is $.617/.107 = 5.766$, showing that cabinet members made nearly six times more than their statistically expected share of moves back into the cabinet. Quite clearly, a spot in the cabinet furnished tremendous leverage for getting a spot in the cabinet.

As a matter of fact, the predominant pattern throughout the entire table underscores the likelihood of repetition in the same office. Subcabinet officials had a .333 chance of remaining in the subcabinet, as well as a .333 chance of moving up to the cabinet. Men in other federal posts had a .235 probability of staying in such posts, slightly less than the .250 chance of getting a seat in the Chamber of Deputies. The tendency to repeat was particularly marked in other so-called elective positions: .627 for senators, .649 for deputies, .556 for governors. All in all, nearly half of the 674 transitions—49.1 percent, to be exact—involved repetition within the same office. Given the range of opportunities this figure is extremely high, and it carries an unambiguous message: the prerevolutionary system, as suggested in the general literature, was extraordinarily static. If you had to make a move, the best bet was that you would end up where you started.

To illustrate prerevolutionary patterns of mobility, Figure 5-1 plots two types of interpositional transitions. One, shown by solid arrows, consists of those with probabilities of .20 or more, meaning that any person in office A had at least a twenty percent chance of going to office B. The choice of the .20 threshold is slightly arbitrary, but because of the possible number of office-to-office moves (10 in Table 5-1) I consider these to be "well-defined" routes.[7] The second type, shown by a broken arrow, comprises moderate paths, defined as those with raw probabilities of less than .20 but with probability ratios of at least

[7] The choice of the .20 threshold is not completely arbitrary. With 10 possibilities for each transition, a .20 probability means that the likelihood of the particular move in question is exactly twice as high as would have been expected had the marginals been equal. Transition matrices for the revolutionary and postrevolutionary cohorts have more than 10 rows and columns, however, so the criterion is less neat in those instances.

TABLE 5-1

Probabilities of Interpositional Mobility for Prerevolutionary Cohort, 1900-1911
(N transitions = 674; N individuals = 96)

FROM \ TO	Cabinet	Subcabinet	Other Federal Post	Senator	Deputy	Governor	Other State Government	Municipal Government	Military Assignment	Other	Total
Cabinet[a]	.617	.000	.133	.067	.083	.067	.017	.000	.000	.000	60
Subcabinet[b]	.333	.333	.048	.190	.048	.048	.000	.000	.000	.000	21
Other federal post[c]	.103	.059	.235	.088	.250	.059	.059	.059	.015	.074	68
Senator	.080	.040	.053	.627	.053	.093	.000	.027	.027	.000	75
Deputy	.021	.031	.068	.052	.649	.058	.058	.010	.026	.026	191
Governor	.069	.000	.042	.111	.139	.556	.000	.014	.069	.000	72
Other state government post	.010	.000	.099	.000	.198	.168	.436	.059	.020	.010	101
Municipal government	.025	.050	.100	.050	.200	.025	.325	.200	.000	.025	40
Military assignment	.095	.048	.095	.000	.143	.380	.048	.048	.143	.000	21
Other	.080	.000	.120	.240	.200	.000	.120	.040	.000	.200	25
Total	72	23	64	87	197	93	77	25	18	18	674
Overall distribution	.107	.034	.095	.129	.292	.138	.114	.037	.027	.027	1.000

[a] Offices with scale value 8 for HIGHEST OFFICE variable (see Appendix A, Table A-3).
[b] Offices with scale value 4 for HIGHEST OFFICE variable (see Appendix A, Table A-3).
[c] Includes a wide variety of positions and appointments, including membership on the Supreme Court.

2.0. That is, a person in office A had twice the statistically expected chance of following this type of route to office B, but the relatively small number of openings in office B meant that he could not gauge this as a one-in-five chance. For this reason I regard these routes as "discernible," but not well-defined.

Figure 5-1 clarifies and confirms the impressions drawn from the transition matrix in Table 5-1. Almost every single position offered a well-defined chance of repeating in the same position, as represented

Figure 5-1: Patterns of Interpositional Mobility: Prerevolutionary Cohort, 1900-1911

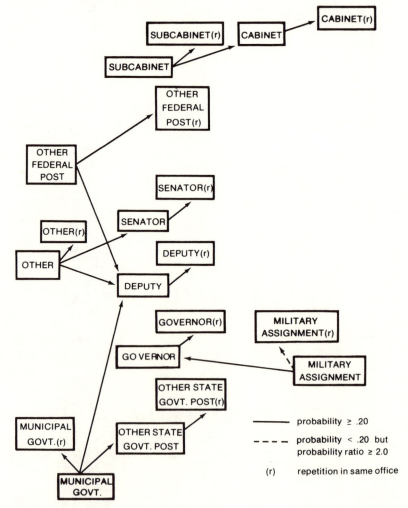

140

by the symbol (r); the sole exception was military assignment, which furnished a discernible chance of repetition.[8] At almost every point in the system, the prevailing pattern of mobility was immobility.

There were, of course, exceptions to this rule. The subcabinet provided a channel to the cabinet. Other federal posts could lead incumbents into the Chamber of Deputies, as could the miscellaneous "other" positions—which also comprised a pathway to the Senate. Military assignments often produced governors of states, as Díaz readily employed the army to quell local disturbances or resolve political disputes, a practice used in subsequent eras as well. Municipal government yielded two plausible outlets, aside from repetition—one to the state-level bureaucracy, another to the Chamber of Deputies. Notwithstanding patterns of this kind, one of the most remarkable aspects of Figure 5-1 is the absence of linkages between the various types of office. In the late Díaz era, an aspiring politician could not plausibly hope (for example) to move from a municipal government position to the Chamber of Deputies, from there to the Senate, on to the subcabinet, and finally into the cabinet. In this kind of recruitment structure, horizons had to be narrowed, career aspirations were necessarily limited. There was a ladder of power and prestige, so to speak, but the rungs were so far apart that hardly anyone could climb it.

Although the evidence is indirect, the patterns in Figure 5-1 cast additional light on one of the impulses behind the revolutionary movement. The high rate of repetition in offices means that a relatively small number of political opportunities were appearing in the 1900-1911 period, so it was difficult for an aspiring young man to attain a position on the national level. And even if he did, the absence of interoffice linkages meant that it would be hard to move up through the system toward the top. Such conditions were bound to give rise to frustration. Accordingly, one of the main components of the anti-Díaz leadership consisted of eager young men (as shown in Chapter 3), often highly educated, some of whom held office in the *Porfiriato*, all of whom resented the restrictions on their opportunities. Once in power, too, they wrought substantial changes in the structures of political careers.

REVOLUTIONARY PATTERNS, 1917-40

Data on 2,444 interpositional moves by 472 members of the 1917-40 cohort appear in Table 5-2. It is a transition matrix, exactly analogous to Table 5-1, with the addition of five extra categories—two for the

---

[8] Of course, some people repeated in office more than once.

TABLE 5-2

Probabilities of Interpositional Mobility for Revolutionary Cohort, 1917-40
(N transitions = 2,444; N individuals = 472)

FROM \ TO	Cabinet	Sub-cabinet	Other Federal Post	Party Leader	Other Party Post	Director Semi-public Agency	Employee Semi-public Sector
Cabinet[a]	.390	.027	.154	.011	.016	.022	.027
Subcabinet[b]	.252	.217	.148	.017	.009	.043	.009
Other federal post[c]	.052	.069	.386	.002	.005	.014	.026
Party leader[d]	.167	.056	.167	.028	.056	.028	.000
Other party post	.077	.000	.038	.154	.038	.077	.000
Director of semi-public agency[e]	.115	.115	.231	.038	.000	.192	.038
Employee in semi-public sector	.031	.031	.344	.000	.000	.094	.188
Senator	.074	.022	.141	.074	.044	.030	.030
Deputy	.044	.029	.162	.019	.029	.006	.013
Governor	.103	.049	.191	.034	.010	.034	.005
Other state government post	.020	.027	.115	.014	.003	.000	.007
Municipal government	.016	.000	.129	.000	.000	.000	.016
Functional organization[f]	.043	.043	.087	.043	.000	.000	.000
Military assignment	.040	.020	.070	.010	.010	.000	.010
Other	.076	.036	.131	.004	.000	.008	.012
Total	218	112	458	44	33	42	43
Overall distribution	.089	.046	.187	.018	.014	.017	.018

[a] Offices with scale value 8 for HIGHEST OFFICE variable (see Appendix A, Table A-3).

[b] Offices with scale value 4 for HIGHEST OFFICE variable (see Appendix A, Table A-3).

[c] Includes a wide variety of positions and appointments, including membership on the Supreme Court.

[d] National Executive Committee of the semiofficial party (the PRI and its predecessors).

[e] Includes some agencies in addition to those listed among the offices with scale value 7 for the HIGHEST OFFICE variable (see Appendix A, Table A-3); as a result, my information on directorships is actually less than complete.

[f] Refers to offices in unions and *sindicatos* (the most notable in recent years being the CNOP, the CNC, and the CTM).

Senator	Deputy	Governor	Other State Government	Municipal Government	Functional Organization	Military Assignment	Other	Total
.044	.060	.077	.000	.005	.005	.022	.137	182
.017	.070	.096	.035	.017	.000	.017	.052	115
.052	.150	.057	.071	.026	.005	.017	.067	420
.194	.083	.167	.000	.000	.000	.000	.056	36
.231	.192	.077	.000	.038	.077	.000	.000	26
.038	.077	.077	.000	.038	.000	.000	.038	115
.031	.125	.094	.031	.000	.000	.000	.031	32
.200	.074	.193	.044	.015	.007	.015	.037	135
.101	.343	.084	.078	.034	.008	.006	.042	475
.123	.103	.088	.034	.010	.010	.118	.088	204
.054	.244	.234	.051	.003	.119	.024	.095	295
.048	.194	.089	.242	.129	.000	.048	.089	124
.087	.391	.087	.043	.000	.174	.000	.000	23
.040	.070	.330	.060	.030	.000	.220	.090	100
.060	.255	.100	.056	.048	.004	.036	.175	251
190	466	249	205	82	18	86	198	2,444
.078	.191	.102	.084	.034	.007	.035	.081	1.000

official party, two for the semipublic sector, one for labor unions and *sindicatos*. These new positions reflect, though only slightly, an expansion and complication in the availability of opportunity.

The most striking characteristic of the table, in sharp contrast to the prerevolutionary pattern, emerges from the evident flexibility of interpositional mobility. First, there was a marked reduction of repetition within the same office. The probability of staying in the cabinet, for instance, was .390, compared to .617 for the prerevolutionary cohort; for the subcabinet it was .217, compared to .333 before. Because of the "no-reelection" rule, formally adopted in 1917, the low rate of repetition was especially apparent for the governors (.088). Since the ban on reelection did not apply to the national congress until the 1930s, the rates were somewhat higher—.200 for senators, .343 for deputies—but they were still far below prerevolutionary levels. In total, only 25.9 percent of all transitions for the 1917-40 cohort represented repetitions in office, compared to 49.1 percent for the 1900-1911 group. The rate of repetition had been cut in half.

Second, Table 5-2 shows a great expansion in the range of interpositional movement. Cabinet members, to start with one example, moved to every square on the checkerboard, with the lone exception of "other state government posts." Senators, deputies, and governors moved on to every conceivable spot. People in other state government posts could entertain the hope of going almost anywhere, and it was even possible (though not common) for men in municipal government to vault into a cabinet job. In short, one of the central propositions of this chapter finds ample confirmation in the data: the Revolution opened up the recruitment system and increased interpositional mobility and flexibility.

On the other hand, some regularities existed. To emphasize the point, Figure 5-2 depicts the most thoroughly traveled interpositional routes. As before, solid arrows indicate well-defined paths, with probabilities of .20 or more; broken arrows represent discernible paths, with raw probabilities of less than .20 but probability ratios of at least 2.0.

The figure conveys, in graphic form, an almost bewildering variety of interpositional transitions, especially in contrast to the stark simplicity of the prerevolutionary structure (Figure 5-1). Yet there also emerge, in hazy outline, three identifiable networks. One, which I shall call the "electoral" network, includes positions in seven separate institutions: municipal government, state bureaucracy, functional organizations, the official party, the Chamber of Deputies, the Senate, and governorships. Typically, a person might join this circle by getting a position in a labor or peasant (functional) organization, moving to

Figure 5-2: Patterns of Interpositional Mobility: Revolutionary Cohort, 1917-40

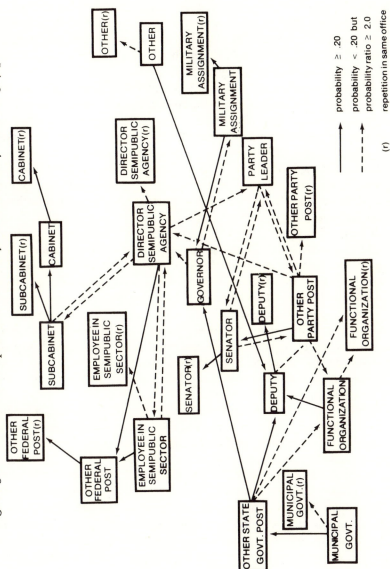

PART II: RESULTS OF REVOLUTION

the Chamber of Deputies and perhaps repeating there, or then assuming a post in the party hierarchy. Another might start in municipal government, move to a spot in the state bureaucracy, and go from there to the Chamber—or to a governorship. Though there was considerable motion *within* the electoral network, there was very little systematic connection *between* this set of offices and other (usually higher) ones, with the exception of one weak link between governorships and directorships of state-supported agencies.

A second network could be called "administrative," and contains essentially the semipublic sector. Employees in this sector showed some tendency to move around within the hierarchy or assume agency directorships, though the most frequent single move was to the federal bureaucracy. Directors repeated in office to some extent, but they also went into the subcabinet, and, like their subordinates, they most commonly transferred over to the federal bureaucracy. Still in its early years, the semipublic sector was not nearly as autonomous as it would later become.

The third network, which I shall refer to as "executive," connects three kinds of institutions: the national bureaucracy (other federal posts), the subcabinet, and the cabinet. The subcabinet-to-cabinet pathway was established and well recognized, and both offices held out substantial likelihood of repetition. It is revealing, however, that neither of these institutions drew its personnel in any perceptible measure from the category of other federal posts. In fact there was only one route leading into either one, a moderate path from directorships in the semipublic sector to the subcabinet. Other than that, the upper reaches of executive authority stood in relative isolation from other institutions in the political system.

What this means, among other things, is that access to the cabinet was highly diverse—not to say random. Of the 218 cabinet appointments made to members of the 1917-40 cohort, 71 went to current cabinet officials; 29 went to subcabinet officers; 22 went to other federal bureaucrats; 6 to party leaders; 3 to directors in the semipublic sector; 10 to senators; 21 to deputies; 21 to governors; 6 to other state-level officials; 2 to leaders in municipal government; 4 to soldiers on military assignment; and 19 to people in miscellaneous other posts. The routes to upper-level office were neither orderly nor tightly structured. For this cohort there was no sure, or even highly probable, means of getting to the top.

So these networks existed, but they should not be overemphasized. Table 5-2 has revealed a broad range of transitional probabilities. Table 5-3 makes the same point in another way, by showing the percentage of moves from all offices within each track that follow identifiable routes. The data in the "total" row reveal that only 38.5 percent of all the moves took place along *any* discernible paths, either well-beaten or moderately so, compared to 58.6 percent for the 1900-1911 cohort.[9] Less than a third (32.5 percent) fell within the well-defined routes, whereas the prerevolutionary figure was close to twice as high (58.6 percent again). Not only did the Revolution bring a sharp drop in within-category repetition; it also reduced the predictability of interpositional mobility by a large and significant margin.

TABLE 5-3

Distribution of Interpositional Moves along Established Routes,
As % of Moves from Offices within Each Track:
Revolutionary Cohort, 1917-40

Track	Moves along Well-Defined Routes[a]		Moves along All Discernible Routes[b]	
	Moves Entirely within Track, as %[c]	All Moves along Routes, as %[d]	Moves Entirely within Track, as %[c]	All Moves along Routes, as %[d]
Executive[e]	40.0	40.0	40.7	44.2
Administrative[f]	0.0	29.3	25.9	62.1
Electoral[g]	28.1	28.5	31.9	34.4
Total	31.4	32.5	34.7	38.5

[a] Transitions with probabilities $\geq$ .20.

[b] Transitions with probabilities $\geq$ .20 or probability ratios $\geq$ 2.0.

[c] Moves to offices exclusively within the same track.

[d] Includes moves from one track to another, and also moves to Military Assignment and Other offices, as plotted in Figure 5-2.

[e] Offices included: Other Federal Post, Subcabinet, Cabinet (see notes to Table 5-2).

[f] Offices included: Employee in Semipublic Sector, Director of Semipublic Agency (see notes to Table 5-2).

[g] Offices included: all those not listed in notes *e* or *f*, with the exception of Military Assignment and Other (see notes to Table 5-2).

Table 5-3 further hints at differences between the officeholding networks. As implied in Figure 5-2, within-track moves along well-defined routes were most common for the executive network (40 percent). In other words, two-fifths of all moves from executive-type offices followed relatively predictable paths to other positions within the same network. This reveals a fairly high degree of autonomy for the executive track—and a concomitant lack of systematic links with other institutions. The fledgling semipublic sector exhibited absolutely no such internal cohe-

[9] There was no "administrative" network on the prerevolutionary period, so the 58.6 percent figure applies only to transitions involving the "executive" and "electoral" tracks.

sion at the time, as shown by the zero percent figure, while the electoral network displayed an intermediate level of 28.1 percent.

Despite its relative autonomy, the executive network was not a bastion of security or stability. Most moves from executive positions did not follow any discernible route at all, and only 44.2 percent occurred on any sort of discernible path. The corresponding figure for the electoral track was even less, 34.4 percent, meaning that only one-third of these job changes followed discernible routes. Paradoxically enough, although the administrative network displayed the lowest level of within-network cohesion, it showed the highest level of total movement along discernible routes (62.1 percent). At this juncture, the semipublic sector did not offer much career autonomy, but it provided substantial outlets in many and varied directions.

In sum, the prevailing features of political careers in the 1917-40 period combined range of opportunity with flexibility of movement—and a relative absence of security or predictability. How did the subsequent institutionalization of Mexico's authoritarian regime affect these processes?

POSTREVOLUTIONARY PATTERNS, 1946-71

To begin responding to this question, Table 5-4 displays a transition matrix for 3,300 moves by 708 members of the 1946-71 cohort. The data show marked continuity with the patterns for 1917-40 in two fundamental respects. First, there was relatively little repetition. The chance of moving from one cabinet post to another was .393, almost exactly the same as for the revolutionary cohort (.390) and far below the prerevolutionary level (.617). Generally low levels of repetition prevailed throughout the system, and by this time they extended to legislative office, now that the "no-reelection" rule had taken full effect: the likelihood of repeating in the Senate (after at least a six-year interim) was .040, and for deputies (after a mandatory three-year interim) it was .200. Overall, only 24.6 percent of interpositional moves for the postrevolutionary generation could be classified as repetitions, compared with 25.9 percent for the revolutionary generation—an almost identical figure—and 49.1 percent for the prerevolutionary group. Clearly, one of the results of institutionalization and stabilization in the 1930s and 40s was to preserve the low levels of within-office repetition that the Revolution had achieved.

Second, the recruitment pattern for the 1946-71 cohort, like that of its immediate predecessor, revealed great flexibility. Cabinet members could go almost anywhere within the system, excluding municipal government and state-level bureaucracies (most of the moves to "other" positions were to ambassadorial posts). Subcabinet officials went everywhere except to municipal government and functional organizations. People in "other state government posts" transferred to all locations except military assignment. And as befits a residual category, those in "other" offices scattered themselves all over the place.

The impression of widely dispersed motion finds confirmation in Figure 5-3, which plots transitions along well-defined routes (solid arrows) and other discernible routes (broken arrows) for the postrevolutionary generation. Like the pattern for the 1917-40 cohort, this one conveys a vivid sense of complexity and variety, not to say confusion. From almost any location in the political system, it appears, one could entertain at least some hope of moving to almost any other location.

And yet a close look at the diagram, especially in comparison to the revolutionary pattern (Figure 5-2), implies a kind of tightening within the interpositional networks. The "electoral" track continued to be rather self-contained and isolated from the other offices. As before, people moved with relative ease from posts in the party hierarchy or *sindicatos* or municipal governments (via state-level bureaucracies) to the Chamber of Deputies, there to repeat or retire. It might be noted, in passing, how this finding confirms the idea, set forth in Chapter 2, that the PRI, in contrast to its widespread reputation, has not functioned as a channel to high-level posts. One also gets the impression that seats in the Chamber came to furnish rewards for loyal service in the party and in local government, and they may also have served to cut off rising union leaders from their grass-roots constituencies, thus making them dependent on the centralized hierarchy for further political advancement. Except for a weak link to the Senate, the Chamber has not provided much of a springboard to higher office.[10]

The process of intranetwork tightening is plainly visible within the so-called administrative track. Whereas employees and directors in the semipublic sector formerly made their most frequent moves into the federal buraucracy (Figure 5-2), there was now a marked tendency for both of them to repeat in office, as well as to exchange positions among themselves. True, employees in the semipublic sector often transferred over to other federal posts, and directors had a moderate path into the cabinet (in contrast to the subcabinet in 1917-40), but the data still

---

[10] In this context the ambiguities of the data on military assignment become especially conspicuous, since it is well known that military men monopolized the presidency of the PRI for quite some time—but no transitions from military assignment to PRI leadership appear in Table 5-4. On the relationship between the army and the PRI see Robert E. Scott, *Mexican Government in Transition*, 2nd ed. (Urbana: University of Illinois Press, 1964), pp. 133-134.

TABLE 5-4

Probabilities of Interpositional Mobility for Postrevolutionary Cohort, 1946-71
(N transitions = 3,300; N individuals = 708)

FROM \ TO	Cabinet	Sub-cabinet	Other Federal Post	Party Leader	Other Party Post	Director Semi-public Agency	Employee Semi-public Sector
Cabinet[a]	.424	.035	.106	.024	.012	.047	.035
Subcabinet[b]	.242	.258	.125	.016	.008	.063	.070
Other federal post[c]	.035	.097	.393	.003	.025	.017	.068
Party leader[d]	.140	.018	.140	.105	.053	.035	.018
Other party post	.005	.014	.055	.028	.101	.009	.028
Director of semi-public agency[e]	.104	.063	.104	.021	.000	.292	.125
Employee in semi-public sector	.006	.043	.210	.000	.043	.074	.302
Senator	.110	.040	.130	.140	.060	.090	.030
Deputy	.019	.022	.108	.038	.084	.016	.027
Governor	.130	.022	.163	.076	.022	.043	.000
Other state government post	.004	.004	.103	.013	.064	.002	.004
Municipal government	.000	.000	.061	.000	.065	.007	.007
Functional organization[f]	.005	.002	.047	.016	.082	.005	.016
Military assignment	.021	.064	.170	.000	.021	.000	.043
Other	.022	.040	.152	.004	.045	.018	.018
Total	143	137	515	68	182	80	145
Overall distribution	.043	.042	.156	.021	.055	.024	.044

[a] Offices with scale value 8 for HIGHEST OFFICE variable (see Appendix A, Table A-3).

[b] Offices with scale value 4 for HIGHEST OFFICE variable (see Appendix A, Table A-3).

[c] Includes a wide variety of positions and appointments, including membership on the Supreme Court.

[d] National Executive Committee of the semiofficial party (The PRI and its predecessors).

[e] Includes some agencies in addition to those listed among the offices with scale value 7 for the HIGHEST OFFICE variable (see Appendix A, Table A-3); as a result, my information on directorships is actually less than complete.

[f] Refers to offices in unions and *sindicatos* (the most notable in recent years being the CNOP, the CNC, and the CTM).

Senator	Deputy	Governor	Other State Govern- ment	Municipal Govern- ment	Functional Organi- zation	Military Assign- ment	Other	Total
.047	.047	.047	.000	.000	.012	.012	.153	85
.039	.031	.086	.023	.000	.000	.016	.023	128
.047	.127	.025	.052	.013	.043	.005	.050	600
.158	.175	.053	.035	.000	.053	.000	.018	57
.065	.300	.023	.097	.092	.157	.005	.023	217
.063	.063	.125	.000	.000	.000	.021	.021	48
.043	.117	.031	.043	.006	.068	.000	.012	162
.040	.040	.230	.030	.000	.050	.010	.000	100
.170	.200	.062	.076	.024	.114	.000	.041	370
.152	.076	.076	.011	.033	.011	.098	.087	92
.028	.246	.043	.278	.092	.073	.000	.045	467
.022	.173	.032	.245	.209	.144	.000	.036	278
.045	.305	.012	.096	.077	.261	.000	.031	426
.128	.064	.128	.085	.000	.000	.255	.021	47
.045	.184	.022	.130	.081	.099	.054	.085	223
205	603	147	368	193	330	42	142	3,300
.062	.183	.045	.112	.058	.100	.013	.043	1.000

Figure 5-3: Patterns of Interpositional Mobility: Postrevolutionary Cohort, 1946-71

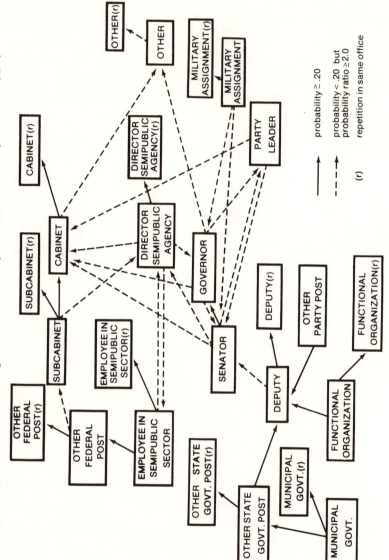

convey a sense of increased coherence and autonomy within the network.

The same holds true for the "executive" track, linking the federal bureaucracy to the subcabinet and cabinet. The novel feature of the 1946-71 pattern is the channel, albeit a weak one, from other federal posts to the subcabinet—from which it would then be possible to move on to the cabinet. More than before, it appears that people underwent a period of training, or apprenticeship, for specific kinds of offices. In a word, politics was becoming professionalized.

In this context Figure 5-3 also isolates the pivotal roles of offices that provided opportunities for moving from one network to another —particularly the Senate, which now offered a strong chance of moving to state governorships and better-than-average chances of moving to national party leadership, directorships of semipublic agencies, or the cabinet itself. This stands in contrast to the situation for the 1917-40 cohort, for which it was only the governorships that furnished a systematic outlet from the electoral network; by 1946-71 they continued to function as intermediary offices, as did party leadership, but to a lesser degree than the Senate. This change is neither overwhelming nor dramatic, but I think it represents a basic trend: a process of centralization. For the revolutionary cohort, governorships provided institutional resources for the accumulation and expression of local power, and their linkages to other offices offered channels through which local leaders (or bosses) could gain access to upper levels of the national political system. The Senate, by contrast, is a central institution. Admission to it is closely controlled by the president,[11] it is small (with two representatives for every state), it is located in Mexico City—and its members can be submitted to constant scrutiny, grooming, and preparation by the inner elite. Thus the elevation of the Senate to a pivotal role in the recruitment process for the revolutionary cohort reflects an increase in the (already overbearing) role of the president and his staff. The fact that senators should become governors provides an especially poignant illustration of the cutting away of local power bases.[12]

For further interpretation of the structure of the postrevolutionary

[11] According to Frank R. Brandenburg, the president used to appoint about 60 percent of the senatorial candidates. Brandenburg, *The Making of Modern Mexico* (Englewood Cliffs, N.J.: Prentice-Hall, 1964), p. 155.

[12] On this point see also Roderic Ai Camp, "Mexican Governors since Cárdenas: Education and Career Contracts," *Journal of Interamerican Studies and World Affairs* 16, no. 4 (November 1974): 454-481; and, for an inside view, Manuel Moreno Sánchez, *Crisis política de México* (Mexico: Editorial Extemporáneos, 1970), pp. 160-162.

networks, Table 5-5 presents the proportion of moves from offices within each track that followed discernible routes. Perhaps the central finding is that 48.5 percent of all transitions for the 1946-71 cohort fell along one kind of identifiable route or another—up from 38.5 percent in 1917-40, thus reflecting an increase in the predictability of job changes. Actually, transitions for the executive track showed relatively little alteration, as the data bear close resemblance to the figures for the revolutionary cohort in Table 5-3. The rate of regularity for moves along the electoral track went up markedly, as the total share of moves along all discernible routes moved from 34.4 percent to 46.7 percent. But the sharpest change took place within the administrative track. Whereas there were *no* within-network moves along well-defined paths for the semipublic sector of the 1917-40 generation (Table 5-3), this figure reached 30 percent for the postrevolutionary group. And of all moves made from offices within this network, 46.2 percent went along well-defined paths, compared to 29.3 percent for the preceding generation. The process of tightening applied to all tracks, but most of all it happened to the semipublic sector.

Yet there were limits to these patterns of predictability. If Table 5-5 shows that 48.5 percent of all moves took place along some kind of track, this still means that the majority of transitions for the 1946-71

TABLE 5-5

Distribution of Interpositional Moves along Established Routes,
as % of Moves from Offices within Each Track:
Postrevolutionary Cohort, 1946-71

Track	Moves along Well-Defined Routes[a]		Moves along All Discernible Routes[b]	
	Moves Entirely within Track, as %[c]	All Moves along Routes, as %[d]	Moves Entirely within Track, as %[c]	All Moves along Routes, as %[d]
Executive[e]	41.3	41.3	48.5	50.1
Administrative[f]	30.0	46.2	38.6	60.0
Electoral[g]	38.6	38.6	43.9	46.7
Total	38.7	39.8	44.8	48.5

[a] Transitions with probabilities $\geq$ .20.

[b] Transitions with probabilities $\geq$ .20 or probability ratios $\geq$ 2.0.

[c] Moves to offices exclusively within the same track.

[d] Includes moves from one track to another, and also moves to Military Assignment and Other offices, as plotted in Figure 5-3.

[e] Offices included: Other Federal Post, Subcabinet, Cabinet (see notes to Table 5-4).

[f] Offices included: Employee in Semipublic Sector, Director of Semipublic Agency (see notes to Table 5-4).

[g] Offices included: all those not listed in notes *e* or *f*, with the exception of Military Assignment and Other (see notes to Table 5-4).

group fell *outside* of *any* track. Figure 5-3 reveals the existence of multiple moderate paths to the cabinet—one for senators, one for governors, one for directors of semipublic agencies, one for party leaders. Of the 143 cabinet-level appointments for this generation, in fact, 36 went to incumbent cabinet officers; 31 went to members of the subcabinet; 21 to other federal bureaucrats; 13 to governors; 11 to senators; 8 to national party leaders; 7 to deputies; 5 to directors of semipublic agencies; 2 to state-level bureaucrats; 2 to *sindicato* leaders, and the rest to people in various other offices. Some of the technical posts, and the most important cabinet positions, have had clearly established training routines. As a rule, however, Mexico's governmental leaders have tended to undergo extensive political experience, rather than intensive preparation for specific roles.[13]

Interestingly enough, this diversity in officeholding does not contradict the notion of career professionalization. Rather, it has been part and parcel of it. As I shall stress in Chapter 7, Mexican politicians of the 1946-71 generation pursued their careers as full-time vocations, not avocations: they started young, they held offices in close succession, they built their lives around the political realm. The point, as I shall maintain below, is that diversity of experience was a valued political resource—and it was an integral part of the training process.

But if diversity has been the rule, there have also been some boundaries on the types of training and experience. And as the networks have tightened and become more exclusive, the boundaries have become increasingly restrictive. One specific consequence of this process is that politicians with electoral experience, the classical *políticos*, have found it harder to gain access to upper-level offices (defined, again, as positions with scale values of 7 or 8 for the HIGHEST OFFICE variable). Among the members of the prerevolutionary cohort (1900-1911) who reached upper-level posts, 84.4 percent had ·at one time or another held elective office, most notably as governors of states. For the revolutionary cohort (1917-40) the figure dropped to 70.4 percent, partly because the instability and upheavals of the era made it possible for some individuals to move into positions of prominence directly, without working up through an elaborate hierarchy. For the postrevolutionary cohort, though, careers had become hierarchical, and aspirants to power usually had to serve out fairly lengthy apprenticeships. Nonetheless, the proportion of upper-level officeholders with

---

[13] One of the most celebrated routes has been from Undersecretary of *Gobernación* to Secretary of *Gobernación* and on to the presidency; revealingly enough, the *destapamiento* in 1975-76 of Jose López Portillo, a treasury minister, contradicted even this longstanding practice (see Chapter 10).

elective experience declined again, this time to 53.7 percent. To turn the figures around, they mean that 46.3 percent of upper-level leaders in the postrevolutionary cohort had never held any elective office, compared to 29.6 percent for the revolutionary generation. What this reflects, quite clearly, is the *bureaucratization* of Mexico's topmost elites, as well as the process of centralization. There is no reason to suspect that these trends will not persist.

CONCLUSION

In this chapter I have tried to examine change and continuity in the structures of political careers, in order to test the notion that the attainment of high office might be related to one's strategic location within the bureaucratic system. For the prerevolutionary cohort of 1900-1911, the proposition was half true and half untrue. By the turn of the century, the distribution of high office was an accomplished fact. Those who had positions by and large retained them. Repetition was the order of the day, and it was in this sense that the possession of one office determined what the next one would be. But institutional location did not determine the direction of mobility, precisely because there was so little movement of any kind. The system was static, rigid, and closed.

The Revolution inaugurated a completely different era. Repetition was greatly reduced, though by no means eliminated. Careers acquired flexibility, and people moved rapidly around the interpositional checkerboard. There were some recurrent regularities, to be sure, especially in relation to three clusters or networks of offices—electoral, administrative, and executive. But there were no certain routes to success; not a single office offered any significant advantages for getting to the cabinet. Improvisation and diversity prevailed.

Subsequent institutionalization and stabilization of the system introduced new elements of predictability. Basic career patterns for the 1946-71 cohort closely resembled those of the 1917-40 group, with low repetition and flexible forms of advancement, but the number of moves along identifiable routes showed a marked increase. In keeping with this trend, career patterns and recruitment processes revealed some signs of three distinct but closely related characteristics: professionalization, centralization, and bureaucratization. But even as these developments took place, it has remained breadth of experience, not narrow specialization, that has been the general rule. For the postrevolutionary cohort, even though it was operating within a strong tutelary regime, interpositional mobility retained a sense of uncertainty and surprise. In contrast to officeholders in the prerevolutionary era, Mexican politicians of the post-1946 era could never count on staying where they were. They had constantly to look ahead and wonder what might happen next.

In this sense the Mexican regime bears close resemblance to the prototypical authoritarian model sketched out by Juan J. Linz. "While the elite is relatively open" to the members of contending power groups, according to Linz, "predictable ways of entry are lacking, which frustrates the ambitions of many." And since competition for office does not follow a clear set of rules, "paths to [power] are obscure: neither devoted partisan service and ideological conformity, nor a steady career through elected office, is available. Success in nonpolitical spheres, identification with groups like religious associations, particularistic criteria of who knows whom, even accident, may be more important." Though such considerations are present in all systems, they usually coexist with broader, more universalistic recruitment criteria.[14]

Insofar as post-1946 Mexico shares obscurity in paths to power with other authoritarian regimes, it necessarily contrasts with different kinds of systems. In totalitarian societies ideological conformity and, more specifically, active service in the monolithic party are requisites for power: in the USSR, for instance, more than 80 percent of the Politburo have served as party functionaries. In democratic polities, such as Britain and the United States, elective office and the civil service play key roles in the formation of careers. In either case, there is a relatively clear *cursus honorum*, and, as a consequence, careers are fairly predictable. (Let it be understood, in passing, that elections do not create all that much uncertainty: about two-thirds of the positions in Congress and the House of Commons are "safe seats." Compare that with the no-reelection law in Mexico!)[15]

This does not mean that there are no rules of any kind in Mexico, that political careers have no shape at all. On the contrary, I have devoted considerable effort in this chapter to determining that shape, and to showing that the patterns have been more discernible for the 1946-71 cohort than for the 1917-40 one. Rather, it means that the

[14] Linz, "An Authoritarian Regime: Spain," in *Mass Politics: Studies in Political Sociology*, ed. Erik Allardt and Stein Rokkan (New York: The Free Press, 1970), p. 274.

[15] See Robert D. Putnam, *The Comparative Study of Political Elites* (Englewood Cliffs, N.J.: Prentice-Hall, 1976), pp. 49-50 and 54; and, for additional data on the predictability of careers in the United States, Schlesinger, *Ambition*, esp. pp. 34 and 90-96.

rules are different from those in many other places. There is no senior-ity system, no examination system, and no system of genuinely com-petitive elections. Things are slightly unpredictable in Mexico, and this element of uncertainty has itself become institutionalized. As I shall argue later on, this fact constitutes a central aspect of the coun-try's authoritarian regime.

· 6 ·

CONTINUITY AND
TURNOVER

The preceding chapters of Part II have focused primarily on ways that Mexican politicians have gained access *to* the national elite and on paths that they have traced *within* the officeholding networks. Here I deal with a complementary problem: patterns of exit *from* the elite. How long have people stayed within the national elite? What have been the rates of continuity? Has the "no-reelection" principle led to constant rotation of political leadership in Mexico, or has it merely provided a means for concentrating authority in the hands of a small group?

Questions of this kind have prompted a considerable amount of speculation and disputation, but surprisingly little research. A common interpretation, perhaps the most widely accepted, sees constant circulation in Mexico's upper-echelon elites. Ever since adoption of the "no-reelection" slogan of the Revolution, it is held, national leadership has undergone a rhythmically consistent (usually sexennial) renovation. This process has tended to invigorate policy formulation and, more important, the periodic reopening of career opportunities has greatly strengthened the stability of the country's one-party system. As Frank Brandenburg has argued, "Permanent revolution thus depends on a political system that opens top bureaucratic positions every three years at the local level and every six years at the state and national levels."[1]

A contrasting view maintains that the doctrine of "no-reelection" merely serves to disguise the political monopoly of an exclusive, tightly closed elite. According to one observer, only the president makes a genuine exit from office. All other politicians are "master acrobats" who, on the "trapeze" of opportunity, leap easily from one post to another, from the Chamber of Deputies to the Senate and back again, from municipal presidencies to governorships to state legislatures,

Portions of Chapter 6 have been published in *Contemporary Mexico: Papers of the IV International Congress of Mexican History*, ed. James W. Wilkie, Michael C. Meyer, and Edna Monzón de Wilkie. Copyright © 1976 by the Regents of the University of California; reprinted by permission of the University of California Press.

[1] Frank R. Brandenburg, *The Making of Modern Mexico* (Englewood Cliffs, N.J.: Prentice-Hall, 1964), p. 159.

concentrating power and prestige within their inner circle. In this "directed democracy," therefore, "suffrage is the effective monopoly of *caciques* and nepotistic patrimony, and 'no-reelection' is the object of derision and constant ridicule, by none other than those who proudly claim to be the paladins of constitutional principles."[2] Political mobility, in short, is but a figment of the imagination; the pervasive fact is domination.

The aim of this chapter is to resolve this controversy, and to amplify the other findings in this book, through a statistical examination of the extent of turnover and continuity in national office from 1900 to 1971. Since I perceive changes in turnover and continuity as being independent of socioeconomic transformation, I shall concentrate on the presumed causal influence of political variables. Specifically, I shall attempt to evaluate the relative impact of the Revolution and of consolidation of Mexico's tutelary system, with occasional reference to implications for elite behavior (a theme to be more fully developed in Chapter 9). The empirical portions of my analysis have required numerous and delicate methodological decisions, and they are set forth and discussed in Appendix B.

RATES OF CONTINUITY

To measure the degree of "continuity" in officeholding on the national level I have, as a first step, taken the names of all incumbents in the following offices during every presidential term from 1900 through 1971: presidents, vice-presidents (whenever there were any), members of the cabinet, members of the subcabinet, heads of selected decentralized agencies and state-supported companies, leaders of the official party, governors of states and territories, and senators. Then, for each group of incumbents in each presidential term, I have computed the percentage of individuals who held any one of these offices at *any* prior time.[3] As explained in Appendix B, the resulting figure provides a fairly valid general measure of *continuity*. (Subtracting this figure from 100 would give an equally usable measure of *turnover*.) A high rate of continuity, as reflected by this index, would tend to support the idea that a relatively small group of individuals has been maintaining tight control on governmental office; a low figure would indicate the importance of political mobility.

[2] R. A. Sosa Ferreyra, "El mito de la 'No Reelección,'" *Excélsior*, 22 May 1956.
[3] As indicated in Chapter 1, I have collated the names of every incumbent in every office at every point in time (according to official rosters and other sources) and thus managed to create a *complete* dossier on interpositional mobility within this pool of offices for every single individual.

The initial findings appear in Table 6-1, which presents the rates of continuity in officeholding, or degrees of "prior elite experience," during each presidential regime. For easy reference, and to emphasize the chronological dimensions of change, Figure 6-1 also plots the percentage figures over time.

The overall pattern is clear. Confirming widely held impressions, the continuity rate under Porfirio Díaz was exceedingly high, 61.3 per-

TABLE 6-1

Continuity Rates, by Presidential Regimes, 1904-71

Presidential Regime[a]	N Incumbents	N with Prior Elite Experience	% with Prior Elite Experience
Díaz, 1904-10	132	81	61.3
Díaz, 1910-11	87	60	68.9
De la Barra, 1911	58	8	13.8
Madero, 1911-13	150	49	32.6
Huerta, 1913-14	144	32	22.2
Convention, 1914-15[b]	121	8	6.6
Carranza as First Chief, 1915-17	84	14	16.7
Carranza as President, 1917-20	181	54	29.8
De la Huerta, 1920	56	18	32.1
Obregón, 1920-24	205	75	36.6
Calles, 1924-28	170	61	35.9
Maximato, 1928-34[c]	291	96	32.9
Cárdenas, 1934-40	234	83	35.4
Ávila Camacho, 1940-46	181	71	39.2
Alemán, 1946-52	190	46	24.2
Ruiz Cortines, 1952-58	168	65	38.7
López Mateos, 1958-64	178	56	31.4
Díaz Ordaz, 1964-70	203	69	33.9
Echeverría, 1970-76[d] (as of 1971)	164	43	26.2

NOTE: As described in Appendix C, the pool of offices in this analysis corresponds to those with scale values from 8 to 2 for the HIGHEST OFFICE variable (see Appendix A, Table A-3).

[a] The 45-minute term of Pedro Lascuráin, in 1913, has been excluded from these and all subsequent calculations.

[b] Includes the regimes of Francisco Carbajal, Eulalio Gutiérrez, Roque González Garza, and Francisco Lagos Cházaro.

[c] Includes the regimes of Emilio Portes Gil, Pascual Ortiz Rubio, and Abelardo Rodríguez; this period is known as the *Maximato* because of Plutarco Elías Calles' alleged domination of the political scene from his position as *Jefe Máximo* of the Revolution.

[d] Here and in subsequent calculations throughout this chapter it should be understood that data on the Echeverría elite are incomplete.

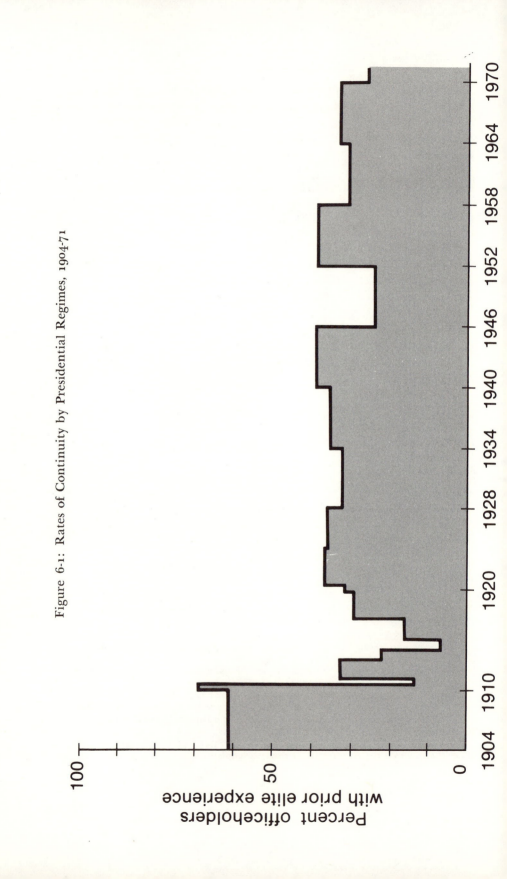

Figure 6-1: Rates of Continuity by Presidential Regimes, 1904-71

cent in 1904-10 and 68.9 percent in his truncated regime of 1910-11. Francisco Madero, moderate that he was, permitted fully one-third of his elite (32.6 percent) to come from prerevolutionary administrations,[4] and Victoriano Huerta also brought a number of old *porfiristas* back into office.[5] It was not until the era of the peripatetic and ill-fated Convention (1914-15) that revolutionary activists gained unchallengeable control of national office. After that, as men moved from one revolutionary regime to another, the rate of continuity climbed quickly upward, reaching the neighborhood of 35 percent by 1920—and there it has remained. Fluctuations have occurred, of course, but the figures have usually stayed between 30 and 40 percent.

The data yield a straightforward conclusion about the impact of the Revolution (and its doctrine of "no-reelection") on the process of elite recruitment. My evidence indicates that, after eliminating the prerevolutionary elite and reaching a new equilibrium, *the Revolution cut the rate of continuity in half,* reducing it from a level of 60-70 percent in the late Díaz era to a level of 35 percent or so since 1920.

Although this finding may seem unambiguous, its substantive meaning is not. Is 35 percent a "high" or "low" rate of continuity? From one perspective, it would be possible to argue that the rate is high. The blockage of elites under Díaz presumably helped precipitate the Revolution—and since then, despite the "no-reelection" formula, the situation has become "half as bad" as it was before. The myth of mobility would thus appear to be laid bare.

Upon further consideration, however, I would maintain that these findings reveal a very high rate of turnover, not continuity, in contemporary Mexico. A 35 percent figure means that, during each presidential term, approximately two-thirds of the high national offices have been held by complete newcomers to the elite circles. This is a striking fact, especially since political advancement depends largely on the formation and accumulation of personal friendships and alliances, a requirement which might seem more conducive to gerontocracy and immobility than to elite rotation. Moreover it seems likely that, for the

[4] "Prerevolutionary administrations," in this context, include the De la Barra regime of 1911. Of the 49 individuals under Madero who had held office during previous presidencies, 19 came from the De la Barra regime; 28 had served under Díaz in 1910-1911; and 17 had served under Díaz in 1904-1910. Most of the *porfirista* holdovers occupied seats in the *maderista* Senate (and there were others in the Chamber of Deputies too); no member of the Díaz group ever sat in Madero's cabinet. So Madero actually *permitted* porfiristas to take seats in the legislature, rather than actively seeking them out.

[5] Of the 32 Huerta holdovers, 13 were in the Díaz regime of 1910-1911, and 17 had been in the Porfirian regime of 1904-1910.

sake of stability, any political system would require some minimal degree of continuity (say, 10 percent). For these reasons the high rate of turnover in Mexico is all the more impressive.

In general, then, the Brandenburg proposition seems to be correct. Since the Revolution, the pattern of officeholding has borne more resemblance to a revolving door than to a game of musical chairs. Political patronage has been constantly available, and its benefits widely distributed. The potential for elite cooptation has remained high, a situation which has doubtless contributed to the stability and durability of the Mexican polity (leaving aside Brandenburg's dubious notion about "permanent revolution").[6]

The relatively high rate of turnover also helps elucidate the phenomenon of political "corruption," or what might be called (in less normative terms) self-enrichment through public office. From the standpoint of the individual officeholder, the mathematical probabilities would yield a clear guideline: if the chances of returning to the national elite are not much more than one out of three, you better take what you can while you're there. And in their turn, opportunities for self-enrichment have facilitated the process of turnover, since people who have reaped substantial private benefits during a single term in office would be willing to step down from their positions—and thus make room for newcomers.

A corollary implication of the revolving-door model is that, with elite-level tenure so short, there has been little opportunity for individuals to accumulate much job-related expertise. Indeed, from a personal standpoint, the acquisition of such skills would seem to be a wasteful investment of energy and time. In a sense, therefore, the Mexican political system has purchased continuing stability (through widespread patronage) at the expense of skilled experience. Whether this formula will continue to function smoothly, as socioeconomic development imposes further demands for technical and other expertise, remains an open question.

QUALITIES OF CONTINUITY

Despite the prevalence of turnover since the 1920s there has also been a fair amount of continuity, and at this point the concept calls for qualification. In the first place it appears that, to the extent that it has

---

[6] For a critical view of the process see Bo Anderson and James D. Cockcroft, "Control and Cooptation in Mexican Politics," republished in Cockcroft et al., eds., *Dependence and Underdevelopment: Latin America's Political Economy* (Garden City, N.Y.: Doubleday, 1972), ch. 8.

existed at all, continuity since the Revolution has not extended much beyond two consecutive presidential terms. Once the mass violence and turmoil began to fade, in fact, a remarkably consistent pattern emerged. Among all the officeholders in a given presidential regime, as shown in Table 6-2, about 20 percent usually came from the immediately preceding regime; about 10 percent came from the group before that; 5 percent came from the one before that; and smaller proportions came from still earlier regimes. To take a specific illustration: of the 203 high officeholders under Díaz Ordaz (1964-70), 42 had appeared within the same institutional pool under López Mateos (1958-64); 26 belonged to the same circle under Ruiz Cortines (1952-58); and only 20 had held similar elite positions under Alemán (1946-52).[7]

TABLE 6-2

Rates of Continuity between Individual
Presidential Regimes, 1917-71

Presidential Regime[a]	Total N Incumbents	% Recruited from Previous Regimes[b]			
		R-1	R-2	R-3	R-4
Carranza, 1917-20	181	18.2	—[c]	—[c]	—[c]
Obregón, 1920-24	205	24.4	8.3	—[c]	—[c]
Calles, 1924-28	170	30.0	10.0	5.3	—[c]
Maximato, 1928-34	291	24.4	12.0	4.8	1.7
Cárdenas, 1934-40	234	26.5	9.4	6.0	3.4
Ávila Camacho, 1940-46	181	27.1	12.7	5.0	5.5
Alemán, 1946-52	190	14.7	8.4	6.8	1.6
Ruiz Cortines, 1952-58	168	22.0	7.7	7.1	8.9
López Mateos, 1958-64	178	20.8	12.0	5.1	2.8
Díaz Ordaz, 1964-70	203	20.7	12.8	9.9	4.4
Echeverría, 1970-76 (as of 1971)	164	18.9	6.1	2.4	3.6
Averages	—	22.5	9.9	5.8	4.0

NOTE: As explained in Appendix C, the pool of offices in this analysis corresponds to those with scale values from 8 to 2 in the HIGHEST OFFICE variable (see Appendix A, Table A-3).

[a] The transitional regime of Adolfo de la Huerta (1920) has been deleted from these computations.

[b] Regimes have been taken in chronological order, as listed in the table. R-1 refers to the immediately previous regime; R-2 to the one before that; R-3 to the one before that; and R-4 to the still preceding one. The Carranza regime of 1915-17 has been counted as "immediately previous" (R-1) to the Carranza presidency of 1917-20.

[c] No computation made, since the chronological juxtaposition (and political uncertainty) of regimes prior to 1915 would bring more confusion than clarity into the picture.

[7] These figures do not refer to elite status in consecutive terms. Not all the repeaters from the Alemán era, for instance, held office under Ruiz Cortines and López Mateos while en route to the Díaz Ordaz elite.

Such figures suggest that the duration of top-level careers has generally been restricted to only one presidential term, in some cases it has extended to two, and in rare instances it has covered three or more (this point receives additional treatment below). Equally important, the data also indicate that on the average *national elites in contemporary Mexico have undergone 90 percent renewal over the course of every three presidential terms*. The significance of this fact is slightly modified by the tendency for longtime elite members to occupy particularly key positions, but the basic pattern holds: the Mexican political elite has been self-renewing as well as self-perpetuating.

Exceptions to this rule come easily to mind. Antonio Carrillo Flores, professor of law at the UNAM, became the director of Nacional Financiera under Ávila Camacho, in 1945, at the age of 36. He held this post through the Alemán administration (1946-52), then was made Secretary of the Treasury under Ruiz Cortines (1952-58). During the López Mateos regime (1958-64) he served as ambassador to the United States, and under Díaz Ordaz (1964-70) he was Secretary of Foreign Relations. All in all, Carrillo Flores held major national offices for 26 consecutive years (at the end of which time he took up an important position in the United Nations!). His career has been extraordinary—it might not be over yet—but he is a person of exceptional gifts, and he has played the game with skill and tact. His powers of political survival are remarkable precisely because they are so rare.

At any rate, the process of constant renewal offers considerable insight into pendulumlike patterns of national policy, for it helps make possible the oft-noted swings from "radical" to "moderate" to "conservative" positions and back again.[8] An 80 percent rate of renewal between every two terms, and a 90 percent renewal between every three terms, means that very few architects of one policy are on hand to take part in the design of subsequent policies. As a result each presidential administration has a great deal of flexibility for making policy, so long as it adheres (at least rhetorically) to the basic tenets of the Revolution.[9]

[8] So many writers have commented upon this phenomenon that citation seems superfluous, but for one fairly recent (and very explicit) formulation see Martin C. Needler, *Politics and Society in Mexico* (Albuquerque: University of New Mexico Press, 1971), pp. 46-49.

[9] These observations pertain only to the availability of policy *options*, and say nothing about the direction or content of presidential decisions. Nor do they explain why every other regime should occupy an intermediate position on the policy-making scale, since 80 percent turnover between consecutive administrations would appear to permit a direct shift from "conservative" to "radical" stances (or vice versa). The role each president has in determining his successor, the persistence of key structural conditions, and the generalized desire to maintain an appearance of

But some regimes have more flexibility than others, depending upon socioeconomic circumstances and a host of other factors. One further source of flexibility is revealed by the rate of turnover, and here I call attention to the especially low degrees of prior elite experience for high officeholders under Miguel Alemán (1946-52) and also under Luis Echeverría (1970-76). According to Table 6-1, the continuity rate under Alemán was only 24.2 percent, a drop of 15 points from the level under Ávila Camacho (1940-46). And on the cabinet level, Alemán recruited only 6.3 percent from prior cabinet members—2 individuals out of 32, and he himself was one of them![10] One can thus begin to understand the ease and thoroughness with which he put through novel and "conservative" pro-business policies so shortly after the end of the "radical" Cárdenas regime (1934-40). Similarly, the Echeverría elite was relatively new, with an overall continuity rate of 26.2 percent. (The figure of 22.2 percent for the cabinet is less striking, but Echeverría ousted a number of holdovers after taking office, so this number may be a bit inflated.)[11] Whether or not these data correspond to the implementation of genuinely new policies—presumably in a "radical" direction—was still a matter of debate after the conclusion of the Echeverría regime.

A second major qualification to the concept of continuity entails the degree of internal mobility within the overall phenomenon of continuity. To deal with this question Table 6-3 lists the number of holdovers between immediately consecutive presidential regimes, and gives the percentages of those who seem to have moved upward, stayed on the same level, or moved down. (For these particular computations I have amplified the pool of offices studied to include the Chamber of Deputies. Individuals have been coded according to the "highest" office held during each presidential administration; for a discussion of the HIGHEST OFFICE variable, which provides the basis for judging the direction of mobility, see Appendix A and especially Table A-3.)[12]

---

continuity in purpose doubtless have an impact on this situation, but this is a topic that demands much further research.

[10] The "cabinet-level" posts correspond to those with scale value 8 for the HIGHEST OFFICE variable.

[11] In a private communication Roderic Ai Camp has reported that by 1976 the continuity rate for the Echeverría regime had risen to 35 percent, but I have not had a chance to verify this figure.

[12] As noted in Appendix C, this pool extends to offices with scale values from 8 to 1 for the HIGHEST OFFICE variable. The Chamber of Deputies has been included here because of its relatively important role in the system of recruitment and cooptation, but ambassadorships (scale value = 0) have been excluded because of their ambiguous position within the officeholding hierarchy—as they were also excluded from the analysis in Chapter 4.

TABLE 6-3

Directions of Mobility between Consecutive Presidential Regimes, 1904-71

Presidential Regime[a]	Total N Incumbents[b]	N Held over from Preceding Term[c]	% Moving Upward	% on Same Level	% Moving Down
Díaz, 1904-10[d]	430	283	6.0	91.2	2.8
Díaz, 1910-11	316	248	4.0	91.5	4.4
Madero, 1911-13	373	47	12.8	80.9	6.4
Huerta, 1913-14	357	35	34.3	60.0	5.7
Carranza, 1917-20[e]	581	132	27.3	59.1	13.6
Obregón, 1920-24	618	134	23.9	70.1	6.0
Calles, 1924-28	574	156	29.5	60.9	9.6
Maximato, 1928-34	720	223	26.0	68.2	5.8
Cárdenas, 1934-40	542	141	44.0	33.3	22.7
Ávila Camacho, 1940-46	475	100	44.0	27.0	29.0
Alemán, 1946-52	463	81	46.9	32.1	21.0
Ruiz Cortines, 1952-58	482	81	50.6	37.0	12.3
López Mateos, 1958-64	500	88	39.8	46.6	13.6
Díaz Ordaz, 1964-70	610	103	46.6	44.7	8.7
Echeverría, 1970-76 (as of 1971)	369	77	54.5	40.3	5.2

[a] Transitional presidencies, particularly those lacking in a full array of associated political institutions, have been deleted.

[b] The pool of offices in this analysis corresponds to those with scale values of 8 through 1 for the HIGHEST OFFICE variable (see Appendix A, Table A-3).

[c] Unless otherwise indicated, the "preceding term" corresponds to the one appearing immediately above in the list of presidential regimes.

[d] The preceding term for this presidency was the Díaz regime of 1900-1904.

[e] The preceding term for this presidency is taken to be the period when Carranza reigned as "First Chief" of the Revolution (1915-17), with delegates to the Constitutional Convention of 1916-17 included as deputies (unless they held some other position, that is, they were given scale values of 8 for their HIGHEST OFFICE during this presidency).

Among the many implications in Table 6-3, one clearly is that a major change in political practice took place during the Cárdenas period. Before that time, from the Díaz era through the *Maximato*, the dominant mode of continuity was to stay on the same institutional level, if not always exactly in the same office; the percentages of this category range from a high of 91.5 percent for the last Díaz presidency to a low of 59.1 percent for the Carranza presidency. Since 1934, however, the prevailing form of continuity has usually entailed more upward mobility than self-perpetuation within a particular stratum. Among 103 elite-level repeaters under Díaz Ordaz, for example, 46.6 percent held higher positions than they had formerly held under López

Mateos; 44.7 percent were on the same level; only 8.7 percent were moving down the ladder of importance and prestige. There has still been a considerable amount of continuity on the same levels, but the high proportions of upward mobility and the consistently low proportions of downward mobility combine to suggest the existence of two fundamental guidelines for political careers in modern Mexico: (1) up or out, usually out, and (2) if up, then out, and rarely down.

One implication of these rules would appear to be an increase in the centralization of political authority. In order to stay in the national elite, since 1934 it has generally been necessary to get a promotion—which, in turn, can only be obtained from the president or the members of his immediate circle. And it has been correspondingly difficult (though not impossible) to gain a near monopoly on some office or other. Unlike the U.S. Congress or the British House of Commons, as pointed out above, there are few "safe seats" in contemporary Mexican politics.

Thus political careers in Mexico, even the most durable ones, have come to exhibit increasing degrees of dependence on presidential largesse. The chronological timing of this development, moreover, suggests that it is more a result of institutional and other changes in the 1930s than of the Revolution itself. The most crucial factor was undoubtedly the formation of the official party in 1928-29, which began to challenge the position of local *caciques* and strengthen the power of the national decisionmaking apparatus. Application of the "no-reelection" law to the national legislature in 1934 also disrupted congressional tenure, though it still has been possible to take seats in alternate sessions.[13] Cárdenas' own reorganization of the official party, his struggle with the entrenched "Northern Dynasty," and his commitment to central government also lent accentuation to the trend.

Concurrent with these changes, there came a decided transformation in the national political environment. With the passage of time, the declining use of violence as a political instrument meant that fewer people could literally force their way into high office. In its way, the up-or-out pattern of elite mobility reflects the process of professionalization in Mexican politics. Since the Cárdenas era very few individuals have entered topmost positions (e.g., the cabinet or an important governorship) without doing prior service on a lower level. But as shown in Chapter 5, political apprenticeship in contemporary Mexico —for both the revolutionary and postrevolutionary cohorts—has

---

[13] Since there are two legislative sessions during every presidency, a person taking alternate turns in the Chamber of Deputies would still show up as having repeated "on the same level" between one presidential term and the next.

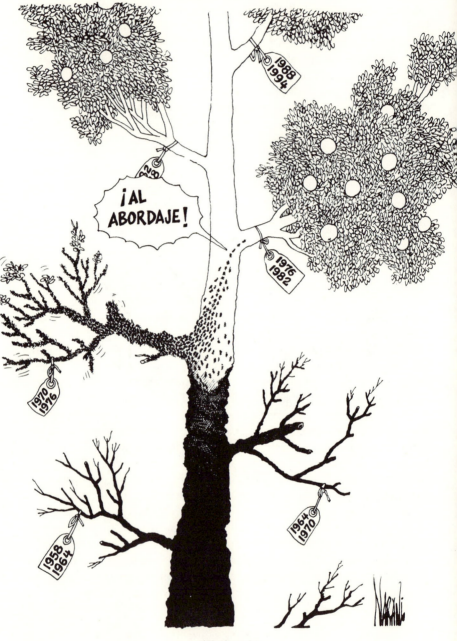

"All aboard!"

tended to be a diffuse experience, involving a series of unrelated jobs. In quality, then, professionalization has largely been limited to the establishment of requirements for moving up the officeholding hierarchy. Except for the case of some *técnicos* it probably has not, for the most part, encouraged the accumulation and application of task-related skills.

THE DURATION OF CAREERS

Whereas the previous discussion has analyzed degrees and types of continuity between presidential *regimes,* I now approach the problem from a different angle by focusing upon the continuity of individual *careers.* How have politicians been affected by the rates of turnover? How many have survived the up-or-out system, and for how long?

To begin, Table 6-4 presents data on successive probabilities for reentering the national elite for members of each of the prerevolutionary, revolutionary, and postrevolutionary officeholding cohorts. The "raw" probabilities for reentry refer to the statistical chance that, once a person has held elite status under a given number of presidential regimes, he will appear again within the elite at a subsequent time. In the case of the prerevolutionary cohort, for instance, 69.8 percent of all individuals holding elite status during one presidency then went on to occupy an elite position during a second presidency; accordingly, the demonstrated probability of repeating was .698. For those appearing in two regimes, the probability of going on to a third was .578. For those appearing in three regimes, the likelihood of going on to a fourth was .374. And so on, down to the end of the column, the maximum number of appearances for any member of this cohort being nine. Note, however, that the figures do not exclusively refer to appearances in chronologically *successive* presidencies; they refer to the total number of presidencies during which national offices were held over the entire course of lifetimes.[14]

As explained in Appendix B, the "adjusted" probabilities make some allowance for the presumed incidence of mortality. Instead of presenting the number of subsequent elite officeholders as a proportion of *all* officeholders in a given number of regimes, the adjusted probabilities compute the number of subsequent elite officeholders as a

---

[14] As explained in Appendix B, the offices for this analysis include those with scale values for the HIGHEST OFFICE variable ranging all the way from 8 to 0. Here, as in other similar instances, I have deleted from calculations all those who (a) first reached national office under Díaz Ordaz, or (b) held any national office under Echeverría.

proportion of all officeholders in a given number of regimes *who are presumed to be alive* and still eligible for reincorporation into the elite. For this reason I shall devote my attention to the adjusted probabilities, instead of the raw ones, though a look at the table shows that there is usually not a great deal of variation between the two sets.

TABLE 6-4

Probabilities for Reentering Political Elite, by Cohort

Nth Presidential Regime during which an Elite Position Held	Probabilities for Reentering Political Elite					
	Prerevolutionary Cohort, 1900-1911		Revolutionary Cohort, 1917-40		Postrevolutionary Cohort, 1946-71	
	Raw	Adjusted	Raw	Adjusted	Raw	Adjusted
1	.698	.811	.330	.355	.356	.380
2	.578	.689	.382	.415	.374	.407
3	.374	.460	.387	.425	.424	.479
4	.435	.556	.306	.343	.329	.390
5	.475	.633	.265	.300	.261	.333
6	.316	.462	.111	—	.167	—
7	.500	—	—	—	—	—
8	.333	—	—	—	—	—

NOTE: Lines represent maximum number of regimes during which positions held by members of each group under consideration (see Appendix B, especially Tables B-6, B-7, and B-8).

As would be expected from the prior findings, dramatic differences emerge between the cohorts. For the Díaz group there was a strong probability that, once in the elite, one would reappear in the elite. At a couple of points the adjusted figures fell below .50, meaning that the chances of permanent exit were greater than fifty-fifty, but in most cases the likelihood of reentry was extremely high: .811 from the first appearance, .689 from the second appearance, .556 from the fourth appearance, .633 from the fifth. Officeholding was, under Díaz, a relatively secure enterprise—that is, up until the Revolution.[15]

Not so for the revolutionaries and their political descendants, for whom the likelihood of permanent exit from office—even allowing for mortality—was always greater than the likelihood of staying on. For the 1917-40 cohort, the probabilities for reentry range from a low of

[15] Though the Revolution obviously shortened the political careers of many *porfiristas*, I have for two reasons not eliminated from these calculations all those holding office in mid-1911: first, numerous members of the Díaz elite could and did reappear in subsequent regimes (such as those of Madero and Huerta); and second, experimentation showed that elimination of officeholders in 1911 would merely reduce the number of observations without substantially altering the results.

.300 to a high of .425. For the 1946-71 group, they range from .333 to .479. At no point do they go higher than 50 percent.

These figures are remarkable for several reasons, the chief one being their consistency. As a rough average, the likelihood of reentering the political elite, for both revolutionary and postrevolutionary cohorts, was constantly around .40; the likelihood of permanent exit was about .60.[16] This means that, for these generations, the accumulation of political experience—not to say accomplishment—has never provided any overwhelming advantage in the quest for additional office. No matter how long or venerable the political career, that is, the current position in the national elite was likely to be the last.

In elaboration of these points, Table 6-5 presents percentage figures on the proportional distribution of elite appearances for members of the three officeholding cohorts. The data indicate a sharp transition between the prerevolutionary era and the post-1917 years. Among the Díaz group, only 30.2 percent made merely one appearance on the national level; 29.5 percent made two appearances, 25.2 percent made three, and 15.1 percent—hard-core veterans by any standard—made four or more appearances. The picture is different for subsequent cohorts. For revolutionaries and postrevolutionaries alike, about two-thirds made only one appearance; one-fifth made two appearances; 7 or 8 percent made three, and 5 or 6 percent made four or more.

TABLE 6-5

Distribution of Continuity in Political Elite, by Cohort

N Presidential Regimes in which an Elite Position Held	Prerevolutionary Cohort, 1900-1911 (N = 610)	Revolutionary Cohort, 1917-40 (N = 2,282)	Postrevolutionary Cohort, 1946-71 (N = 1,239)
1 only	30.2%	67.0%	64.4%
2	29.5	20.4	22.3
3	25.2	7.7	7.7
4 or more	15.1	4.9	5.6
Totals	100.0	100.0	100.0

These contrasting portraits correspond to major differences in recruitment styles and system processes. The prerevolutionary regime was a coalition carefully orchestrated by Díaz himself. Seeking an optional balance among political forces, he allocated offices with care—

16 This process has all the basic properties of a Markov-chain model, which provides an extraordinarily good approximation of the actual data.

and would alter the allocation only in response to a change in the balance of forces. (His evident inattention to such matters after 1900 increased the rigidity of his regime, and this was one of the reasons for his downfall.) He also tended to favor cronies, many of whom had fought under him in the war against French intervention in the 1860s or had joined his camp during the storm-tossed 1870s. Hence the coexistence of great individual power, concentrated in Díaz himself, along with a longstanding team of trusted associates.

The picture for the revolutionary and postrevolutionary cohorts depicts another type of process. Also attempting to maintain and protect a coalition, post-1917 leaders have evidently distributed political patronage as far and wide as possible by giving most aspirants (about two-thirds of the total) only one opportunity to possess national office. Some have come back a second time. A small proportion has repeated three or more times—about 13 percent—and this may well represent the group that dominates the power structures of the polity. At any rate it is clear that only a few politicians, such as Carrillo Flores, have played the up-or-out game with much success.

From another perspective, the data in Tables 6-4 and 6-5 plus other previous findings indicate that, in the whole, *the Mexican Revolution led to an abbreviation of political careers on the national level.* For instance, members of the 1900-1911 cohort came to hold national office, during separate presidential regimes, an average number of 2.4 times. For the 1917-40 cohort, the figure fell to only 1.5 times—and it stayed in that vicinity, barely moving up to 1.6 times for the 1946-71 cohort. This truncation of tenure on the national level was one of the most basic and lasting consequences of the Revolution, and, as I shall argue below, it was bound to have profound effects on the implicit behavioral codes of political leaders.

Some implications of this point find further expression in Table 6-6, which offers information on the duration of careers for the three cohorts. As computed here, the length of a career is defined as the entire time span between the initiation of any recognizable political activity and the last year of the presidential regime during which the final office was held.[17] Because these calculations required a fairly thorough amount of information, they relate to only a fraction—around 10 percent or so—of the complete cohorts; because of the bias in my sources, it is certain that the data pertain to disproportionately prominent

---

[17] This procedure is necessary because of the frequency of missing data for the final year of officeholding. It produces a slight inflation in the year of exit, since some people left their final office before the conclusion of the relevant presidential term.

TABLE 6-6

Duration of Political Careers, by Cohort

N years	Prerevolutionary Cohort, 1900-1911 (N = 50)	Revolutionary Cohort, 1917-40 (N = 253)	Postrevolutionary Cohort, 1946-71 (N = 226)
0-9	8.0%	18.2%	10.2%
10-19	28.0	24.5	18.1
20-29	24.0	27.3	21.2
30 or more	40.0	30.0	50.5
Totals	100.0	100.0	100.0

subsets of the respective elites. Even so, the figures in the table are revealing.

The truncation effect of the Revolution clearly emerges from contrasts between the 1900-1911 and 1917-40 cohorts. Only 8.0 percent of the Díaz elite had careers lasting less than 10 years, compared to 18.2 percent of the revolutionary group. Similarly, fully 40 percent of the prerevolutionary cohort had been in politics for more than 30 years—meaning that they started in or before the 1870s—while just 30 percent of the revolutionaries stayed in public life that long. Paradoxically, however, careers for the 1946-71 cohort appear to have undergone a process of lengthening, especially in comparison to the 1917-40 group. Only 10.2 percent of the postrevolutionaries had careers of less than 10 years, and *over 50 percent* pursued political activity for more than 30 years. Together with the findings in Table 6-5, this means that members of the 1946-71 cohort had to work for a relatively long time on the subnational level before breaking into the national elite—but notwithstanding all that struggle, their tenure on the national level would still be relatively short. For the system to maintain stability, the rewards would obviously have to be worth the effort.

Again, the different patterns in career duration correspond to the varying political styles of the historical periods. Members of the Díaz elite began their political activity, on the average, at the age of 34—often after launching full-fledged careers in law, landholding, or business—and they stepped down around the age of 61 (many would doubtless have stayed on longer, had they not been ousted by the Revolution). In keeping with the youthful character of the Revolution, members of the 1917-40 cohort started at the average age of 28, with many beginning as teenagers in the Revolution itself, and they left office at around 51, a full decade earlier than their prerevolutionary predecessors. Members of the 1946-71 cohort, by contrast, pursued their careers in the relatively stable, institutionalized environment fostered by the one-party system, and politics was for them a full profession. Like the revolutionaries they started fairly early, at the average age of 28, but they stayed on longer, until the average age of 57. Even then, this was a fairly young age for retirement, whether forced or voluntary: as of 1960 Mexican males who reached the age of 55 could expect to live another 20 years.[18] What would they do for the rest of their lives?

At face value, this combination of long apprenticeship, short supremacy, and early retirement might appear as likely sources of alienation and resentment among members of the postrevolutionary cohort. This outcome has been prevented, however, in two fundamental ways. First, the economic rewards of officeholding have been extremely generous. Corruption, or whatever one might want to call it, has done much to soften the blows of exit from office. Second, for those who leave the national elite there has almost always remained the possibility of returning to it again. Among the individuals (in Tables 6-4 and 6-5) who reached high office more than once, a fair number did so after attaining their posts and then being skipped over by one or more presidents. To take but one example from the data in Tables 6-1 and 6-2: of the 69 members of the Díaz Ordaz group (1964-70) who had held prior elite experience, 42 had appeared in the immediately previous López Mateos elite—and 27 had made comebacks after being out of national office during the entire 1958-64 sexennium. Some people— not too many, but some—have thus managed to play a game of leapfrog. So when officeholders have been ejected from the system, they can continue to entertain the possibility, or at least the dream, of getting back on top. Hope springs eternal, and as long as this is true there is very little likelihood that ousted politicians will mount a major challenge to the system.

COMPARATIVE PERSPECTIVES

Throughout this chapter I have been arguing that elite continuity since the Mexican Revolution has been low, that turnover has been high, and that the rate of renewal has been relatively steady. To be confirmed, however, these judgments require cross-national compari-

---

[18] Eduardo E. Arriaga, *New Life Tables for Latin American Populations in the Nineteenth and Twentieth Centuries* (Berkeley: Institute of International Studies, University of California, 1968), p. 206.

son. This is a difficult task, and there is not much cumulative research in this area: as Robert D. Putnam points out, "Little is known systematically about how turnover rates vary from country to country."[19] Our understanding of the Mexican pattern demands it, however, and a poor effort is better than none.

It seems possible, at the outset, to establish relative *degrees* of continuity. In a comparative study of postwar Western Europe and the British Commonwealth, Valentine Herman has calculated rates of persistence on the ministerial level for 18 separate systems. Defining continuity as the proportional rate of holdovers between immediately successive governments (that is, the percentage of ministers in government 1 who hold portfolios in government 2), he finds that the highest average rate of continuity appears in Sweden (93.5 percent); that all but two of the systems have mean continuity rates of 40 percent or more; and that the lowest, during the Fourth Republic in France, was 27 percent.[20]

Mexico presents a startling contrast. From 1946 through 1971, the average proportion of cabinet ministers[21] who had served in *any* previous cabinet, not just the immediately preceding one, was only 20.7 percent; discounting the Alemán period, which witnessed an exceptionally high rate of renewal, the average for 1952-71 was 24.3 percent, still below the figure for the Fourth Republic. Coming closer to Herman's computational procedure, one also finds that the average proportion of ministers in Mexico who had served in the immediately previous cabinet was only 17.9 percent. To be sure, this contrast is mitigated by the relatively long, six-year duration of Mexican administrations,[22] but the conclusion is inescapable: in comparison to multiparty parliamentary systems, Mexico's one-party system has an exceptionally high degree of turnover.

Cutting across a more divergent range of polities, John D. Nagle has compiled data on personnel turnover in West Germany and the United States (with relatively open, pluralistic competition), the Soviet Union (a closed system), and Mexico ("semi-open," in Nagle's

[19] Robert D. Putnam, *The Comparative Study of Political Elites* (Englewood Cliffs, N.J.: Prentice-Hall, 1976), p. 65.

[20] Valentine Herman, "Comparative Perspectives on Ministerial Stability in Britain," unpublished paper (University of Essex, 1973), Table 5. (Note that Herman and I use the terms "continuity" and "turnover" in different ways.)

[21] Offices with scale values of 8 according to the HIGHEST OFFICE variable (see Appendix A, Table A-3).

[22] One useful attempt to compare continuity rates between offices with terms of varying length appears in Joseph A. Schlesinger, *Ambition and Politics: Political Careers in the United States* (Chicago: Rand-McNally, 1966), pp. 38-41.

term).[23] He measures rates of renewal as the proportion of cabinet ministers (or their equivalent) in government 2 who did not hold similar portfolios in previous government 1. The results are in Table 6-7, and they present a somewhat mixed picture. First, they indicate that, for government-to-government changes, the average Mexican rate of renewal has been the highest of all: 75.3 percent, just ahead of the United States (75.0 percent), substantially more than in West Germany (59.6 percent) and far greater than in the USSR (43.0 percent). Second, however, the data for annual average turnover brings Mexico down to third place, with 12.5 percent, behind the United States and West Germany (18.8 and 14.9 respectively) but still ahead of the Soviet Union (9.1 percent).

In comparison to other nations, cabinet ministers in Mexico have thus enjoyed relatively high security of tenure *within* presidential administrations, but they have faced relatively low probabilities for staying on *between* presidential administrations. Once in office, during the 1946-70 period, they could usually expect to finish out their term. Once out of office, they could usually expect to stay there. This set of probabilities contrasts sharply with parliamentary regimes, where the likelihood of gaining a portfolio depends upon the strength of one's party, and where the existence of multiparty coalitions can (as in the Herman study) often lead to high rates of intergovernmental continuity, with the same individuals frequently taking part in successive coalitions. It also contrasts with the presidentialist system of the United States, where a victory by Party B would lead to the near-total expulsion of leaders from Party A. (This process shows up in the cabinet-level data in Table 6-7, and in other studies too: according to one count, only 6 percent of the 64 "top" civilian officials in the Eisenhower administration had been top leaders under Truman, while another 10 percent had held lesser posts in the Truman government; similarly, about 6 percent of the top officials under Kennedy had been at the top under Eisenhower, and only 5 percent more had held second-level jobs under Eisenhower.)[24]

These differences suggest that patterns of continuity can vary in *shape*, or *form*, as well as in degree. To pursue this point, Figure 6-2 presents a general outline of trends in continuity within "top" leadership posts in three countries: Mexico, the United States, and the So-

---

[23] John D. Nagle, "System and Succession: A Generational Analysis of Elite Turnover in Four Nations" (paper presented at the annual meeting of the Southern Political Science Association, Atlanta, 1973).

[24] Zbigniew Brzezinski and Samuel P. Huntington, *Political Power: USA/USSR* (New York: Viking Press, 1965), p. 174.

TABLE 6-7

Turnover and Continuity in Four Nations:
the United States, West Germany, the Soviet Union,
and Mexico

	% Turnover	% Continuity
United States (cabinet)		
1949-53	100	0
1953-57	100	0
1957-61	25	75
1961-65	100	0
1965-69	50	50
Average per change:	75.0	
Average per year:	18.8	
West Germany (cabinet)		
1949-53	58	42
1953-57	44	56
1957-61	43	57
1961-65	59	41
1965-69	94	6
Average per change:	59.6	
Average per year:	14.9	
Soviet Union (politburo)		
1952-56	73	27
1956-61	36	64
1961-66	36	64
1966-71	27	73
Average per change:	43.0	
Average per year:	9.1	
Mexico (cabinet)[a]		
1946-52	89	11
1952-58	89	11
1958-64	50	50
1964-70	73	27
Average per change:	75.3	
Average per year:	12.5	

SOURCE: John D. Nagle, "System and Succession: A Generational Analysis of Elite Turnover in Four Nations" (paper presented at the annual meeting of the Southern Political Science Association, Atlanta, 1973), Table 1.

[a] Adapted, by Nagle, from Roderic Ai Camp, "The Cabinet and the *Técnico* in Mexico and the United States," *Journal of Comparative Administration* 3, no. 2 (August 1971): 201.

viet Union—representing, respectively, authoritarian, democratic, and totalitarian systems. To establish comparability between the curves, the data base refers to roughly similar offices: for Mexico, the cabinet and other upper-level posts;[25] for the United States, the cabinet and other high appointive positions; for the USSR, the politburo, the secretariat, and the central committee.[26] It should be understood that the trends, as I have drawn them, depict *abstract models* which are derived from factual information, rather than tracing empirical data themselves.[27]

As already shown above, Mexico has maintained a high level of turnover with a consistent, steady shape. The rate of continuity has hung around the 30-35 percent level, for cabinet ministries as well as for the broader pool of offices reflected in Figure 6-1. Except for the Alemán cabinet, which made a sharp break with the past, there has been relatively little fluctuation: continuity has almost always hovered between 20 and 40 percent.

The Russian case is altogether different. For the most part continuity has been much higher than in Mexico, fluctuating between 65 and 80 percent (on the central committee), presumably in accordance with the centralized, monopolistic tendencies of such a state. In times of crisis, however, particularly crises of succession, Soviet leadership has been subject to dramatic changes. (The relationship between crisis and turnover also holds in Communist China.)[28] In the 1930s, when Joseph Stalin carried out his infamous purge, continuity on the central committee dropped to 22.5 percent; as Nikita Khrushchev consolidated power in the late 1950s and early '60s, it plunged again to 37 percent. So the Soviet system has shown great continuity, but it has been subject to erratic transformations. Even then the figures are revealing: continuity rates *during Soviet crises*, even in the purges of the 1930s, have been within the *normal* range of continuity for Mexico! For a

[25] As explained in Appendix B, trends for nine different pools of offices are much the same, so it does not matter very much which pool is used for this analysis.

[26] Brzezinski and Huntington, *Political Power*, pp. 173-182; and Brzezinski, *The Permanent Purge: Politics in Soviet Totalitarianism* (Cambridge: Harvard University Press, 1956). It is unclear whether Brzezinski and Huntington define continuity precisely as I do—as prior elite experience at *any* point in time, rather than in the immediately preceding period—but for these broad purposes the difference is negligible.

[27] The time units for all three cases are not exactly the same: usually six years for Mexico, four years for the United States, and (on the average, with notable fluctuation) three years in the USSR. These differences could lead to some distortion but, again, I must stress the general nature of this comparison.

[28] See George C. S. Sung, *A Biographical Approach to Chinese Political Analysis* (Santa Monica, Cal.: Rand Corporation, 1975), esp. pp. 33-35.

Figure 6-2: Comparative Patterns of Elite Continuity: Mexico,
the USSR, and the USA

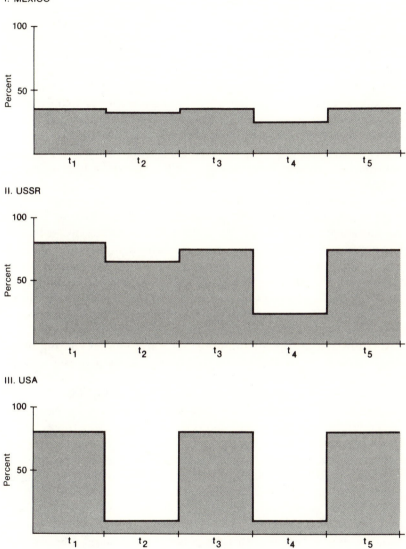

NOTE: The subscripted letter *t* refers to successive periods of time.

one-party system, Mexico seems to have an absolutely minimum amount of continuity.

Illustrating still another pattern, the U.S. shows a series of sharp but regular oscillations in elite recruitment. As drawn in the figure, the curve begins at a high point—around 80 percent—to represent the general tendency for second-term presidents to retain top officials from one administration to another (let us say that this is Party A). If the opposing Party B wins the following election, however, a near-complete catharsis then takes place, as implied in Table 6-7, and the curve accordingly drops to 10 percent or so (quite a bit lower than in Mexico). Reelection of this president, and retention of his partisan entourage, would push the rate of continuity back up again. A subsequent victory by Party A would bring in a new team and push the curve back down; and so on, as long as effective two-party competition persists.

It should be emphasized, in passing, that these patterns for the U.S. refer to top-level appointive positions, prototypically the cabinet. On the congressional level, especially among the major leaders of both houses, the United States tends to exhibit high continuity and long tenure—in studied contrast to Mexico, where the "no-reelection" rule prevails.[29] Inclusion of key legislators would substantially reduce the American turnover rates, and also tend to flatten out the curve, though I strongly suspect that the overall pattern of oscillation would remain.

Notwithstanding this qualification the variations in continuity, in regard to both degree and shape, correspond closely with the types of political system. A democratic presidentialist polity, such as the U.S., produces steep fluctuations, changes from high to low continuity, at regular intervals (the intervals would be less steep in a parliamentary system, but the basic principle would still obtain). A totalitarian state, such as the Soviet Union or China, is characterized by high continuity and sudden convulsion. In an authoritarian regime, such as Mexico, turnover is steady and smooth: as Juan Linz has written, referring to Franco's Spain, "a change in the elite's composition [under authoritarianism] can go on more silently and smoothly than under totalitarianism, where changes in leadership are associated with crises. Turnover in authoritarian regimes can take place without purges, by retiring people to secondary or honorary positions, if not to private life."[30]

[29] Brzezinski and Huntington, *Political Power*, pp. 175-176; Nagle, "System and Succession," Table 1; and Schlesinger, *Ambition*, p. 40.

[30] Juan J. Linz, "An Authoritarian Regime: Spain," in *Mass Politics: Studies in Political Sociology*, ed. Erik Allardt and Stein Rokkan (New York: Free Press, 1970), pp. 273-274.

But if the *shape* of Mexico's turnover pattern is typical of authoritarian regimes, its *level* of renewal rates is not. According to Linz, authoritarian systems are generally "slow" to renew elites; according to any standard, international or otherwise, and particularly in comparison to Spain,[31] Mexico has a rapid turnover rate, especially during transitions between presidential administrations. At least in this sense, and possibly in others, Mexico appears to have developed a genuinely unique tutelary regime.

Conclusion: The Results of Revolution

Taken together, Chapters 3 through 6 have focused on a set of unified questions: How has the composition and selection of political elites in twentieth-century Mexico varied over time, and what have been the sources of that variation? What has been the impact of socioeconomic variables, such as urbanization and industrialization? How did the Mexican Revolution affect patterns of elite recruitment and selection? What kind of difference did the Revolution make? How long did those differences last? And what has been the consequence of consolidation of the tutelary system?

According to Chapter 3, the social background of national elites has not undergone any cataclysmic change. There has been, instead, a slow and steady transformation. The upper class has faded from the scene, the lower class has assumed a (minor) role, and the middle class has (if anything) strengthened its control of public office. This trend appears to comply with analogous patterns in other industrializing societies, regardless of political system, and it would appear to reflect the result of socioeconomic change rather than of political events.

But if socioeconomic changes established and delimited the broad outlines of elite transformation, at least regarding social composition, the Revolution filled in many specific and important details. While it drew most of its leaders from the middle class—sons of middle-class fathers, usually university graduates and often lawyers—it clearly represented those segments of the middle class which had been previously excluded from the Porfirian system. Revolutionary leadership was substantially younger and more rural (or less urban) than the Díaz clique, and it came from different geographical regions, especially the northern tier. In sum, the Revolution did not alter, in any fundamental

31 See Linz, "Continuidad y descontinuidad en la élite política española: de la restauración al régimen actual," in *Estudios de ciencia política y sociología* (Madrid: n.p., 1972), pp. 361-423; and Paul H. Lewis, "The Spanish Ministerial Elite, 1938-1969," *Comparative Politics* 5, no. 1 (October 1972): 83-106, esp. 91-93.

way, the class composition of the national political elite, but it did lead to an effective reallocation of political power *within* the country's upper strata.

In another sense, the Revolution has also placed the state almost completely at the service of middle-class groups. On the basis of socioeconomic trends in Mexico, one might expect that rising capitalists, particularly industrialists (of either upper- or middle-class status), would be moving into positions of political power. This has not happened, and I shall explore the implications of this nonevent in Chapter 7. My point, for the moment, is that the Revolution has brought about a separation of political and economic elites.

The social character and homogeneity of the ruling group since 1917 offer a suggestive, though incomplete, explanation for the persisting reluctance with which national elites have pursued structural change in behalf of laborers and *campesinos*.[32] This is not to imply a deterministic relationship between elite composition and public policy. But at first glance, the evident failure of Mexican leaders to fulfill the pro-working-class goals of the Revolution might seem perplexing; the contradiction between rhetoric and action becomes less surprising, if not wholly understandable, when it is realized that, ever since Carranza's triumph, the governing elite has been largely of middle-class extraction. One can also appreciate the words of Artemio Cruz, a fictional character in a well-known novel by Carlos Fuentes:

> A revolution is shaped on battlefields, but once it is corrupted, though battles are still won, the revolution is lost. We have all been responsible. . . . Those who wanted a true revolution, radical and uncompromising, are unfortunately ignorant and bloody men. And the literate element want only a half-revolution, compatible with what interests them, their only interest, getting on in the world, living well, replacing Don Porfirio's elite. There you have Mexico's drama. Look at me. All my life reading Kropotkin, Bakunin, old Plekhanov, reading since childhood, and discussing, discussing. And at the really critical moment I had to side with Carranza because he is the only one who seems a decent sort of person, a person who won't frighten me. See what a damned effeminacy . . . I'm afraid of the tough bastards, Villa and Zapata. "I will continue being an impossible person so long as those persons who today are possible go on being possible. . . ." Ah, yes. Why not?[33]

[32] See especially Ramón Eduardo Ruiz, *Labor and the Ambivalent Revolutionaries: Mexico, 1911-1923* (Baltimore: Johns Hopkins University Press, 1976).

[33] Carlos Fuentes, *The Death of Artemio Cruz*, trans. Sam Hileman (New York: Farrar, Straus, and Giroux, 1964), p. 186.

Neither Fuentes nor I wish to imply that specific policy preferences, such as a decision on agricultural credit, are closely related to social background. The point is that basic values—both normative and cognitive orientations, such as a belief in the virtues of capitalism—bear a relationship to social class, and this factor helps explain the cautiousness of public policy during the revolutionary era.

This same principle would apply to leaders of the postrevolutionary cohort, also dominated by the middle class, with additional effects from institutionalization. As shown in Chapters 5 and 6, stabilization of the system in the 1930s and '40s obliged members of the 1946-71 group to undergo relatively long periods of political apprenticeship, and this training process no doubt imposed a set of established norms on office-seekers. As ambitious young aspirants adapted to and abided by the rules of the game (to be spelled out in Chapter 9), the mechanisms of recruitment and selection acted as agents of socialization. This phenomenon further contributes to the general continuity of post-1940 public policy despite the proportional (though modest) increase in the number of people of lower-class extraction. Not only are they often kept on lesser levels of the political hierarchy, as revealed in Chapter 4; more important, they are taught that the road to success lies in the acceptance and promulgation of middle-class norms. Thus the relationship between social class and political values has in recent years been mitigated by the intervening effect of institutionalization and patterns of recruitment.

Despite this cooptation of the lower class, fragmentary as it has been, institutionalization of the tutelary system has, if anything, tightened the social requirements for admission to the ruling circles. Higher education and a professional occupation have almost become a *sine qua non* for access to the elite. Though relationships between social background and political attainment have remained weak, as already noted, people of modest origins have found it disproportionately difficult to move up beyond the Chamber of Deputies. As a matter of fact, with the exception of age structures and the incidence of military officers, the postrevolutionary cohort bore a substantial resemblance to the prerevolutionary group. Both elites were born and raised in predominantly urban, middle-class environments; they were trained in universities; and they held professional occupations, especially in law and (more recently) economics. One senses, in this connection, a return to Porfirian practices.

Perhaps the most far-reaching effect of the Mexican Revolution concerned the structure of political careers. At no time in twentieth-century Mexico, as argued in Chapter 4, has social background been a

185

strong determinant of relative political success. But as shown in Chapters 5 and 6, the shape of officeholding careers has undergone a profound change. By the late Díaz years, when the system was highly centralized, the recruitment and selection processes had become extremely static. There was hardly any turnover, and there was hardly any movement from office to office. Díaz had established his preeminence, he reigned supreme, and he apparently saw little need to alter the composition of his regime.

The Revolution changed all this. Members of the 1917-40 cohort moved frequently from one office to another, and, though there were some fairly well-established job-to-job routes, the pattern of movement for individuals consistently defied easy prediction. Moreover the "no-reelection" rule and associated practices sharply reduced the rate of continuity within elites, cutting it approximately in half. In sum, the Revolution may not have led to major changes in the social composition of those who received national political offices, but it brought about a major alteration in the manner of distributing those offices.

Career structures for the postrevolutionary cohort have been similar in many ways to those of the 1917-40 group. As before, careers have been characterized by diversity of experience, rather than concentrated preparation; by frequent and far-ranging interpositional movement, rather than repetition in one office; and by early exit from the elite, rather than longevity. Yet there have been some additional developments which, in combination, point to a steady increase in the centralization of the recruitment and selection processes. Because of its social, political, and geographic location, the UNAM accumulated great importance as a training ground for members of the national elite. A background in elective office has become something of a liability in the quest for admission to the upper-level circles of power and prestige, whose ranks have become dominated by lifelong bureaucrats who have gradually worked their way up through the national government hierarchy. Concurrently, a pivotal role in career formation has moved from the state governorships to the Senate. Once people have made it into the elite, they have faced the persistent threat of being forced out of it. And to the extent that they have stayed in, they have usually had to do so by moving up, a fact which has placed them at the constant mercy of their superiors. Since the 1940s, recruitment and selection procedures under the tutelary system have thus enhanced and strengthened the role and power of centralized authority.

There has been a constant circulation of elites, therefore, but not in the sense that Vilfredo Pareto used the term. In Mexico the process has involved the rapid rotation of individuals, but mostly of individuals within a single class, the middle class (and its component fractions). Circulation has not entailed the kind of social mobility, open opportunity, and extensive incorporation of lower-class elements which, in Pareto's view, would lead to institutional stability. Rather, the circulation of elites, together with cooptation of potential dissidents, has combined to strengthen the predominance of the middle class and to accelerate the tendency toward centralization.

Through the use of novel mechanisms, that is, the Mexican political system has regained the level of centralized control that it formerly exhibited under the Díaz regime.[34] To be sure, power has come to reside in a monolithic presidential *system* rather than in the person of an omnipotent *individual*, and this is a substantial difference, but the *degree* of effective centralization is much the same. Ironically enough, the PRI has not really institutionalized the Revolution, as its name proclaims. What it has done is to find a new formula for reinstitutionalizing the essence of the *Porfiriato*.

[34] See also the essay by Lorenzo Meyer, "Historical Roots of the Authoritarian State in Mexico," in *Authoritarianism in Mexico,* ed. José Luis Reyna and Richard S. Weinert (Philadelphia: ISHI, 1977), pp. 3-22.

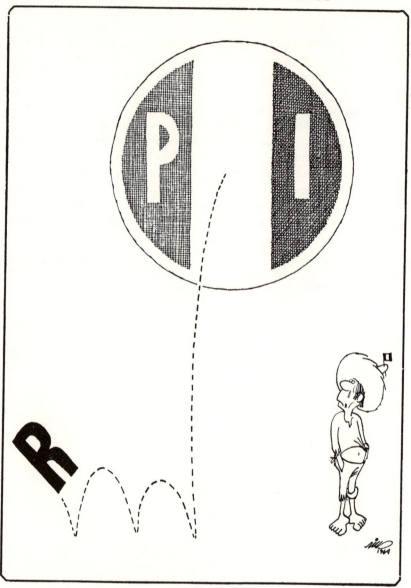

PART III

ASPECTS OF AN
AUTHORITARIAN SYSTEM

· 7 ·

IS THERE A POWER ELITE?

The various chapters of Part II all focused on patterns of historical change affecting, and affected by, both the Mexican Revolution and the subsequent formation, by the 1940s, of an apparently stable, tutelary, authoritarian political system. Granted the existence of this regime, Part III now sets out to explore, in some detail, selected aspects of its structure and operation since 1946: first, the relationships between the nation's economic and political elites; second, the role and composition of the national Chamber of Deputies; third, the tacit codes for political survival and advancement; and finally, the procedures for presidential succession, as exemplified in the transition from Luis Echeverría to José López Portillo in 1976. The analytical perspective is no longer longitudinal and dynamic, as it was in Part II. It is cross-sectional and static, and, excepting Chapter 10, the data on political elites refer almost exclusively to what has hitherto been known as the "postrevolutionary" officeholding cohort of 1946-71.

The linkages between economic and political elites, to be dealt with in this chapter, comprise a central aspect of any political system, and they are especially germane to systems with restricted competition. Under the contemporary Mexican regime do major economic interests have direct voice in the councils of government? If so, which ones? Or do they stand outside the circles of political decisionmaking? Such problems raise critical issues about the *form* and *function* of the "limited pluralism" that exists in Mexico. And even if these questions defy unequivocal answers, they nonetheless have to be asked.

For better or for worse, the whole subject of interconnections between economic and political elites (and, by indirection, the interplay of economic and political power) is one of the most complex and hotly debated themes in contemporary social science. Marxists have argued that economic power creates political power, and that, in capitalist societies, the state is at the service of the bourgeoisie. Pluralists have contended that power is fractured, not concentrated, that diverse groups can enter the decisionmaking process, and that government

An earlier version of Chapter 7 has been published in slightly different form in *Authoritarianism in Mexico*, ed. José Luis Reyna and Richard S. Weinert. Copyright © 1977 by ISHI, Institute for the Study of Human Issues, Philadelphia; reproduced by permission of the Institute.

transcends the interests of any dominant class (itself divided into competing factions). From Marxian viewpoints, Ralph Miliband[1] and Nicos Poulantzas[2] have offered bold new formulations—and become locked in a dispute of their own.[3] Questions sprout and opinions abound, but facts are fairly scarce.

If relatively little has yet emerged from this welter of confusion, one thing at least is clear: the relationship between political and economic elites can take on varied forms. Consider, for a moment, the following range of possibilities, by no means exhaustive in itself:

1. Those who control the modes of economic production—that is, the wealthy—control the state directly. They enjoy a near-monopoly on public office and they make all major political decisions. This situation typically prevailed in preindustrial societies, where landed aristocracies held sway, such as eighteenth-century England[4] or Argentina up to 1912 or 1916.[5]

2. Members of the economic elite take an active part in government, without monopolizing office, they have inordinate (though not always paramount) influence, they are partners in what C. Wright Mills has called the "power elite" (about which more below).[6] The prototypical case is, of course, the United States: more than 60 percent of cabinet officers between 1889 and 1949 were businessmen of one sort or another,[7] and a recent study has demonstrated that, as of 1970 or so, fully 40 percent of the nation's top 3,572 corporate leaders had held major government posts at one time or another.[8] The ebullient style of Mark Hanna might have given way to the graceful manners of Douglas Dillon and Cyrus Vance, but the structural pattern remains the same. In

---

[1] Ralph Miliband, *The State in Capitalist Society* (New York: Basic Books, 1969).

[2] Nicos Poulantzas, *Political Power and Social Class*, trans. Timothy O'Hagan (London: NLB and Sheed and Ward, 1973).

[3] Poulantzas, "The Problem of the Capitalist State," *New Left Review* 58 (November-December 1969): 67-78; Miliband, "The Capitalist State: Reply to Nicos Poulantzas," *New Left Review* 59 (January-February 1970): 53-60; Miliband, "Poulantzas and the Capitalist State," *New Left Review* 82 (November-December 1973): 83-92; and Poulantzas, "The Capitalist State: A Reply to Miliband and Laclau," *New Left Review* 95 (January-February 1976): 63-83.

[4] Miliband, *State*, p. 59 and 59n.

[5] Peter H. Smith, *Argentina and the Failure of Democracy: Conflict among Political Elites, 1904-1955* (Madison: University of Wisconsin Press, 1974), esp. pp. 26-27.

[6] C. Wright Mills, *The Power Elite* (New York: Oxford University Press, 1959).

[7] Harold D. Lasswell, Daniel Lerner, and C. Easton Rothwell, *The Comparative Study of Elites: An Introduction and Bibliography* (Stanford: Stanford University Press, 1952), p. 30.

[8] Thomas R. Dye and John W. Pickering, "Governmental and Corporate Elites: Convergence and Differentiation," *Journal of Politics* 36, no. 4 (November 1974): 900-925, esp. 911-912. See also Robert D. Putnam, *The Comparative Study of Political Elites* (Englewood Cliffs, N.J.: Prentice-Hall, 1976), p. 48.

Colombia, too, at least 14.1 percent of the cabinet ministers from 1900 to 1975 had gained prominence primarily as landowners, merchants, or businessmen, and many others—perhaps as many as 30 percent—had secondary occupations of this kind.[9] It is important, in this regard, to distinguish between three subtypes of recruitment: simultaneous interlocking, where people occupy positions of political and economic power at the same time; sequential interlocking, where they make a single move from one sphere to another; and repetitive interlocking, where they shuttle from corporate boardrooms to government offices and back again.[10]

3. The economic elite plays little or no visible role in the government, operating behind the scenes if at all, while the political elite willingly protects the interests of the wealthy. Miliband maintains that this affinity is due to social origin, since government leaders and top businessmen alike tend to come from upper- and middle-class backgrounds, and he supports his point with evidence from contemporary France, Britain, Germany, and elsewhere.[11] According to this view economic and political elites might even engage in conflict (as during the New Deal) but, because of common class interests, the conflict would always be kept within strict limits (as during the New Deal).

4. The political and economic elites are separate, in background and attitude, they have little interaction with each other, and they engage in genuine struggles for supremacy. This confrontation is most obviously found in revolutionary situations—Cuba, China, Russia—but it could also obtain, at least theoretically, in other instances. One key problem here concerns the measurement of conflict: how much is a lot? Miliband has argued that even when rival elites have *thought* they were locked in meaningful combat, as in France under the Popular Front (1936-37), they really were not, since there was no effective structural challenge to the existing socioeconomic order.[12] This all-or-nothing view of conflict seems a little simplified to me. Even within the confines of a capitalist society, it might well be possible for deep-seated struggles to take place between monied interests and the politicians, as exemplified, I think, by Argentina during the first Perón regime (1946-55).[13]

9 John I. Laun, "El reclutamiento político en Colombia: los ministros de estado, 1900-1975" (Bogota: Universidad Nacional de los Andes, 1976), p. 15 and Cuadro 22.

10 One could also distinguish between *horizontal* interlocking, in which individuals hold positions of equal importance in different spheres; and *vertical* interlocking, in which individuals hold high-level positions in one sphere and medium- or lower-level positions in the other one(s).

11 Miliband, *State*, pp. 59-65.   12 Ibid., pp. 102-106.

13 Smith, *Argentina*, esp. pp. 106-108.

What has been the case in Mexico? There is little doubt that the Mexican state has, over the years, encouraged, promoted, and defended the development of a capitalistic economy. Circumstantial evidence gives rise to a compelling syllogism: as shown in Chapter 2, national entrepreneurs have benefited from government policy; politicians have made government policy; *ergo*, politicians have been purposely serving the interests of the entrepreneurs. Political power goes hand in hand with economic power, and, as in option (2) above, Mexico remains under the firm control of a united, purposeful, exclusive power elite.

A forceful and articulate formulation of this idea has come from Alonso Aguilar, who, along with other contributors to *El milagro mexicano*, identifies the nation's ruling stratum as "the bourgeoisie." Neither homogeneous nor monolithic, this class has various components, mainly defined by control over means of production—landowners, merchants, industrialists, financiers, and, last but not least, politicians:

> . . . if one could speak of a bureaucratic or governmental bourgeoisie, it would contain the numerous current and former public functionaries who have made great fortunes through their offices (*a la sombra de sus puestos*) and who have sizable investments in farms and ranches, in urban real estate, in luxurious homes, in national and foreign banks and in businesses of the most varied kinds, but who are fundamentally considered to be politicians. To this sector would belong well-known ex-presidents of the Republic, prominent cabinet members, directors of national institutions and state-supported companies, high military officials, governors, deputies, senators, many municipal presidents and not a few labor leaders.[14]

Accounting for less than 2 percent of the economically active population, by Aguilar's estimation, the Mexican bourgeoisie constitutes "a well-defined class, which has grown out of a long historical process and which possesses an ever-clearer sense of its common interests." It is led, at the top, by *la verdadera oligarquía*, a close-knit group of uppermost leaders from each of the component sectors, perhaps a thousand families in all.[15] "The fundamental thing" about this group, continues Aguilar, "is not the tie to any particular activity, either by itself or in conjunction with others, but the close intercommunication, even the

[14] Alonso Aguilar M., "Problemas y perspectivas de un cambio radical," in Fernando Carmona et al., *El milagro mexicano* (Mexico: Editorial Nuestro Tiempo, 1970), p. 311.

[15] On this point see Alonso Aguilar M. and Fernando Carmona, *México: riqueza y miseria* (Mexico: Editorial Nuestro Tiempo, 1970), ch. 2, esp. pp. 66-80.

fusion of interests that exists among the upper strata of the bourgeoisie."[16]

But is this true? Does Mexico have a power elite? Here it is important to remember, and Aguilar would appear to agree, that a "power elite" is not just a minority of people who possess predominant shares of power. As C. Wright Mills defined the concept, referring to the United States of the mid-1950s: "By power elite, we refer to those political, economic, and military circles which *as an intricate set of overlapping cliques* share decisions having at least national consequences. In so far as national events are decided, the power elite are those who decide them" (emphasis added). It was the linkages between the political, economic, and military hierarchies that provided the basis for unified action, and the consequent existence of a monolithic elite, and these linkages took three fundamental forms. One was common social background: "In so far as the power elite is composed of men of similar origin and education," Mills wrote, "in so far as their careers and their styles of life are similar, there are psychological and social bases for their unity, resting upon the fact they are of similar social type and leading to the fact of their easy intermingling." A second linkage grew out of institutional connections, as men moved smoothly from one circle to another, articulating common points of interest and creating complex webs of interlocking directorates. Third, particularly in times of crisis, component segments of the power elite engaged in explicit coordination of various sorts.[17]

Given this framework, I shall here explore the linkages, real or imagined, between political and economic decisionmaking groups in Mexico. Specifically, in keeping with Mills's (and Aguilar's) formulation of the problem, I shall examine relationships between these sectors by focusing upon their *social background*, their *career patterns*, and their *modes of interaction*. For data on political leaders, I shall concentrate on the "postrevolutionary" cohort of 1946-71 (N = 2,008) and the "upper-level" officeholders of that era (N = 159). For data on the economic elite I shall rely largely, almost exclusively, on Flavia DeRossi's study of *The Mexican Entrepreneur*. One drawback of the DeRossi book is that it deals with a sample (N = 143) of leaders in

---

[16] Aguilar, "Problemas y perspectivas," *El milagro mexicano*, pp. 312, 315. For another comment on the existence of a power elite see Robert E. Scott, "Mexico: The Established Revolution," in *Political Culture and Political Development*, ed. Lucian W. Pye and Sidney Verba (Princeton: Princeton University Press, 1965), pp. 377-384 and esp. p. 380.

[17] Mills, *Power Elite*, pp. 18-20. Aguilar does not make explicit reference to *The Power Elite*, but his depiction of Mexico's ruling class has a definite Millsian ring (note, for instance, the phraseology on p. 315 of the essay on "Problemas y perspectivas").

the *industrial* sector in the late 1960s, and touches only in passing on bankers, merchants, and other economic groups.[18] Nevertheless, it is the manufacturing sector which, among privately dominated areas of the economy, has grown most rapidly since the 1940s, as revealed above in Chapter 2, and it is this sector which would therefore seem to have gained the most from government policy. If there has been collusion between the state and private capital, it ought to show up first—and most strikingly—as collusion between the politicians and the industrialists.

The limitations of this analysis should be self-evident. Unlike Mills, I shall omit explicit consideration of the Mexican military. I shall also leave out foreign investors, despite their great importance, since my primary concern lies with the structure of power within *Mexican* society.[19] I shall concentrate exclusively on the national level, and my approach is, of necessity, static rather than dynamic. Aside from weaknesses in data, there are also conceptual and methodological problems in the Mills approach.[20] This is a difficult task, and my findings must be regarded as tentative.

Social Background

As indicated above, one of the central characteristics of a power elite is common social origin. The question seems deceptively simple: Do

[18] Flavia DeRossi, *The Mexican Entrepreneur* (Paris: OECD, 1971). DeRossi interviewed a stratified random sample (N = 143) of owners or general managers of private Mexican industrial firms with at least 5 million pesos capital as of 1965 in four regions: the Distrito Federal and state of Mexico, Nuevo León, Jalisco, and Puebla. It is not quite clear what was the scope of her total target population: owners and/or general managers of the 662 such firms in all of Mexico, owners and/or general managers of the firms of that size in the four particular regions, or "important industrialists" in general. By contrast, my political elites are not samples—except for missing data they represent total populations in themselves. Note that the total elite (N = 2,008) embraces a group that might be roughly similar in size to DeRossi's target population (whatever that might be); and the upper-level elite (N = 159) is nearly the same size as the sample which she interviewed. One way or another, I hope that the comparisons are satisfactory. (Note, incidentally, the similarity between my political elite and the officeholders mentioned by Aguilar "Problemas," p. 311.)

[19] It is not uncommon, however, for Mexicans to function in behalf of foreign interests (as, for instance, *prestanombres*). To this extent international forces, both private and governmental, have gained indirect representation within Mexican society, and it is accordingly impossible to exclude foreign influence completely from any rigorous conceptual consideration of the country's social structure. See also the excellent essay by Richard S. Weinert, "The State and Foreign Capital," in *Authoritarianism in Mexico*, ed. Reyna and Weinert, pp. 109-128.

[20] For ample presentation of these matters see G. William Domhoff and Hoyt B. Ballard, eds., *C. Wright Mills and the Power Elite* (Boston: Beacon Press, 1968).

politicians and industrialists in contemporary Mexico come from the same sort of background? Would they be likely to have, in Mills's phrase, "psychological and social bases for their unity"? Or do they represent divergent social types?

It appears, in this regard, that Mexico's industrialists and politicians differ in basic respects. According to DeRossi, about 20 percent of the entrepreneurs were foreign-born. Considering the birthplace of parents and grandparents, too, it appears that 44 percent of the industrialists were of foreign origin, and to this extent they were newcomers (or outsiders) to Mexican society.[21] In sharp contrast, and partly owing to legal restrictions on officeholding, governmental leaders were overwhelmingly native-born, with well under 1 percent of either political elite having been born abroad. I do not have solid data on the birthplaces of their fathers or grandfathers, but my impression is that Mexico's political decisionmakers have tended to come from native stock.

The fathers of entrepreneurs and politicians also differed in their occupations. Table 7-1 displays the DeRossi findings plus my own effort to arrange available data in a comparable way.[22] DeRossi's categories might seem questionable, especially insofar as they distinguish between the middle and the upper class, but the value of the table does not hinge entirely upon the precision of the groupings.

The implications are profound. For one thing, it is clear that neither industrialists nor political leaders came in substantial measure from the lower class. Though a fair share (24 percent) of the total officeholding elite came from lower-class backgrounds, *none* of the upper-level politicians had fathers in such occupations, and the same is true for the industrialists. For people starting at the bottom of the social ladder, upward mobility has been almost as hard to attain through politics as through business.[23]

At the same time, it is equally clear that industrialists and politicians came from separate strata. According to DeRossi's scheme, 54 percent of the entrepreneurs were from the upper class, while the political elites were predominantly middle class in origin (64 percent for the total group, 82 percent from the top-level group). Even more revealing

[21] DeRossi, *Entrepreneur*, pp. 143-144. For supplementary evidence see Raymond Vernon, *The Dilemma of Mexico's Development: The Roles of the Private and Public Sectors* (Cambridge: Harvard University Press, 1963), p. 156.

[22] As the table indicates, data are available for only small fractions of the political elites, and I have no way of knowing whether the distribution of existing vs. missing data follows any underlying pattern. Accordingly I cannot say whether the politicians for whom we have data on father's occupation constitute genuinely random samples of the total (target) populations.

[23] On entrepreneurs see also the data in Vernon, *Dilemma*, p. 157.

TABLE 7-1

Father's Occupation for Entrepreneurs and Politicians

		Politicians	
Occupation[a]	Entrepreneurs (N = 139)[b]	Total Elite (N = 192)	Upper-Level Elite (N = 33)
Upper Class:			
Industrialist	60	2	1
Banker	3	1	0
Rentier	3	1	0
Landowner	9	17	4
Other	0	2	1
Subtotal	75 (54%)	23 (12%)	6 (18%)
Middle Class:			
Merchant	33	8	4
Employee	18	5	1
Civil Servant		5	2
Professional	13	47	10
Military	0	16	2
Politician	0	25	3
Other	0	17	5
Subtotal	64 (46%)	123 (64%)	27 (82%)
Lower Class:			
Worker	0	7	0
Peasant	0	22	0
Other	0	17	0
Subtotal	0 (0%)	46 (24%)	0 (0%)
Totals	139 (100%)	192 (100%)	33 (100%)

[a] Categorizations and class groupings based on DeRossi, *Entrepreneur*, p. 160.
[b] Raw figures computed from percentage data in DeRossi, ibid.

are the specific kinds of fathers' occupations. Nearly half the industrialists (46 percent) had fathers who were industrialists. Another sizable share (24 percent) had merchant origins. Just about one-half of the governmental officeholders, for their part, came from backgrounds in the professions, civil service, politics, or the military—occupations that brought their fathers into, or at least close to, the political arena. To a considerable extent, therefore, both the economic and political elites have tended to pursue the same sorts of occupations their fathers had. This does not necessarily attest to the existence of family dynasties (though there have surely been some). What it does show is that, with respect to occupation, economic and political leaders have emerged from distinctly separate and partly self-perpetuating social backgrounds.

In some other respects, however, the two groups had similar backgrounds. Both came from urban areas. According to DeRossi, 69 percent of the industrialists were born in cities.[24] Though my data have been compiled in a different manner, it is clear that national political leaders were overwhelmingly of urban origin: nearly half (45.8 percent) of the total elite came from relatively major cities, very often the state capitals, while three-fifths of the upper-level group came from sizable cities (see Table 3-3 above). In short, Mexico's entrepreneurs and officeholders both shared the manifold advantages of urban life, one of which is access to education.

Presumably in cumulative fashion, the middle-to-upper class backgrounds and urban life styles of the two elites combined to produce similar educational profiles. According to Table 7-2, both the entrepreneurs and the politicians achieved extremely high levels of education, 68 percent of the industrialists having gone to a university, compared to 73 percent of the total officeholding elite and 87 percent of the upper-level elite. Parenthetically, the data contain some further implications—suggesting, for instance, that a university experience is a more stringent requirement for political success than for economic attainment—but the basic message is uniquivocal. In a society where less than 3 percent of the literate adult male population had attended a university (as of 1960), the industrialists and the politicians both

TABLE 7-2

Educational Background of Entrepreneurs and Politicians

Level of Education	% among Entrepreneurs (N = 143)[a]	% among Politicians	
		Total Elite (N = 1,371)	Upper-Level Elite (N = 151)
Primary or less	2	6	0
Secondary	13	3	3
Higher	17	18	11
University	68	73	87
Totals	100	100	101[b]

[a] DeRossi, *Entrepreneur*, p. 164n.
[b] Percentage details do not add up to 100 because of rounding.

[24] DeRossi, *Entrepreneur*, pp. 164-165. DeRossi defined urban communities as those with 2,000 or more inhabitants, presumably as of 1960. (See also Vernon, *Dilemma*, p. 157.)

tended to come from the uppermost stratum of advantage. To the extent that educational opportunity reflects "class" status, that is, the distribution of "life chances," then it must be concluded, as Aguilar maintains, that Mexico's economic and political elites have grown out of a single and highly privileged class.

But this does not necessarily mean that they went to school together, or that they forged lifelong ties of friendship while at university. Impressionistic evidence suggests that many of the industrialists attended technical universities, such as the Instituto Politécnico Nacional in Mexico City or the Instituto Tecnológico de Monterrey. The politicians, as we have already seen, showed a strong tendency to cluster together at the UNAM. And even if budding entrepreneurs and future officeholders attended the same institution, their paths may still not have crossed. Among the university-educated industrialists in the De-Rossi sample, 75 percent had "technical" training, 12 percent had studied the "humanities," and 13 percent had majored in "business."[25] Since the distinction between technical and humanistic subjects is not spelled out, I cannot order my data in strictly comparative fashion, but my information demonstrates that political cadres tended to specialize in selected fields: the *políticos* had studied law (by far the most common), engineering, medicine, and education; almost by definition, the *técnicos* had gone to schools of economics (which is to be distinguished from business or accounting). The material implies that the economic and political elites tended to concentrate in different faculties, even when at the same university, and the chances for forming friendships—or what Mills would call the "psychological and social bases for their unity"—would thereby be diminished.

This point finds further reinforcement in the occupational patterns followed by the politicians (aside from the pursuit of governmental office). Table 7-3 yields two suggestive findings: first, that politicians engaged heavily in the professions (as doctors, teachers, journalists, and especially as lawyers), and second, that they did not, as a rule, join the "ownership" stratum of Mexican society.[26] Though many officeholders made (or took) small fortunes during their incumbencies, made significant investments, and frequently acquired substantial amounts of wealth, they did not become participating members of the genuinely upper economic circles. It is my impression that, when they invest, pol-

[25] DeRossi, *Entrepreneur*, p. 164n.

[26] Occupational data are rough and sometimes contradictory. For Table 7-3 the strata were ranked from low to high, from "worker or peasant" to "owner," and individuals with separate occupations in different strata were placed in the highest stratum attained.

iticians tend to deal in certain sorts of activities—such as real estate, communications, or construction, rather than manufacturing or commerce—and that they operate within implicit boundaries. Perhaps for this reason the capital accumulations of politicians, contrary to gossip and widespread assumption, are not, as Aguilar points out, among the largest ones in Mexico. And the ones that are—such as those of Miguel Alemán (real estate, television), Aarón Sáenz (sugar, banking), and Nazario Ortiz Garza (grapes, wine)—are conspicuous precisely because of their scarcity.[27]

TABLE 7-3

Highest Occupational Stratum Achieved by Politicians

Occupational Stratum	% for Total Elite (N = 1,429)	% for Upper-Level Elite (N = 153)
Worker or Peasant	6	less than 1
Employee	4	less than 1
Professional	84	91
Owner	6	8
Totals	100	100

In summary, the data on social background produce paradoxical results. On the one hand, it appears that Mexico's economic and political elites have emerged from a common class background—with middle-to-upper-class fathers, urban life styles, and exceptional educational privilege. On the other hand, they have also differed—in their national origins, in the specific occupations of their fathers, in the subjects they studied and the occupations they pursued. Following the De-Rossi notion of class (reflected in Table 7-1), one might conclude that industrialists came from upper-class backgrounds and politicians from middle-class backgrounds. Adopting a somewhat broader view of class, placing the upper and middle strata together in a common category, one might alternatively conclude that *entrepreneurs and officeholders emerged from a single class, but from demonstrably different segments of that class.* Either way, the basic inference remains: the starting points for the two groups were not the same.[28]

[27] Aguilar and Carmona, *México: riqueza y miseria*, pp. 67-70, 79.

[28] For additional observations on this point see Roger D. Hansen, *The Politics of Mexican Development* (Baltimore: Johns Hopkins University Press, 1971), ch. 5, esp. pp. 97-98

CAREER PATTERNS

The hallmark of the industrialists' careers in Mexico has been consistency. As already noted, especially in Table 7-1, entrepreneurs tended to follow occupational patterns established by their fathers. Perhaps reflecting the achievements of their parents, who might have provided necessary start-up capital, more than a third of the industrialists in the DeRossi sample (34 percent) went directly into business without acquiring any prior job experience. This pattern was more apparent among those of urban origin than among the rural group, whose fathers and grandfathers were often engaged in agriculture, but it still represents a substantial portion of the total sample.[29]

Of the two-thirds that acquired prior experience, most took jobs in private Mexican-owned industry (43 percent of the entire sample). Some worked for foreign-owned firms, either in Mexico or abroad (14 percent combined). Others started out as self-employed professionals (7 percent), and some engaged in commerce. Only a tiny portion (1 percent) gained experience in the semipublic sector—a figure suggesting that, contrary to my own expectation, state-supported companies have not provided an arena for steady interaction between entrepreneurs and politicians.[30]

It thus appears that most aspiring young businessmen set out in determined pursuit of particular skills, either technical or organizational. The apprenticeship could take quite a long time, often more than 10 years, but by the end of this period the great majority had performed important leadership functions. DeRossi cites some illustrative cases of deviations from the norm—such as the highly trained electronic technician who went into the cosmetics industry for a fortuitous reason (he married the boss's daughter!)—but the general rule still holds: these men began as entrepreneurs, they worked as entrepreneurs, and they achieved as entrepreneurs.[31]

One thing they have *not* done frequently has been to take overt part in politics. Among the DeRossi group only 12 percent actively participated in political organizations of one sort or another (she does not say which ones).[32] Though precise figures are unavailable, there can be little doubt that an even smaller proportion of the country's leading businessmen acquired governmental office. This says absolutely nothing about the kinds of interaction that might have taken place

[29] DeRossi, *Entrepreneur*, p. 165. Note also the prevalence of family control of enterprises (pp. 101-102, and, more generally, pt. I, ch. III).

[30] Ibid., p. 165.　　　　　　　　　　　[31] Ibid., pp. 165-166.

[32] Ibid., pp. 187-188.

between the entrepreneurial and political spheres, a theme that I will take up further below, and it begs a host of questions about alternative forms of political participation. Nonetheless, it does indicate that there has been very little positional crossover from business careers to political ones—in contrast with the United States, where lateral entry into politics has been fairly commonplace.

The careers of Mexican politicians have been similar in ways to those of the entrepreneurs. Like their industrial counterparts, would-be officeholders started pursuing their goals shortly after finishing their education (and some began while still in school). Within the entire 1946-71 political elite, for example, over 50 percent are known to have started taking active part in politics before the age of 30, most frequently in their late twenties. Again reflecting the small degree of lateral entry, less than 10 percent of the group entered formal politics beyond the age of 50, and many of these were labor union activists whose roles had long been quasi-political. Though aspiring politicians often began in other occupations, or engaged in professional practice (such as law) even while holding office, a basic dictum has nevertheless been apparent: those who get ahead start young.

Political careers in Mexico have been extremely intense. The norm has been for people, once started in government, to hold between 4 and 8 positions, frequently 10 to 15, usually in rapid-fire succession. As I have argued in Chapter 5, these posts have often been unrelated to each other. True, there have existed three discernible institutional grooves or "tracks": the executive track, linking the federal bureaucracy to the cabinet; the administrative track, encompassing the semipublic sector; and the electoral track, tying the official party to legislative and other elected positions. Individuals moving along one of these institutional routes would seem, like the budding industrialists, to have acquired specific, task-related skills in a cumulative fashion. Nevertheless, the majority of job changes have not taken place within the tracks (see Table 5-5). From almost any location in the political system, an ambitious officeholder could entertain at least some hope of moving to almost any other location. Diversity and breadth of exposure, rather than concentrated apprenticeship, have set the predominant pattern.

Just as political careers have started early, they have also tended to end speedily. For a variety of reasons, including the principle of "no-reelection," turnover in office has been extraordinarily rapid. Once a person reaches national office under one president, as seen in Chapter 6, his chance of holding a comparable position under another president has been just over one in three. A large-scale change in personnel has taken place with every sexennial change in the presidency, and those who disappear from the national scene rarely return at subsequent times.

Consequently, most Mexican politicians have left their last major national office while still fairly young—on the average, around the age of 57. To state the point another way: nearly 25 percent in the total 1946-71 elite left their last office before the age of 50, over 34 percent did so while in their fifties, and the rest (a minority of about 40 percent) did so at a later age. For most officeholders, the likelihood of such a relatively youthful exit has no doubt offered profound implications—making it both desirable and reasonable, for instance, to accumulate as much wealth as possible before one's tenure is up.

But the age of exit raises another critical question: What have the politicians done afterward? Unfortunately, I do not have any solid data on this matter. It appears, impressionistically, that many of them have set up private professional practices, most commonly in law. Some have moved into private industry, but in restricted ways, usually in fields, such as construction, where they can make use of their political contacts. Others have obtained minor but useful jobs as "advisers" to friends still holding political office. At any rate, it does not appear that ex-politicians have crossed over into industrial positions any more than industrialists have gained lateral entry into politics. Skills for the two careers have rarely been viewed as interchangeable, and the "intermingling" between the groups, in Mills' sense, would be accordingly reduced. Yet it is still plausible to suppose that ex-politicians have often served as functional *intermediaries* between the private sector and the state. That is a topic for further research.[33]

There is reason to suspect that, among officeholders in the public sector, *técnicos* have had greater opportunities for crossing over to the private sector than have the *políticos*. Government officials have often held multiple jobs, with economic specialists frequently sitting on the boards of state-supported companies and other corporations, and in return they have received handsome fees. By relaying tips on policy to private companies, some decisionmakers have no doubt used public knowledge for private gain. And as almost all observers have stressed, bribery—of both *políticos* and *técnicos*—appears to have been widespread. Such ties between public officials and private interests have been, in Raymond Vernon's view, "part and parcel of Mexican life. . . . Any major shift in the existing relations between the private and the public sectors could well disturb the characteristically profitable ties which key public officials have managed to develop with the private

[33] See also the comments in Hansen, *Politics*, pp. 124-129.

sector." The situation, he concludes, offers little incentive for a radical reorientation of governmental economic policy.[34] Within this context, though, the question remains: What has been the nature of relationships between officials and businessmen in Mexico?

MODES OF INTERACTION

One of the central postulates in the Mills formulation was that, in times of crisis, component segments of the power elite would act in conscious and explicit coordination. Yet it was precisely on this point that his analysis was weakest. As Robert Dahl insisted, Mills never explored the decisionmaking process during any crisis, so there is no demonstrable evidence of any such coordination.[35] Referring loosely to the "big decisions" of the 1940s and '50s, Mills mentioned the dropping of the A-bomb on Japan, the reaction to Korea, the ultimately fateful response to Dienbienphu—issues involving foreign policy, it should be noted, usually decided by the president and his close advisers.[36] To explore actual linkages between public officeholders and private investors in Mexico, therefore, we cannot rest content with information on social background and careers. Even if the leaders of the sectors are distinct in these respects, as the data so far show, they might still have acted in collaboration.

Since the mid-1940s, in fact, Mexican entrepreneurs and politicians seem to have agreed on at least two basic guidelines for governmental economic policy. One has held that the state should permit the entry of desirable foreign capital but at the same time protect national industry from excessive international competition, principally through import controls and regulations on foreign investment.[37] The other guideline has assigned to the state the role of controlling and, when necessary, repressing the masses: the workers, the peasants, and the poor. Together, these policy orientations have furnished a reasonably coherent and workable prescription for maintaining the country's capitalist system.

Within this general consensus, however, specific measures have prompted frequent and substantial disagreement. In the first place, the government has taken steps of its own design that have met with wide-

---

[34] Vernon, *Dilemma*, p. 153.

[35] Robert A. Dahl, "A Critique of the Ruling Elite Model," republished in *C. Wright Mills*, ed. Domhoff and Ballard, pp. 25-36.

[36] Mills, *Power Elite*, p. 22.

[37] Whether the limitations on foreign enterprise have been sufficient or successful is, of course, a separate question. For a positive assessment see Weinert, "The State and Foreign Capital."

spread opposition from the business community, some of whose members hold profound laissez-faire convictions.[38] Second, and probably more important, the entrepreneurial sector has been far from monolithic—what is good for industrialist A has not always been good for industrialist B (tariff protection for A, for instance, could increase production costs for B). In illustration of these points, respondents in the DeRossi sample came up with the results in Table 7-4 when asked for their opinions of governmental policies. Clearly, industrialists have often been at odds with the state (though not so much regarding labor policy); almost as frequently, they have been at odds with themselves. Regrettably, DeRossi did not explore the relationships between responses, so we cannot tell if individual businessmen tended to support or oppose the government across the board, or hold selective opinions on specific issue-areas; we do not know how they viewed the policies most directly related to their own companies; nor can we judge the intensity of the responses. Despite these shortcomings, the message still seems unambiguous: there has been considerable conflict between the private and the public sectors.

TABLE 7-4

Entrepreneurs' Evaluations of Government Economic Policies

Policy	Evaluation (by %; N = 143)			
	Favorable	Neutral	Unfavorable	Total
Credit	46	23	31	100%
Fiscal	40	24	36	100
Pricing of finished products	33	36	31	100
Pricing of raw material	19	27	54	100
Import	27	33	40	100
Customs Duties	20	30	50	100
Export	25	45	30	100
Labor	41	35	24	100

SOURCE: DeRossi, *Entrepreneur*, p. 61.

From the entrepreneurs' point of view, cases of disagreement have been exacerbated by the temporary and discretionary quality of governmental decisions. Once given, permits and licenses can always be

---

[38] See Robert J. Shafer, *Mexican Business Organizations: History and Analysis* (Syracuse, N.Y.: Syracuse University Press, 1973), ch. IV; and Merle Kling, *A Mexican Interest Group in Action* (Englewood Cliffs, N.J.: Prentice-Hall, 1961), ch. VII.

revoked, a situation that has made private investors dependent on the state. As an example, listen to the complaint of this entrepreneur:

> The price of containers, both metal and cardboard, is excessive in Mexico. In Mexico metal containers for food cost approximately double their price in America. *At one stage I was allowed to import cans in bond but the permit was not renewed* and I had to fall back on the high-priced domestic article. . . . Were the government to allow the import of Japanese sheeting the price of cans would be halved. (Emphasis added.)[39]

Such disputes have often centered on the implementation of existing law, rather than on the formulation of new laws, and the state relies upon its regulations as a source of strength. "The important point," as Raymond Vernon said some years ago, "is that the private sector operates in a milieu in which the public sector is in a position to make or break any firm."[40] In order to defend themselves industrialists have engaged in various maneuvers, including bribery, to influence the judgment of the bureaucrats and politicians.

Combined with the data in Table 7-4, the discretionary aspect of decisionmaking implies a shifting pattern of conflicts and alliances. To present a simplified picture of the situation, Figure 7-1 depicts four possible patterns of alignment between four sets of actors: two groups within the public sector, $Public_1$ and $Public_2$, which could represent any conceivable pair (*políticos* and *técnicos*, the central bank and the treasury, Nacional Financiera and PEMEX, etc.); and two groups within the private sector, equally undefined as $Private_1$ and $Private_2$ (importers and exporters, bankers and realtors, etc.). The solid lines in the diagrams indicate lines of conflict, the connecting arrows represent alliances.

Pattern A arrays both public groups against both private groups in a total confrontation between the state and business. This situation has no doubt occurred but, given the fragmentation of entrepreneurial responses in Table 7-4 (and well-known rivalries between some government agencies), it surely has not happened all the time. Pattern B, on the other hand, allows for these divisions, with $Public_1$ and $Private_1$ joined against $Public_2$ and $Private_2$. Pattern C extends the range of possibilities by portraying a war of all-against-all, with no alliances of any sort; this may well occur at the early stages of any given decision, but the ingrown preferences for accommodation (plus, again, the data in Table 7-4) suggest that this would be a transient phase. Finally,

[39] DeRossi, *Entrepreneur*, p. 61.
[40] Vernon, *Dilemma*, p. 26.

Figure 7-1: Hypothetical Patterns of Public-Private Conflict

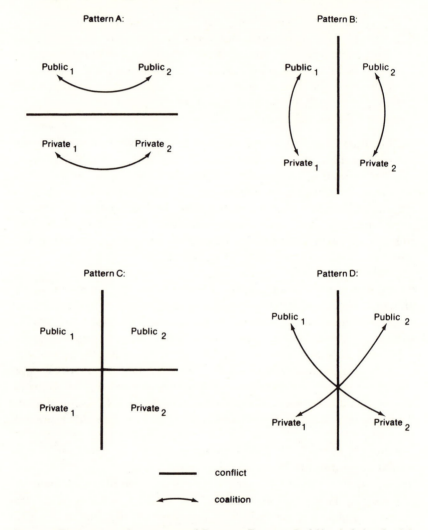

Pattern D presents the reverse of Pattern B: now Public$_1$ is joined with Private$_2$, and Public$_2$ is linked with Private$_1$.

My guess would be that all of these patterns occur. If so, the next step is to determine which alignments take place when, and under what conditions, but that is a matter for further research. (The presence of foreign capital adds another dimension to this situation, opening up the possibility of triangular struggles and complex coalitions—

IS THERE A POWER ELITE?

which seem in fact to emerge.[41]) For the moment, it appears that economic elites participate in the Mexican process of "limited pluralism" as political outsiders, not as insiders; that they often find themselves in conflict with political elites; and that, in advancement of their interests, they engage in fluid alliances of temporary duration.[42]

These multiple interactions between entrepreneurs and officeholders are further conditioned by the rapid and periodic rotation of political personnel. For one thing, the high rate of turnover has increased the element of risk for industrialists. To the extent that their investments depend on some sort of permit, or on a transient alliance, they accept the chance that the future holder of the relevant office might or might not extend the particular license (or the coalition). In order to forestall any unfavorable change, therefore, the logical strategy for entrepreneurs would be to identify, and curry the favor of, the up-and-coming politicians—as well as the current incumbents. This kind of activity demands skill, tact, and usually some inside information. It is an area where ex-politicians could play important roles as go-betweens.

Paradoxically, turnover in politics would also appear to give the industrialists a significant advantage in some situations. Because the personnel in upper-level private industry is (or seems to be) stable,[43] it has been possible for entrepreneurs to develop relatively coherent demands, to unify their forces, to muster appropriate technical documentation, and to maintain steady pursuit of incremental concessions and gains. Politicians, by contrast, because they change office so frequently, have often found it difficult to accumulate comparable amounts of expertise, though this problem has been less acute for highly trained *técnicos* than for others. Even more important is the fact that each new set of officeholders must strike its own bargain with the entrepreneurs. If the politicians appear to be favorably disposed toward business, private-sector leaders can seize the opportunity to form an alliance, step up their demands and seek ever-greater concessions. But if the predisposition of the politicians appears to be unfavorable, private-sector

[41] Weinert, "The State and Foreign Capital."

[42] See also Robert T. Aubey, *Nacional Financiera and Mexican Industry: A Study of the Financial Relationships between the Government and the Private Sector of Mexico* (Los Angeles: UCLA Latin American Center, Latin American Studies, vol. 3, 1966), pp. 76-78.

[43] Susan Kaufman Purcell has found fairly high rates of turnover among leaders of CONCAMIN, but it is not clear what effect this has on the organization's policy. In any case, I would guess that the leadership of individual *firms* is very stable indeed. Purcell, *The Mexican Profit-Sharing Decision: Politics in an Authoritarian Regime* (Berkeley and Los Angeles: University of California Press, 1975), p. 29.

leaders have the option of refusing to negotiate and waiting out the difficulty; at least within the short run, time is on their side. This kind of advantage, strategic as it may be, probably pertains only to specific issue-areas that (a) have low public visibility and (b) involve cohesive segments of the entrepreneurial sector. On broad questions of governmental policy, as shown in Table 7-4, the private sector can suffer internal division, thus affording politicians the chance to play businessmen off against each other.

Given the importance of individual discretion in government policy-making, it is revealing, and somewhat surprising, that industrialists have tended to seek redress for grievances largely through institutional means. According to Table 7-5, fully one-half of the respondents in the DeRossi sample said they would seek to counteract unfavorable policies through formal industrial associations (CONCAMIN, COPARMEX, CANACINTRA, etc.). A fairly small minority (12 percent), apparently disaffected, felt that no meaningful action would be possible. About one-quarter, 23 percent to be exact, would rely on an informal pressure group. Only 15 percent thought that individual action might be useful.

TABLE 7-5

Modes of Action to Counteract Unfavorable Government Policies, as Perceived by Entrepreneurs

Mode	% of Responses (N = 136)
No action possible	12
Action possible	
on individual basis	15
Through informal	
pressure group	23
Through industrial	
associations	50
Total	100

SOURCE: DeRossi, *Entrepreneur*, p. 40n.

To an extent the tendency to rely on associations is entirely rational. Regulated by national law, Mexico's business organizations have considerable resources at their disposal. Membership in one or another of the key associations is obligatory (there are in addition voluntary groupings). Partly as a result of this requirement, the national peak organizations have solid financial resources with which they can maintain a paid staff. Their leaders maintain informal contact among themselves, and sometimes act in coordination. Moreover, representatives of these associations often sit on government boards, they consult with political leaders, and they have developed varied channels of communication with policymaking officials.[44]

Even so, the responses to the DeRossi survey convey two further messages. One is the assumption, based on the numbers in Table 7-4 and diagrams in Figure 7-1, that relationships with political decisionmakers could often be of an adversary character. Another is the entrepreneurs' sense of social distance from the politicians. A combined total of 62 percent of the respondents thought effective action was either impossible or attainable solely through a formal institution. Only 38 percent believed that informal approaches would work, mostly through a collective pressure group, and informality, it should be noted, does not always bespeak harmony: bribery is needed primarily to soften discord. Though a great majority of entrepreneurs (88 percent) expressed feelings of efficacy in dealing with the politicians, they would mostly do so on an adversary basis.[45] The evidence does not present a picture of relaxed and intimate chats among old boyhood chums.

In further testimony to the social distance between the two elites, Mexico's entrepreneurs appear to have an extremely low opinion of political officials. One item in the DeRossi survey solicited views on the relative prestige of various occupational groups. The respondents displayed considerable esteem for bankers, industrialists (that is, themselves!), and intellectuals and professionals, in that order. Only 9 percent rated politicians and public officials as commanding the highest prestige, and 34 percent ranked government officeholders as the group of lowest prestige. (See Table 7-6 for a full summary of the data.) Attitudes of this sort would hardly seem consistent with the easygoing, familiar intermingling of decisionmaking cliques that C. Wright Mills detected within the North American power elite.

Unfortunately, I do not know of any solid data on the politicians' perceptions of Mexican entrepreneurs. Quite clearly, government pol-

---

[44] Shafer, *Organizations*, esp. ch. v. It would seem especially sensible for entrepreneurs located at considerable distance from the Federal District to rely on the interest-group organizations. Unfortunately DeRossi has not partitioned responses on modes of countering policy according to region, so we cannot explore this point here.

[45] Shafer, *Organizations*, ch. v. Note also that while Kling asserts that his conservative-minded businessmen had "ready access to key government officials," his evidence actually reveals that members of the Instituto de Investigaciones Sociales y Económicas attended political and governmental functions in rather formal capacities. Kling, *Interest Group*, pp. 41-43 and 66.

TABLE 7-6

Ranking of Prestige Groups by Entrepreneurs

Group	% Rankings of Highest Prestige (N responses = 136)	% Rankings of Lowest Prestige (N responses = 129)
Bankers	42	2
Industrialists	26	1
Intellectuals and professionals	18	7
Politicians and public officials	9	34
Priests	4	7
Army generals	1	20
Landowners	0	8
Union leaders	0	18
Merchants	0	3
Totals	100	100

SOURCE: DeRossi, *Entrepreneur*, pp. 182, 186.

icymakers have regarded a vital private sector as essential to national economic growth and as a bulwark against excessive inroads by foreign oligopoly interests. And yet the terms of this collaboration with the business community—what Clark Reynolds has called an "alliance for profits"[46]—seem to reflect suspicion. Making exhortation sound like accusations (or vice versa), presidential speeches and official pronouncements have often urged Mexican capitalists to act for the national good instead of for private gain (the latter being the presumption).[47] Vernon reported, in the early 1960s, a generalized picture of businessmen as "ruthless, money-grubbing opportunists, utterly devoid of social consciousness, without culture or refinement, imitating the worst in North American society, extravagant without limit." Even the *técnicos*, committed to mixed-economy growth and presumably friendly to the private sector, tended to view businessmen as narrow-minded, unskilled, and, above all, untrained.[48]

Impressionistic evidence further suggests that the separation of eco-

[46] Clark W. Reynolds, *The Mexican Economy: Twentieth-Century Structure and Growth* (New Haven: Yale University Press, 1970), pp. 185-191.

[47] See, for example, the declaration by Secretary of the Treasury Mario Ramón Beteta in *Excélsior*, 11 March 1976.

[48] Vernon, *Dilemma*, pp. 157, 147. For one illustration of a politician's resentment of the private sector see Braulio Maldonado, *Baja California: comentarios políticos*, 3rd ed. (Mexico: Costa-Amic, 1960), pp. 36 and 55-57.

nomic and political elites extends to their private lives as well. Well-informed Mexicans have repeatedly told me that there is relatively little intermarriage between the two sectors: economic and political leaders do not, as a rule, strike alliances through the matching of their daughters and sons. Nor does it appear that individual families become engaged in both business and politics, with one son becoming a governor, for instance, and another running a top corporation. (It *is* likely that the governor's brother would deal in some lucrative business, but not, once again, within the uppermost reaches of the private sector.) Needless to say, the social and political functions of family and kinship in Mexico comprise yet another subject for future research.

Despite their agreement on certain issues, their unquestioned need for each other, and their common commitment to a capitalistic pattern of growth, it thus appears that entrepreneurs and politicians interact within an atmosphere of uncertainty, distrust, suspicion, and even disdain. They are locked in a struggle for supremacy. The industrialists have been seeking to expand their profits, accumulate capital, and keep governmental regulation to a necessary (albeit critical) minimum. The politicians, for their part, have been attempting to gain and assert their control of the entrepreneurial sector. Toward this end they have established (and regulated) the business associations, they have set up an impressive array of licensing arrangements—and, symbolically enough, they have kept big business out of the PRI, thus maintaining the ability to apply autonomous pressure against the industrial community.[49]

In summary, relations between entrepreneurs and politicians have rested upon three tacit premises: (1) the popular masses, especially labor, should be kept under control; (2) the public and private sectors must often act in explicit coordination; and given these conditions, (3) entrepreneurs and politicians can still compete for relative superiority. These triple assumptions, paradoxically related to each other, find expression in mutliple ways, one of the best-known instances being the profit-sharing decision of 1961-63. In belated fulfillment of a key clause in the 1917 Constitution, this law seemed on face value to constitute a major victory for labor, since workers would henceforth share in the profits of the company owners. The amount of profits to be shared was so small as to be acceptable to employers, however, and the law was never strictly enforced. So labor had a paper triumph and business had successfully defended its own interests. By proposing the legislation without consulting business leaders, however, the politicians displayed their willingness and ability to take autonomous ac-

---

[49] Shafer, *Organizations*, p. 135.

tion. And by getting the law on the books, the politicians acquired another weapon with which they could, in the future, threaten or challenge private capital.[50] A subtle game, this.

CONCLUSION

Much of the contact between economic and political elites in Mexico remains invisible, at least to scholarly eyes, so it is impossible to draw any firm conclusions about the hypothetical existence of interlocking directorates. The subject stands in need of research, and we need solid information on specific types of elite relationships: socialization patterns, informal associations, kinship networks, decisionmaking processes. Within the limits of available data, however, we can still focus on the question: Does Mexico have a power elite?

The answer appears to be no. This does not mean that Mexico is an egalitarian society. To the contrary, the data on father's occupation (Table 7-1) indicate that people of lower-class origin have virtually no chance of gaining access to the upper circles of influence and authority. Moreover, as shown in Table 7-2, university training constitutes a near-requisite for entering either the economic or political elite, with the result that power is restricted to a tiny fraction of the population. Despite the rhetorical legacy of the Revolution, Mexico remains under the effective control of a small and classbound minority.

Yet a defining characteristic of the power elite, as Mills used the term, was the existence of *overlapping cliques* that, by virtue of their common origin and training, intermingled with each other. This does not seem to hold true for entrepreneurs and politicians in Mexico. Members of the two elites came from separate segments of the upper-plus-middle class, if not from separate classes, as suggested by the data on father's occupation and also by the prevalence of foreign origins among the industrial group. They went to different schools, even while reaching comparable levels of educational achievement. They started their respective careers at relatively early ages, and, once started, they tended to concentrate exclusively upon their separate arenas. Entrepreneurs hardly ever moved into politics and, to the best of our knowledge, governmental officeholders (with the possible exception of some *técnicos*) did not cross over into private industry (Table 7-3) before retiring from politics—if even then. Throughout their dealings with

[50] See Susan Kaufman Purcell, "Decision-Making in an Authoritarian Regime: Theoretical Implications from a Mexican Case Study," *World Politics* 26, no. 1 (October 1973), 28-54; Purcell, *Mexican Profit-Sharing Decision*; and Shafer, *Organizations*, pp. 167-168.

each other, often marked by conflict (Table 7-4), the industrialists and politicians seem to have maintained a sense of social distance (Table 7-5) plus an admixture of mutual disdain (Table 7-6).

Instead of a unified power elite, Mexico therefore appears to have a fragmented power structure that is dominated, at the uppermost levels, by two distinct and competitive elites. They have specific common interests, most notably in the continuing subordination and manipulation of the popular masses and in the promotion of capital accumulation. But aside from this tacit consensus, and the collaboration needed to maintain it, these elites are at the same time struggling for control of the country's development process—and for supremacy over each other, as illustrated by the public-private tensions of the Echeverría years.[51] While the leaders of the Mexican state thus attempt to stimulate growth and change within a *capitalistic framework*, they are not operating primarily in behalf of the *capitalist class* (not to mention individual entrepreneurs). From the viewpoint of the state, after all, the private sector represents the major source of rival power.

It appears, in addition, that the processes of political recruitment in Mexico may well have tended to foster the articulation of a relatively autonomous "state interest." Officeholders have come from reasonably uniform social origins and they have carved out whole careers together within the political realm. It would therefore seem natural for them to identify their interests with those of the state, as distinct from any other social sector. As it turns out, what has been good for the state has been good for the country's capitalists. But this concurrence is a result of governmental policy, rather than the guiding motive for it. In principle this relationship could change at any time, at least in degree if not in kind, and the threat of such a change constitutes one of the public sector's major weapons in dealing with the private sector.

In operation, Mexico's authoritarian regime thus reflects constant interplay between a relatively coherent state interest and a somewhat less coherent set of business interests. One consequence of this situation has been a considerable degree of flexibility for the formulation of state policy; and in its turn, the ability to play off one actor (or businessman, including the foreign investor) against another has enhanced the stability and strength of the regime. In recent decades the political and economic elites have maintained an implicit alliance, though an uneasy one, in part because of a lack of perceived plausible alternatives. It is entirely possible that the active pursuit of state interests will increase the level of conflict in the future.

[51] Carlos Arriola, "Los grupos empresariales frente al Estado (1973-1975)," *Foro Internacional* 16, no. 64 (April-June 1976): 449-495.

In the long run, this bifurcation of the national power structure may constitute one of the most important consequences of the Mexican Revolution. Available evidence indicates that the Díaz regime created a genuine power elite, an interlocking of the political and economic domains, with private-sector families moving easily into government and public-sector families doing the reverse.[52] In contemporary Mexico this is simply not the case, and, in the absence of further information, I am inclined to attribute this outcome primarily to the social and political changes wrought by the Revolution: the displacement of the Porfirian elite, the elevation to power of disaffected segments of the middle class, the formation of full-time careers in politics. The subsequent course of Mexico's economic development, with its reliance on state participation for large-scale capital investment, would in my view be a secondary cause. And whatever its origin, the separation of Mexico's political and economic elites stands as a central and defining characteristic of the country's authoritarian regime.

[52] See, for instance, James D. Cockcroft, *Intellectual Precursors of the Mexican Revolution, 1900-1913* (Austin: University of Texas Press, 1968), ch. 1, esp. pp. 26-27.

· 8 ·

SERVING THE SYSTEM:
DEPUTIES AND SECTORS
OF THE PRI

Like most other authoritarian systems, the Mexican regime draws much of its stability and strength from the performance of its middle-level institutions. In general, intermediate agencies tend to serve and support the allocation of power throughout the entire polity—sometimes by implementing policy decisions made at the top, sometimes by providing symbolic support, sometimes in other ways. And it is at the lower and middle range of the bureaucracy that most politicians necessarily operate, since only a small minority manage to reach the upper echelons of preeminence. Accordingly the distribution of rewards at the intermediate level acquires a critical role in the satisfaction of ambitions among the active political strata, and the question therefore arises: Who has access to middle-level offices? In an empirical effort to confront the issue, this chapter focuses upon a single institution in the middle range: the national Chamber of Deputies.

Functions of the Chamber

Under the formal provisions of the Mexican Constitution, the Chamber is the lower house in a bicameral legislature, the upper house being the Senate. Deputies are elected every three years to represent their local districts, and the size of state delegations varies with population size: from 1951 until 1973 there was to be one deputy for each 200,000 inhabitants or fraction over 100,000—so the number of congressional districts has varied over time, reaching a total of 178 as of 1970.[1] For each seat in the Chamber there is an alternate, or *suplente*, as well as an incumbent. In accordance with the principle of "no-reelection," applied to the national congress in 1934, deputies cannot win reelection for consecutive terms.

Despite all the elaborate provisions for popular representation and (presumably) the expression of opposition views, the Chamber has actually been an integral part of the ruling coalition. Since the mid-

[1] In 1973 the rule was amended to provide one seat for every 250,000 inhabitants or fraction over 125,000—but because of population growth the number of districts nevertheless went up to 196.

1940s candidates of the PRI, with or without resort to electoral fraud, have consistently won around 95 percent of the contested races. The high point for the opposition came in 1952, when dissident parties captured a grand total of 10 seats—out of 162.[2] In 1963 a constitutional amendment laid down a complex formula for awarding deputyships to opposition parties according to their share of the national vote. First applied in 1964, the provision gave 20 seats to the PAN, 10 to the PPS, and 5 to the PARM—while the PRI retained 175 for itself.[3] Similar patterns have persisted since then. Without any meaningful interruption, the Chamber of Deputies has consistently been dominated by the forces of the government.

More significant than the presence of the opposition is the allocation of seats to the three component parts or "sectors" of the PRI. As its name suggests, the peasant sector contains the *campesinos*, organized mainly through the massive CNC. The labor sector represents the workers and their unions, by far the largest being the CTM. Third is the so-called popular sector, organized principally by the CNOP (Confederación Nacional de Organizaciones Populares), a broad-based institution whose eclectic constituency includes civil servants, teachers, small farmers, small businessmen, professionals, intellectuals, soldiers, women's organizations, youth groups, and others. The distribution of PRI seats among the sectors merits thorough scrutiny, not because it reflects popular preference (which it doesn't) and not because their respective spokesmen engage in overt conflict over legislation (which they don't). Rather, the significance of the seats lies in the way that they can furnish proxy evidence about the relative weight of the sectors within the governmental apparatus.

It is important to understand, in this context, that Mexican deputies are not elected in any strict sense of the term; they are appointed. According to one source, control of the deputyships held constant from the 1940s to the early '70s. The president personally picked about 20 percent of the deputies. Governors and regional strongmen named another 15 percent. Opposition parties were granted 5 percent. The remaining 60 percent emerged directly from the sectors of the PRI.[4] How the nominations are decided within the party councils is unknown. Presumably some major unions control some seats in the

[2] Donald J. Mabry, "Mexico's Party Deputy System: The First Decade," *Journal of Interamerican Studies and World Affairs* 16, no. 2 (May 1974): 222; and a memorandum on "Diputados de mayoría" supplied to me by an official of the Chamber of Deputies in 1970.

[3] Mabry, "Mexico's Party Deputy System."

[4] Frank R. Brandenburg, *The Making of Modern Mexico* (Englewood Cliffs, N.J.: Prentice-Hall, 1964), p. 155.

Chamber: the petroleum workers have regularly claimed at least one seat from the oil-producing state of Tamaulipas, movie actors and radio announcers have had seats from the Federal District, miners have had deputies from northern states like Zacatacas and San Luis Potosí, and peasant spokesmen have come out of predominantly rural states. Aside from allocations of this sort, it appears that most other seats have been granted through favoritism and bargaining.

Whatever the decisionmaking processes, the results are fairly consistent—and they will form a central concern of this chapter. As revealed in Table 8-1, which gives the party and sectoral affiliation for state and regional delegations during the legislative session of 1970-73,[5] most delegations have had a mixture of bias and balance. Hardly any major state has been entirely captured by any sector of the PRI, virtually all have had deputies from each of the three groupings, and the balance between the groupings has shifted over time within state delegations. On the other hand, definite tendencies emerge. The Federal District, for instance, has had strong delegations largely from the popular and labor sectors. Guanajuato, Sinaloa, and the state of México have had consistent representation of the peasant sector. Michoacán has drawn most of its deputies from the popular and peasant sectors, while Puebla and Veracruz have granted a steady forum for the labor group. To an extent these patterns comply with regional and local socioeconomic structures—peasant-sector deputies come from states with lots of peasants, labor-sector deputies come from states with lots of workers, popular-sector deputies come from states with complex economies and social structures.

But only to an extent, for the selection of national deputies responds to preferences from above, not on expressions of mass support from below. According to Manuel Moreno Sánchez, himself a former deputy and senator, the designation of legislators by sector tends to favor centralization at the expense of local interests, since deputies need not come from the districts they represent. As Moreno Sánchez argues,

> The manipulation of the "sectors" has permitted the allocation of candidacies for elective posts on a national scale, at the expense of local interests. Little has it mattered, for example, whether a deputy candidate "sent" by the party to a district should belong to the popular, worker, or military sector, while the district is preponderantly peasant, or the other way around. The use of the "sectors" has been a magnificent instrument for designating candidates without paying

[5] Throughout most of this chapter I shall rely on data for the 1970-1973 session; similar information for the 1964-1967 legislature appears in Appendix C.

attention to their local stature or influence, in the same way that, in congress under the *Porfiriato*, individuals from one state used to represent some other state or region where they had never been and about which they knew nothing at all. Sometimes the handling of the sectors was criticized as a form of political "parachutism," as candidates fell down on districts as though they had come from the

TABLE 8-1

Constituency, by Party and Sector, 1970-73

State and Region	PRI			PAN	PARM	PPS	Unknown	Totals
	Peasant	Labor	Popular					
Pacific North:								
BC Norte	1	1	1	0	0	0	0	3
BC Sur	1	0	0	0	0	0	0	1
Nayarit	1	0	1	0	0	0	0	2
Sinaloa	2	1	1	0	0	0	0	4
Sonora	1	1	2	0	0	0	0	4
Subtotals	6	3	5	0	0	0	0	14
North:								
Chihuahua	2	1	3	0	0	0	0	6
Coahuila	0	1	2	0	0	0	1	4
Durango	3	0	1	0	0	0	0	4
Nuevo León	1	1	3	0	0	0	0	5
San Luis Potosí	1	2	1	0	0	0	1	5
Tamaulipas	1	2	2	0	0	0	0	5
Zacatecas	1	1	2	0	0	0	0	4
Subtotals	9	8	14	0	0	0	2	33
Center:								
Aguascalientes	1	0	1	0	0	0	0	2
Guanajuato	2	2	5	0	0	0	0	9
Hidalgo	2	0	3	0	0	0	0	5
Jalisco	3	3	6	0	0	0	0	12
México	4	3	2	0	0	0	0	9
Michoacán	3	0	6	0	0	0	0	9
Morelos	1	0	1	0	0	0	0	2
Puebla	3	4	3	0	0	0	0	10
Querétaro	1	0	1	0	0	0	0	2
Tlaxcala	1	1	0	0	0	0	0	2
Subtotals	21	13	28	0	0	0	0	62
Federal District:	1	8	13	0	0	0	2	24

TABLE 8-1 *(cont.)*

State and Region	PRI			PAN	PARM	PPS	Unknown	Totals
	Peasant	Labor	Popular					
Gulf:								
Campeche	1	1	0	0	0	0	0	2
Quintana Roo	0	0	1	0	0	0	0	1
Tabasco	0	0	2	0	0	0	0	2
Veracruz	3	3	8	0	0	0	0	14
Yucatán	2	0	1	0	0	0	0	3
Subtotals	6	4	12	0	0	0	0	22
Pacific South:								
Chiapas	1	0	5	0	0	0	0	6
Colima	1	0	1	0	0	0	0	2
Guerrero	0	0	5	0	0	0	1	6
Oaxaca	2	1	6	0	0	0	0	9
Subtotals	4	1	17	0	0	0	1	23
No constituency:	0	0	0	20	5	10	0	35
Totals	47	37	89	20	5	10	5	213

sky, often just before elections. The forces of central political power found that the sector system offered yet another opportunity for domination by bargaining off the available seats to candidates and placing them throughout the country. This system has ended up by turning the PRI into a means for facilitating the distribution of secondary politicians into electoral posts according to the personal desires, or with the acquiescence, of the true head of the party *(instituto)*—the president of the republic—and also of crushing any sign of insurgency in local politics.[6]

In addition to imposing outsiders on congressional districts, the recruitment process can also work to the disadvantage of local interests in precisely the opposite way: by drawing up-and-coming leaders with local bases of support into the promotion system. To serve in the Chamber of Deputies, a person must go to Mexico City, thereby losing

[6] Manuel Moreno Sánchez, *México: 1968-1972. Crisis y perspectiva* (Austin: Institute of Latin American Studies, University of Texas, 1973), pp. 4-5. Because of its close ties to the government, Moreno Sánchez often refers to the PRI not as a party but an "institute."

vital contact with any grass-roots base at home. The "no-reelection" rule makes it impossible to establish a career in the congress itself, as Moreno Sánchez also notes, so the novice deputy has to start looking around for another government position soon after reaching the legislature.[7] To obtain another position, as shown in Chapter 6, one usually has to move up, and this can be achieved only at the pleasure of one's superiors. The primary hope for political survival, then, lies in gratifying elites up above, not in representing the interests of people down below. In this way deputyships become instruments for coopting local leaders, for making them dependent on the national hierarchy, and for increasing the centralization of effective political rule.

Partly because of its extensive ties to the establishment, the Chamber performs an extremely passive role in the legislative process. Most bills originate in the executive branch, and most are passed without meaningful debate or substantive revision. As Pablo González Casanova revealed some time ago, the Chamber habitually approves about 95 percent of all proposals sent to it by the president.[8] Rudolph O. de la Garza has recently found a mild increase in legislative activity, primarily due to spokesmen for the opposition, but not enough to make much difference in the final outcomes.[9]

So what does the Chamber do? One of its leading functions is to supply ritualistic ratification for the power structure and decisions emanating from it. As González Casanova put it:

> It seems that the legislative power has a symbolic function. It sanctions the acts of the Executive. It gives them a traditional and metaphysical legitimation. Thus they acquire the status of laws, owing to a very old yet secular symbolic mechanism. The rulers of old governed in the name of the law, which in return was sanctioned by divine powers. This had a symbolic-religious functional significance. In Mexico today, the Chamber of Representatives fulfills a function similar to that of the divine powers. Its theoretical significance to the community is as a visible "sanction of legality."[10]

[7] Ibid., pp. 7-8.

[8] Pablo González Casanova, *Democracy in Mexico*, trans. Danielle Salti (London, Oxford, New York: Oxford University Press, 1970), pp. 18-19. The book was first published in Mexico in 1965.

[9] Rudolph O. de la Garza, "The Mexican Chamber of Deputies and the Mexican Political System" (Ph.D. diss., University of Arizona, 1972), ch. 2. Part of the explanation for the decay of the legislative function, according to Moreno Sánchez, has been the steady curtailment in the length and frequency of congressional sessions: *México*, pp. 9-10.

[10] González Casanova, *Democracy*, p. 20.

In this connection, a prime purpose of the 1963 amendment regarding opposition parties was to improve the performance of this ceremonial function by giving the congress an increasingly "democratic" appearance.[11] Clearly, the Chamber plays a central role in the legitimation of the system.

It also provides an important link in communications between the people and the government. One function of congressional campaigning, in a context where the opposition hardly ever wins, is the exchange of information.[12] Through meetings, conferences, and personal conversations, candidates learn about the preoccupations of their dis-

3. IN THE CHAMBER

Deputy 1: "We'll be working a lot these days."
Deputy 2: "They're right when they say it will be an extraordinary period" (referring to the "extraordinary" session of Congress).

[11] Mabry, "Mexico's Party Deputy System."
[12] Karl M. Schmitt, "Congressional Campaigning in Mexico: A View from the Provinces," *Journal of Inter-American Studies* 11, no. 1 (January 1969): 93-110.

tricts; this procedure acquires special importance from the fact that many of them have never lived in the areas they are about to represent. In return PRI candidates usually make some effort to explain national policies (and, of course, extol the government's fulfillment of the Revolution). Once in office, PRI deputies spend a fair amount of time presenting petitions and demands from their districts to the appropriate agencies of the governmental bureaucracy. As *gestores*, they become informal lobbyists, serving as political brokers between the people—especially the lower classes—and the state.[13]

In addition to these roles, the Chamber of Deputies is also an important source of patronage. Seats in the congress supply substantial income, prestige, perquisites, and the opportunity to engage in other lucrative endeavors.[14] There is also the chance, for some, of advancement to a higher office. The Chamber is particularly efficient in dispensing these benefits because it spreads them far and wide. Since 1961 the PRI has had between 172 and 192 deputies in each legislative session. The Chamber has been renewed every three years, with reelection prohibited (though a few individuals have reclaimed their seats after waiting out the three-year intervals). And for every incumbent there has been a *suplente*, who obtains at least some satisfaction from the designation. In total, association with the Chamber furnished direct gratification to approximately 1,070 active members of the PRI (and perhaps 2,000, counting *suplentes*), in the 25-year period from 1946 to 1971.

In general, it appears that most of these seats are given to party loyalists as a reward for years of faithful service (especially, as shown in Chapter 4, to people of relatively modest educational or occupational background). The prospect of getting a deputyship thus becomes an incentive for maintaining discipline within the PRI. Some seats are also awarded to up-and-coming young politicians, for whom the Chamber represents a probationary introduction into the national elite; as dem-

[13] De la Garza, "Chamber," ch. 3. A skeptical, and convincing, analysis of the relationship between deputies and lower-class constituents is in Susan Eckstein, *The Poverty of Revolution: The State and the Urban Poor in Mexico* (Princeton: Princeton University Press, 1977), pp. 82-83.

[14] As of 1970, deputies received 33,000 pesos for expenses incurred during the course of their three-year period, available in a lump sum at the start of the term. Their monthly salary was $10,000 pesos, which they received throughout the entire year even though the Chamber is usually in session for only four months. Those on the Gran Comisión and the Permanent Commission got extra pay, and many deputies had a double salary because they were granted leaves with pay from their home organizations. By Mexican standards these are large amounts of money (the exchange rate was 12.5 pesos to the U.S. dollar). De la Garza, "Chamber," pp. 156-158. See also the fascinating discussion of congressional salaries and financial emoluments in *Excélsior*, 17 January 1978.

onstrated in Chapter 5, however, the lower house has not been a particularly efficient route to higher office. Finally, some spots are used for cooptation. Potential dissidents, particularly, often wind up in the Chamber.[15] Moreover, those who might start to develop independent power bases, for instance in local labor movements, are frequently brought into the legislature—where they lose touch with their grassroots constituencies and become dependent for further advancement on the power dealers in Mexico City. In all these ways the Chamber of Deputies performs what may well be its paramount functions, the mutually related roles of recruitment and patronage.[16]

It should be noted, parenthetically, that the Senate accomplishes a different set of tasks. Like the Chamber of Deputies, it has a minimal impact on the process of lawmaking. It supports the legitimacy of the system, but not by incorporating members of the opposition. With every seat being held by a member of the PRI, the Senate has in recent years provided symbolic representation for every discernible faction of the Revolution and its successor governments—*carrancismo, zapatismo, callismo, cardenismo, alemanismo,* and so on. Within the 1964-70 Senate, for instance, there were three ex-deputies from the Constitutional Convention of 1916-17 (Juan de Dios Bojórquez, Jesús Romero Flores, and Alberto Terrones Benítez); one symbolic *carrancista* (Hermenegildo Cuenca Díaz, who as a young cadet accompanied Carranza during his flight from the *obregonistas* in 1920); the son of a prominent *convencionista* (Eulalio Gutiérrez Treviño, whose father served as president in 1914-15); one leading *callista* (Luis L. León, who went with Calles into exile in 1935); one well-known *cardenista* (Salvador Corona Bandín); and a former member of the *alemanista* cabinet (Andrés Serra Rojas). Another senator, Ezequiel Padilla, had also served in the *villista* army as a young man, but by 1964 was primarily remembered for his role as opposition candidate against Alemán in the presidential campaign of 1946. Explicit incorporation of a *villista* representative actually came in 1970, with the nomination of

---

[15] Note that the reference is to potential dissidents; active dissidents are usually met with coercion. In an apparent exception to this rule some members of the student movement in 1968 have been coopted with seats in the Chamber of Deputies, and others (such as Francisco Javier Alejo) have been given positions of major importance.

[16] Note the contrast with Argentina, where the Chamber of Deputies has at various times served as a critic of government policies and as a training ground for cabinet members: Peter H. Smith, *Argentina and the Failure of Democracy: Conflict among Political Elites, 1904-1955* (Madison: University of Wisconsin Press, 1974), pp. 16-22. For additional reflections on the comparative roles of legislatures see Weston H. Agor, ed., *Latin American Legislatures: Their Role and Influence* (New York: Praeger, 1971).

Martín Luis Guzmán, a famous writer and once Pancho Villa's private secretary. Thus stressing the unity and continuity of the revolutionary legacy, linking the current regime to a heroic past, the Senate operates as a kind of political museum.

Because of its small size, with only 60 members as of 1970 (plus *suplentes*) elected every six years, the Senate distributes much less patronage than does the Chamber. Its performance as a museum means that quite a few posts have gone to elder men, often as rewards for long and productive careers, sometimes as consolation prizes for those who failed to reach a higher level. And as noted in Chapter 4, the Senate has functioned more actively as a training ground than has the Chamber. If senators move on to other offices, they often go to extremely prestigious ones, most notably state governorships.[17]

In sum, one of the central roles for the Chamber of Deputies, as might be expected for any middle-level institution in an authoritarian system, entails the related functions of recruitment and patronage. But who gets these rewards? What sectors predominate within the PRI? Who goes on to higher office? What is the social composition of the sector delegations?

To begin exploring these questions it is necessary to determine the effective size and composition of the PRI—and that is not a simple task. In order to emphasize national consensus, and also to broaden the dues-paying population, party officials claim the allegiance of huge followings throughout the country. Membership for workers in most unions is automatic and obligatory. By the early 1960s the PRI purported to have around 6 million members, both male and female (the 1960 census listed only 15.9 million adults in all of Mexico!). Of the total membership, about 40 percent belonged to the peasant sector, 32 percent were with the labor sector, and 28 percent were in the popular sector.[18] By 1970, it has been held, party affiliation had swelled to more

---

[17] The upper chamber's function as a training ground might be related to the fact that the president has normally chosen about 60 percent of the senators himself: Brandenburg, *Making*, p. 155. Senators therefore tend to be associated with the president, and—since the president picks the governors—it would seem natural for him to look in the Senate for appropriate candidates.

[18] The percentages are computed from data in Robert E. Scott, *Mexican Government in Transition*, rev. ed. (Urbana: University of Illinois Press, 1964), pp. 166-167. Scott's figures show a total membership in the PRI of 6.6 million; there is no date although, judging from the year of publication of the book, I would guess that the estimate refers to the early 1960s. If so, the number is quite a bit higher than those in a memorandum on PRI membership between 1958 and 1970 that was supplied to me by an official of the PRI in 1970 (who might have tended to downplay the size of membership around 1960 in order to dramatize the results of an affiliation campaign in the latter part of the decade). For an illustration of the difficulty in estimating party membership, see the exchange between Daniel Cosío Villegas and

than 12 million, with some apparent shift in the relative size of the sectors. According to one PRI spokesman (who may have been exaggerating the party's strength among the masses), around 50 percent of members were from the peasant sector, 30 percent from the labor sector, and 20 percent from the popular sector.[19] Since then the PRI has allegedly maintained high rates of growth.

Whatever the true proportions of party membership, it is clear that the popular sector—presumably the smallest of all—has dominated congressional delegations of the PRI. According to Table 8-2, which gives available data on selected election years from 1943 to 1976, the popular sector has generally received more than half of the deputy seats. The peasant group has obtained about one-quarter of all seats in recent years, compared to 30-40 percent during the 1940s. Labor, by

TABLE 8-2

*Sectoral Representation within Congressional
Delegations of the PRI, 1943-76*

	Sector		
Year of Designation	Peasant (%)	Labor (%)	Popular (%)
1943 (N = 147)[a]	31.3	15.6	53.1
1949 (N = 147)[b]	42.2	16.3	41.5
1952 (N = 161)[c]	22.4	21.7	55.9
1964 (N = 178)[d]	27.0	19.7	53.4
1967 (N = 173)[e]	25.4	22.0	52.6
1970 (N = 177)[e]	26.6	20.3	53.1
1973 (N = 192)[f]	27.1	19.8	53.1
1976 (N = 196)[g]	28.6	29.6	41.8

SOURCES:

[a] Raymond Vernon, *The Dilemma of Mexico's Development: The Roles of the Private and Public Sectors* (Cambridge: Harvard University Press, 1963), p. 130.

[b] *La República* (July 15, 1949), p. 9.

[c] William P. Tucker, *The Mexican Government Today* (Minneapolis: University of Minnesota Press, 1957), p. 100.

[d] Estimates by personal informants.

[e] Rudolph O. de la Garza, "The Mexican Chamber of Deputies and the Mexican Political System" (Ph.D. diss., University of Arizona, 1972), p. 146. Slightly different figures for 1970 appear in Bertha Lerner Sigal, "Partido Revolucionario Institucional," in Antonio Delhumeau A. et al., *México: realidad política de sus partidos* (Mexico: Instituto Mexicano de Estudios Políticos, 1970), p. 80.

[f] *Excélsior*, 12 February 1976.

[g] *Excélsior*, 1 March 1976.

Miguel Alemán in *Miguel Alemán contesta* (Austin: Institute of Latin American Studies, University of Texas, 1975), pp. 12-13.

[19] Personal interview, Mexico City, 21 August 1970.

contrast, has increased its share, moving from around 15 percent in the 1940s to the 20 percent range in the '50s. By implication, at least, the data suggest a restructuring of party strength during the Alemán administration (1946-52), with the labor group gaining at the expense of the peasants and the popular sector asserting its supremacy.[20] Ever since then, at least up to the mid-1970s, the composition of deputy delegations remained remarkably constant. (The slight deviation in 1976 will be discussed in Chapter 10.)

Plainly enough, the distribution of deputyships does not reflect the composition of the membership. The peasant sector has been severely underrepresented: with 40 to 50 percent of the members, it has been getting only 25 percent of the seats. Labor has also been underrepresented, though perhaps to a lesser degree: 30 to 40 percent of the members, and 20 percent of the seats. The popular sector has emerged triumphant, picking up nearly twice its fair share of positions in the Chamber. With 20 to 30 percent of PRI members, it has usually controlled 50-55 percent of the seats. The allocation of rewards, to put it mildly, has been highly skewed.

This situation is subject to varying interpretations. It could be argued that the internal mechanisms of the PRI have led to a sustained and systematic denial of just representation for the peasants and the laborers. It could be argued that party members from the peasant and labor sectors have only a pro forma affiliation with the PRI, owing to union obligations, whereas more people in the popular sector tend to join up out of personal conviction; accordingly, they dominate the effective or actively participant party membership, and the congressional delegations provide a fair and accurate representation of that fact. It could be argued that leaders of the popular sector have been more adept than spokesmen for labor and the peasantry, who have failed to capitalize upon their political resources in meetings of the inner councils.[21] From a slightly Machiavellian posture, it could be argued that labor and the peasants really dominate the party, and deputyships are thrown to the popular sector merely as a sop. Finally, of course, it could be argued that the allocation reveals absolutely nothing: the Chamber of Deputies is meaningless and so is the distribution of seats in it.

In my own view it is relatively clear that the distribution of deputy-

[20] Alemán's tendency to favor the CNOP is mentioned in L. Vincent Padgett, *The Mexican Political System* (Boston: Houghton Mifflin, 1966), p. 125; and in Bertha Lerner Sigal, "Partido Revolucionario Institucional," in Antonio Delhumeau A. et al., *México: realidad política de sus partidos* (Mexico: Instituto Mexicano de Estudios Políticos, 1970), p. 78.

[21] For this hypothesis see Padgett, *Mexican Political System*, p. 125.

ships reveals a systematic bias within the PRI in favor of the popular sector at the expense of the labor sector and especially the peasant sector, although the mechanisms producing this result are not at all apparent. Seats in the Chamber carry considerable prestige in political circles, they are highly valued, and, as I have tried to show, the legislature performs important functions on behalf of the regime.

This pattern of official preference not only finds expression in the relative size of PRI delegations to congress. It also shows up in their roles within the assembly. As an indication of this point, Table 8-3 offers data on the distribution of positions on the most powerful committee in the Chamber, the Gran Comisión, for the 1970-73 session.[22] The Gran Comisión controls the allocation of legislative patronage: it makes all committee assignments, names the presidents of all committees, hires all administrative staff, and sets all wages for administrative personnel. Every state delegation elects one of its own members to serve on the Gran Comisión, so deputies from small states have better random chances of getting on the committee than do legislators from large states (while Quintana Roo and Baja California Sur each had only one deputy, who automatically went on the Comisión). For this reason Table 8-3 categorizes membership on the committee according to the size of the state delegations.

Once again, the data demonstrate the preeminence of the popular sector. Of the 29 members of the Gran Comisión with known sectoral affiliation in 1970-73, 19—nearly two-thirds—were from the popular group. Labor placed only one member on the committee. The peasant sector fared somewhat better, with 9 spokesmen on the Comisión, though most of them came from small or medium states. (According to Table C-2, in Appendix C, the 1964-67 session revealed a similar pattern: domination by the popular sector, with 19 out of 28 identifiable slots; severe underrepresentation of labor, with only 3 positions; and a low to middling share for the peasants). People in the popular sector thus not only enjoyed disproportionate advantage in the quest for seats in the Chamber. Once in congress, they held disproportionate advantage in the race for the Gran Comisión. Of all 89 identifiable delegates from the popular sector in 1970-73, for instance, 21.3 percent made it to the Comisión; the corresponding figure for labor was 2.7 percent, and for the *campesinos* it was 19.1 percent.

[22] The totals for sector delegates in this and subsequent tables, including those in Appendix C, differ ever so slightly from those in the sources for the 1964 and 1970 designations given in Table 8-2. The discrepancies are due to (*a*) missing data and (*b*) the difficulty of ascertaining sectoral affiliation; but they are extremely minor and, in general, the closeness between my figures and those in the other sources is most encouraging.

TABLE 8-3

Membership on the Gran Comisión,
by Party and Sector, 1970-73

Committee Status	Party							
	PRI							
	Peasant	Labor	Popular	PAN	PARM	PPS	Unknown	Totals
Nonmember	38	36	70	20	5	10	3	182
Member from small state delegation[a]	4	0	6	0	0	0	0	10
Member from medium state delegation[b]	2	1	7	0	0	0	1	11
Member from large state delegation[c]	3	0	6	0	0	0	1	10
Totals	47	37	89	20	5	10	5	213

[a] Delegations with 1 or 2 members.
[b] Delegations with 3 to 5 members.
[c] Delegations with more than 5 members (actual range: 6 to 24).

The inequalities run even further than that: once in the Chamber, delegates from the popular sector have better prospects than their colleagues for moving on to higher posts. To demonstrate this pattern, Table 8-4 gives data on the subsequent political attainments of nearly 500 members of the 1946-71 officeholding cohort within known sectoral affiliations. As presented in the table, "level of attainment" refers to the highest level of political office ever held within the national hierarchy: some went on to upper-level posts, some moved on to other positions, most never got beyond the Chamber itself. The figures reveal that delegates from the three sectors went on to higher office (either upper-level or other national posts) in nearly equal proportions, though the ratio was somewhat greater for the popular sector, .176 (since $6 + 33 = 39$, and $39/222 = .176$), than for labor (.141) and the peasantry (.132).[23] The disparity sharpens, however, regarding access

[23] Note that Table 8-4 refers to political attainment at any time in the course of a career, not merely to moves made directly from the Chamber of Deputies. Also, some of the sector delegates in the table were in the 1970-1973 session, so they had hardly any chance to attain subsequent office before the end of the data-gathering phase of this study; this would produce a slight downward bias in the proportion of the popular-sector deputies who went on to higher office, since the popular sector dominated the 1970-1973 session.

to topmost positions on the national level: out of the 9 who are known to have made it to the upper-level elite, 6 were from the popular sector.

In passing, the data in Table 8-4 convey another message: activity in the electoral realm, either in congress or the PRI, does not provide much of a channel to the uppermost levels of office. Of the 174 individuals of unknown sectoral affiliation who made it to high office, just about one-half (to be precise, 49.4 percent) are known to have *never* held any position in the PRI, and quite a few others held only temporary, ad hoc party jobs. This finding fully confirms the implications of Figure 2-2, in Chapter 2, and it further supports some of the conclusions in Chapter 5. In Mexico, the party does not run the state. Rather, it is a tool of the state, an instrument of those who truly command the governmental apparatus.

Within these limits, it thus appears that recruitment and selection processes of the PRI lead to a systematic bias in favor of the popular sector. Party members from this sector have disproportionate access to the congress, disproportionate control over the working of the Chamber, and disproportionate chances of going on to higher office (especially to topmost office). Taken together, these findings tend to undermine Frank Brandenburg's oft-quoted deduction that the PRI cannot

TABLE 8-4

Political Attainment, by Sectors of the PRI, 1946-71

Level of Attainment	Sector			No Known Sectoral Affiliation	Totals
	Peasant	Labor	Popular		
Upper-level office[a]	2	1	6	174	183
Other national position[b]	15	18	33	497	563
Chamber of Deputies	112	116	183	829	1,240
Other[c]	0	0	0	24	24
Totals	129	135	222	1,524	2,010[d]

[a] Includes positions with scale values 7 and 8 for HIGHEST OFFICE variable (see Appendix A, Table A-3).
[b] Includes positions with scale values 2 through 6 for HIGHEST OFFICE variable (see Appendix A, Table A-3).
[c] Positions (that is, ambassadorships) with scale values 0 for HIGHEST OFFICE variable (see Appendix A, Table A-3).
[d] Sum exceeds the total number of officeholders in the 1946-71 cohort (N = 2,008) because two individuals are known to have represented more than one sector of the PRI at different times in their careers.

have much influence on the decisionmaking process because, if it did, more would be done to benefit the laborers and *campesinos* who account for most members of the party.[24] What the data here indicate is that, through its internal mechanisms, the PRI has elevated the popular sector to a position of preeminence—and, on the leadership level, the party is quite in step with the pro-middle-class policies emanating from other agencies within the governmental apparatus.[25] It does not appear to be a worker- and peasant-dominated institution that is constantly rebuffed and denied by the bureaucracy. Rather, it seems to employ means at its own disposal to curtail, control, and manipulate the vast majority of its own members.

In this connection former president Miguel Alemán has furnished a remarkably (perhaps inadvertently) clear statement on the functions of the party and its sectors. In the decades just after the Mexican Revolution, he recalled, there were some attempts to create a powerful lower-class coalition of workers and peasants, a prospect which he interpreted as a serious threat to the system, and the popular sector was created in order to prevent this possibility. In Alemán's own words:

> There was an effort to merge the peasant organizations with those of the workers. With that, the political stability of Mexico would have practically disappeared. Who would have appeased this group? This would have produced a mass movement directed by a single sector. Would we have been able to preserve stability in such a situation? Most probably, the progress of the country would have stopped. Given those circumstances, the popular class had to act as a conciliator (*debió ser la conciliadora*), in order to guide political and social forces. . . . What would have happened to Mexico without that stability? We would not have had economic prosperity. . . . There did not exist sufficient political awareness for those groups [workers or peasants] to be able to lead the country. On the other hand, workers and peasants have received all the benefits, all the programs have taken place basically in order to improve their collective and individual condition.[26]

That is to say, the purpose of maintaining separate sectors for workers and peasants was to head off the formation of a lower-class coalition, to prevent the stimulation of class consciousness, and to forestall the dangers of class conflict. As the "conciliator" of national interests, the

[24] Brandenburg, *Making*, p. 144.

[25] As Brandenburg himself reveals (pp. 281-283), the upper echelons of party leadership have been controlled by the popular sector.

[26] Alemán, *Miguel Alemán contesta*, pp. 32-33.

popular sector—that is, the middle class—would determine the course of policy. Workers, peasants, and lower-class people would have hardly any direct influence on the decisionmaking process, although they would receive the benefits dispersed from up above (which, in fact, they have yet to attain).[27] To put it in a nutshell: Mexico would have a corporate state, and the PRI and its sectors would comprise its fundamental pillars.

To gain further insight on this process and its implications, it is necessary to understand the social composition of the sectoral delegations. Do representatives for the PRI sectors differ in their social extraction? Do they tend to reflect the backgrounds of their presumed constituencies? Or do all sector spokesmen come from the same origins? And how do they compare to the opposition parties?

Social Differentiation

To begin, Table 8-5 offers data on the rural vs. urban origins of the congressional delegations in 1970-73. A correlation exists between the background of the delegations and the composition of their constituencies, but it is not very strong. About 66 percent of the peasant-sector deputies with known birthplaces came from rural areas, compared to 45 percent of the labor representatives and 53 percent of the popular-sector delegates. As the most rural group, the peasant deputies were also the least urban, only 9.1 percent coming from urban or highly urban communities. By contrast 36.4 percent of the labor delegates were from such cities, as were 25.9 percent of those from the popular sector.

The opposition parties reveal vague and contradictory patterns. The PARM clearly draws its leaders from rural roots, with 3 out of 4 delegates of known birthplace in the 1970-73 congress being from such areas. The PAN delegation displays considerable variance in its urban-rural composition, though most were from urban or highly urban backgrounds. And the PPS—somewhat surprisingly, given its prolabor stance—recruited 8 out of its 10 members from rural backgrounds.

On this urban-origin dimension it thus appears that sector delegates from the PRI differ according to the composition of their presumed constituencies. Peasant-sector leaders tend to be from rural areas, where *campesinos* live by definition. At the same time, they are much less

[27] Upon hearing Alemán's statement, Daniel Cosío Villegas expressed (with characteristic humor) his dissatisfaction: "It seems rather doubtful to me that this popular sector has introduced an element of conciliation, unless one could believe that, in a quarrel between two children over the division of a cake, you can conciliate things by bringing in another child who takes a piece for himself; that is to say, the slice of cake is smaller." *Miguel Alemán contesta*, p. 33.

TABLE 8-5

Urbanization of Birthplace, by Party and Sector, 1970-73

Level of Urbanization	PRI			PAN	PARM	PPS	Unknown	Totals
	Peasant	Labor	Popular					
Rural[a]	29	15	46	6	3	8	1	108
Semirural[b]	4	5	4	0	0	0	0	13
Semiurban[c]	7	1	15	2	0	0	0	25
Urban[d]	3	5	14	7	1	2	2	34
Highly Urban[e]	1	7	9	3	0	0	0	20
Unknown	3	4	1	2	1	0	2	13
Totals	47	37	89	20	5	10	5	213

[a] Communities with less than 10,000 inhabitants as of 1921 (according to Departamento de la Estadística Nacional, *Resumen del censo general de habitantes de 30 de noviembre de 1921* [Mexico: Talleres Gráficos de la Nación, 1928], pp. 166-182),

[b] Communities with 10,000-19,999 inhabitants as of 1921.

[c] Communities with 20,000-49,999 inhabitants as of 1921.

[d] Communities with 50,000-499,999 inhabitants as of 1921.

[e] Communities with 500,000 or more inhabitants as of 1921.

rural than the *campesinos* themselves; the presence of agrarian delegates from urban and highly urban backgrounds testifies, once again, to the imposition of deputies upon constituencies by centralized fiat. Labor spokesmen are most heavily from cities, where the working-class movement has its base. And, reflecting the diversity of its constituency, the popular-sector delegation varies in this regard, though it shows a tendency in favor of the cities (this was especially true in 1964-67, as shown in Table C-3 of Appendix C). Opposition party delegations are less easy to interpret since, being party deputies, they do not have clearly defined constituencies.

The congressional delegations show considerable discrepancies in levels of educational attainment. As revealed in Table 8-6, leaders of the popular sector have consistently been the most highly educated, 73 percent of the 1970-73 cohort having been to university. The labor sector has had the least educated representatives: only 7 out of the 36 members of known educational achievement (19.4 percent) had been to university.[28] Perhaps more revealing are the proportions of labor spokesmen known to have had modest educational training: 44.5 percent of the 1970-73 group never got beyond primary school. Interest-

[28] The corresponding figure for 1964-67 was substantially higher (43.8 percent), but this may well be a result of missing data. See Appendix C, Table C-5.

ingly enough, deputies from the peasant sector, with certainly the least educated mass base, occupied an intermediate position in regard to schooling, with a fairly high proportion (46.5 percent) having been to universities.

TABLE 8-6

Level of Education, by Party and Sector, 1970-73

| Level | Party | | | | | | | |
| | PRI | | | | | | | |
	Peasant	Labor	Popular	PAN	PARM	PPS	Unknown	Totals
None	0	1	1	0	0	0	0	2
Primary	7	15	3	1	2	0	0	28
Secondary	2	3	1	0	0	0	0	6
Special, trade, or normal school[a]	12	5	15	2	0	6	0	40
Preparatory	2	5	3	0	1	1	0	12
University[b]	20	7	66	15	1	3	4	116
Unknown	4	1	0	2	1	0	1	9
Totals	47	37	89	20	5	10	5	213

[a] Schools of commerce, agriculture, technology, and music; and normal schools.
[b] Includes all those who are believed to have attended a university, whether or not they are known to have received degrees.

If the labor-sector deputies seem to bear a closer resemblance to the working-class constituency than the peasant-sector leaders have to the country's *campesinos*, it should nevertheless be remembered that both delegations are far more educated than the groups they represent. For the entire nation, as pointed out in Chapter 3 (Table 3-5), only 3 percent of the literate adult male population as of 1960 had ever been to university—while the figure for the labor deputies, by far the lowest of all, came to nearly 20 percent. In short, variations in the educational profiles (and, by implication, the "life chances") of the labor and peasant sector delegations have occurred within restricted limits, and neither group of deputies has furnished an accurate reflection of the classes they represent. As a matter of fact the most representative delegation, in this sense, is that of the popular sector—not because of any democratic aspect of the recruitment process, but because the educational level of the popular-sector constituents is relatively high.

Limited variation in social backgrounds of the deputies is also apparent in Table 8-7, which presents the incidence of professional titles by party and sector in 1970-73. As in the case of education, there was substantial difference among sectoral delegations. Only 16.2 percent of the labor deputies wore professional titles of any kind, in striking contrast to 61.7 percent of the peasant-sector deputies. As might have been expected, in view of the data on educational attainment, the popular sector had the greatest frequency of titles, 75.6 percent in 1970-73.

TABLE 8-7

Professional Title, by Party and Sector, 1970-73

Professional Title	Party							
	PRI							
	Peasant	Labor	Popular	PAN	PARM	PPS	Unknown	Totals
Licenciado en derecho (lawyer)[a]	16	3	34	8	1	0	2	64
Licenciado (other or unknown)	1	0	8	0	0	0	1	10
Doctor (medicine)	0	0	14	3	0	0	0	17
Profesor	7	2	5	2	0	6	0	22
Ingeniero (engineer)	3	0	2	1	0	2	1	9
Other	2	1	3	2	0	0	0	8
None	18	31	23	4	4	2	1	83
Totals	47	37	89	20	5	10	5	213

[a] Includes some *doctores en derecho* (doctors of law).

Equally significant is the specific nature of the titles themselves. The majority of degrees held by labor-sector leaders is in the field of law, which may well correspond to the importance of labor lawyers. The popular-sector delegates have had titles in various fields, again reflecting the diversity of their constituency—law (by far the most common), medicine, education, engineering, and incidental other disciplines. Most telling, however, are the data on the peasant sector. There have been some *ingenieros*, usually agronomists; some teachers or *profesores*, who may or may not have taught in rural areas; only a couple of doctors; and, by far the largest number, lawyers! In 1970-73 at least 16 out of the 29 title-holders from the peasant sector had been trained as lawyers (and as revealed in Table C-5, a similar pattern obtained in 1964-67). Of course some of these lawyers may have been active in defending *campesino* interests, though the sheer magnitude of their number makes it unlikely that all of them had done so. Whatever the case, one thing is plain: it was neither peasants nor farmers who were getting into congress, it was the politicians—who may or may not have had genuine experience in the Mexican countryside.

These observations find impressionistic support in some fragmentary data on occupations. At least 21 of the 31 labor-sector deputies in 1964-67 had actually been workers in factories or activists in unions, and at least 17 of the 37 labor spokesmen in 1970-73 had also had this practical experience. By contrast only *one* of the peasant-sector spokesmen in each session claimed to have been a *campesino*, though several had apparently been farmers. The information is paltry and the inference is tenuous, but the evident conclusion is that the labor sector has tended to elevate its own workers and constituents to the Chamber of Deputies to a greater degree than has the peasant sector. To state the point another way: both groups appear to be bureaucratized and hierarchical, but the labor sector would appear to be more open—or at least less closed—than the peasant sector.

Additional clues on this point emerge from data on the age structures of the party and sectoral delegations, presented in Table 8-8. Many of the deputies from the peasant sector tended to be relatively young: 17 out of the 44 delegates of known age (38.6 percent) in 1970-73 had not reached the age of 40 by the beginning of the legislative session, and a total of 26 (59.0 percent) had not reached the age of 50. The labor sector was a bit older: only 6 out of 35 (17.1 percent) were

TABLE 8-8

Age, by Party and Sector, 1970-73

| | Party | | | | | | | |
| | PRI | | | | | | | |
Age[a]	Peasant	Labor	Popular	PAN	PARM	PPS	Unknown	Totals
20-29	3	0	4	0	0	0	0	7
30-39	14	6	28	6	0	2	1	57
40-49	9	9	29	3	0	5	2	57
50-59	13	13	24	9	2	1	1	63
60-69	5	6	3	0	0	2	0	16
70-plus	0	1	1	0	3	0	0	5
Unknown	3	2	0	2	0	0	1	8
Totals	47	37	89	20	5	10	5	213

[a] As of 1970.

still under 40 in 1970, and 42.9 percent were under 50. (There were
similar differences in 1964-67, as revealed in Table C-6.) The data do
not submit to facile interpretation, but one implication seems to come
through: seats in the Chamber of Deputies came fairly rapidly to some
activists in the peasant sector, while they may have been given as rewards for years of steady service (hence at later ages) to members of
the labor sector. As with some other indicators, the popular sector
stands in the middle, with the bulk of its deputies arriving between
the ages of 30 and 50—by comparison, neither young nor old.

The significance of age structures becomes a bit more clear in Table
8-9, which gives data on the relationship between age and professional
title within sectoral and party groupings (note that categories have
been collapsed for ease of presentation). Seen in this perspective, the
peasant-sector delegation consisted of three distinct types: young people (under 40) with degrees, mainly in law; a middle-aged (40-59)
bracket, almost evenly divided between those with and without degrees; and an older (60-plus) cohort, mostly without degrees. The labor delegation did not reveal any such coalition: regardless of age,
labor deputies tended not to have professional titles. The popular-

TABLE 8-9

Age and Professional Title, by Party and Sector, 1970-73

Age	Peasant Sector				Labor Sector			
	None	Law[a]	Other	Totals	None	Law[a]	Other	Totals
Under 40	1	10	6	17	5	1	0	6
40-59	10	6	6	24	19	2	1	24
60 and over	4	0	1	5	6	0	1	7
Unknown	3	0	0	3	1	0	1	2
Totals	18	16	13	47	31	3	3	37
Age	Popular Sector				PAN, PARM, and PPS			
	None	Law[a]	Other	Totals	None	Law[a]	Other	Totals
Under 40	7	16	9	32	1	3	4	8
40-59	14	20	19	53	4	5	11	20
60 and over	2	0	2	4	3	1	1	5
Unknown	0	0	0	0	2	0	0	2
Totals	23	36	30	89	10	9	16	35

NOTE: Five individuals with unknown sectoral affiliation are omitted from this table.
[a] Includes some *licenciados* who are not definitely known to have been lawyers.

sector group was the reverse: regardless of age, CNOP spokesmen tended to have professional titles. (As shown in Table C-8 of Appendix C, the same pattern prevailed in 1964-67.)

A cross-tabulation between age and level of education (not reported here) produces an almost identical result. Such findings seem to indicate, again, that the peasant-sector delegation to the legislature has been highly permeable, that it frequently takes into its circles ambitious young men with professional degrees who might have little first-hand contact with country life. The labor delegation has been somewhat more autonomous and self-contained, rewarding its own kind in return for years of faithful service. The popular sector is difficult to characterize in this respect. My guess is that it has been permeable, given the eclectic and relatively unorganized nature of its constituency, but that the kind of people who make it into congress nevertheless provide a reasonable facsimile of popular-sector membership at large.

SUMMARY

As a middle-range institution that has no major role in making policy, Mexico's Chamber of Deputies has served and supported the national political structure in various ways. Though its members are appointed rather than elected, it provides a democratic and representative veneer to an authoritarian system. It lends an aura of legitimacy to acts of the executive. It facilitates communication between the public and the state (in the interests of both). It functions as a training ground, though to a lesser degree than some other institutions. Perhaps most important, the Chamber is a source of patronage, a means of rewarding loyal service to the regime. It is also an instrument for coopting potential dissidents and independent local leaders. Seats in the lower house confer prestige, perquisites, and other opportunities; they are, in short, a form of political payoff.

Like most other things in Mexico, these benefits are distributed primarily to members of the middle class. Despite the composition of total PRI membership, it is the so-called popular sector that dominates the delegations to the congress and reaps the largest share of the rewards. In a pattern that has persisted since the 1940s, labor and the peasant sector have been severely underrepresented in the legislature. Moreover the superiority of the popular sector extends to control of the workings of the Chamber (through the Gran Comisión) and also to the chances for subsequent political attainment. At all levels, the PRI recruitment system operates in favor of the popular sector—at the expense of the labor and peasant groupings of the party.

These findings derive considerable significance from the social differentiation between the sectoral delegations to the congress. Each of the groups bears a vague resemblance to its constituency. Peasant spokesmen tend to come from rural areas, labor leaders come from cities, popular-sector deputies come from diverse urban-rural origins. Labor and peasant delegates are less highly educated than their popular-sector colleagues. And it appears, in general, that deputies from all three sectors have worked their way up through their sectoral organizations before receiving seats in the Chamber, except for youthful peasant-sector deputies. In view of the data on age, and on the relationship between age and professional title, it seems especially true that the labor sector rewards its members for active service in unions and other worker institutions.

Yet these variations occur within severely restrictive limits. Labor and peasant sector delegates, not to mention their popular-sector colleagues, are much more highly educated than the adult population at large. Many of them have obtained university degrees in law, which is not exactly a lower-class profession, and only a moderate number have actually worked among the people whom they purport to represent. Urban workers and rural *campesinos* thus have far less than their legitimate share of members in the congress; and they do not have spokesmen from their own ranks. In other words, the recruitment and selection system of the congress operates in consistent behalf of the middle class, heterogeneous though it might be: about one-half the deputies have come from the popular sector, and a substantial number of peasant- and labor-sector delegates have themselves come from middle-class origins. As befits a corporate state, lower-class people do not represent themselves; they are led by groups who stand above them in the social hierarchy. The Chamber of Deputies, like the rest of the Mexican system, offers little opportunity for genuine upward mobility. It is an institution of, by, and for the ruling elite.

"Izquierda" means "Left."

· 9 ·

THE RULES OF
THE GAME

So far I have concentrated almost exclusively upon the structural characteristics of political recruitment and selection processes in twentieth-century Mexico. Separate chapters have focused on patterns and changes in the requirements for admission to the elite, the conditions for advancement, the duration of careers, relationships between political and economic power groups, and internal biases within the PRI. Now it is time to raise another question: How have these structures affected the *behavior* of Mexican politicians? As a logical extension of this inquiry, this problem establishes a connection between my empirical data on elites and the ways in which they act, make policy, and relate to the people at large.

Specifically, I shall in this chapter attempt to derive a series of "rules" for self-advancement within the tutelary authoritarian regime that Mexico established by the 1940s. I shall therefore be dealing with members of the postrevolutionary cohort, and in so doing I adopt three premises. First, that officeholders in Mexico have sought to climb upward on the ladder of power and prestige. Second, that they have developed a reasonably accurate (if sometimes unconscious) perception of the structures set forth in the previous chapters—which is a way of saying that they have always known what I claim to have discovered through statistical procedures. And third, that they have shaped their behavior in accord with those perceptions. To justify the use of these assumptions, I shall wherever possible rely upon the testimony of political actors themselves.

The primary purpose of this analysis is not to offer practical or even meaningful advice to would-be politicians. I am a scholar, not a politician, and a North American at that, so it would be wholly improper for me to put on avuncular airs of omniscience and condescension. I employ the notion of "rules of the game" as a literary device, as a kind of metaphor, not as a list of literal instructions, and some of the rules that I propound will seem trivial and self-evident, especially to seasoned Mexican *políticos*. Rather, it should be understood that my intent is to explore the relationships between elite *behavior* and the structural *environment* within which politicians operate. So I have asked myself: Given feature X or Y of the recruitment system, what would be the most logical way for individual officeholders (or office-seekers) to proceed? And have they actually reacted in that way? Thus I am attempting to uncover *rational* modes of behavior, not to prescribe desirable ones. The difference is important.

As the basic conditions of Mexican politics have undergone change, it is apparent that the rules of the game, such as they are, have also altered over time. To gain some historical perspective on the situation of the postrevolutionary cohort, it would be useful to present some brief notes on the circumstances and norms that guided the prerevolutionary and revolutionary generations.

Past Patterns

During the late Porfirian era, as Chapter 3 has shown, there was considerable advantage in having attended a university, as had the *cientificos*, or in having accompanied Díaz in his early military campaigns. The prerevolutionary elite displayed a sharp generational bias, with important governorships and upper-level posts being controlled by men (like Díaz) in their 60s and 70s. For those who met the qualifications for entrance into the elite, the basic rule for political survival was a simple one: curry the favor of the old man. There was very little movement from one position to another, as revealed in Chapter 5, so it was difficult to use one kind of office as a springboard to a higher one. From the late 1880s onward Díaz maintained strict control of the recruitment and selection process, and the only way to get ahead was through his personal approval. In demonstration of his power, Porfirio handpicked his ministers, governors, and even senators and deputies. "His electoral system," Luis Lara Pardo has written,

> was a marvel of precision, in its numerous and complicated details. The lists were made in the office of his private secretary, whose chief, Rafael Chaussal, had more influence than did the majority of ministers. The candidates were put forth by their friends, their ministers, their governors, their military leaders, or their favorites. Each governor could count on one or two seats in the legislature, and these were generally given to sons or near relatives of the incumbents. With some of his ministers Díaz was more generous. From his old friends and faithful followers he chose some deputies and senators himself. For each election it was necessary to renew the recommendations and requests, and Díaz always refrained from making definite commitments, only offering "to do whatever is possible."
> Naturally the candidates outnumbered the positions and he him-

self, with "Chaussalito," made up the final lists. He did this entirely according to caprice, without following any rule other than the conveniences of his system. . . .

After the lists were composed, their distribution was handled by the minister of Gobernación, who sent them to the respective electoral districts. The date of the elections passed completely unnoticed. Nobody voted. Nobody stopped it. From the districts came the certificates of election, with total regularity, without the slightest error.[1]

Thus recruited, the legislature—or *caballada* (horseherd), as it was popularly known—was thoroughly docile. Its members had achieved their position through subordination to Díaz, and their only hope for continuation or promotion lay in further subordination (which was frequent enough, judging from the high rates of continuity revealed in Chapter 6). The rule was clear, straightforward, and widely known: "each of these appointments was due to Porfirio, and gratitude, in consequence, was due to him." Those who broke it by attempting to establish independent power bases, such as Bernardo Reyes, were punished for their violations. Others paid a subtle price, as shown, for instance, by this heartfelt note to Díaz from Francisco M. Arredondo, a supreme court magistrate, in 1900:

> My daughter Concha has melted into a flood of tears because she has not seen the name of her husband, Ing. Manuel F. Villaseñor, listed for any of the electoral districts for deputies. . . . My wife and children think that I have fallen from your good graces.[2]

In this regime, prospects for a son-in-law could depend entirely upon personal relations between the father-in-law (aptly known in Spanish as the *padre político*) and the man at the top.

The Revolution not only ousted Díaz, it also disrupted the rules of the game. As shown in Chapters 3 and 4, the social conditions for admission and promotion underwent some changes. Coming from an urban community furnished less of an advantage than before, and the revolutionary cohort placed somewhat of a premium on youth instead of age. The system also allowed greater opportunity for people of humble background (according to Tables 3-4 and 3-7), but there were

[1] Luis Lara Pardo, "Un sistema electoral a la Porfirio Díaz," *Excélsior*, 5 May 1934.

[2] The quotes are from Daniel Cosío Villegas, *Historia moderna de México: El porfiriato. La vida política interior, parte segunda* (Mexico: Editorial Hermes, 1972), pp. 424 and 425; a complete analysis of the Porfirian electoral system runs from p. 404 to p. 493.

limits to these alterations. University training was still a valued political commodity, degrees in law provided exceptional mobility, and people with professional occupations continued to dominate the upper levels of the hierarchy (see Tables 4-5 and 4-6).

Despite these continuities in the social composition of the elite, the Revolution brought a drastic change in the mechanisms for parceling out political positions. As demonstrated in Chapters 5 and 6, careers became highly flexible—and rather short. People could move easily from office to office, and they felt little structural constraint upon their aspirations. For the 1917-40 cohort public life was a free-wheeling affair, and it no doubt had one cardinal rule: be ready to move fast.

Power was fragmented, not centralized as under Díaz, so a primary task of political aspirants was to identify effective power-holders. The strongest single group, of course, consisted of the president and his inner clique. Another set of power-wielders contained military men, ex-revolutionary generals who, in the 1920s and '30s, maintained their personal armies. As shown in Figure 3-4 it was during this era that soldiers took their largest share of upper-level posts, sometimes in exchange for tacit promises to desist from attempting to overthrow the government. A third important power group consisted of regional strongmen, local *caciques* and state bosses, sometimes military men as well. As indicated in Chapter 5, governors occupied key positions in the 1917-40 epoch. The most powerful among them—men such as Adalberto Tejeda in Veracruz, Tomás Garrido Canabal in Tabasco, or Gonzalo Santos in San Luis Potosí—not only ran their states like fiefdoms; they could also place their favorites in prestigious positions in the national hierarchy.

The revolutionary cohort struggled through a time when political currency was primitive: the most valued goods were force, money, and connections. The military chieftains drew their power from the size and strength of their armies, they traded offices for cash, they dispensed political appointments as a form of outright patronage, they openly favored their friends and relatives.[3] The rules of the game were unambiguous: get close to a powerful person by whatever means, stick to him for as long as possible, and be ready to abandon him if he starts to lose his strength.

[3] On this period see Emilio Portes Gil, *Autobiografía de la Revolución Mexicana. Un tratado de interpretación histórica* (Mexico: Instituto Mexicano de Cultura, 1964); the classic by Ernest Gruening, *Mexico and Its Heritage* (New York: D. Appleton-Century, 1928); and John W. F. Dulles, *Yesterday in Mexico* (Austin: University of Texas Press, 1961). A short but suggestive analysis also appears in Gustavo de Anda, "La carreta burocrática de la Revolución," *Excélsior*, 25 September 1958.

As I shall argue below, some of these precepts have continued to be in force for the postrevolutionary cohort, but the style and content of their application have undergone some major changes. One of the most vivid illustrations of this alteration comes from a sketch of governors by Fernando Díaz de Urdanivia. The quotation is lengthy but the images are strong:

> One day I was waiting for a friend in one of the quieter hotels of Mexico City. I was putting up with my boredom in an armchair in the vestibule. Suddenly there appeared a number of self-important fellows, with peculiar gray hats pulled down over their faces, carrying mysterious suitcases. Joining in a group, they started to unpack the strange bags, taking from them a lovely collection of submachineguns. With prudent apprehension I got up and hid in the hotel office, where I asked the attendant: "What does this mean?" She replied: "That the governor of Jalisco is about to leave." Sure enough, soon afterward the elevator discharged another group of repulsive-looking individuals with pistols on their hips. One of them was, of course, the *señor gobernador*. He crossed the vestibule rapidly and got into his automobile. Behind him there followed, headlong and trampling, the frightful gang. When the blood finally came back to my veins, I thought about Jalisco, poor and admirable, beneath that ignominious yoke.

Then, in what appears to be the era of the postrevolutionary cohort:

> Years later, circumstances brought me to a dance that was being given in a metropolitan social center for another *señor gobernador*. I knew him only by his picture, I must say for the satisfaction of my conscience. When the grand ballroom was jammed with an excited crowd, the guest of honor made his spectacular arrival. He was sporting the most outlandish hat to be imagined: with immense brims raised in front and back, in the napoleonic style; from his shoulders fell a cape beyond definition, too short to be the classic Spanish cape and too long for him to pass for one of those so-called *alguaciles* (officers) who lead the promenade in the bullring; the trimmings were mulberry velvet. His fawning courtesans, who came in a mad rush at his heels, removed and received, with veneration, the marvelous hat. There stood the elegant figure of the *señor gobernador*, wearing a blue smoking jacket and pearl-colored pants; his hands looked like a display case of jewelry, so full were they of dazzling rings. The crowd broke into applause. All the better! And for the little time that I could endure that party, while the courtesans were

dying to speak to the hero and win one of his smiles, and to be seen next to him, I thought of the poor province, with its wretchedly poor people, its dusty streets, its barefoot inhabitants. . . . The Revolution was for *this*?[4]

For the postrevolutionary generation, as the passage implies, politics has become a subtle art. The appearances are genteel, the *señores gobernadores* put on elegant airs, the PRI hegemony is undisturbed—but there exists a struggle for advancement, power, and prestige. What have been the rules of this game?

Making It

The empirical analysis in previous chapters has established several basic features of political recruitment and mobility in Mexico since 1946. In the first place, as Chapter 3 has shown, there have existed rigorous social prerequisites for admission to the national political elite. As in the Díaz era, urbanization of birthplace and level of education have acted as social filters in the recruitment process; particularly important has been attendance at the UNAM. Occupational data on both the officeholders and their fathers (in Tables 3-3 and 3-6) clearly indicate the middle-class character of elite origins. Yet for those who made it into the elite, social background has exerted a relatively minor impact on the prospects for political attainment, the strongest determinants of success being the possession of a professional title and —once again—a degree from UNAM (Chapter 4). In the second place, a strategic position in the institutional chain of offices has had a discernible effect on the likelihood of political achievement, more so than for the revolutionary generation, and cabinet officials in the postrevolutionary cohort have tended to move up through the "executive" network (Chapter 5). But it has still been possible to move from any given position on the political checkerboard to almost any other position and, in view of the statistical probabilities, predictions would be precarious. In the third place, one of the most common moves has been to retirement, or to an honorific sinecure, at a relatively early age. In order to stay in the elite, as Chapter 6 has demonstrated, it has generally been necessary to move up—and then be ready to move out.

All these conditions combine to create a kind of political environment, or ambience, that has profound implications for the norms and guidelines of contemporary elite behavior. What these conditions indi-

[4] Fernando Díaz de Urdanivia, "Pausas del camino. Los señores gobernadores," *Excélsior*, 1 October 1954.

cate is that aspirants to office—or *buscachambas*, as they are called in Mexico, the positions being known as *chambas*—have been struggling in an atmosphere of perpetual uncertainty. There have been no clear-cut blueprints for success, and active politicians have been acutely aware of this fact. As one of my informants kept insisting, to my initial disbelief, "There are no rules, *señor*! There are no rules!" Another individual, a man of considerable experience, has told me that political careers depend entirely upon the whim and caprice of the ruling president. Another long-time politician put it to me in another way: "The only rule," he said, "is that there are no rules." And in a recent interview, a national deputy took note of the unpredictability of the system as well as the cultural proclivities of social scientists from the United States: "North American researchers are very detailed in their work; they are very precise, but they never understand the real intimacies. For example, I just told you what I should do to continue with my career, but I might do all these things and then not make it. In your individual political development there are many other factors, many other factors. *It is almost random.*"[5]

Under these circumstances, then, the most that one can do is to maximize the opportunities. But how? What are the prescriptions? Do they vary? To some extent the maximization of opportunity is bound to depend on past performance and present location—that is, on where you are and where you have been. This raises the difficult problem of differentiation in the rules. As presented in Table 9-1, for instance, it would make a priori sense to distinguish (*a*) the institutional network of the incumbent's current office, using the classification established in Chapter 5, (*b*) the level of office held within that network, and (*c*) type of education and past performance, as reflected in the much-noted difference between *políticos* and *técnicos*. One might suppose, on the basis of this typology, that what is best for a middle-range *político* in the electoral network may not necessarily be best for an upper- or lower-level *técnico* in the administrative apparatus.[6] I shall therefore try to make appropriate distinctions wherever necessary, though not as many as one might expect. It is my suspicion that the rules of the game have broad application in Mexico, that legislators and administrators act alike in many ways, that *técnicos* often bear a close resemblance to *políticos*.

[5] Rudolph O. de la Garza, "The Mexican Chamber of Deputies and the Mexican Political System" (Ph.D. dissertation, University of Arizona, 1972), p. 168; emphasis added.

[6] As here conceived, the "lower" level does not include "base" employees whose jobs are protected by labor unions.

TABLE 9-1

A Typology of Officeholders in Mexico

Level of Office Held	Institutional Network					
	Electoral		Administrative		Executive	
	Político	*Técnico*	*Político*	*Técnico*	*Político*	*Técnico*
High						
Medium						
Low						

For stylistic convenience I shall cast my views in the form of "recommendations." As stated above, these statements do not convey my personal opinion of what is desirable for Mexico or any other country. Nor do they represent prescriptions for elite behavior in the future, since Mexico's political system may well undergo some significant changes in the years ahead. Instead, the recommendations present my notion of the sort of advice that a prescient Mexican observer or politician might have offered to an ambitious young man around the year 1940. (But note, in this regard, that I shall be moving back and forth in time. The rules themselves depict guidelines for action to be taken in the future. The derivation and explanation of the rules relies on materials and patterns seen from the vantage point of the 1970s.)

On Getting Started

1. GO TO A UNIVERSITY, PREFERABLY THE UNAM

Chapter 3 plainly reveals that a university career has become a practically indispensable condition for admission to the national political elite, especially the upper-level elite. According to Table 3-5 three-quarters of the entire postrevolutionary officeholding cohort had been to a university, as had 86.8 percent of the top-echelon elites. UNAM proved to be particularly important as a training ground. As many prominent officials would later recall, the national university was an excellent place for making contacts, alliances, and friendships —especially during the 1920s and '30s, when classes were still small. Professors and students were able to observe each other's talents, they often met informally, they introduced one another to friends and acquaintances in government, and they provided one another with *pa-*

lancas for subsequent use.[7] Table 3-5 tells the story again: nearly one-half the total 1946-71 elite studied at the UNAM, and the figure may have been as high as 70 percent for upper-level officeholders.

Once at UNAM, or whatever institution, *choose a discipline with care.* Law has traditionally offered the optimal prospects for a political career (as implied by Table 3-6) and economics has steadily gained importance over time. Engineering can be useful, but mainly for technical careers in the federal ministries. Medicine has furnished entrees to limited areas of political life, principally in social security and public health.[8] Of course, not everyone could get to UNAM, given its middle-class tendencies, and not everyone could go to university: for people of disadvantaged background, schoolteaching has offered the most promising avenue into political life.

Of course, part of this is just plain luck. If you happen to have a future president of Mexico in your class at university, the chances of reaching high office improve dramatically. For instance, Roderic Ai Camp has established that nearly 20 percent of Miguel Alemán's classmates from the UNAM law school went on to attain high national office, most frequently through Alemán's own intervention.[9] It has been apparent, too, that members of Luis Echeverría's UNAM class have reached positions of prominence—including José López Portillo. But for other classes, those which have not produced presidents or other politically powerful alumni, the career advantages of a UNAM education would be somewhat reduced.

2. JOIN THE PRI

The PRI's hegemony remains unchallenged to this day. This step is pretty much essential for those who become involved in the electoral network, and the PRI hierarchy has often dispensed seats in the national congress as rewards for years of faithful service to the party (see Chapter 8). On the other hand active affiliation with the PRI is not an absolute requirement, as shown in Figure 2-2, especially for *técnico* types who are moving upward through the administrative or executive institutional tracks. Sealtiel Alatriste, for one, obtained several major positions—including an upper-level post, the directorship of the Insti-

[7] On this subject see Roderic Ai Camp, *The Education of Mexico's Revolutionary Family* (forthcoming). It is possible that UNAM may be losing (or have lost) its importance as a training ground for future leaders, partly because of the expansion of the student body, but the effects of this process remain to be seen.

[8] For a typical career of a successful doctor-in-politics see José Báez Villaseñor et al., *Doctor Salvador Zubirán: 50 años de vida profesional* (Mexico: Asociación de Médicos del Instituto Nacional de la Nutrición, 1973).

[9] Roderic Ai Camp, "Education and Political Recruitment in Mexico: The Alemán Generation," *Journal of Interamerican Studies and World Affairs* 18, no. 3 (August 1976): 295-321.

tuto Mexicano del Seguro Social (IMSS)—without ever holding any formal position in the party.[10] So it is possible to get ahead without a visible connection with the PRI, and association with the party can be more of a symbolic act than an active commitment. But it should be remembered that the PRI retains its virtual monopoly on electoral politics, and it is impossible to get very far by linking up with the PAN, PARM, or PPS (beyond an occasional deputy seat, as discussed in Chapter 8). Accordingly, the rule about PRI membership has a corollary to it: whatever else you do, *do not join an opposition party!*

3. TAKE ANY OFFICE IN POLITICS OR GOVERNMENT THAT YOU CAN GET, THE SOONER THE BETTER

As revealed in Chapter 5, specifically in Table 5-4, it is possible to move from position to position with great flexibility, though less so than for the 1917-40 group. To the extent that career patterns have tightened up, the electoral track has become rather removed from routes to high-level offices in the administrative and executive tracks, so ambitious politicians should be wary of the network binding party posts to functional organizations to the Chamber of Deputies (see Figure 5-3). But as one legislator said, there is always hope:

> I did not want to be a deputy. It is not something you want. If politics is getting what you want, it would be very easy. Being a deputy is one step in my career. I think politics is a career, and being a deputy is part of that career. It is like being a doctor. You do not ask him if he wants to perform an appendectomy. You do not ask a politician if he wants to serve in the Chamber. You play with different possibilities as your career develops. You gain political maturity and this provides a series of options, and you accept or reject these. *All my political history is one of trying to achieve higher positions without focusing on a specific post. This is what I think a political career is.* (Emphasis added.)[11]

The important thing is getting into the system, where you can make contacts and start building a career.[12] Remember, too, that politics in Mexico is not an old man's game. Time is short, and it is best to get an early start.[13]

10 Interview with Roderic Ai Camp (23 July 1974). Apparently the president sometimes nominates people who are not members of the PRI for deputyships and brings them into the popular sector. De la Garza, "Chamber," p. 139.
11 De la Garza, "Chamber," pp. 153-154.
12 Ibid., p. 154.
13 There is a slight negative correlation (Pearson's $r = -.109$, $N = 384$) between the age of starting one's career and HIGHEST OFFICE for the postrevolutionary cohort.

4. BE READY TO COMPETE

The university or UNAM degree that helps you get into the system will not help you much in getting to a high position. There are many more aspirants than high offices, as reflected by the opportunity structure in Table 5-4 (and also by the figures in Table A-3 of Appendix A). The struggle is intense: the chances for mobility might expand as one moves from "lower" to "middle-level" positions, but then they contract sharply as one approaches the "upper" range—and it is here that the competition is the strongest. In the view of one well-placed official, "It's a blood-filled battle, a constant fight of one against the other."[14]

On Moving Up

5. STUDY THE SYSTEM

Once you get an office, figure out the best chances for your next move and find a way to maximize those chances. As a matter of fact, Mexican politicians have been constantly engaging in this task, as though they are implicitly computing the probabilities for office-to-office movements displayed in Table 5-4. Almost any discussion of any public figure turns to a description of his *curriculum vitae*, which informed officeholders and observers usually know by heart. As one Mexican colleague explained to me, politicians tend to be veritable *archivos políticos*, thoroughly versed in the intricate movements of their rivals and companions. Because of this habit members of the elite have developed definite (and usually accurate) perceptions of the opportunities afforded by their offices. A legislator described the value of his congressional seat in these terms: "If you have political ambitions it is better to be a deputy than a technical adviser. *Much better.*"[15] Another member of the Chamber, sensing that the Senate would have opened up more opportunities, confessed his disappointment: "I did not want to be a deputy. I was originally slated to be a senator, but other more important political interests intervened and another candidate received the nomination. So, the governor called me in and asked me to be a deputy. What I was interested in was being a state party officer, and since I already had that post I accepted."[16] This man had made his calculations about the relative roles of the two houses

14 Merilee Grindle, "Patrons and Clients in the Bureaucracy: Career Networks in Mexico," *Latin American Research Review* 12, no. 1 (1977): 42. Most of the material in this article also appears in ch. 3 of Merilee Serrill Grindle, *Bureaucrats, Politicians, and Peasants in Mexico* (Berkeley and Los Angeles: University of California Press, 1977).
15 De la Garza, "Chamber," p. 154. Actually this is not saying very much, since the position of technical adviser is generally known to be a low-mobility post.
16 Ibid.

of the congress, and his conclusions closely matched the implications of Table 5-4 in Chapter 5.

6. WHENEVER POSSIBLE, TRY TO GET A POSITION IN MEXICO CITY

This is the place where the president lives, it is the location of the national bureaucracy (and the institutions in the executive and administrative networks), it is the locus of critical decisions. A PRI deputy has put the matter succinctly: "Serving in the Chamber gives you contacts. As a comparison, I have spent 20 years in politics in ————. If I had been in Mexico City I would likely have a more important national position. The fact that I am here allows me to get to know who is active in national politics and, more important, it is an opportunity to have them get to know me. Coming here is really the first step in a national career."[17] What is being measured is not geographical distance; it is a kind of political and social space, counted in units of proximity to the president. The closer one gets to presidential favor, the better one's chances in politics. And to approach the president, or at least the presidential circle, one must go to Mexico City.

7. MAKE ALL THE FRIENDS YOU CAN,
ESPECIALLY AMONG YOUR SUPERIORS

This is crucial because jobs are distributed on a personal basis. Contacts from the UNAM, if you have them, can provide useful entrees and introductions. As an example of these connections, one CONASUPO official got his position through an old school chum: "Don Roberto and I are *compadres*," he said. "We have been friends ever since preparatory school days—we really got to know each other at the university. We worked together in the PRI and then Don Roberto asked me to collaborate with him here."[18] Other politicians have made use of different contacts, of course, but the point is that everyone needs them. A recent study by Merilee Grindle has shown that *none* of the high-level officials in CONASUPO obtained their posts without some sort of introduction or *palanca*, and only 19.5 percent of the middle-level administrators used open recruitment in order to get their jobs; all of the others attained their positions through a direct or indirect personal tie.[19]

It is primarily in this respect, I think, that *técnicos* bear close resemblance to *políticos*. To be sure, aspirants for technical positions must have sufficient training and preparation for the job: to do some engineering, one has to be an engineer. But technical expertise is

17 Ibid., pp. 154-155.
18 Grindle, "Patrons and Clients," p. 43.
19 Ibid., p. 49.

merely a necessary condition for getting the job; it is by no means sufficient in itself. There are still more candidates than openings, competition exists, and the winner—in most cases—is the one with the best personal contacts.[20] Just as do *políticos,* the *técnicos* need friends.

8. MAKE THE MOST OF FAMILY RELATIONSHIPS

According to widespread stereotype, family connections play a central role in Mexican politics, as in the rest of Mexican society, and one of the major weaknesses in the analysis thus far has resulted from my inability to locate solid, empirical data on this question. Fortunately, however, Roderic Camp has compiled usable information on approximately 1,000 officeholders since 1935, a group roughly analogous to my postrevolutionary cohort. According to Camp's count, about 25 percent of national politicians in Mexico have had relatives by blood or marriage in some other public office. Of these relationships, 60 percent were intergenerational, the most common pattern being father-child (mainly father-son), which accounted for 40 percent of the total. The remaining relationships involved members of the same generation, the most frequent bond being brother-brother, which came to one-third of the total.[21] These figures reveal, on one hand, the prevalance of family connections, which furnish an immediate and automatic basis for alliances and loyalties. But on the other hand, they also indicate some limitations of kinship networks. Most prominent politicians have *not* been related to other practicing politicians, though some have been able to extend connections through the institution of *compadrazgo* (godfatherhood),[22] and rather few have been able to get headstarts through their fathers.[23] Hence one corollary: don't rely on family contacts alone.

[20] See Martin Harry Greenberg, *Bureaucracy and Development: A Mexican Case Study* (Lexington, Mass.: D. C. Heath, 1970), esp. p. 100; and the example in Susan Kaufman Purcell, *The Mexican Profit-Sharing Decision: Politics in an Authoritarian Regime* (Berkeley and Los Angeles: University of California Press, 1975), pp. 95-96.

[21] Roderic Ai Camp, "El sistema mexicano y las decisiones sobre el personal político," *Foro Internacional* 27, no. 1 (July-September 1976): 75-78; and Camp, *Education.* Given the difficulty of tracing family connections, Camp's data may well understate the incidence of kinship relations within the political elite. On the other hand, he has counted officeholders with political kin as a percentage of all members of the elite, rather than computing the frequency of family connections as a percentage of all pairwise relations among all politicians, and his procedure might tend to produce a higher figure.

[22] These are also hard to trace: when Hugo Cervantes del Río announced, in 1976, that he and Leandro Rovirosa Wade, another cabinet member, had been *compadres* for years, the news was a surprise. *Excélsior,* 30 April 1976.

[23] Nepotism in Mexico is usually indirect, and relatives are put into agencies *other* than that in which the "placer" is employed. See Greenberg, *Bureaucracy,* pp. 129-130.

For those without any kin relationship to leading politicians, consanguineal or otherwise, there is yet another recourse: gain the confidence of someone who does. One demonstration of this principle comes from the recollections of Praxedis Balboa, whose hopes for an appointment as subdirector of PEMEX were temporarily dashed because the president's mother intervened:

> . . . doña Tomasita Valdés, President Alemán's mother, asked don Antonio [Bermúdez, then director of PEMEX] to lend a helping hand to don Juan Gray, who held an intermediate position; don Antonio, who was very eager to please the lady, decided that it would be useful for his personal interests to nominate Gray for the subdirectorship, even though he lacked the training and capacity for the job. . . . nevertheless, don Antonio achieved his purpose, and I had to give up the illusions that I had concocted for myself.[24]

Balboa later got the appointment, but only after Gray had put his incompetence on public display.

One might also note, in passing, the impact of marriages upon careers. In most instances, marrying the daughter of a prominent officeholder can provide an instant entrée into politics, furnishing the groom with access to all the political capital accumulated by the father-in-law. But liaisons of this sort have been fairly infrequent (accounting for less than 3 percent of the connections uncovered by Camp), and they can also backfire: if the father-in-law falls out of favor with his superiors, the young husband might go down with him as well. If this happened under the *Porfiriato*, it could also happen later on.

9. IF YOU JOIN AN *equipo* OR A *camarilla*, PICK YOUR LEADER WITH CARE

The fate of your boss may well prove to be your own, so it is imperative to choose a winner. Calculate his chances, assess his resources, then make a judicious selection. One insider has described the situation:

> If someone has a chief who is capable and has the prospects for a good future, then that person will probably think, "Perhaps I can go with him at the *sexenio*"; and it happens in reverse, too, if someone has a chief who is not particularly capable but who has influential friends, some will want to follow him. There are a lot of changes and it affects our program, especially when people stop working [in order] to pursue their futures.[25]

---

[24] Praxedis Balboa, *Apuntes de mi vida* (Mexico: n. p., 1975), p. 178.
[25] Grindle, "Patrons and Clients," p. 37.

The choice of a leader has especially weighty consequences for office-holders at the middle and lower echelons, who may never get to make an upward move unless they make an accurate selection.

This process becomes magnified and intensified near the end of presidential *sexenios*, when officeholders of all types—at all levels, but most conspicuously at upper levels—try to figure out who is the *tapado*, the person destined to be the next president. A primary goal of much political activity during these periods is to identify oneself with the eventual winner before the name is released, capitalize upon this early loyalty, and wind up with a lucrative post; many take the cautious road, declaring their support as soon as the *tapado* is known. In general, the later you join the bandwagon, the less the chance for a good job. And as the Arreola cartoons show, those who make a wrong bet are usually the ones to lose out.

10. DON'T MAKE ANY ENEMIES

Be loyal to your leader, at least always *demonstrate* loyalty to him, but don't get too close to him unless you are willing to accept the risks. There is always the possibility that he will not survive the next roll of the dice, as Chapter 6 has demonstrated, so you should try to establish and maintain an independent set of social contacts. As one person in CONASUPO has reasoned: "What if the director general should get 'sick' and have to leave CONASUPO? I have to think of that eventuality and be prepared for it."[26]

The most efficient way of coping with this prospect, of course, would be to keep up good relations elsewhere. Even in one of the most technically oriented agencies of the Mexican government, the Secretaría de Recursos Hidráulicos (SRH), such politicking is widespread and intense. According to one study,

> changing sides and coalitions is tolerated, although abusing this privilege can earn a man the reputation of being a "fair weather friend." Once a man who commands a large political following is clearly out of favor with the power structure, it is permissible for his adherents to drop him for a better prospect. Switching while the issue is still in doubt takes place, but it is a risky undertaking. Political activity in the Ministry is constant, but it reaches fever pitch at the end of each six-year presidential term. Who the President will be is of crucial importance to the members of the bureaucracy, for it will be the high-ranking friends of this man within the SRH who will in all probability be appointed to the top posts. There are few

26 Ibid., p. 39.

Captions: (top): "A cousin of a friend of one of my uncles wants me to tell him . . . but the *compadre* of the friend of my nephew hasn't told me yet."

(Bottom): "If I could only meet the nephew of the friend of the *compadre* of the uncle of the *tapado's* brother . . . I would ask him for a job as assistant to the servant of the subsecretary of the secretary's secretary of the *jefe de intendencia.*"

6. THE STAKES OF THE GAME

Marquee: "Today—The Designation of the Cabinet."
(From left to right): "How happy I am—it's a magnificent comedy!"
"My God! What a horrible tragedy!"

(Labels, from left to right):
Minister
Tapado
Deputy
He Didn't Know Who the
Tapado Was

"Give him a job as a servant of the assistant to the secretary's secretary—he's been wrong for two *sexenios* in a row! Have some pity on the poor man."

surprises in these appointments . . . [but] high-level administrators are often changed after the new term has begun, and it is therefore of primacy that an ambitious man affiliate himself with more than one "leader."[27]

The implication is clear: if you want to keep on moving, keep on looking around.

The trick is to do this without making enemies. Years after Praxedis Balboa had broken with the initial leader of his *camarilla*, Emilio Portes Gil, who thenceforth viewed him as an enemy, he discovered that the former president no longer had the ability to put his friends in influential places—but "he did not lack means or resources to prevent his enemies from getting there."[28] Himself an astute politician, Balboa survived by cultivating the friendship and respect of Adolfo López Mateos. Eventually, he was rewarded with the governorship of Tamaulipas.

11. DON'T ROCK THE BOAT

This is the golden rule of Mexican politics, it has many corollary principles, and several of the rules set forth in this chapter are merely variations on this theme. Power originates in the presidency, designation to office comes down from above, the structure is hierarchical, and one admonition should be self-evident: Don't create problems or difficulties for your superiors, since they control your destiny.

It is this injunction, more than any other, that produces an incentive for effective job performance. For *técnicos* in administrative or executive posts, effectiveness usually relates to the satisfactory completion of a specific task. If an engineer designs a bridge, it ought to stand up; if an economist computes an index, the calculations should be accurate. Failure and gross incompetence can affect and embarrass the boss, since he must bear responsibility for the actions of his underlings. If the bridge falls down, he must answer to his own superiors— and by creating a problem for him, you've created one for yourself.

On occasion, however, *técnicos* must take stands that contradict their own professional judgment. If some technical matter (on, say, terms of agricultural credit or the location of a bridge) is in dispute, a highly trained *técnico* can bring the weight of his intellectual credentials to bear upon the decision, thus earning the gratitude of the person whose position he supports and the enmity of the one whom he opposes. Under these circumstances the *técnico* must make his choice not so much

---

[27] Greenberg, *Bureaucracy*, pp. 118-119.
[28] Balboa, *Apuntes*, p. 175.

on the substantive merits of the case on the basis of a political cal-culation.[29] Among *técnicos*, as among other circles, loyalty is a prized commodity.

For *políticos*, especially those in electoral posts, the definition of ef-fective performance varies with the office. One role of deputies, for in-stance, is to establish communication with the people in their districts. "The party asks that you be a *gestor*," a legislator has explained, "but does not do so explicitly. . . . Those who do not comply with this are not punished, they just do not continue advancing."[30] Senators have other obligations, sometimes serving as brokers between state govern-ments and the national bureaucracy. Governors have yet another set of formal and informal responsibilities.[31]

But the primary task of all Mexican *políticos*, whatever their posi-tion, is to contain, control, and mediate conflict—so as not to engage the attention or concern of their superiors, especially the president. By this criterion, an effective politician is one who does not let crises get out of control. In this sense governors occupy an especially vulnerable position, since they can be held responsible for mass uprisings and pop-ular movements within their states: of the 27 governors who were forced out of office between 1940 and 1964, almost always because of presidential disapproval, 11 lost their jobs at least partly because of their inability to contain protests, riots, or disturbances.[32] The func-tion of politicians is to keep the lid on, by whatever means,[33] and this may be the meaning of advice which Ramón Beteta, a former profes-sor and cabinet minister, is reported to have given Sealtiel Alatriste in his student days: "No matter how great a problem is, remain calm."[34] If you lose your cool, you may well lose your job.

12. AVOID MISTAKES

Tenure in office is brief and insecure, as shown in Chapter 6, and a flagrant error—especially one that becomes public knowledge—can bring a career to an end. Rather than take any chances, many Mexi-can politicians prefer to avoid the public eye, in stark contrast to their

[29] Greenberg, *Bureaucracy*, p. 118.   [30] De la Garza, "Chamber," p. 97.

[31] See Roger Charles Anderson, "The Functional Role of the Governors and Their States in the Political Development of Mexico, 1940-1964" (Ph.D. dissertation, Uni-versity of Wisconsin, 1971).

[32] Anderson, "Governors," ch. VII.

[33] In the hypothetical illustration presented by Kenneth F. Johnson, an aspiring young politician regains favor with his superiors—and a seat in the Chamber of Deputies—by successfully controlling a student outbreak at the national university. Johnson, *Mexican Democracy: A Critical View* (Boston: Allyn and Bacon, 1971), p. 80.

[34] Interview between Sealtiel Alatriste and Roderic Ai Camp (23 July 1974).

limelight-seeking counterparts in the United States. As one deputy has remarked, "Speaking in the Chamber is dangerous. You can make a mistake. You can promote yourself in other ways. If you make a mistake up there, that can be the end."[35]

Publicity, in fact, constitutes a form of insubordination, since it threatens to disturb the hierarchical distribution of authority. "Because of this," according to Manuel Moreno Sánchez,

> it has once again become obligatory for politicians not to speak out, and to try to work always from behind the scenes (*en tono menor y sin relieve*). The more outstanding the activity of any member of the legislature, the more certain that this quality will be the first obstacle for the continuation of his political career. The politician who is diffuse, confused, silent, disciplined, *agachado*, as popular expression says, is the one who takes the lead in the quest for other positions, since he has proven his capacity for reverence and obedience.[36]

If you stay in line, follow orders, and keep quiet, you cannot make a mistake. And if you don't make any mistakes, you cannot embarrass your boss—you win some points for loyalty instead. This axiom is universal, and it applies to all types of politicians at all levels in all types of offices.[37]

13. DON'T MAKE CONTROVERSIAL STATEMENTS IN PUBLIC

This is a specific form of the previous rule, since public declarations can turn into disastrous mistakes. If there is any chance that a statement to the media might annoy some superior, don't make it. A poignant illustration of this principle took place in early 1976, when General Eliseo Jiménez Ruíz, a PRI candidate for a Senate seat, spontaneously answered a reporter's unexpected questions about the army's antiguerrilla campaign in the state of Guerrero that Jiménez Ruíz had led two years before. This whole business had raised something of a public furor, since the rebel leader, Lucio Cabañas, had become a popular hero for radicals, and it was widely thought that he had been murdered in cold blood, perhaps as a result of orders from the presidential palace. After giving details about the way his troops had battled the guerrillas, rescued a kidnapped politician, located most of the ransom money, and killed Cabañas (who allegedly went down fighting, without even a *coup de grace*), the general came to a close:

---

[35] De la Garza, "Chamber," p. 165.

[36] Manuel Moreno Sánchez, *México: 1968-1972. Crisis y perspectiva* (Austin: Institute of Latin American Studies, University of Texas, 1973), p. 8.

[37] See Grindle, "Patrons and Clients," p. 42.

There followed a moment of confusion. The general was nervous at the end. His round face, very dark-complexioned (*moreno*), looked a little pale. Between smiles, he commented:

"I didn't think that they would set this trap for me. *I should not have talked.*"

"But you already did," answered Rodolfo Echeverría Zuno [the president's son, and a key person in the PRI].

"And in front of ten qualified witnesses," concluded the reporter.[38] (Emphasis added.)

Now that the word was out, Jiménez Ruíz might have to answer for his declaration. And if the revelation brought consternation in the upper circles, as he himself realized, he would have to pay. As things turned out, he made it to the Senate, but it was nevertheless clear that his public statement had placed his career in jeopardy.

14. IF YOU HAVE TO MAKE A PUBLIC STATEMENT, USE THE APPROPRIATE LANGUAGE

The rhetorical legacy of the Revolution contains a rich collection of symbols, heroes, and myths—the Constitution, Madero, Zapata, Cárdenas, and so on. Invocation of these images is an essential part of public discourse in Mexico, since it provides a means of identifying any contemporary position on policy with a heroic and unassailable tradition. Potentially controversial statements instantly become noncontroversial. When Adolfo López Mateos declared in 1960 that his regime would be "of the extreme left," for example, he quickly added that this stance would be "within the Constitution."[39] Who could challenge that?

Deference to the president is also mandatory. When José López Portillo formally opened his presidential campaign, in October 1975, he made efficient use of available symbolism. The meeting took place in Querétaro, site of the constitutional convention of 1916-17, with four surviving members of that congress there as honored guests. López Portillo gave a winding, extemporaneous exegesis of the Constitution, then looked ahead to the election under the PRI: "The Party of the Mexican Revolution"—referring to the party by a previous name—"the one that brought Cárdenas and Echeverría to power"—thus identifying Echeverría with the populist and much-revered Cárdenas—"intends to keep pursuing Mexican ways in order to carry its banners more onward and upward"—echoing the slogan of Echeverría's 1970 campaign, *arriba y adelante*—and the party's efforts in the election

---

[38] *Excélsior*, 26 April 1976.   [39] *Excélsior*, 2 July 1960.

would reaffirm the national commitment to justice, freedom, peace, and progress.[40] It would be hard to vote against a candidate and party like that!

15. PASS DIFFICULT DECISIONS ON TO YOUR SUPERIORS

Yet another corollary of the injunction against mistakes, this rule can accomplish two goals: first, it provides you with a chance to demonstrate deference and loyalty; and second, if the decision turns out to be incorrect—that is, if it incurs displeasure at the upper reaches of the hierarchy—you can escape responsibility. There is a built-in disincentive for initiative, as one ambitious officeholder clearly recognized: "If you do more than your boss you're in real trouble."[41] Application of this rule helps account for some of the delays that occur within the Mexican bureaucracy, since delicate decisions must climb upward until they reach a level where they can be handled, await resolution, and then filter back down to the level of implementation.

Instances of decision-passing can be difficult to find, since most public figures like to talk, if at all, about decisions that they made. One anecdotal illustration emerges from my own efforts to do the research for this book. From an academic colleague I had heard that one government office had biographical records on a group of officeholders. When I asked the head of the archive about these materials, he flatly denied their existence; I pressed the inquiry, he continued his denial, and then I gave up. Some time later, through another contact, I made friends with a fairly senior official (the *oficial mayor*) of that same institution. In the course of one conversation I asked him about the biographies, he said they existed, took me over to meet the head of the archive (as though we'd never met before), and ordered him to get the records—and this the archivist did, courteously and graciously, without a flicker of recognition or hesitation. The point of the story is not that the archivist was being deceitful, since that would be grossly unfair. My point is that he was being smart, protecting himself until commands came from above. After all, he had nothing to gain from helping a foreign researcher, and, if some politician objected to the release of biographical data, possibly a lot to lose.

16. BUT WHILE AVOIDING MISTAKES, THE MEDIA, AND EXCESS RESPONSIBILITY, TRY TO DISTINGUISH YOURSELF

This can be a delicate task. In order to get ahead, you have to capture the notice of the higher-ups—without appearing to challenge or

---

[40] *Excélsior*, 10 October 1975.

[41] Susan Eckstein, *The Poverty of Revolution: The State and the Urban Poor in Mexico* (Princeton: Princeton University Press, 1977), p. 87.

threaten them in any way. That is, you want to gain a reputation for being exceptionally able—and willing to carry out orders as well.

In practice, this stricture leads officeholders to seek out projects
a. that are highly visible, and can thus enhance the reputation of the incumbent;
b. that can be finished fairly quickly, before the tnure in office is up;
c. that require no hard or controversial choices, such as having to favor one group or sector over another, since this would create conflict and adverse publicity;
d. that offend no higher-level politicians; and
e. that do not cost much money.

Especially on lower (and local) levels, these criteria typically stimulate efforts at "beautification"—public parks, fountains, malls, and so forth. Such projects may not have much developmental value, but they meet all the requirements for building a career, and they furthermore provide an opportunity for the incumbent to curry someone's favor by naming the plaza after him (or at least including his name on a dedicatory plaque). This phenomenon is so widespread, in fact, that two scholars have come up with a name for it: *plazismo* (plaza-ism).[42]

For bureaucrats and *técnicos* who may not have much chance to indulge in public works, this syndrome takes on different forms. One of the most common manifestations of it is the publication of numerous and voluminous reports, extolling the accomplishments of the incumbent's own department, and also praising the inspirational (Revolutionary!) leadership of the *señor presidente*.[43] The PRI offers another outlet for literary talent by putting out a number of magazines and *anuarios* and by publishing miscellaneous volumes from time to time. Another recourse for ambitious office-seekers is oratory: many politicians start out as champions in this at school, they get invited to give speeches for a candidate, and during the campaign they can display their talents and start making useful contacts. Yet another is to write a book, usually on an innocuous topic (history will do), and thus acquire the prestige and renown of being an intellectual. (Mario Moya Palencia, who nearly won the presidential designation in 1976, began attracting attention with, among other things, the publication of a

[42] Richard R. Fagen and William S. Tuohy, *Politics and Privilege in a Mexican City* (Stanford: Stanford University Press, 1972), pp. 28-29; and Tuohy, "Centralism and Political Elite Behavior in Mexico," in *Development Administration in Latin America*, ed. Clarence E. Thurber and Lawrence S. Graham (Durham, N.C.: Duke University Press, 1973), pp. 260-280, and esp. pp. 273-274.
[43] See Greenberg, *Bureaucracy*, pp. 51, 54.

book on *La reforma electoral* in 1964.)[44] Thus it is possible to combine exhibitions of talent and expertise with demonstrations of political acuteness.

There is a premium, then, on discreet visibility, and the quest for it partakes of many forms. Officeholders and office-seekers attend a myriad of ceremonies and functions, the most conspicuous, perhaps, being the political breakfast. During campaign years they struggle for positions in the candidate's entourage, where they can capture the attention of the incumbent-to-be (or at least of his subordinates). After a day-long trip with the López Portillo group in 1976, for instance, I asked one participant why everyone had so willingly endured the 20-hour schedule: "It is important," he said, "to see and to be seen. That is *very important*." From an earlier era, too, Frank Tannenbaum recalled a similar incident:

> There was once a man who was one of the large group that always accompanied the President on his trips through the country. This man suffered from the heat and from the difficulties of living in a train or traveling on horseback over the mountains. He was obviously uncomfortable. I inquired: "What is he doing here?" The reply was: "He is acquiring merit." "What does he want merit for?" "He wants to be governor of Chihuahua." This man did not acquire sufficient merit and did not become governor.[45]

There was never any question, though, about the logic or propriety of his behavior; he was simply beaten out by someone with more "merit."

17. WORK FAST

This is a uniform commandment for all officeholders, regardless of level or location. Local offices and deputyships have only three-year terms, and even the six-year tenure of most other positions puts incumbents under pressure to perform. "You know how we all come in and get thrown out at the *sexenio*," one federal official has remarked. Another has explained that "We want to do away with programs which are subject to the *sexenio*," and a third has expressed his determination to "set this program in motion before the next *sexenio* so that it will really be carried out."[46] Besides, bureaucrats fully understand that their positions depend entirely upon the continued favor of their superiors, and they know they could be fired on a moment's notice.[47] Politicians not only have to distinguish themselves within the limits al-

44 Mario Moya Palencia, *La reforma electoral* (Mexico: Ediciones Plataforma, 1964).
45 Frank Tannenbaum, *Mexico: The Struggle for Peace and Bread* (New York: Alfred A. Knopf, 1960), p. 86.
46 Grindle, "Patrons and Clients," pp. 37, 41.
47 Greenberg, *Bureaucracy*, p. 130.

lowed by the system; they also have to do it rapidly. (This premium on haste, it should be noted, is totally antithetical to long-run planning. Speed and short-run efficiency are exalted at the expense of purpose, persistence, and long-range vision.)

18. INSTEAD OF LOSING EXCESSIVE TIME ON THE JOB,
KEEP ON MAKING FRIENDS

Beyond the need to work fast and avoid mistakes, it is not really necessary to acquire a thorough mastery of all the details and requirements of your present office. Positions are won primarily through contacts, not merit, and (as indicated in Table 5-4) there is only a modest chance that the skills required by your next position will have much to do with the nature of your current one. One high official in the semi-public sector described his own qualifications:

If you would look at my professional *curriculum vitae* you would find little reason for me to be here. But if you were to look at my political *curriculum* you would see much more clearly why I occupy this position. What kind of politics? Well, party politics doesn't really matter all that much since it's effectively a one-party system. What counts is group politics and the politics of personal relations.[48]

Similarly, when a deputy recounted the advantages of serving on the Permanent Commission, which conducts congressional business while the legislature is not in session, it was in terms of making contacts. "During the regular session the Chamber's activities are carried out by around 200 deputies; here they are carried out by 15. That gives you a mathematical response. You have closer contact with individuals and with other branches of government."[49]

Despite the quality of their training and their jobs, *técnicos* must also concentrate on making friends. They are highly mobile individuals and they move frequently from job to job. As Martin Harry Greenberg has pointed out, "Mexican engineers are trained as generalists instead of specialists as in the United States. Engineers can thus be shifted from one position to another within the bureaucracy, giving them a great deal of flexibility and insuring that they will find a position *somewhere* within the system."[50] To be sure, officeholders who are moving along the executive and administrative routes may spend less time on contacts and friendships than do politicians on the electoral track, and, as argued in Chapter 5, some professionalization in career patterns appears to have taken place. But this is a matter of degree, not kind. The fact is, all Mexican officeholders have to put a consider-

[48] Grindle, "Patrons and Clients," p. 51.
[49] De la Garza, "Chamber," p. 167.   [50] Greenberg, *Bureaucracy*, p. 53.

able amount of energy into the continual cultivation of their social networks.

19. RESPECT THE LAW OF PRODUCTIVE INEFFICIENCY

This principle stipulates that an inefficient agency can prove to be a useful instrument for making friends and accumulating political capital. An efficient office, as I use the term, is one that fulfills all its formally assigned tasks and satisfies the needs and demands of its relevant clientele. An inefficient agency cannot perform all its assigned functions, a situation which permits the director to decide which jobs shall be done—and, more important, it allows him to make those decisions on the basis of personal favoritism. "It will be difficult," one often hears from an administrator, "but for you I'll make a special effort." Alternatively, officeholders sometimes accept money, rather than the promise of a political payoff, in exchange for the fulfillment of a task.

The principle of productive inefficiency finds most frequent application in agencies with ample discretionary power, especially those that issue licenses and permits. Customs agencies are veritable hotbeds of productive inefficiency. Also, the principle tends to be most fully implemented by officials at the middle level of authority: they have enough power to make the key decisions, but they are not so visible that they run much risk of negative publicity. Not everyone applies this law, of course, but almost everyone respects it. So if you see someone else engaging in productive inefficiency, you don't blow the whistle —remember that it's a part of the game.

On Accepting Defeat

20. IF YOU DO NOT RECEIVE THE OFFICE THAT YOU WANT, BE PATIENT

Don't complain. Wait. There is a great deal of turnover in the Mexican system, and new opportunities are bound to arise. As documented in Chapter 6, more than one person has made a political comeback. As Ramón Beteta put it, the only political sin without pardon has been affiliation with the reactionary regime of Victoriano Huerta (1913-14). "We have forgiven everything else: some of us were with Carranza, others were with Villa, others with Zapata; some were for Obregón, some were against Obregón," but those are things of the past. People from every side—except the Huerta group—could work in total harmony.[51] In recent periods, too, politicians have continued to display resiliency. "I began by selling newspapers in the streets," a

---

[51] As quoted in James W. Wilkie and Edna Monzón de Wilkie, *México visto en el siglo XX: entrevistas de historia oral* (Mexico: Instituto Mexicano de Investigaciones Económicas, 1969), p. 27.

prominent official has recalled, "and worked my way up to be a manager in three government companies. Then I lost out and was reduced to being a mere department chief . . . then a submanager and now I have risen to being a manager again. There is what you might call a great deal of capillary action in Mexico."[52]

On the other hand, repeated chances are available only for those who accept disappointment silently and stoically. According to Braulio Maldonado, former governor of Baja California, the price of a transgression can be great: "May God keep him from getting into a rebellion, because his political relegation will then be sealed for many years! For those who are sacrificed, there remains no alternative to accepting one's fate and getting the greatest advantages from demonstrating disinterest and 'discipline.' "[53]

It is in this light that one might best comprehend the plight of Carlos Armando Biebrich, the youthful governor of Sonora who was forced to resign in October 1975 under intense pressure from federal authorities in Mexico City. Explanations for presidential displeasure with Biebrich are various. One view is that he engaged in too flagrant corruption (thus violating rule 21, mentioned below); another is that he was unable to control the violence that accompanied *campesino* seizure of land (see rule 11); another refers to a personal dispute between himself and Echeverría; and a fourth interpretation, the one that I myself accept, is that he had misidentified the presidential *tapado*, backing Moya Palencia instead of López Portillo (see rule 9), and his punishment was intended as a warning to other *moyistas* (see Chapter 10).

Whatever the source of the problem, Biebrich sealed his fate by giving a remarkable interview to the newspaper *Excélsior*. Declaring himself to be the victim "of an openly manipulated demagogic attack," Biebrich accused the director of Agrarian Reform, Agustín Gómez Villanueva—by name—of fomenting violence and disorder in the countryside, and of instigating the disturbance that led to his resignation. He charged Celestino Salcedo, president of the national peasant organization (the CNC), of complicity in this design, referring to him as "an incompetent *campesino* leader and an irresponsible demagogue." He asserted that Salcedo, like Gómez Villanueva, was conspiring with large-scale *latifundistas*. Perhaps most remarkably, he did not exculpate the president—"History will have to make its own judgment on President Luis Echeverría"—though he did shower praise on the successor-to-be, José López Portillo, for his "clear sense of history" and

[52] Grindle, "Patrons and Clients," p. 39.

[53] Braulio Maldonado, *Baja California: comentarios políticos* (Mexico: Costa-Amic, 1960), p. 16.

commitment to "revolutionary transformation" (see rule 14).[54] But the damage was done. With this interview Biebrich had broken several rules of the game: by making controversial public statements (13), by making enemies (10), by rocking the boat (11). Disgraced, he lost much of his property, as well as his governorship, and for some time there was a warrant out for his arrest. Whether he could ever recover from these multiple transgressions seems, at most, a dubious prospect.

For people who don't obtain any office at all, one of the most promising alternatives has been to take a professorship at the UNAM, even on a part-time basis. There you can cultivate a following among students, renew your credentials as an intellectual, keep up your contacts in the government—and wait.

21. ONCE IN THE NATIONAL ELITE, PREPARE YOUR EXIT FROM IT

Chances are that your first office on the national level will also be your last one, and the odds are not much more than one out of three that you will ever hold a comparable position under another president. Moreover you can never be sure of staying on: no matter how many presidents have given you positions in the past, the greatest single likelihood is that you will not hold any similar position in the future (see Table 6-4).

The moral here is obvious: *take what you can while you're there.* Self-enrichment through public office is a time-honored tradition in Mexico, it is expected of officials, and it constitutes a kind of self-protection or insurance. But there are also limits, as to both method and amount. As Ramón Beteta has described it, self-enrichment (not to call it corruption) has become a subtle art:

> I don't know how some people can believe that the minister of the treasury, the president of the republic, or some other minister can say on one fine day:
>
> "Well, from this or that appropriation of the budget send one half to my home."
>
> There are some who believe this, I tell you, there really are. After resigning from the government [in 1952] I personally was accused, for example, of taking the gold reserves of the Bank of Mexico when I went to Europe as ambassador.
>
> I say it is absurd, but there are people who believe it. As you say, there is no need to do it in this way, which is, let's say, the crudest way to take advantage of the government.
>
> There are many ways, unethical but legal, that an officeholder

---

[54] The interview is in *Excélsior*, 13 November 1975.

can make himself rich. Take, for instance, a public official who knows that a new highway will be constructed and who knows the person in charge of building or directing the project. He can buy, directly or indirectly, the land that will be affected by the highway and thus obtain a profit. Ethically, this is not correct; but legally, it is not a crime. And these things are commonplace, much more so than people think. . . .

On the lower levels of government, as in customs and inspections agencies, inspectors do receive what is known in Mexico as a *mordida*, or bribe, a tip for doing or not doing a certain thing. This has various degrees: there is the *mordida* for doing quickly what a person can rightfully request, and this is really a tip; there is the *mordida* for doing something slowly, not rapidly, and this is a serious thing; then there is the third kind of *mordida*, for doing something that a person cannot rightfully request, like letting merchandise into the country without paying duty.

This, unfortunately, does exist, but Mexico is not the only country where it does, and it does not happen at the ministerial level. That is to say, there has not been any president or minister within, let us say, the last five or six administrations who has ever gained a significant advantage for himself through really illegal means.[55]

But the opportunities are widespread as well as diverse, and temptations come in varied forms: within the ministries there can be kickbacks on purchases, payoffs for contracts, internal bribes and "year-end gifts," payoffs for special services.[56] Given the probability of imminent retirement in middle age, it seems only natural for officeholders to seize the advantages before they disappear.

One of the consequences of this pervasive pattern of self-enrichment is to increase control and discipline within the political elite. If a powerful politician wants to attack a rival, or justify the removal of an underling, he can usually trot out charges of "corruption" (as happened in the Biebrich case). The chances are that there will be some truth in the accusation, but even if there isn't most people *think* the charge is accurate (as it would be for most officeholders) and some damage is still done. Thus the opportunities for self-enrichment become a systematic source of tacit blackmail. And not surprisingly, this tends to discourage political insurgency.

[55] In Wilkie and Wilkie, *México visto*, p. 67. For a slightly different translation of this passage see James W. Wilkie, *The Mexican Revolution: Federal Expenditure and Social Change since 1910* (Berkeley and Los Angeles: University of California Press, 1967), pp. 8-9.

[56] See Greenberg, *Bureaucracy*, pp. 70-77.

Matriarcado

POR MARINO

"Corruption."

22. EVEN AS YOU REACH THE PEAK OF YOUR CAREER,
ALWAYS BE KIND TO YOUR SUBORDINATES

Chances are that you will be leaving national office before the age of 60, and you will need their help when they have risen to prominence. It appears, from Chapter 7, that the private sector does not offer many opportunities to ex-politicians. So you will have to rely on favors and appointments, perhaps as one of the countless "advisers" in Mexican officialdom. (This practice has become institutionalized in the SRH, where the office of "technical adviser" on the eighteenth floor is known as "the nest of the fallen eagles.")[57] If you go into business on your own, pick an industry where you can make full use of your contacts in the government (construction is highly recommended). Law is a promising field. "As a lawyer," one deputy has said, "I will have met all the government officials in the Federal District. When I hear of some work they are doing in my state I can call them and ask for the assignment. They might give it to me."[58] Lawyers can also operate as intermediaries between the public and the private sectors.

But no matter what you do, you are bound to need the assistance of your underlings, and you can never predict when one of those connections might bear fruit. One of the country's most distinguished engineers, Antonio Dovalí Jaime, held a subcabinet post during the Alemán administration and in 1952 returned to his professorship at UNAM. There he accumulated further honors and recognition, but no public offices, until 1970—when, it is reported, one of his former students remembered him and put him up for an important spot in the incoming Echeverría regime.[59] The recommendation went through, and, at the age of 65, Dovalí Jaime suddenly became the head of PEMEX. The moral is: Never lose hope.

Agustín García López did not have that much luck. A man of humble background, he managed to get a law degree from UNAM, earned a reputation as a brilliant professor, and became Secretary of Public Works under Alemán in 1946-52. According to a reliable source he retired from the cabinet with 200 million pesos, a huge fortune at the time, and then his troubles began. First he invested in manganese mines in Tamaulipas; apparently out of hostility to members of the *alemanista* group, perhaps for excessive corruption, the Ruiz Cortines government promptly nationalized the mines—without compensation. Next, García López joined some Americans in land investments in Colima; these were nationalized too. Third, he purchased a huge plot

---

[57] Ibid., p. 68.   [58] De la Garza, "Chamber," p. 158.
[59] Interview of former cabinet member with Roderic Ai Camp (28 July 1974).

of land, practically a whole mountain, on the outskirts of Mexico City. He intended to develop it as a low-income housing district, but was unable to obtain a license for construction and the investment was lost. Even as a former cabinet officer, and a figure of presence and prestige, García López had been unable to maintain effective political contacts, notwithstanding his personal friendship with Alemán. When he died in January 1976, he left no will, no fortune, and a pile of debts. "If he had put the money under a mattress," said one descendant ruefully, "we would still be rich."[60]

Thus my recommendations, a total of 22 in all. They are overstated and oversimplified, and they do not begin to capture the complexity of public life in Mexico. My basic point, as stated before, is that these guidelines constitute an absolutely rational, if not wholly desirable, response to the structural environment within which politicians have to operate.

One of the most obvious implications of this behavior pattern is that, in building their careers, Mexican politicians pay scant attention to their popular constituencies (except in order to control them). They are forever dealing with each other, they are seeking favor from their superiors, and they are communicating in a language of exaggerated deference. At times the quest for office becomes thoroughly demeaning, and Braulio Maldonado has written a poignant description of that self-abasement. Although the president appoints the leading officeholders, Maldonado begins, getting the appointment is a painful process since

> to become a viable candidate for a public position, one must go through a rather droll, but rigorously definite, procedure. The would-be candidate has to enter the battle early, he has to appeal to friends and use political influences; he has to become a hardened *antesalero* [in anterooms to offices] and wait hour after hour, day after day, in order to be received by functionaries high and low; he must suffer countless humiliations; he must smile and be polite to everyone, from the doorman to the boss. This prior task is popularly known as "leaving no stone unturned" (*picar piedra*).
>
> It is also indispensable for the aspirant to figure in the "political file," that is, for his name to appear on the list of contenders, with full and precise information about his background: where he was born, who were his parents, what were his revolutionary or reactionary origins, which group or party that he had served; who might be

60 As reported by informants who wish to remain anonymous.

his political sponsors (*padrinos*) and what interests they might have in his career. These look, more than anything else, like police files on a criminal. The thankless job of the *antesalero* and *picapedrero* requires patience and resignation for weeks, months, and even years.

A further requirement is that the president should know the candidate, or be a relative or friend. If he can get an endorsement through family connections, then the aspirant draws closer to his goal. But when this happens, that is, when he is on the threshold of the designation, the contender has by this time given the shirt off his back, he has made countless promises, often at the price of his own dignity. He has been mercilessly exploited by hundreds of politicians, labor bosses, peasant leaders, and by mercenary journalists. He has had to parade a line of behavior that is "revolutionary" without parallel. He has already made arrangements for the disbursement of the public budget, or even for his own salary, for the period of his incumbency.

Only after suffering this calvary does the aspirant get presidential approval. From there on the process is exceedingly easy, the battle is won, victory having been secured in governmental anterooms. Now the labor unions, the peasant organizations, the popular sector and the party declare him to be the Official Candidate, and thus it is that our political hopeful becomes the man of the day, a person of talent, honored in every respect, a figure of great revolutionary merits.[61]

One has to wonder, after absorbing a passage like that, about the emotional strains and stresses of the recruitment and promotion processes.

A further implication of my analysis lies in the extension of its basic premise: that, given the exisiting institutional environment, Mexican officeholders have complied with these rules as a rational means for maximizing power and success. I myself remain skeptical of attempts to explain Mexican patterns of political behavior purely as functions of "national character," *machismo* drives or other cultural propensities. Such interpretations are often tautological (Mexicans act like Mexicans because they are Mexicans) and they sometimes suggest, if only indirectly, that the behavior under study is somehow quixotic or irrational. On the contrary, this analysis urges the conclusion that Mexico's office-seekers and officeholders have adopted functional, and in this sense entirely rational, modes of responding to the structure of opportunities that they confront. Cultural norms, of course, are important: they provide systematic codification of rules, they formulate

61 Maldonado, *Baja California*, pp. 14-15. For an unsympathetic description of Maldonado and his governorship see Johnson, *Mexican Democracy*, pp. 134-140.

prescriptions for behavior, and they can have an independent impact on patterns of action and response. What I am here suggesting is that "culture" is in this case only a secondary causal agent. The primary one is the political environment, the formal and informal structure of opportunities.[62]

The existence and acceptance of these rules confirm yet another fundamental proposition: that the long and arduous pursuit of high-level office has a strong influence on the socialization of Mexican politicians, providing them with a key for appropriate responses to any given set of cues. It is in this sense that social background, or class origin, has relatively slight impact on values or premises among Mexico's top-echelon officials. Having survived the rigors of promotion, these people have gone through an extensive and intensive training process, achieving success in accordance with the rules of the game. Consensus prevails at the pinnacles of power, and this is in part a consequence of socialization through institutionalization.

It is hard to know, in the absence of rigorous comparative data, what might determine the rules of the game. Certainly the Mexican codes differ from standard procedure in open democratic polities, where aspirants to power usually try to build grass-roots support, sometimes by combative exploitation of a single issue (as Joe McCarthy did in the United States). They also differ from seniority systems, as in military establishments that place such premiums on professional conduct; one reason that Juan Carlos Onganía was the undisputed leader of the so-called Argentine Revolution in 1966 was his reputation as a "soldier's soldier." It is possible, too, that totalitarian systems, with thoroughly planned economies, place more emphasis on task-related skill than is the case in Mexico.

But there are also similarities, especially in other countries of the Third World. To take but one example, Mexico's *camarilla* system bears an uncanny resemblance to the Brazilian *panelinha* system as described by Anthony Leeds. Seeking a structural explanation for the Brazilian phenomenon, Leeds maintains that it results from the juxtaposition of "static-agrarian" and "expansive-industrial" societies, a situation that (*a*) leads to the simultaneous usage of traditional (personalistic) and modern (bureaucratic) modes of conduct, and (*b*) expands and complicates the range of opportunities, leading individuals to acquire numerous (or generalized) skills and to join together in

---

[62] Note the recognition of institutional factors in James E. Payne and Oliver H. Woshinsky, "Incentives for Political Participation," *World Politics* 24, no. 4 (July 1972): 546. One problem with the Payne-Woshinsky approach is that it stresses only the *types* of incentives, without saying much about the origins or *causes*.

collective groups (*camarillas* or *panelinhas*). There are differences between Brazil and Mexico, and these should not be overlooked, but Leeds has presented a major hypothesis—that *camarilla*-type systems are associated with specific patterns of socioeconomic development, those found currently in the Third World.[63] Only comparative analysis can prove or disprove this idea, but Mexico is one case that strongly confirms it.

A further determining factor would appear to be the style and structure of authoritarian regimes, themselves perhaps related to the existence of social structures in which expansive "modern" sectors are attempting to contain and repress the static "traditional" ones. Authoritarianism is entirely compatible with the personalized and deferential Mexican rules of the game, which both limit the range of the political agenda and stress the need for cohesiveness within the ruling groups. Here it is difficult to isolate the causal process—to figure out whether authoritarianism produces such rules, in order to maintain the pattern of "limited pluralism," or whether such rules produce authoritarian regimes. Probably both factors reinforce each other, though I tend to view the political system itself as the stronger causal agent. Regimes tend to impose their rules.

As set forth in this chapter, the rules of the Mexican game have pertained specifically to the postrevolutionary generation of 1946-71. After the inauguration of the Echeverría regime in 1970 there was much talk about the need for structural change, and about means of altering the institutional environment of politics. Chapter 10 will attempt to discuss the impact of the 1970-76 *sexenio* and of the presidential succession of 1976.

[63] Anthony Leeds, "Brazilian Careers and Social Structure: A Case History and a Model," in *Contemporary Cultures and Societies of Latin America*, ed. Dwight B. Heath and Richard N. Adams (New York: Random House, 1965), pp. 379-404. In contrast to Mexican *camarillas*, Brazilian *panelinhas* generally include businessmen as well as politicians, and participants often hold multiple jobs simultaneously —whereas Mexicans tend to do so in sequential fashion.

· 10 ·

RETROSPECT AND PROSPECT:
FROM ECHEVERRÍA
TO LÓPEZ PORTILLO

The presidential succession is the paramount event in contemporary Mexican politics. It involves the transfer of the nation's highest office from one person to another, but it signifies far more than that. It can bring new directions in policy, within the generous limits prescribed by revolutionary rhetoric, even fairly sharp departures from the recent past. More directly, and necessarily, it means a realignment in the distribution of power and prestige throughout the country, a rearrangement in the relative standing of cliques and *camarillas*: those who are close to the new president move up near the top, those who are not move either out or to the bottom. The succession thus sets the rhythm of political life, marking time according to *sexenios*, the six-year limits of incumbencies. The object of endless speculation and discussion, the transition is imbued with deep symbolic value. Ever since Madero's challenge against Díaz, it has been taken as a measure of the nation's political health: a peaceful transfer of power means that the system is working, that "no-reelection" is in force, that the government is complying with the heritage and obligations of the Revolution.

In this chapter I describe and analyze the presidential succession of 1976, the transition from Luis Echeverría to José López Portillo. Through a fairly detailed reconstruction of events, I attempt to explore the *operation* of the system, relating the structural characteristics of the regime (as described in prior chapters) to an immediate series of choices and decisions—moving from macroanalysis to microanalysis, illustrating general tendencies through the study of a single case. In particular, I focus on the *process* of political recruitment, and the ways that elite formation can affect (and reflect) the system's capacity for adaptation, absorption, and change. Because of constraints on time, as well as space, the narrative concentrates on events up through December 1976.

I assume, at the outset, that the outgoing president selects his own successor after consulting with leaders of power groups, euphemistically known in Mexico as "public opinion." This means that the president cannot impose a truly unpopular candidate. It also means that, among those who are deemed to be acceptable, the president makes the final and determining choice. As Alfonso Corona del Rosal, an able, experienced, and powerful *político*, once said, it is the president who "selects his successor, supports him, and sets him on his course."[1] I take this view to be correct.

THE ECHEVERRÍA REGIME (1970-75)

When Luis Echeverría took the presidential oath on December 1, 1970 he looked like the supreme embodiment of Mexico's political elite. Almost to the very letter, he had obeyed all the rules of the game. Born in Mexico City in 1922, he had studied at UNAM, taken a degree in law, and, like so many of his colleagues, taught courses there as well. He married into a prominent political family from the state of Jalisco. He promptly entered the PRI and, more important, joined the *camarilla* of Rodolfo Sánchez Taboada, a revolutionary general and old-time political figure. When Sánchez Taboada became president of the PRI, in 1946, Echeverría became the party's press secretary; when Sánchez Taboada became Secretary of the Navy, in 1952, Echeverría became director of a department in that ministry. In 1955 Sánchez Taboada died and Echeverría, then holding a post in the secretariat of education, had to expand his network. Two years later he reentered the PRI as *oficial mayor*, he worked hard during the López Mateos campaign, and, in 1958, he landed a crucial position: Subsecretary of Gobernación, under Gustavo Díaz Ordaz. When Díaz Ordaz assumed the presidency, in 1964, Echeverría received the post of secretary. Six years later, Echeverría repeated the move that Alemán, Ruiz Cortines, and Díaz Ordaz had all made before, from Gobernación to the presidency. It seemed to be a tradition.

Throughout his career, Echeverría had labored intensively and steadily behind the scenes. Aside from his positions in the PRI, he had stayed resolutely on what I have called the "executive" officeholding track (Chapter 5). He was the first constitutional president since the end of the Mexican Revolution who had *never* held a single elective position. He had become, over the years, a master of bureaucratic maneuvering. Only one event—the massacre of students in 1968—had brought him into the limelight, and, though many held him responsible for that wanton display of force, his actual role was not at all clear. An austere, ambitious man, balding, bespectacled, nonsmoking, teeto-

---

[1] See the discussion of this theme in *Excélsior*, 14 September 1975. Recent analyses of the subject include Roderic Ai Camp, "El sistema mexicano y las decisiones sobre el personal político," *Foro Internacional* 27, no. 1 (July-September 1976): 51-83; and Daniel Cosío Villegas, *La sucesión presidencial* (Mexico: Joaquín Mortiz, 1975).

taling, and trim, he was the consummate expression of Mexico's new breed: the bureaucrat-turned-president.[2]

Once in office, Echeverría started to reveal the power of his personality. Impatient and energetic, he took to his work with passion, exhorting his countrymen to labor with "creative anguish." Apparently hoping to become a latter-day Cárdenas, he went everywhere, saw everyone, gave speeches, made pronouncements, talked and talked some more: as Daniel Cosío Villegas wryly observed, talking seemed to be a "physiological necessity" for Echeverría, a need requiring periodic satisfaction. Ironically enough, Echeverría's style of rule was neither institutionalized nor bureaucratized. It was extremely, urgently, and intensively personal.[3]

In the international arena Echeverría sought to establish Mexico as a leader of the Third World countries, with himself as major spokesman. Often (if not always) with good reason, he was critical of the United States. He traveled widely, reaching China in 1973. He traded visits with Salvador Allende, welcoming hundreds of Chilean exiles after the coup of 1973 (including Allende's widow) and eventually withdrawing recognition of the military junta. At the United Nations, he promoted a Charter of Economic Rights and Obligations and, in 1975, he instructed the Mexican ambassador to support the anti-Israeli denunciation of Zionism as a form of "racism." Greatly overestimating his prestige, Echeverría also presented himself as a candidate for the secretary-generalship of the U.N. near the conclusion of his presidential term.

At home, Echeverría pursued an activist, growth-oriented economic policy. In keeping with his *tercermundista* pronouncements, Mexico passed new laws to regulate—but by no means eliminate—the actions of foreign enterprise, especially the multinational corporations. The role of the state, already large (see Chapter 2), expanded sharply. Mainly as a result of tax reforms, total government revenue went from around 8 percent of the gross domestic product in 1970 to roughly 12.5 percent in 1975.[4] Public spending poured into housing, schooling, and

[2] A brief portrait of Echeverría appears in John Womack, Jr., "The Spoils of the Mexican Revolution," *Foreign Affairs* 48, no. 4 (July 1970): 677-687, esp. 684-686; on the student movement of 1968 see Ramón Ramírez, *El movimiento estudiantil de México: julio-diciembre de 1968*, 2 vols. (Mexico: Ediciones Era, 1969), and Elena Poniatowska, *La noche de Tlatelolco* (Mexico: Ediciones Era, 1971).

[3] Daniel Cosío Villegas, *El estilo personal de gobernar* (México: Joaquín Mortiz, 1975); the quote is from p. 31.

[4] Note that slight discrepancy between these figures and the ones in Table 2-9. A brief analysis of the tax reform is in John F. H. Purcell and Susan Kaufman Purcell, "El estado y la empresa privada," *Nueva Política* 1, no. 2 (April-June 1976): 230-232.

other development programs. Agricultural credit increased. The nation doubled its capacity to produce crude oil, electricity, and iron and steel. As a result, Echeverría proudly pointed out, the GDP grew at an annual average rate of 5.6 percent.[5]

The expansion of state activity was not without its problems. It brought Echeverría into constant conflict with the domestic private sector, caught in a squeeze between multinational corporations and the Mexican state.[6] Only the strongest local firms could survive, and the government bought out many of the weaker ones (almost incredibly, the number of state-owned corporations swelled from 86 to 740 during Echeverría's regime). Between 1970 and 1976 the money supply grew about 18 percent a year, compared to previous rates around 12 percent, and the federal deficit increased sixfold. This contributed to a inflationary spiral, as prices rose about 22 percent a year, and this, in turn, priced Mexican goods out of international markets. As a result, the deficit in balance of payments tripled between 1973 and 1975—thus placing great, ultimately overbearing pressure on the value of the peso.[7]

Just as the state increased its role in the economy, so did Echeverría strengthen and consolidate his own political power. From the outset, he strove to isolate and dismantle some rival *camarillas*, especially old-time machines. Rather conspicuously, he failed to give a cabinet appointment to the old war horse, Alfonso Corona del Rosal. In June of 1971, the bloody assault on students by paramilitary thugs gave him an opportunity to expel Alfonso Martínez Domínguez, then head of the Federal District, in what some observers have interpreted as the "great political coup" of the sexennium. Echeverría ousted no less than five state governors from office (in Guerrero, Nuevo León, Puebla, Hidalgo, Sonora), and he made frequent changes in his cabinet: by November 1976, only 6 out of the 17 secretaries still occupied their original positions.[8]

To amplify his political base, Echeverría appears to have relied upon two major groups. One was a cadre of young men, mostly in their early 30s, to whom he gave top-level, sensitive posts: Francisco Javier Alejo, Juan José Bremer, Ignacio Ovalle, Fausto Zapata, figureheads for what came to be known, with derision at the end, as a "youthocracy" (*efebocracia*). It was, according to Manuel Camacho, a "new

[5] In his sixth and final state-of-the-nation address, the transcript of which appears in *Excélsior*, 2 September 1976.

[6] Carlos Arriola, "Los grupos empresariales frente al Estado (1973-1975)," *Foro Internacional* 16, no. 64 (April-June 1976): 449-495.

[7] Richard A. Shaffer in the *Wall Street Journal*, 23 November 1976.

[8] *Proceso* 1, no. 1 (6 November 1976): 7.

generation," defined by both outlook and age, nurtured and brought to power by the president, a group that would presumably remain in his debt for many years to come. The second base was organized labor. For the first couple of years, Echeverría and his group tried to restrict the power of labor's *jefe máximo*, Fidel Velázquez, partly by encouraging the insurgent independent workers' movement, but in time the government reversed itself: the *independentistas* were repressed, wage hikes were made, and Velázquez remained supreme. "The labor movement has received great impetus and great support from this administration," according to one union leader; "extraordinarily advanced," said another of Echeverría's labor policy.[9]

There were signs, too, that the president intended to broaden and perpetuate his influence. Five of his cabinet secretaries left office in order to assume state governorships, and a sixth started running for another one just after the conclusion of the *sexenio*.[10] Several members of the subcabinet became governors of other states as well. Almost all observers caught the point: these politicians, *echeverrista* to a man, would be solidly ensconced in state capitals well after the president stepped down.

It was in this context that Echeverría broke all precedent by publicly calling attention to the forthcoming presidential succession. "It is useful," he stated in late 1974, "for public opinion [!] to analyze and evaluate men in relation to the presidential succession, and it is good for it to be that way. . . . I should think that public opinion will start to define its preferences sometime in the latter part of next year; but in the meantime, everyone should be the object of study, observation, and judgment. That is democratically healthy."[11] He returned to the subject on subsequent occasions, even going so far as to describe the necessary qualities for leadership. The next president of Mexico, he said in January 1975, "should be a person who gets up early and stays up late (*muy madrugador y muy desvelado*), that is, a person who works hard and has a great capacity for work." The following month he amplified upon this theme, adding that the next president should have "climbed slowly up the ladder of political or administrative opportunities," in order to fully understand the workings of the govern-

9 Ibid., 7-9.

10 On the departures see Miguel Angel Granados Chapa, "¿Por qué se fueron los que se fueron?," *Excélsior*, 3 December 1975. The sixth cabinet minister, Hermenegildo Cuenca Díaz, died suddenly in 1977.

11 The text is from Andrés Montemayor H., *Los Pridestinados* (Monterrey, N.L.: Avance Editorial, 1975), p. 8, though Montemayor gives the wrong date for the statement; the correct date is in Daniel Cadena Z., *El candidato presidencial 1976* (Mexico: n.p., 1975), p. 20.

ment, and he should also be able to reach decisions rapidly.[12] Among all possible aspirants, of course, no one fit this description better than Echeverría himself.

As speculation mounted, Leandro Rovirosa Wade, the Secretary of Hydraulic Resources, startled the press in April 1975 by announcing the names of plausible contenders—in Mexican parlance, the *tapados* or "hidden ones." The move was so novel that it could only have been prompted by Echeverría, perhaps to demonstrate his own control of the selection process. Thus revealed before "public opinion," the so-called *tapados* were seven:

Mario Moya Palencia, 42, Echeverría's successor as Secretary of Gobernación.[13] Trained in law at UNAM, where he made friends with Miguel Alemán's son,[14] he immediately launched on a political career. During the López Mateos campaign, in 1957-58, he created his own political base by establishing the Plataforma de Profesionales, a dependency of the CNOP. In 1964 he assumed directorship of a department in Gobernación, took over the federal newsprint monopoly (PIPSA) in 1968, became Subsecretary of Gobernación in 1969 and Secretary in 1970. An able politician, he put through several electoral reforms, and he appeared to have won Echeverría's confidence and respect. Partly because four out of the five previous presidents had come out of Gobernación, and partly because of his support among political leaders, Moya Palencia was generally regarded as the front runner.

Hugo Cervantes del Río, 49, Secretary of the Presidency. A law graduate from UNAM and later a professor, he had become friends with Echeverría in the late 1940s, when they both belonged to Sánchez Taboada's *camarilla*. A man of considerable administrative experience, former governor of the territory of Baja California Sur (an appointive position), he maintained a low political profile. Whenever he spoke, which was rare, he tended to quote or paraphrase his superiors.[15] He had no visible enemies and a close relationship with Echeverría, qualities that made him a serious contender.

José López Portillo, 54, Secretary of the Treasury. Another UNAM lawyer and professor, he had known Echeverría since their early boyhood days. As law students they had traveled together on a scholarship to Chile, and their friendship was extremely close. Having entered the

[12] Montemayor, *Los Pridestinados*, pp. 7-8.

[13] Ages for the *tapados* are calculated as of the time of Rovirosa Wade's announcement.

[14] Montemayer, *Los Pridestinados*, p. 12.

[15] Daniel Cosío Villegas, *La sucesión: desenlace y perspectivas* (Mexico: Joaquín Mortiz, 1976), pp. 29, 104.

283

government in 1959, López Portillo held a series of relatively minor posts until 1968, when he became Subsecretary of the Presidency. Though his leader and boss, Emilio Martínez Manautou, was Echeverría's closest rival in the precampaign of 1969, López Portillo received another subsecretaryship, in Patrimonio Nacional, in 1970. From there he moved to the Comisión Federal de Electricidad (CFE), in 1972, and from there to the treasury in 1973. In that capacity he had managed Mexico's exchange policy and helped implement the tax reform, earning some opposition from the private sector. An affable, outgoing, intelligent and forceful individual, he was thought to be well endowed for the presidency—but lacking any political base.

Porfirio Muñoz Ledo, 41, Secretary of Labor. A UNAM-trained lawyer and a well-known professor of politics and history, he held a series of advisory and minor posts until 1966, when he landed an important position in the social security institute (IMSS). It was not until the campaign of 1970 that he joined Echeverría's inner circle, principally as a speechwriter and ideologue.[16] Appointed Subsecretary of the Presidency under Cervantes del Río in 1970, Muñoz Ledo was suddenly made Secretary of Labor in 1972. After some initial disagreements with Fidel Velázquez, he eventually gained strong support among the unionists.

Carlos Gálvez Betancourt, 54, director of the social security institute. Yet another graduate of the UNAM law school, where he had known Echeverría, he became an active member of the PRI in 1945. He started collaborating with Echeverría in 1957, serving as *oficial mayor* in Gobernación from 1964 to 1968, when he became governor of Michoacán. While reforming the law on social security he worked with both labor and management, apparently obtaining the respect of both, but, because his position at IMSS did not give him the stature of a cabinet member, he was given little chance of getting the nomination.

Augusto Gómez Villanueva, 44, Secretary of Agrarian Reform. Trained in political science (not law) at UNAM, where he had been an active student leader, Gómez Villanueva was both a university professor and a seasoned *político*. Joining up with the *camarilla* of Enrique Olivares Santana, governor of Aguascalientes, he served as the boss's private secretary (1962-64), received a deputyship (1964-67), and moved to the PRI when Olivares Santana became secretary general of the party. Both in PRI and in the government, Gómez Villanueva was closely identified with the peasant sector. In 1969, as head of the CNC, he had been the first to publicly proclaim support for Echeverría's own

---

[16] Montemayor, *Los Pridestinados*, p. 103.

candidacy, an act that had presumably earned him a large measure of presidential gratitude.

Luis Enrique Bracamontes, 51, Secretary of Public Works. An engineer (with a UNAM degree) and *técnico*, he had joined the ministry of public works in 1950 and stayed there ever since. A subsecretary at the age of 29, he was regarded as extremely able—but, because of the narrowness of his career, most unlikely to become the presidential candidate.

"Any one of them is excellent," concluded Rovirosa Wade after listing all the names. "Each one has managed admirably to perform the tasks with which President Echeverría has entrusted him."[17]

Just around the time of this announcement, Jesús Reyes Heroles, president of the PRI, proclaimed the party's intention to draft a "Basic Plan of Government" for the 1976-82 administration. The idea would be to forge a platform, a series of policy commitments by the government. With Echeverría's evident approval, Reyes Heroles revealed that the plan would be ready by late September and submitted to the party leadership for ratification. The candidate would be selected in October, presumably as the person most capable of carrying out the Plan. The slogan went forth: "First the program, then the man!" At Echeverría's urging, one state governor even suggested that the seven candidates ought to publicly "confront" the Plan, in order to permit a full evaluation of their views.[18] It seemed, to some, that Echeverría had found a novel way to tie the hands of his successor.

Tension mounted as the months went by. Members of the private sector demonstrated their political ineptitude on more than one occasion, taking Echeverría's statements about "public opinion" at face value. One group of private-sector spokesmen issued a "Declaration of Principles" in April, incurring the wrath and disdain of officialdom.[19] And in a remarkable display of either malice or naiveté, another private organization actually took a *survey* of popular views on the succession![20] A few politicians made cautious statements about desirable attributes for the next president, but, for the most part, the posture was one of expectation. As David Gustavo Gutiérrez, leader of the CNOP, put it, this was no time to enter in any "debate about names.

17 *Hispano-Americano*, 21 April 1975, p. 7. In referring to any one as *bueno* (here translated as "excellent") Rovirosa Wade was playing on words, since in Mexico *el bueno* also means "the right one" or "the real one."

18 Cosío Villegas, *La sucesión: desenlace*, pp. 81-86 esp. pp. 81-82.

19 Ibid., pp. 64-78.

20 See *Excélsior*, 7 and 10 December 1974, and 8 May 1975. For one of many disdainful comments about the survey see Cadena Z., *El candidato*, pp. 220-221.

Intérpretes del Informe

[from top to bottom]:

"Well, I think it came clearly through the address: *el bueno* (the real one) is Mario [Moya Palencia]."

"Well, I think it came clearly through the address: *el bueno* is Hugo [Cervantes del Río]."

"Well, I think it came clearly through the address: there's no one besides Pepe [José López Portillo]."

"Well, I think it came clearly through the address: *el bueno* is Porfirio [Muñoz Ledo]."

"Well, I think the address left no doubts: *el bueno* is Luis Enrique [Bracamontes]."

"Well, I think it was clear in the address: the *amarrado* (literally, fastened one, or tied-in one) is Carlos [Gálvez Betancourt]."

"Well, I think it came clearly through the address: there's no one other than Augusto [Gómez Villanueva]."

. . . For the moment, the leaders of the PRI should take an attitude of observation, of watching and examining, without expressing their opinions."[21] Who was the truly favored one, the *verdadero tapado*? When would Echeverría give the word?

FROM SELECTION TO ELECTION
(SEPTEMBER 1975–JULY 1976)

On the morning of September 22, right on schedule, Jesús Reyes Heroles was chairing a meeting about the PRI's "Basic Plan" when he received a hot-line call from Los Pinos, the presidential residence. He returned to the session, disconcerted and surprised, and hurried out to Los Pinos for a brief visit at midday. In the afternoon, three of the presidential hopefuls—Moya Palencia, Cervantes del Río, and Gálvez Betancourt—were together with Echeverría at a ceremonial lunch. When interrupted by an aide, according to one report, Moya Palencia turned pale and quickly left the table.[22]

It was López Portillo.

Downtown, Fidel Velázquez was publicly proclaiming labor's support for the Secretary of the Treasury, and others were rapidly joining the ranks. For some the *destapamiento* ("uncovering") was a surprise, for others it was a shock. Celestino Salcedo Monteón, leader of the CNC, was asked if the peasant sector would add its backing: "To

21 Cosío Villegas, *La sucesión: desenlace*, p. 43.
22 These details are given in *ibid.*, pp. 91-93; and *Latin America* 9, no. 41 (17 October 1975): 323.

whom?" he inquired. Shown a copy of an afternoon paper, with López Portillo's name in the headline, he merely nodded and said: "Of course." Fidel and other party leaders went to the treasury building to offer their congratulations, and at 6:10 p.m. a crestfallen Moya Palencia came to express his own capitulation: "José López Portillo is the best man that the Mexican Revolution has. Let us believe in him."[23]

Then the bandwagon began, as thousands pushed their way into the building in order to join the *cargada*. Declarations of adhesion came from all sides, including the other *tapados*, and López Portillo—hitherto a dark-horse prospect—became the man of the hour. Sara Ornelas, head of the lottery workers' union, arrived in a shirt with López Portillo's name stitched into the material, as though to show that she had favored his candidacy long before the *destape* itself. Observers thought the ruse too transparent: surely, she had seven different shirts, and she was merely waiting for the day.

Even as they proclaimed their loyalty, people in the political world kept wondering: Why López Portillo? In his relatively brief career he had never been in a position to curry the favor of labor or the peasant sector; and, if anything, his fiscal reforms had earned him some disfavor among the "popular" or middle-class groupings. Admittedly, he was an intimate, lifelong friend of the president, but it seemed unlikely that *amiguismo* could override all other considerations. Cosío Villegas reflected on the similarity between the two men—"they are very much alike, physically, mentally, and maybe even morally"—a questionable statement, but one that, even if true, provides only a partial explanation.[24]

In mid-November Echeverría himself offered a clue, when he made the remarkable declaration—breaking all precedent again—that López Portillo won out "because he was the one with the fewest political attachments, the one who had not reached any secret or discreet agreement, the one who dedicated himself to the service of the country without engaging in cheap politics (*política barata*)."[25] The denunciation of *política barata* was widely interpreted as a rebuke to Moya Palencia, generally regarded as the *tapado* with the widest political support. But even at face value, the statement is revealing. López Portillo's greatest asset was also his greatest liability: he did not have a team of his own.[26] From Echeverría's point of view, this would be the

---

[23] *Excélsior*, 23 September 1976.

[24] Cosío Villegas, *La sucesión: desenlace*, p. 106.

[25] *Excélsior*, 13 November 1975.

[26] As noted by Miguel Angel Granados Chapa in *Excélsior*, 26 September 1975.

easiest person to control, manipulate, or, in Corona del Rosal's word, "to set on course" (*orientar*).

Echeverría's intention to retain command of the political scene became clear in many ways. The timing of the *destape*, on the same day that the PRI was still completing the "Basic Plan,"[27] could only have come as a humiliation to Reyes Heroles and other party leaders. As though to emphasize the point, Echeverría moved Reyes Heroles from the presidency of the PRI over to the social security institute. Muñoz Ledo, Secretary of Labor and one of the precandidates, took over the PRI. Gómez Villanueva, of Agrarian Reform, assumed the party's number two post. Cervantes del Río was put in charge of the PRI organization in the Federal District. One impact of these changes was to demonstrate concern for the elections scheduled for July 1976; the PAN had shown surprising strength in the 1973 congressional campaign,[28] and the PPS had nearly won the governorship of Nayarit in 1975.[29] Upset by these signs, and alarmed by the possibility that the PAN might nominate Francisco Madero's own grandson as its presidential candidate, Echeverría was putting the PRI electoral machine in charge of men most able to mobilize the vote. But another implication was unsettling: López Portillo would not be able to run his own campaign. It would be largely controlled, instead, by his former rivals, all of them, despite their disappointment, still beholden to Echeverría. (As Muñoz Ledo stated while taking possession of his party post, the task of the future would be "to deepen, amplify and continue the work of President Echeverría.")[30] López Portillo eventually placed a number of his most trusted associates in the Instituto de Estudios Políticos, Económicos y Sociales, an agency of the PRI, and IEPES assumed a major role in the campaign, but it was hardly a traditional bastion of strength.

It was in this setting, too, that the Biebrich affair might best be understood. As described in Chapter 9, Carlos Armando Biebrich, another member of the *efebocracia*, was dumped from the governorship of Sonora after violent repression of some peasants. These events took place in October, one month after the *destapamiento*, and Biebrich was known to be an ardent *moyista* (backer of Moya Palencia). Many interpreted Biebrich's ouster, not as a reflection of official concern about peasants, but as a warning to *moyistas*: accept López Portillo or

---

[27] A summary of the "Basic Plan" is in *Excélsior*, 23 September 1975.

[28] Rafael Segovia, "La reforma política: el Ejecutivo Federal, el PRI y las elecciones de 1973," *Foro Internacional* 14, no. 3 (January-March 1974): 305-330.

[29] Miguel Angel Granados Chapa, "Nayarit: consolidación del monopartido," *Foro Internacional* 16, no. 64 (April-June 1976): 429-448.

[30] As quoted by Samuel I. del Villar in *Excélsior*, 30 September 1976.

else. Echeverría himself was openly demanding "elementary loyalty" from his collaborators, "even though there have been many political disenchantments since September 22."[31] Disappointment, yes, but neither opposition nor subversion. Moya Palencia and his supporters, still in control of Gobernación and therefore in charge of the election, had better step in line.

Fully aware of his tenuous position, López Portillo inaugurated his campaign in early October, nearly nine months before the election. In recent decades such campaigns have almost all been long and intense, partly as a ritual, partly as learning experience, and partly to give the candidate a chance to select members of his team, from cabinet ministers to city mayors. This last function was especially urgent for López Portillo, and he alluded to it in his opening speech:

> We do not need to steep ourselves in foreign orthodoxies or nonsensical geometries, we have our own way to realize our desire and calling for justice; we have our own form to mold our future; with one condition: that the process of distribution should be by legal means, to avoid any risk of dictatorship or a government of technocrats, because the constitution, our wise constitution, states that regulation or distribution requires legislation by congress, to establish the general condition, because our revolution, based on people and the law, is a democratic one.[32]

Despite his own lack of legislative experience, in other words, López Portillo would respect the congress, he would work with *políticos*, he would not surround himself with a small band of *técnicos*.[33] If the language was convoluted, the message—and the appeal—were clear enough.

As the campaign progressed, Echeverría continued to demonstrate his mastery of the situation. In contrast to previous transition periods, when lame-duck executives let the incoming president choose PRI candidates for congress, Echeverría appeared to control the selection process that took place in early 1976. Two designations were spectacular—Cervantes del Río for the Senate, Gómez Villanueva for the Chamber of Deputies—both former presidential hopefuls, committed *echeverristas*, now in positions to dominate the congress that López Portillo had promised to respect. Numerous other officeholders in the Echeverría regime were also slated for legislative seats, where they would be for three to six years. Whatever the precise composition of

---

[31] *Excélsior*, 13 November 1975.   [32] *Excélsior*, 10 October 1975.
[33] A theme that he repeated more than once, as in an interview published in *Excélsior*, 20 June 1976.

the chambers, the relative weight of *echeverristas* and *lopezportillistas* (of whom, again, there were precious few to begin with), the selection process seems to have been more centralized than before.[34] According to one anecdote, a prominent state governor was discussing the deputy-ships with Muñoz Ledo, and asked the PRI leader when it might be time for him to express his own opinions on the candidates. Replied Muñoz Ledo: "You already did."

As in previous years, the popular sector continued to receive a dis-proportionate share of the PRI's deputy nominations, with 41.8 per-cent of the total. To be sure, this represented somewhat of a decline from past practice, when the popular sector usually got more than 50 percent (see Table 8-2), and it is revealing that the slack was taken up by labor—which now received 29.6 percent, slightly more than the peasant sector (28.6 percent). Thus Echeverría continued to cultivate the favor of the trade unionists, without, however, seriously reducing the political preeminence of the middle class. (This was even more marked in the Senate, where the popular sector obtained 56.3 percent of the nominations, compared to 20.3 percent for labor and 23.4 per-cent for the agrarians.)[35] What changed, then, was not so much the sectoral distribution of the nominations. It was the manner in which it was done.

And so it continued, up until the election itself: Echeverría in the spotlight, López Portillo in the shadows. The election was a desultory affair, partly because an internal schism had prevented the PAN from fielding any candidate at all. It was a race between López Portillo and abstentionism, and if it is true that 69 percent of the eligible popula-tion went to the polls, with 94 percent casting ballots in favor of the PRI candidate, this would have to go down as a triumph for López Portillo.[36] Throughout the campaign, he had shown himself to be easygoing, friendly, sincere, *simpático* in every sense of the word. It appears that some voters, apprehensive about Echeverría's intentions, went to the polls in order to give López Portillo a mandate of his own.

After the voting was over, most political observers settled down for

[34] For analyses of the nominations see Jorge Hernández Campos in *Excélsior*, 23 February, 1 March, and 8 March 1976; Vicente Leñero in *Excélsior*, 18 February 1976; Manuel Moreno Sánchez, "Selecciones y ratificaciones, las formas y los prece-dentes: el Partido y sus listas," *Siempre!*, no. 1123 (25 February 1976): 18, 70; and Daniel Cosío Villegas, "Los llamados y los escogidos del PRI," *Plural* 5, no. 6 (March 1976): 47-49.

[35] Figures on sectoral representation among the congressional nominations are given by Jorge Hernández Campos in *Excélsior*, 1 March 1976. Biographical data on approximately half of the new deputies appear in *Excélsior*, 20-31 August 1976.

[36] *Facts on File* 36, no. 1861 (10 July 1976): 498, and no. 1870 (11 September 1976): 677; also a personal communication from Rafael Segovia.

a regular sexennial obsession—*gabinetitis* or *gabinetomanía*, feverish preoccupation with and daring prediction of the composition of the cabinet. The stakes in this game are exceedingly high, for the naming of people to high-level posts reveals a basic outcome of the presidential succession: who is in, who is out, which *camarillas* are up and which are down. Actually, as revealed by the Quezada cartoon of September 1975, the speculation began as soon as the *destape* took place.[37] The guessing continued for more than a year, reaching its highest pitch just before the inauguration on December 1, 1976. Some of the predictions went astray—one of the most persistent rumors being that Corona del Rosal would return to prominence as Secretary of Defense—but most guesses were accurate up to a point. That is, they got the right names of *individuals*, but they sometimes put them in the wrong *posts* (especially the lesser ones).[38] Prospects for recruitment, then, did not concern preparation for specific jobs; the question was whether you were in or out. As already argued in Chapter 5, an aspiring politician could move from almost any square on the checkerboard to almost any other, and this pattern found confirmation in the symptoms of *gabinetitis*. So the guessing continued, bets were made, and, by the middle of July 1976, things seemed fairly normal. Not for long.

CRISIS! (JULY–NOVEMBER 1976)

A sense of malaise, that something was wrong, started to spread by mid-July. Early in the month a rebellion erupted within the staff of *Excélsior*, Mexico City's leading daily newspaper, owned collectively as a cooperative venture. The insurgents resorted to numerous illegal tactics, but governmental authorities—from Echeverría on down—refused to take any action. The uprising succeeded, the directorship changed hands, and what had become a proud, independent, critical voice was now stilled.[39] By itself, the outcome was disheartening, especially to the country's intellectuals. The coup also eliminated a poten-

[37] It is revealing that eight of the 26 people on Quezada's list eventually received "upper-level" posts in the López Portillo government, and several others became advisers to the president. The implication is that the immediate circle of López Portillo's closest collaborators was visible from the start; what remained to be seen was how he would construct a coalition around that central core.

[38] Sample predictions appear in the magazine ¡Ya!, no. 294 (September-November 1976); *Excélsior*, 2 November and 26 November 1976; *Proceso* 1, no. 4 (27 November 1976): 20-23; *El Universal*, 29 November 1976; and *El Heraldo*, 29 November 1976.

[39] The full sequence of events is described in *Proceso* 1, no. 1 (6 November 1976): 12-14, though it should be understood the *Proceso* is published by those who were ousted from *Excélsior*. As footnotes in this chapter show, however, *Excélsior* remained a fairly useful and reliable source of factual information.

El Futuro es de Ellos

—POR ABEL QUEZADA—

RESUELTA LA ADIVINANZA PRESIDENCIAL, QUEDA EL DEPORTE DE HACER GABINETES. — ESTA TEMPORADA DEPORTIVA DURARÁ UN POCO MAS DE UN AÑO.

POR LO PRONTO,
ESTÁ ES LA
PRIMERA LISTA
DE POSIBLES.

J. RODOLFO MOCTEZUMA CID.
CARLOS TELLO
JOSÉ LUIS BECERRA
JORGE TAMAYO
OSCAR REYES RETANA
ENRIQUE VELAZCO IBARRA
FRANCISCO LÓPEZ SERRANO
ARSENIO FARELL
PORFIRIO MUÑOZ LEDO
AUGUSTO GÓMEZ VILLANUEVA
HUGO CERVANTES DEL RÍO
MARIO MOYA PALENCIA
MARIO RAMÓN BETETA
LUIS CORREA SARABIA
MANUEL MARCUÉ PARDIÑAS
JORGE DÍAZ SERRANO
RICARDO MARTÍNEZ DE HOYOS
DAVID GUSTAVO GUTIÉRREZ
RODOLFO LANDEROS
CARLOS REAL ENCINAS
GUSTAVO ROMERO KOLBECK
FERNANDO PÉREZ GAVILÁN
ANTONIO ENRÍQUEZ SAVIGNAC
MANUEL TELLO
HÉCTOR MEDINA NERI
JOSÉ JUAN DE OLLOQUI
Y USTED.

"For now, this is the first list of *posibles* (possibilities for high office). J. Rodolfo Moctezuma Cid [plus other names] . . . and you."

tial source of opposition to Echeverría's apparent designs on maintaining power through a *maximato*, as Calles had done in 1928-34. And when it was remembered that Echeverría had become a major shareholder in a new newspaper group controlling 37 dailies, the implications became ominous.[40]

On August 11 an unidentified terrorist organization, possibly the leftist September 23d League, attacked a car that was carrying Margarita López Portillo, a sister of the president-elect. She was unhurt but one of her bodyguards was killed, three others were wounded, and the leader of the gang was shot to death. Viewed in isolation, the incident was unsettling enough, but the unanswered questions were deeply disturbing: Who was really behind the attack? What if Margarita had been killed? What if López Portillo had been the real target? How could this happen in broad daylight in Mexico City?

There followed a crushing blow. On August 31, after months of official denial, the government devalued the peso for the first time in 22 years. The drain on the country's foreign reserves had reached intolerable limits, there had been large-scale capital flights since the previous April, and exports remained overpriced. As a result the government finally decided to "float" the peso, letting it find its new level—which the Bank of Mexico pegged at 19.90 to the dollar on September 12, a 37 percent drop in value from the longstanding rate of 12.50. As though this were not enough, the government refloated the peso a second time, on October 26, and the exchange rate quickly jumped to 26.50 to the dollar. Within two months, the international value of the peso had been cut in half. For those who viewed the currency's position as a sign of strength and stability, a manifestation of "the Mexican miracle" and a hallmark of national pride, this was bitter medicine indeed.

It was around this time that the rumors started to intensify. To a considerable extent, Echeverría himself helped foment them. In his final report to the nation, delivered on September 1, he repeatedly chastised (unnamed) opponents of the regime, and warned of plots by sinister forces. "In the fulfillment of our noble task," he declared at one point,

> we have faced unjust and superficial attack, calumny and insult. Powerful economic interests, within Mexico and against Mexico, have financed these insidious attacks.
>
> Removed from our great problems and national aspirations, small

[40] As reported by Alan Riding in the *New York Times*, 16 May 1976, and as generally known within Mexican political circles.

groups within the country have rejoiced in the aggressions we have suffered from abroad, and they have actively joined in the vain attempt (*empeño*) to undermine the independent decisions of the Nation.[41]

Echeverría thus pictured himself, and Mexico, as the targets of an international conspiracy, the victims of betrayal, innocent forces of good against the sinister forces of evil. What would happen? Who would do what? When?

All sorts of answers came forth. There would be an attack on Echeverría's wife. There would be an attack on López Portillo's wife. Someone would try to murder Hermenegildo Cuenca Díaz, Echeverría's Secretary of Defense. A local boss in Jalisco had put out a contract on the life of Marcelino García Barragán, Díaz Ordaz's Secretary of Defense.[42]

But the chief rumor, the one that captured the popular imagination, was the most implausible of all: there would be a military coup. The first time around, the coup was to occur on September 16, the anniversary of Mexico's independence. After that day went by, attention fastened on another date: November 20, the anniversary of the Revolution, only 10 days before the end of Echeverría's term. With historical perspective, it seems impossible to conjure up an even faintly realistic scenario for such an event, given the low profile and relative weakness of the Mexican military, but there were those who were willing to try.[43]

Especially during November, events in the north created further tension and exacerbated popular gullibility. Around the middle of the month, peasant groups seized extensions of land in Sonora, Sinaloa, and Durango. The actions reflected longstanding grievances, and agrarian resentment had been smoldering for years; what was novel about the confrontations and threats of violence was their timing, only days before the end of a regime. On November 20 Echeverría, not about to give up power till the final minute, suddenly expropriated nearly 100,000 hectares of rich, privately owned land in Sonora for collective *ejidos*. Outraged by this action, landowners protested, and, in Sinaloa, 28,000 owners announced a stoppage in the fields. In a demonstration of solidarity with the landowners, businessmen and merchants in Puebla, Chihuahua, and Nuevo León joined in brief work stop-

[41] *Excélsior*, 2 September 1976.

[42] The variety of rumors is described by Jorge de la Garma Lopetegui in the magazine *Impacto*, no. 1397 (5 December 1976): 9.

[43] See the comments by Alberto Domingo in *Siempre!*, no. 1223 (1 December 1976): 32-33; and Abraham Zabludovsky, "¡La historia oculta detrás del rumor del golpe!," *Siempre!*, no. 1224 (8 December 1976): 17, 86.

pages. Encouraged by the outcome in Sonora, hoping for similar expropriations, peasants invaded other lands in Durango and Jalisco.

As the confrontation mounted in the north, the rumors of a coup developed one plausible form. The Mexican military would not intervene by itself, nor would it stage a barracks revolt in Echeverría's behalf. Rather, it was held, Echeverría would declare the country to be in a state of emergency, and invoke a constitutional clause that would allow him to stay in power for two more years. That was why he had stirred up all this trouble, dwelling on anxiety and fomenting (presumably) the seizures of land. Everything now fit together. Except for one problem: the constitution contained no such clause.[44]

Near the end of November, when it appeared that there would be no coup, there were rumors about the rumors. Who had started them? Why? Echeverría seemed to have an answer: the Monterrey group of industrialists, whom he had accused of being "bad Christians" on October 15.[45] The Chamber of Deputies launched a series of accusations against Andrés Marcelo Sada, head of COPARMEX and a leader of the Monterrey group, charging that he had started the rumors (perhaps in order to profit by speculation against the peso). Asked to comment on the accusations, Echeverría replied: "Where there's smoke, there must be fire." Then he continued, denouncing "those neofascist groups" who were using the same tactics here as they had in Allende's Chile: "these interests may be very powerful economically, but morally they are very small."[46]

For his part, López Portillo was unable to take any steps to dispel the atmosphere of crisis and tension. Echeverría had so preempted the scene, had taken so many startling actions, that the president-elect could only wait. López Portillo made not a single speech between the day of his election and the inauguration. One of his rare statements, attributed to him by another politician, was hardly comforting: "We have the risk of Southamericanization; I do not want us to run it. We do not want fascism."[47] Indirectly, if not directly, this looked like a rebuke to Echeverría. Their lifelong friendship, according to many observers, was undergoing strain.

[44] The confusion may have stemmed from Article 84 of the constitution, which lays down procedures for installing a provisional president in the event that the president-elect is unable to assume office during the first two years of the term; on the other hand, Article 85 clearly states that the outgoing president must step down anyway, even if the incoming president cannot take the oath of office, so the rumor was entirely devoid of any constitutional foundation.

[45] *Latin America* 10, no. 43 (5 November 1976): 341.

[46] *Excélsior*, 27 November 1976; and see the article by Renward García Medrano in *El Sol*, 29 November 1976.

[47] *Excélsior*, 27 November 1976.

As the *sexenio* was nearing its end, Echeverría looked back on his administration. In response to one reporter's question, he attempted to give a rationale for his regime, especially, perhaps, the tension-riddled final months:

> We had to choose stability, which favors the strong in times of inflation and scarcity, or choose crisis, with all its consequences, in order to get the nation ready for the absolute necessity of its own transformation.
>
> I chose the latter path because I thought, and now I believe it more firmly than ever, that it would mean working for the future of the country, making the way more fruitful for governments that follow mine. My greatest objectives therefore have yet to be fulfilled.[48]

In Echeverría's view, his regime was one of "transition." Having put the country through a necessary crisis, he had prepared the way for structural change. The future would absolve him.

To judge from contemporary opinion, Echeverría's vindication would take quite some time. The events of the last three months had stripped him of his popularity. Public confidence was at its lowest ebb in years; within political circles there was constant talk of "crisis." The conservative magazine *Impacto* would ultimately, if ludicrously, accuse Echeverría of "secret but effective complicity with international communist subversion."[49] Manuel Sánchez Vite, former governor of Hidalgo and ex-president of the PRI, reached the opposite conclusion: the Echeverría regime was "fascist," he wrote in a nearly unbelievable public statement, "FASCIST IN CAPITAL LETTERS."[50] And Gustavo Díaz Ordaz, the ex-president who had selected Echeverría as his successor, delivered a judicious but biting critique. Mexico's current situation "is extremely serious," he said, "with regard to matters economic, political, social, juridical, administrative. . . . In all respects."[51]

The question was whether Echeverría would still retain his influence, whether his efforts to perpetuate his power would succeed. He had been scheming, many thought, to impose another *maximato*. With puckish humor, one wag suggested Echeverría would be capable of no more than a *minimato*. But the problem was there, and observers were watching closely for signs of continuity and change. Iñigo Laviada, among others, urged López Portillo to make a total break with the

48 *Excélsior*, 30 November 1976.
49 *Impacto*, no. 1397 (8 December 1976).
50 *Siempre!*, no. 1222 (24 November 1976): 20-21.
51 *Excélsior*, 2 December 1976.

Echeverría group, to exclude *echeverristas* completely from top-level posts—"because of the crisis of confidence, the rumor about a new *maximato*, and the need for a spectacular change that would have magical effects on public opinion. . . . The change of government on December 1 is a unique opportunity to achieve an irresistible impulse of confidence and popular support, based on our magical conception of government."[52]

On the night of November 29, a series of explosions rocked commercial buildings in various parts of Mexico City, causing extensive damage and injuring at least one person. Finally, the month of November drew to a close.

THE RETURN TO NORMALCY (DECEMBER 1976)

The inauguration was scheduled for December 1. Early in the morning, guests and spectators, including Henry Kissinger and Rosalynn Carter, began filing into the Auditorio Nacional. At 10:50 a.m. Echeverría arrived and received a respectful ovation. Around 11:00 López Portillo drew near the auditorium, and the crowd burst into a crescendo of applause. His right arm raised, a smile on his face, López Portillo acknowledged his reception, and, in time, the audience fell silent. Augusto Gómez Villanueva, at this time the leader of the Chamber of Deputies, administered the oath of office. Echeverría surrendered the presidential sash, and the crowd gave an audible sigh of relief. Gómez Villanueva turned the rostrum over to López Portillo, and the president addressed the multitude.[53]

The speech was a tour de force. At the outset, López Portillo signaled his intention to govern by himself. "By the will of the Mexican people," he proclaimed, "I assume the office of President of the Republic and, with that, my personal and indivisible responsibility toward its history and its future."[54] An innocuous enough beginning, one might think, but the immediate meaning was plain. López Portillo had received his mandate not from Echeverría but from "the people" —a statement that was questionable as to accuracy, but not as to intent—and his responsibility was "indivisible." There would be no *maximato*, not even a *minimato*. A new regime had taken hold.

Having proclaimed his authority, López Portillo attempted to re-

[52] *Excélsior*, 29 November 1976.
[53] The description is taken from the magazine *Tiempo* 70, no. 1805 (6 December 1976).
[54] The full text of the speech appears in *El Nacional*, 2 December 1976.

store public confidence. The devaluation of the peso had been a blow, he conceded, but it should not be overemphasized: "It is neither a disaster nor a panacea. It states, objectively, the terms of our exchange with the rest of the world. . . . Mexico needs to reaffirm its values, its strength, and the assurance that its destiny does not depend on monetary whimsy or on some magical number that sets the parity of the peso with foreign currencies." To the private sector, so chastised by Echeverría, he offered an olive branch, referring to "legitimate expectations" of businessmen within the "mixed" economy. In a stirring conclusion, he begged for "pardon" from the poor and dispossessed, pledging to redouble efforts to bring them out of their prostration. Throughout, he spoke in tones of moderation. "I ask all Mexicans, every one, to believe in my good faith. I will have to demonstrate my ability and intelligence through my service. For that I need time. Give it to me."[55] The emphasis was on collaboration rather than divisiveness, harmony instead of conflict, an eloquent exegesis of his campaign slogan: *La solución somos todos* (loosely, "The answer lies in our cooperation").

Even more important than the speech was the composition of the new administration. Here, in the designation of top-level officeholders, would be a tangible sign of intent, López Portillo's first decisions of far-reaching consequence. This time the designations had a special urgency, too, since it was generally recognized that López Portillo did not command a sizable *camarilla* of his own. If he was not to depend on *echeverristas*, where would he find his collaborators? As the answer to this question unfolded, it not only resolved contemporary doubts and anxieties; it also provided a remarkably clear picture of the Mexican recruitment process.

One source of supporters came out of López Portillo's own political background, people with whom he had worked in the course of his own career. By far the most conspicuous circle of this sort was the staff at the Secretariat of the Presidency from 1965 to 1970, where he himself had been an undersecretary. This group included Rodolfo Moctezuma Cid, whom López Portillo appointed Secretary of the Treasury; Carlos Tello, Secretary of the Presidency; Fernando Solana, Secretary of Commerce; Emilio Mújica Montoya, Secretary of Communications and Transport; Enrique Velasco Ibarra, the presidential private secretary; Mario Ramón Beteta, the outgoing treasury secretary, so discredited by the devaluations that he could only be given a position in the semipublic sector, not quite an upper-level post; and others in less im-

---

[55] Ibid.

portant offices. Several of these people had followed López Portillo to the treasury in 1973-75, and one (Tello) had also worked with him at Patrimonio Nacional in 1960-65.

It was this group, the hard-core *lopezportillistas*, that came into control of economic policy. (One other member of the team, the 34-year-old José Andrés de Oteyza, had first joined up with López Portillo at Patrimonio Nacional in the early seventies.) Diverse in ideological preference, pragmatic in their policies, highly trained as *técnicos*, those in charge of the economy—Moctezuma, Tello, Solana and Oteyza—shared one basic attribute: they were loyal to López Portillo.[56]

Among the appointments to former collaborators, one was by far the most striking, the designation of Emilio Martínez Manautou as Secretary of Health and Welfare. In 1969, as Secretary of the Presidency and López Portillo's immediate boss, Martínez Manautou had been a serious contender for the presidential nomination—losing out to Luis Echeverría. During the 1970-76 *sexenio* he had been totally *quemado* ("burned"), excluded from the system altogether. Some of his supporters, such as López Portillo, had stayed on with Echeverría, and now he himself was back. In a way, this meant that *martinez-manautuismo*, now under López Portillo's direction, had come into power; *echeverrismo* was on the way out.[57]

In addition to his former colleagues, López Portillo drew on another time-honored resource: personal friends, some of whom he had known as a student at UNAM. Arsenio Farell Cubillas, new director of IMSS, for instance, had known both Echeverría and López Portillo in primary school and at law school. After graduation he entered practice together with Echeverría's brother Rodolfo, while maintaining a close personal relationship with López Portillo. When López Portillo became head of the electricity commission, in 1972, he made Farell a top assistant; when López Portillo moved on to the treasury, Farell took his place as head of the CFE. Equally clear cases are Jorge Díaz Serrano, the head of PEMEX; Jesús Reyes Heroles, Secretary of Gobernación, and Pedro Ojeda Paullada, Secretary of Labor, who had also worked with López Portillo at Patrimonio Nacional in the early sixties; and Santiago Roel, the surprise appointee as Secretary of Foreign Relations, a man with absolutely no prior experience in international affairs but a long and warm association with López Portillo.

In order to illustrate these patterns, Figure 10-1 depicts various aspects of López Portillo's personal and political life as a series of circles

[56] See the columns by José Luis Mejías in *El Universal*, 30 and 31 December 1976.
[57] An excellent analysis along these lines, by Carlos Sirvent, is in *Excélsior*, 11 December 1976.

—his UNAM generation, his social network, and the succession of his public offices. Some individuals belonged to more than one of these circles, and arrows indicate such linkages: Velasco Ibarra, for example, overlapped with López Portillo at UNAM (though they were not in the same graduating class) and was later with him in the Secretariat of the Presidency (1966-70). Others had only one place of contact: Gustavo Romero Kolbeck, new head of Banco de México, had been a contemporary at UNAM,[58] and Guillermo Rossell de la Lama, Secretary of Tourism, worked with López Portillo only at Patrimonio Nacional (1959-64). Despite their spareness and simplicity, these circles depict major resources for the recruitment of López Portillo's team: together they account for approximately 47 percent of the "upper-level" positions at the start of his administration.[59]

Another traditional resource was family relations, especially for lesser posts. Margarita López Portillo, the sister who had been attacked in August, became director of communications in Gobernación. Guillermo, a cousin, became director of a sports institute in the ministry of public education. Enrique Loaeza, a nephew (though rather distant) who had collaborated with López Portillo ever since the late 1960s, became head of the airport system. José Antonio Ugarte, another distant nephew and López Portillo's former private secretary, became head of an economic team in Presidencia. It would be incorrect, however, to interpret these appointments as a sign of outright nepotism, or even of paternalistic concern for presidential kin. For some cases, such as Loaeza and Ugarte, the family ties were probably less important than their years of steady service to López Portillo. Rather, the cumulative effect of these designations was to convey a message: the president was putting his own people, those on whom he could rely, in key positions throughout the governmental hierarchy.

In drawing upon this core of friends, collaborators, and relatives, López Portillo constructed a *camarilla* that had, as its common denominator, personal loyalty to himself. For other appointments he relied on other criteria, such as obtaining a political equilibrium. To appease the old-time *alemanistas*, still a powerful group, López Portillo upgraded the national tourist council and left it in the hands of Miguel Alemán, as it had been for many years. Several members of

[58] Though he had come into frequent contact with López Portillo in subsequent years, Romero Kolbeck having been director of the Bank of Mexico while the new president was head of the treasury.

[59] The count excludes López Portillo himself and also Mario Ramón Beteta, since SOMEX was not an upper-level position (that is, one with scale values of 7 or 8 for the HIGHEST OFFICE variable [Appendix A, Table A-3]). These same circles also explain a number of appointments outside the "upper-level" offices.

Figure 10-1: Origins of an Elite: The López Portillo Regime

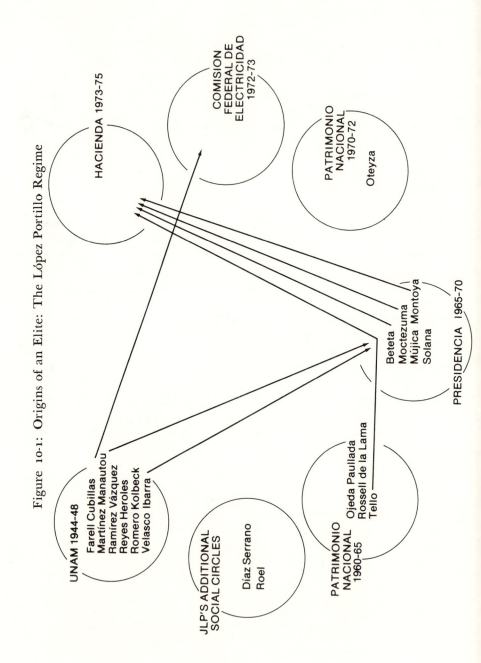

the new administration, most conspicuously Reyes Heroles, had formerly been identified as *lopezmateístas* during the 1958-64 regime. A large number—such as Carlos Hank González, now head of the Federal District, and Oscar Flores Sánchez, the Attorney General—had collaborated with the *diazordacista* government of 1964-70. (Flores had also been a subsecretary under Alemán.) And some, of course, were *echeverrista*, the most conspicuous instance being Echeverría's able young nephew, Rodolfo, appointed a Subsecretary of Gobernación. In these respects López Portillo followed the example of all recent presidents, giving all major factions some access to office and expressing, on a symbolic level, the continuity and harmony of postrevolutionary politics.[60]

López Portillo was particularly careful in his treatment of *echeverristas*. As though in response to Iñigo Laviada's plea for a complete purge, he did not hold over a single cabinet secretary in the same post. But he did reappoint two upper-level officeholders in the semipublic sector—Luis Gómez at national railroads, and Antonio Padilla Segura in the state-owned steel mill. Some of Echeverría's other collaborators, even the *efebocracia*, received middle-level posts. Francisco Javier Alejo was made director of an industrial complex at Ciudad Sahagún, for instance, and Juan José Bremer was made head of the Instituto Nacional de Bellas Artes. These were not topmost positions, of course, and they were almost degrading in some respects. Perhaps López Portillo's attitude was best revealed when he heard that Abel Quezada, the gifted cartoonist whom he had appointed as head of the government television station, had criticized the Echeverría administration in his acceptance speech. Quezada was fired overnight, and the warning spread: no public denunciation of Echeverría. If *echeverristas* were not entirely in, neither were they entirely out.

Similarly, López Portillo gave gingerly treatment to the ex-rival *tapados,* virtually all of whom were *echeverrista* to one extent or another. Muñoz Ledo was given the secretaryship for public education, and Cervantes del Río became head of the CFE. These were important posts, but also fraught with danger—public education because of student strikes and campus violence, the CFE because of insurgency within the electricians' union. One major problem, or one minor slip, and Muñoz Ledo or Cervantes could be through. Gómez Villanueva was temporarily left in charge of the Chamber of Deputies (he would soon be sent off as Ambassador to Italy), and López Portillo played a little

[60] See José Luis Mejías in *El Universal*, 3 December 1976; and Enrique León Martínez, "Características del nuevo gabinete," *Siempre!*, no. 1226 (22 December 1976): 56.

game: he gave the directorship of a major state-run bank to Enrique Olivares Santana, Gómez Villanueva's original *patrón* from Aguascalientes, thus appeasing and containing that entire *camarilla*. Perhaps because of his position as López Portillo's chief rival, Moya Palencia did not get any official appointment, he took up a professorship in law at UNAM, and he later became the director of the newspaper chain reputed to be under Echeverría's control—thus indicating his apparent continual importance within the *echeverrista* clique. The two remaining precandidates, Gálvez Betancourt and Bracamontes, were left out entirely, presumably because they were not strong enough to require cooptation.

Another dimension to the quest for balance came in the arrangement of *políticos* and *técnicos*. The latter group was clearly in command of economic policy, and, as a matter of fact, two-thirds of López Portillo's upper-level appointees had never held any elective office. But for some key posts, the new president relied heavily upon *políticos*. Carlos Hank González, the affable, well-liked former governor of the state of Mexico, would exercise great power as the head of the Federal District. Jesús Reyes Heroles, Secretary of Gobernación, had gained distinction as the leading ideologue of the PRI. The party itself, and the legislative delegations, were in the hands of tough, strong, old-fashioned *políticos*: Carlos Sansores Pérez, Joaquín Gamboa Pascoe, and Gómez Villanueva.[61]

Yet another aspect of the concern for equilibrium related to policy orientation. There were, for instance, ideological divergences among his economic advisers: one reporter categorized Tello and Oteyza as "Marxist" (a questionable judgment, especially regarding Oteyza) and Moctezuma as a Keynesian, while Solana proved difficult to classify.[62] Jorge Rojo Lugo, new head of Agrarian Reform, was closely identified with the peasant movement; but Oscar Flores, the Attorney General, was a wealthy rancher from Chihuahua with a no-nonsense reputation. Men from the labor movement received a number of middle-range appointments, including the leadership of the Senate, but the Secretary of Labor, Pedro Ojeda Paullada, had shown himself to be an extremely tough-minded Attorney General under Echeverría.

In one area López Portillo took unequivocal action: he expelled the youthful *efebócratas*. Of his top appointees, only Oteyza, the Cambridge-trained economist, was in his early thirties. More than half were,

---

[61] *Proceso* 1, no. 7 (18 December 1976): 6-11.

[62] See, particularly, the articles by José Luis Mejías in *El Universal*, 30 and 31 December 1976. Mejías called Solana a "functionalist," but José J. Castellanos referred to him as a "leftist" in *El Heraldo*, 1 December 1976.

like López Portillo, over the age of 50, and the average age of the
entire group was 52. According to Table 10-1, the age structures of the
Echeverría elite and the López Portillo group were actually quite similar, the largest proportion of both groups coming from the same birth
cohort as the presidents (1920-24). But there was one outstanding difference: the role of the very young. Whereas one-sixth of the outgoing
echeverrista elite had been born in the 1940s, this was true for only
one (or 3.1 percent) of López Portillo's 32 men. During the new *sexenio*, callow youth would have to wait its turn.

TABLE 10-1

*Age Structure of Echeverría
and López Portillo Elites*

Year of Birth	Echeverría		López Portillo
	% Entire Elite (N = 34)[a]	% Outgoing Elite (N = 24)[b]	% Entire Elite (N = 32)
1900-1904	5.9	8.3	0.0
1905-09	5.9	4.2	6.3
1910-14	2.9	4.2	6.3
1915-19	14.7	16.7	12.5
1920-24	35.3	29.2	28.1
1925-29	5.9	4.2	18.8
1930-34	17.6	16.7	18.8
1935-39	0.0	0.0	6.3
1940-44	11.8	16.7	3.1
Totals[c]	100.0	100.2	100.2

NOTE: Upper-level elites only (people in offices with scale values of 7 or 8 for the
HIGHEST OFFICE variable in Table A-3, Appendix A).

[a] As of November 30, 1976 (including Echeverría and, as special cases, Bremer,
Cervantes del Río, and López Portillo).

[b] Includes only those individuals of known age who did *not* receive upper-level
positions in the López Portillo administration.

[c] May not add up to 100 because of rounding.

In searching so diligently for harmony and equilibrium, López Portillo appointed a group whose composition fit in neatly with the historical patterns of previous times. About 30 percent of his upper-level
collaborators had held top positions under Echeverría—a holdover rate
that was somewhat higher than in prior years, when it was closer to
20 percent (see Table 6-2), but it was still fairly low, and, as empha-

sized above, some of the *echeverristas* were placed in awkward positions. A total of 36.4 percent had held upper-level posts in any previous administration, a figure closely matching the overall continuity rates presented in Table 6-1.[63] López Portillo neither broke with preceding regimes, nor did he rely on so-called emissaries of the past: he did almost exactly as others had done before.

Trends in social background were either confirmed or accelerated. Approximately 40 percent of the López Portillo group was born in Mexico City, just about twice the share as for the 1946-71 cohort as a whole (Table 3-1), a figure that clearly shows the continuing urbanization of the political elite and the paramount role of the Federal District itself.[64] About 95 percent had enjoyed the benefits of a university education, a proportion that falls almost exactly in line with the generally upward trend of the last 40 years (Figure 3-3). By the 1970s, a university degree had become a prime requisite for the exercise of power on the national level.

But, as before, it was not that any school would do. About *71 percent* of the *lopezportillista* elite had studied at UNAM; 45 percent had been to the national law school, a place where many made their first acquaintance with the future president. Just as remarkably, over half of the elite (54.5 percent) had, like López Portillo, taught courses at the university. Such data provide overwhelming evidence, if any more were needed, about UNAM's role in forming political elites, at least for the generation now in power. It has been the central place for making contacts, creating alliances, and forging political destinies.

The shape of these careers also fit the preestablished mold. Approximately half of the new group were trained as lawyers, a general-purpose skill that lent itself to accommodation and negotiation, the essential keys to success, and the legal profession would furnish further opportunities at the end of their incumbencies. Almost all had entered politics soon after graduation from the university, climbing up the ladder of offices with professional skill and dedication; only a couple, like Farell and López Portillo, had practiced law privately for extended periods before crossing over to the public sector—but, once in, there they stayed. Most of the top-level officeholders in the new regime had, in addition, worked their way up through the "exec-

---

[63] Note, however, that the figures in Table 6-1 refer to a pool of offices that is larger than just the upper-level posts, for which the average rate of continuity was somewhat less (around 30 percent or so, depending upon the regimes included in the average).

[64] The predominance of *capitalinos* was noticed by Enrique León Martínez in *Siempre!* (cited above) and also by Victor M. Salinas in *Últimas Noticias*, 1 December 1976.

utive" network of institutional positions; a few had spent their careers in the "administrative" track. Only one-third had held any office in the "electoral" network, thus illustrating the continuing difficulty of moving from elected posts to cabinet-level jobs (see Chapter 5)—notwithstanding López Portillo's effort to make peace with the *políticos*.[65]

There were some new developments as well. One was the growing number of women in positions of importance—not only in the Chamber of Deputies but, most conspicuously, in subcabinet posts. Luisa María Leal, Rosa Luz Alegría, Emilia Téllez Benoit, and María Lavalle Urbina all received significant subministerial positions, and, as already noted, Margarita López Portillo obtained a crucial office too. This pattern accelerated a trend that had started under Echeverría, and it was a revealing indication of the times. As Beatriz Reyes Nevares observed, "it is a sign of social as well as political evolution. These appointments show that many of the old obstacles have disappeared, and also that we women have not been improvident."[66] Obviously enough, the political participation of females in Mexico was still modest, but it was plainly on the rise.

One other element might or might not be new: the conspicuous appearance of political dynasties. As shown above, López Portillo gave offices to some of his own relatives, and kinship bonds have always played a major role in Mexican politics. But as noted in Chapter 9, many of these connections have, in the past, been intragenerational—brother-brother, cousin-cousin, etc. What the López Portillo group revealed, in contrast, is a sizable number of intergenerational ties, mostly father-son. According to Table 10-2, for instance, Rojo Lugo was the son of a former peasant leader, and he had followed in his father's footsteps as governor of Hidalgo before moving to Agrarian Reform. Carlos Tello, Manuel Tello, and Gustavo Carbajal—as well as Rojo Lugo—were sons of former cabinet ministers, Cuauhtémoc Cárdenas was the son of a president, Rodolfo Echeverría and Mario Calles were nephews of ex-presidents. Joaquín Gamboa Pascoe, leader of the Senate, was the ally and son-in-law of Fidel Velázquez, the *jefazo* of the labor movement. One of the most illustrative appointments, in this respect, was made by Fernando Solana: having worked closely with a former UNAM rector, Javier Barros Sierra, he designated Barros' son

---

[65] Among those who had held elective office, several had done so for the first time by entering the 1976 legislature—most notably the Senate, which seems to have functioned as a kind of "waiting room" during the transition period. See the column by Cirino Pérez Aguirre in *Novedades*, 3 December 1976.

[66] *El Nacional*, 3 January 1977. See also Roderic Ai Camp, "Women and Political Leadership in Mexico: A Comparative Study of Female and Male Political Elites" (unpublished paper).

TABLE 10-2

Kinship Ties in the López Portillo Regime

Officeholder	Kinship Tie
I. CABINET	
Jorge Rojo Lugo, Secretary of Agrarian Reform	Son of Javier Rojo Gómez, former governor of Hidalgo (1937-40), head of the Federal District (1940-46), and leader of the CNC
Carlos Tello, Secretary of the Presidency	Son of Manuel Tello, former Secretary of Foreign Relations (1948-52, 1958-64) and Ambassador to the United States (1952-58)
II. SUBCABINET	
Rosa Luz Alegría, Subsecretary of Budget and Planning (formerly Presidencia)	Former daughter-in-law of Luis Echeverría; divorced from Luis Vicente Echeverría Zuno
Mario Calles, Subsecretary of Health and Welfare	Nephew of Plutarco Elías Calles, former President of Mexico (1924-28)
Gustavo Carbajal Moreno, Subsecretary of Labor	Son of Angel Carbajal, former Secretary of Gobernación (1952-58)
Cuauhtémoc Cárdenas, Subsecretary of Agriculture	Son of Lázaro Cárdenas, former President of Mexico (1934-40)
Rodolfo Echeverría Ruiz, Subsecretary of Gobernación	Nephew of Luis Echeverría
Maria Lavalle Urbina, Subsecretary of of Education	Sister of Eduardo J. Lavalle Urbina, former Governor of Campeche (1944-49)
Carlos Armando Madrazo Pintado, *Oficial Mayor* of Public Works	Son of Carlos Madrazo, former Governor of Tabasco (1959-64) and head of the PRI (1964-65)
Alfonso Rosenzweig Díaz, Subsecretary of Foreign Relations	Member of Rosenzweig family, involved in diplomatic service for generations
Jorge Tamayo, Subsecretary of Industry and Commerce	Cousin (distant) of José López Portillo
María Téllez Benoit, Subsecretary of Foreign Relations	Daughter of Manuel C. Téllez, former Secretary of Gobernación (1931-32) and Foreign Relations (1932)
III. OTHER	
Mario Ramón Beteta, director of SOMEX (Sociedad Mexicana de Crédito Industrial)	Son of Ignacio Beteta, chief of staff under Cárdenas (1934-40), and nephew of Ramón Beteta, former Secretary of Treasury (1946-52)
Alejandro Carrillo Castro, presidential adviser	Son of Alejandro Carrillo Marcor, former federal deputy (1940-43, 1964-67) and senator (1970-76)

TABLE 10-2 (continued)

Officeholder	Kinship Tie
Joaquín Gamboa Pascoe, leader of the Senate and labor spokesman	Son-in-law of Fidel Velázquez, leader of the CTM
Enrique M. Loaeza Tovar, director of ASA (Aeropuertos y Servicios Auxiliares)	Nephew (distant) of José López Portillo
Guillermo López Portillo, director of Instituto Mexicano del Deporte, under Secretariat of Public Education	Cousin of José López Portillo
José Ramón López Portillo, director general in Secretariat of Budget and Planning (formerly Presidencia)	Son of José López Portillo
Manuel López Portillo y Ramos, subdirector of ISSSTE	Cousin of José López Portillo
Margarita López Portillo, director of communications under Secretariat of Gobernación	Sister of José López Portillo
Manuel Tello Macías, Ambassador to England	Son of Manuel Tello, former Secretary of Foreign Relations, and brother of Carlos Tello (see above)
Javier Barros Valero, private secretary to Minister of Commerce	Son of Javier Barros Sierra, former rector of UNAM and patron of Fernando Solana, the Secretary of Commerce

as his own private secretary. And one of the most indicative, in a political sense, was the appointment of Carlos Armando Madrazo Pintado to a subministerial post: his father, Carlos Madrazo, had attempted to initiate political reforms during a brief tenure as head of the PRI (1964-65), and the Madrazo name had ever since been identified with the forces of change.

It is my guess that the extensive formation of multigenerational political dynasties is a relatively recent phenomenon, one that would depend, in part, on the processes of institutionalization and stabilization that have taken hold since the 1940s. If only because of the time spans involved, political tranquility would seem to be a precondition for the regularized transmission of office from one generation to another, especially from parent to child. But this transmission is usually neither automatic nor direct: Manuel Tello and Javier Rojo Gómez, both deceased, could hardly have imposed their sons on López Portillo. Rather, paternal prominence confers aspiring young functionaries with instant connections, immediate visibility, and a "recognition factor" that constitutes a useful career resource—but not much more than that. (Gamboa Pascoe and Rodolfo Echeverría may, by contrast, have been the beneficiaries of more direct intervention, but these would be exceptions to the rule.)

If my hypothesis about the relationship between stability and dynasty is correct, the emergence and strengthening of multigenerational bonds in the postrevolutionary (post-1940) period would be entirely consistent with my argument about the separation of political and economic elites (Chapter 7). Within each realm, sons tend to follow their fathers, rather than crossing from one sphere to the other. Socially, as well as otherwise, the two groups stand apart.

Within the confines of all these changes, processes, and continuities, López Portillo made one brilliant master stroke. In the appointment of Reyes Heroles, he gave the post of Gobernación to a man of considerable talent—who, by virtue of having a foreign (Spanish) father, was constitutionally ineligible to become president. The person in the most advantageous institutional position for the next sexennial campaign was therefore unable to accept its rewards, so it would be impossible for Gobernación to become a center of political intrigue. Coincidentally, Hank González, head of the Federal District, was also disqualified for the same reason, his father having been German. So was Oteyza, the son of Spanish parents. As a result, the picture for 1982 was anything but clear, and it would be senseless to engage in active maneuvering, jockeying, and speculation—known in Mexico as *futurismo*—for several years.[67] All eyes were on the present, and it belonged to López Portillo.

With this tactical coup, López Portillo climaxed his effort to create a political team and establish his own authority. In compliance with long-standing tradition, too, he used top-level appointments in order to issue symbolic statements of unity and continuity, carefully constructing coalitions and alliances. Despite occasional criticism,[68] initial reactions indicated that his political architecture had been a success. The newspaper *Novedades* reported that general impressions about the "intelligently formed" cabinet were "positive, even expressing extensive satisfaction."[69] *El Nacional* noted that the composition of the top-level group had caused "a good impression on public opinion,"

[67] Even so, the temptation for idle guesswork was hard to resist. Early betting was on Ojeda Paullada, Martínez Manautou, Muñoz Ledo, or—in the event of a constitutional amendment—Hank González.

[68] See, for instance, the sharp criticism of Martínez Manautou's appointment by Irene Talamas, "Decepción en el gremio médico," *Excélsior*, 3 December 1976.

[69] *Novedades*, 1 December 1976.

"Confidence"

adding that it would mean "political dynamism within a basic ideological harmony."[70] Perhaps a headline in *El Universal* caught the mood most aptly: "Neither a coup, nor a *maximato*, nor *futurismo*."[71]

By his acceptance speech and through his appointments, López Portillo made a concerted attempt to restore public confidence and, in so doing, gain time for his government. He was playing by all the accepted rules of the game—as Echeverría had not during the previous months—and this fact alone reassured many people. Capital began returning to the country. At a meeting of businessmen, Andrés Marcelo Sada, so thoroughly pilloried in late November, declared that investment would increase because of the atmosphere of calm.[72] By mid-December the dollar value of the peso had climbed from 3.47 cents up to a nickel. Clearly, López Portillo was winning confidence within political circles and among the private sector.

The pattern continued in subsequent months. In early 1977 López Portillo further asserted his control by appointing ex-presidents Díaz Ordaz and Echeverría to ambassadorial posts, thus removing them both from the domestic political scene. Though the designation of Díaz Ordaz as the country's first Ambassador to Spain since 1939 met with substantial opposition, prompting Carlos Fuentes to resign his own ambassadorship in protest, it was a calculatedly ambivalent move, both acknowledging and isolating the strength of the *diazordacista* group. (Díaz Ordaz complicated the picture by resigning the post soon after presenting his credentials, but this would hardly strengthen his political prestige.) Similarly, Echeverría's position as ambassador, first to the Third World and then to UNESCO, provided him with an opportunity to seek actively the secretary-generalship of the United Nations, an office to which he had aspired in 1976, and it would reduce his political presence within Mexico.

If the manipulation of personnel achieved a measure of balance for the regime, and this would include some cabinet-level changes late in 1977, policy problems proved to be intractable. On land reform, the new president moved back and forth: in December 1976 a federal court judge declared Echeverría's expropriation in Sonora to be unconstitutional, López Portillo proclaimed his concern for the law, and in mid-1977 he announced that it would be impossible to return the land to the original owners. On the political front, López Portillo appeared to be opting for change, offering amnesty to political prisoners and instructing Reyes Heroles and other advisers to design a program for

---

[70] *El Nacional*, 3 December 1976.
[71] Above the column by Ortega, *El Universal*, 6 December 1976.
[72] *El Universal*, 3 December 1976; and *El Sol*, 3 December 1976.

political reform—while the president also maintained contacts with conservatives. In recognition of the country's economic needs, he reestablished rapport with the United States and encouraged foreign investment, simultaneously attempting to uphold nationalistic pride. New waves of protest broke out within the universities. At all times, there lurked the specter of inflation, unemployment, and underemployment. The discovery of massive petroleum deposits offered a new source of hope, and gave some ground for optimism, but the projected socioeconomic consequences of large-scale oil revenues were anything but clear.[73] On so many crucial issues, there seemed to be no easy escape.

Plus Ça Change ... ?

In overcoming the problem of presidential succession, and surviving the peculiar crisis of late 1976, Mexico's authoritarian system once again revealed its capacity for adaptation and change. It remained, as before, a regime in which effective competition for power was restricted to a fairly small group—urban-born, middle class, highly educated. The political elite continued to be separate from the economic elite, a point dramatically emphasized by Echeverría himself, though accommodation could be reached, as López Portillo had shown. The rules of the political game remained intact, as revealed by López Portillo's own designation and, even more apparently, in his choices for collaborators. It was a regime in which the middle class predominated, both in personnel and in policy orientations.

Finally, and most important, it remained a regime in which a crisis could be met and resolved in symbolic terms. The anguish of November and the fears of a coup were primarily *political* concerns. There was no talk of a social revolution, of drastic measures to alleviate deep-seated structural problems. This absence of social content made it possible for López Portillo to dispel these anxieties through symbolic means, by his speech and, more especially, by his skillful composition of a *camarilla* and a cabinet. In an ironic way, the crisis of November may have eased the transition because it focused all attention on *whether* the succession would occur and *who* would be in power—rather than on what the policies would be. Merely by acquiring office, López Portillo had secured a grand personal triumph.

As time wore on it began to seem that, in the long run, both López

[73] For a highly controversial assessment of some possibilities see George W. Grayson, "Mexico's Opportunity: The Oil Boom," *Foreign Policy*, no. 29 (Winter 1977-78): 65-89.

Portillo and the system would have to confront the nation's frightful problems of poverty, inequality, and suffering.[74] Radical policies of re-distribution would require sharp redirections for the regime, the application of new priorities and formulas. The basic alternative appeared to be repression, the increasing use of force to quell disturbances. Either outcome would eventually alter the character of Mexico's authoritarian regime.

[74] For some thoughtful forecasts see Susan Kaufman Purcell, "The Future of the Mexican System," in *Authoritarianism in Mexico*, ed. José Luis Reyna and Richard S. Weinert (Philadelphia: ISHI, 1977), pp. 173-191.

APPENDICES

APPENDIX A.
DEFINING A POLITICAL ELITE

The ultimate significance of this entire book depends upon the adequacy of the procedures for defining a "political elite" in twentieth-century Mexico. In spite of its generalized usage, or perhaps because of it, the concept of "elite" has become elusive and vague. This fact has caused me to make numerous (and painful) methodological decisions, and because of their importance to this study I shall spell them out in some detail.

Abstractly, I regard a "political elite" as that group of people which holds the most decisive portion of political power. As stated in Chapter 1, I use the term in a descriptive, not a normative, way. It is *not* my view that those who rule are "chosen" (as the word implies), that they possess superior qualities, or that they necessarily deserve the power they command. Nor do I mean to assume that they must have been united by group consciousness, shared characteristics (other than power-wielding), or a coherent will to act in behalf of common interests. As shown frequently throughout the text, in fact, I believe elites are usually divided and almost always stratified. In speaking of an "elite" I simply intend to indicate the powerful. But even in this relatively neutral sense, the concept raises severe operational problems—figuring out how much power is "decisive," discovering who has power over whom with regard to what issues, and assessing the impact of change over time.[1] The challenge stands: How to identify the members of an elite?

There are three practical approaches to this problem. One is the *reputational* method, pioneered by Floyd Hunter, who isolated an upper stratum of community leaders in Atlanta, Georgia, by asking a panel of presumably well-qualified "judges" to pick out the most important people in the city.[2] A second technique relies on *positional* criteria: those who occupy the "command posts" of a society comprise its "power elite," as C. Wright Mills explained it, so the task of re-

[1] For excellent discussions of the concept of power see Robert A. Dahl, *Modern Political Analysis* (Englewood Cliffs, N.J.: Prentice-Hall, 1964), ch. 5, and the numerous essays in Roderick Bell, David V. Edwards, and R. Harrison Wagner, eds., *Political Power: A Reader in Theory and Research* (New York: The Free Press, 1969).

[2] Floyd Hunter, *Community Power Structure: A Study of Decision Makers* (Chapel Hill: University of North Carolina Press, 1953), esp. pp. 262-271. Hunter also applied this technique in his subsequent study of *Top Leadership, U.S.A.* (Chapel Hill: University of North Carolina Press, 1959).

search is to locate the key organizations and identify their leaders.[3] The third procedure, associated with Robert A. Dahl, is to focus on *decisionmaking*. Distinguishing between the *possession* of power resources and their actual *use*, Dahl argued that power relationships could become evident only through the careful analysis of specific political conflicts—who took part, who fought, who made the decisions, and who won.[4]

All of these methods have their weaknesses. The reputational approach depends too heavily on the perception of informants, who may or may not be well-informed and who might tend to overemphasize the visible trappings of leadership, not to mention political gossip, whereas real power might be exercised behind the scenes. The institutional approach stresses organizations and overlooks informal sources of power. And the decisionmaking criterion, notwithstanding its merits, deals only with overt cases of conflict; it says nothing about the issues which never reach the political arena and which, for that very reason, might be the most crucial of all.[5] There is no way of avoiding the likelihood of error: all you can do is pick your pitfall.

While these different methods seem to entail separate risks, at least in principle, they show substantial similarity in practice. As Frank Bonilla has observed, none of these techniques

> lends itself to unequivocal and easily reproducible selection procedures, and even less to clear-cut rankings of individuals. Although the identification of *positions* according to tables of organizations seems on the surface more readily performed according to objective criteria, it is not hard to show that beyond a handful of top positions the actual operation quickly reduces to a choice of positions *according to their reputation*. Similarly, the examination of any list of individuals to whom judges attribute power quickly reveals that the positions occupied by subjects clearly weigh in the rankings made. Again, even in the most careful studies of decisions with a view to locating influential individuals, the opportunities for making the full range of observations necessary seem plainly absent. Here also inferences on the basis of formal positions occupied and

---

[3] C. Wright Mills, *The Power Elite* (New York: Oxford University Press, 1959).
[4] Robert A. Dahl, "A Critique of the Ruling Elite Model," in G. William Domhoff and Hoyt B. Ballard, eds., *C. Wright Mills and the Power Elite* (Boston: Beacon Press, 1968), pp. 25-36; and Dahl, *Who Governs? Democracy and Power in an American City* (New Haven: Yale University Press, 1961).
[5] See E. E. Schattschneider, *The Semisovereign People: A Realist's View of Democracy in America* (New York: Holt, Rinehart, and Winston, 1960); and Peter Bachrach and Morton S. Baratz, "Two Faces of Power," *American Political Science Review* 56, no. 4 (December 1962): 947-952.

personal reputation inevitably color the evaluations of the meaning of the behavior of participants.[6]

One implication of this view, indeed a sobering one, is that there is no error-free technique. But in a perverse kind of way, another implication is encouraging. If the methods share common faults, maybe they have common virtues too—and when all is said and done, the choice of one approach over the others may not make a lot of difference.

It would be nice if that were true, since, dealing with twentieth-century Mexico, I have found my options limited. Because of the chronological scope of this book I have been unable to consult a panel of judges: firsthand informants for the early decades of the century have died, primary and secondary literature is too sparse to take their place, and many knowledgeable Mexicans of today hold a generalized (and often justified) suspicion of North American social science and its practitioners. Nor has it been feasible to focus on conflict *à la* Robert Dahl. Within Mexico's authoritarian system political struggle has taken place outside the public eye, behind closed doors, with participants and winners known mainly to themselves. In such a context neither the reputational approach nor the decisionmaking method turned out to be viable.

Partly by default, I have therefore elected to identify the national political elite in Mexico as *those people who have held major political office.* One advantage of this criterion is that it has allowed me to apply uniform rules for elite designation and data collection over an extended and sometimes turbulent period of Mexican history. Another is that it produced a large number of individuals ($N = 6,302$), thus making it possible to seek broad patterns in recruitment processes and also to deal with elites at various levels. Despite its apparent simplicity, though, the validity of the positional approach hinges upon one basic and beguiling question: Which positions ought to be selected for analysis?

Significantly enough, I have made my choices on primarily reputational grounds. My first step was to consult the work of Frank R. Brandenburg, who depicted the Mexican political system as a vast and complex network under the control and domination of the so-called Revolutionary Family. Apparently using reputational criteria (that is, informal, unstructured interviews, plus a decade of professional experience) he went on to draw the hierarchy as consisting of twelve distinct levels or rungs which, in an act of sheer intellectual bravado, he

6 Frank Bonilla, *The Failure of Elites,* vol. 2 of *The Politics of Change in Venezuela* (Cambridge: M.I.T. Press, 1970), p. 15.

diputado

¿POR QUÉ LES DICEN "REPRESENTANTES POPULARES", SI SON DE LO MÁS IMPOPULAR..?

embajador

PERSONAJES OFICIALMENTE AUTORIZADOS PARA DENIGRAR AL PAÍS EN EL EXTRANJERO.

exiliado

INDIVIDUO QUE, SIN SER EMBAJADOR, HABLA MAL DE SU GOBIERNO.

46

gobernador

VER VIRREYES

legislador

LOS LEGISLADORES ESTÁN EN EL PODER, PERO NO PUEDEN...

POLÍTICOS

(NO EN BALDE SE LES LLAMA "HOMBRES PÚBLICOS"..)

PRESIDENTE

DESPUÉS DE 60 AÑOS DE REVOLUCIÓN, SE CONVENCE UNO DE LA FRASE DE QUE "CUALQUIERA PUEDE SER PRESIDENTE"...

102

senado

EL ASILO DE LOS POLÍTICOS

tapado

A FIN DE CUENTAS, EL TAPADO ES EL PUEBLO..

virrey

(VER GOBERNADOR)

Diputado (deputy): "Why do they call them 'popular representatives' if they are so unpopular?"

Embajador (ambassador): "Persons officially authorized to insult the country abroad."

Exiliado (exile): "An individual who, without being an ambassador, speaks badly of his government."

Gobernador (governor): "See *virreyes.*"

Legislador (legislator): "Legislators are in power, but they can't do anything." The picture also pokes fun, since the term *borrego* (lamb) is applied to those who follow along like a herd of sheep.

Políticos: "Not in jest are they known as 'public men'. . . ."

Presidente (with a likeness of Díaz Ordaz): "After 60 years of revolution, one can believe in the phrase, 'Anyone can become president.' "

Senado (Senate): "An asylum for politicians."

Tapado: "After all, the *tapado* is the people."

Virrey (viceroy): "(See governor)."

presented in rank order.[7] Ranging from the head of the Revolutionary Family down to municipal councilmen, Brandenburg's scheme furnished a preliminary list of positions—some formal, some informal—that could be used to select an elite. With this in mind, and sometimes in hand, I then proceeded to solicit the opinions of scholars and practicing politicians in Mexico who, occasionally for reasons of their own, thought certain offices to be "important." I also read as widely as possible in primary and secondary literature on Mexican politics. Finally, I decided to identify the national political elite for 1900-1971 as those individuals who held any one of the following positions at any time during the period.[8]

a. President (and vice-president, insofar as the office existed)

b. Members of the cabinet (national secretaries, heads of autonomous departments, governors of the Federal District, attorneys general, and ambassadors to the United States)

c. Members of the subcabinet (subsecretaries and *oficiales mayores* of national secretariats, *Jefes del Estado Mayor*, and heads of the department of Fábricas Militares)

d. Heads of major decentralized agencies and state-supported companies, selected according to the size of their budgets (Comisión Federal de Electricidad, Ferrocarriles Nacionales, Instituto Mexi-

[7] Frank R. Brandenburg, *The Making of Modern Mexico* (Englewood Cliffs, N.J.: Prentice-Hall, 1964), pp. 158-159. On the hazards of such an enterprise see the excellent review article by Carolyn and Martin Needleman, "Who Rules Mexico? A Critique of Some Current Views on the Mexican Political Process," *Journal of Politics* 31, no. 4 (November 1969): 1011-1034.

[8] Unless otherwise indicated, officeholders include incumbents with provisional, acting, or interim status.

cano del Seguro Social, Instituto de Servicios y Seguros Sociales de Trabajadores del Estado, and Petróleos Mexicanos; Altos Hornos de México, Banco de México, Banco Nacional de Crédito Ejidal, Banco Nacional Hipotecario Urbano y de Obras Públicas, and Nacional Financiera)[9]

e. Members of the National Executive Committee of the official party[10]

f. Governors of states and federal territories

g. Senators

h. National deputies (including delegates to special congresses of 1914-15 and 1916-17)[11]

i. Ambassadors in foreign posts (only those with rank of Ambassador or Envoy Extraordinary and Minister Plenipotentiary)

A comparison between my selection and the Brandenburg scheme appears in Table A-1, which presents his version of the hierarchy—with the offices that I have chosen in italics. One difference, of course, is that I have made no effort to identify informal power-wielders (such as "members of the inner circle and factional leaders of the Revolutionary Family"). In the interests of economy, both of money and time, I have omitted some organizational elites, either in the hope that they would turn up somewhere else within my institutional network (as with many labor leaders) or in the conviction that the necessary information was unavailable (as with military zone commanders).[12] Nevertheless I have attempted to include a fairly broad spectrum of offices, from near the top of the Brandenburg hierarchy to near the bottom (rung numbers 2 to 9).[13]

This reliance on position-holding might appear to be unduly treacherous in Mexico because, by definition, it makes no allowance for un-

[9] The data on budgets were taken from Roberto Santillán López and Aniceto Rosas Figueroa, *Teoría general de las finanzas públicas y el caso de México* (Mexico: Universidad Nacional Autónoma de México, 1962), Anexos 18, 20, and 21; and Secretaría de la Presidencia, Dirección de Inversiones Públicas, *México: Inversión pública federal, 1925-63* (Mexico: Talleres Gráficos de la Nación, 1964), Cuadro 11, pp. 111-118. Note that some agencies which have acquired great importance within the past few years, such as CONASUPO, are omitted from my list.

[10] Successively known as the Partido Nacional Revolucionario, the Partido de la Revolución Mexicana, and, since 1946, the Partido Revolucionario Institucional.

[11] Senators and deputies do not include *suplentes* (alternates) unless they are known to have taken office.

[12] My desire to include Jefes de Zonas Militares was thwarted by the Secretaría de la Defensa Nacional, which withheld the names of zone commanders because the information was "of an official character."

[13] As Brandenburg himself points out, the head of the Revolutionary Family is "usually" the president of Mexico—or, if not, is an ex-president—so rung 1 is actually incorporated in rung 2. Brandenburg, *Making*, pp. 3-4.

TABLE A-1

Offices Selected from the Brandenburg Ranking

Level of Rung in Brandenburg's Scheme	Position[a]
1	The head of the Revolutionary Family
2	*The president of Mexico*
3	Members of the inner circle and factional leaders of the Revolutionary Family
4	*Cabinet members, including the governor of the Federal District; the military chief of staff; the private secretary of the president; managers of large state industries; and directors of large semiautonomous agencies, commissions, banks, and boards*
5	*Governors of the big states and the federal territories, ambassadors in prestige posts,* regional strongmen not in the inner circle, *the two presidential legislative spokesmen in the respective houses of congress,* military zone commanders, and *the official-party president*
6	Supreme court justices; *senators; undersecretaries of cabinet ministries* and assistant directors of large state industries, commissions, boards, and dependencies; *the secretary-general and sector heads of the official party;* leaders of major opposition parties; and the secretaries-general of the CTM, CNC, and FSTSE
7	Directors and managers of medium-size state industries; directors of secondary federal boards, commissions, and agencies; *governors of medium and small states; ambassadors, ministers,* and consuls general
8	Municipal presidents in large cities
9	*Federal deputies;* federal judges; the president and members of regional executive councils of the official party; leaders of minor opposition parties; labor, agrarian, and federal credit bank bosses at the state level; and state cabinet officers
10	State deputies, state judges, district official-party officials, federal officials in the states, and local caciques[b]
11	Municipal presidents, local military commanders, and state and federal officials at the local level
12	Local party officials and municipal councilmen

[a] The complete list of positions is taken from Frank R. Brandenburg, *The Making of Modern Mexico* (Englewood Cliffs, N.J.: Prentice-Hall, 1964), pp. 158-159. Offices selected for inclusion in this study are in italics.
[b] The term *cacique* is roughly equivalent to "boss."

deniably important informal leadership. In defense of my approach I would emphasize two points. First, the relatively small number of informal leaders—small even according to the Brandenburg scheme—would have a minimal impact on the statistical composition of the groups under study. Second, despite the frequent absence of decision-making authority, political office in Mexico can be viewed as a kind of trophy or reward. Officeholders have triumphed in the game of office-seeking, they are "winners," and to this extent they constitute a properly defined elite. (In technical terms I am adopting the premise that there is a strong and positive correlation between political office and political power, but the relationship is plainly an imperfect one.) Despite its obvious drawbacks, I believe that my application of the positional technique has produced a solid representation of the national political elite in twentieth-century Mexico.[14]

In addition to identifying the elite as a whole, I have also attempted to explore its internal hierarchy. Various portions of the text focus on "upper-level" elites, and Chapters 4 and 5 concentrate upon the correlates of relative success within the system. For these and other steps in the analysis, I have had to arrange the offices in order of importance or prestige.

My general approach has been to follow the ranking that Brandenburg employed (see Table A-1), with some significant modifications. First, I have grouped members of the cabinet and subcabinet in slightly different ways. Second, given the composition and realities of political resources in Mexico, I have decided to identify "big states" (rung 5) according to the size of their *budgets* rather than the size of populations. And since the relative economic importance of the states has varied a great deal over time, I have selected three separate sets of "big states": one for 1910, one for 1930, one for 1960. There is some overlap between the sets, as revealed in Table A-2, though the individual rank order showed substantial variance. The practical point is this: whether a governorship would be counted as that of a "big state" would depend on (a) the size of the budget, and (b) the chronological proximity of the gubernatorial inauguration to the years 1910, 1930, or 1960.[15] Third, I have elected to omit ambassadorships (except to the

[14] Note the similarity between my political elite and the list of officeholders described as Mexico's "political bourgeoisie" in Alonso Aguilar M., "Problemas y perspectivas de un cambio radical," in Fernando Carmona et al., *El milagro mexicano* (Mexico: Editorial Nuestro Tiempo, 1970), p. 311.

[15] In a previous essay I used population size instead of budgets as a means of categorizing the states. See Peter H. Smith, "La movilidad política en el México contemporáneo," *Foro Internacional* 15, no. 3 (January-March 1975): 379-413, esp. 412-413.

United States) from most of the analysis of success within the system, largely because diplomatic appointments have been ambiguous: they can represent major promotion or, as has so often happened, they can be a subtle form of political exile.

TABLE A-2

States with Largest Budgets in 1910, 1930, and 1960

Rank	1910[a]	1930[b]	1960[c]
1	Jalisco	Veracruz	Chihuahua
2	Yucatán	Baja California Norte	Sonora
3	Puebla	Jalisco	Veracruz
4	Michoacán	Yucatán	Mexico
5	Oaxaca[d]	Puebla	Baja California Norte
6	Mexico	Sonora	Jalisco
7	Veracruz	México	Yucatán
8	Durango	Hidalgo	Nuevo León
9	Guanajuato	Tamaulipas	Puebla
10	Chihuahua	Chihuahua	—
11	Hidalgo	—	

[a] SOURCE: Secretaría de Economía, Dirección General de Estadística, *Estadísticas sociales del Porfiriato, 1877-1910* (Mexico: Talleres Gráficos de la Nación, 1956), p. 38.

[b] SOURCE: Secretaría de la Economía Nacional, Dirección General de Estadística, *Anuario estadístico de los Estados Unidos Mexicanos, 1939* (Mexico: Talleres Gráficos de la Nación, 1941), pp. 678-680.

[c] SOURCE: Secretaría de Industria y Comercio, Dirección General de Estadística, *Compendio estadístico 1960* (Mexico: Talleres Gráficos de la Nación, 1960), p. 143.

[d] No data for 1910; in 1878 Oaxaca ranked fourth in state budgets.

These last two alterations point to a basic difficulty with any ranking scheme. Different offices can perform different functions at different times, and, especially in a society that underwent a revolution, they might occupy different ranks on the ladder of political prestige. Nonetheless the attempt to analyze continuity and change in the determinants of political success requires a consistent definition of the dependent variable, success, measured in this instance by the highest level of office achieved at any time during one's career. Accordingly I have stratified nine levels of office and assigned numerical values to each of them. As illustrated in Table A-3, the resulting variable, known as **HIGHEST OFFICE**, ranges from a value of 8 at the top to o at the bottom.

TABLE A-3

*Offices, Scale Values, and Frequency Distributions
for HIGHEST OFFICE Variable*

Offices[a]	Scale Values for HIGHEST OFFICE Variable	Distribution of Officeholders	
		N	%
President and cabinet members	8	454	7.5
Presidents of the government party plus directors of selected decentralized agencies and state-supported companies	7	60	1.0
Governors of major states[b]	6	292	4.9
National Executive Committee of the government party	5	89	1.5
Subcabinet	4	302	5.0
Senators	3	581	9.7
Governors of other states or federal territories	2	412	6.8
National deputies	1	3,776	62.8
Ambassadors in major posts[c]	0	50	0.8
Subtotals	...	6,016	100.0
Ambassadors in other posts	(not scored)	286	—
Totals	...	6,302	100.0

[a] For full listings of the offices see pp. 4, 5 and Table A-1.

[b] As defined in Table A-2.

[c] The designation of "major" diplomatic posts is based on my own impressionistic judgment, and includes the following: Argentina, Brazil, Chile, China, France, Germany, Great Britain, Guatemala, Italy, Japan, League of Nations, Russia or Soviet Union, Spain, United Nations, or any combination involving these posts.

One technical consequence of this scaling procedure is that, since success was hard to come by, most people clustered near the bottom of the ladder. According to Table A-3, for instance, over 60 percent of the total stratified pool of politicians never got beyond the Chamber of Deputies. Naturally, this concentration led to severe downward skewness in the HIGHEST OFFICE variable.

In the attempt to analyze the attributes associated with political success, especially in Chapter 4, further distortions resulted from the availability of social-background data. To illustrate the problem, Figure A-1 traces the relative incidence of reasonably "reliable" personal

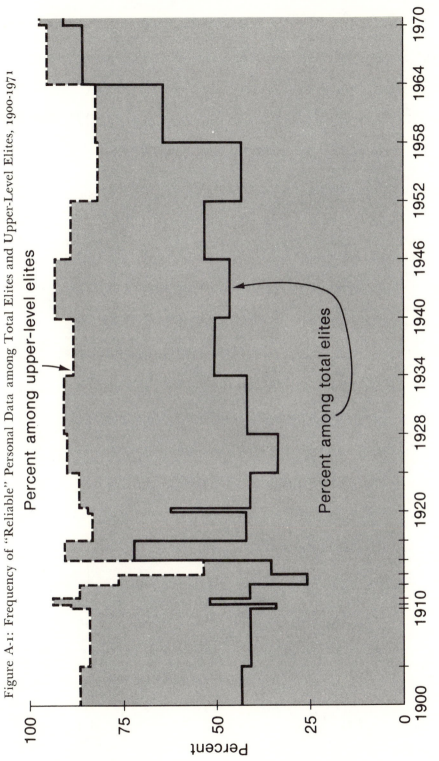

Figure A-1: Frequency of "Reliable" Personal Data among Total Elites and Upper-Level Elites, 1900-1971

Percent among upper-level elites

Percent among total elites

data[16] for (a) all officeholders in successive presidential regimes between 1900 and 1971, and (b) occupants of the "upper-level" offices, defined as those with scale values of 7 or 8 in Table A-3. Demonstrating the law of documentary elitism, which holds that biographical data on only the most prominent people shall find their way into standard historical sources,[17] information has been much more readily obtainable for upper-level officeholders than for the total elites. There is also a bias in time: for the period up to 1958 I was usually able to locate data on something like 40 percent of all the members of presidential elites (with, of course, substantial variance around that figure); for the post-1958 years, the availability of data steadily improved.

Obviously, this means that the data base for my analysis is woefully incomplete. Less obviously, but more seriously, it is apparent that those for whom data have been obtained do not constitute a statistically acceptable random sample of Mexico's twentieth-century political elite: they tend to be more prominent and more recent than the officeholding population as a whole. In order to cope with the prominence bias, if only crudely, I have tried deleting all deputies (scale value = 1) as well as ambassadors (scale value = 0) from all the computer runs for Chapter 4, and found that the results were generally much the same as when only ambassadors were omitted. I also discovered that the correlation between HIGHEST OFFICE and the presence or absence of data for social-background variables tended to be rather weak, and so I let the matter drop. To control for the chronology bias, as well as to examine change over time, I divided members of the elites into separate historical cohorts—as explained in Chapter 1.

[16] Judgments on the "reliability" of data were impressionistic, and they were concerned largely with the presence and the consistency (but not the completeness) of social-background information; a person with believable entries for only three or four personal attributes would be coded as having "reliable" data, even though information might be lacking on all other items.

[17] Although, as shown in the bibliography, I have used unpublished as well as published sources in tracking down biographical data.

APPENDIX B.
MEASURING CONTINUITY
AND TURNOVER

At first glance the measurement of continuity within a political elite seems straightforward enough: you take the members of an elite group at time t_0, you find out how many remained in the group at time t_1, and then compute percentages (or proportions) to establish rates of continuity or turnover. Upon close examination, however, the practical application of this technique requires a number of intricate decisions. In Appendix A I have given my reasons for using the possession of political office as a criterion for membership in Mexico's national political elite, and the material in Chapter 6 accordingly deals with continuity and turnover among officeholding elites. Even within these constraints, in themselves significant, manifold questions remain. *Which* offices? Continuity from what to what?

To illustrate some ramifications of these problems, Table B-1 sets out a range of choices. One dimension, labeled "institutional scope," refers to the selection of offices for study: they can be individual positions (such as the Secretariat of Gobernación), a pool of positions (such as the presidential cabinet), or an entire system (including *all* political positions). Since continuity necessarily involves transitions over time, a second dimension concerns possible changes in the total number of available positions: they can increase, stay even, or decrease. This factor can have crucial operational and interpretative implications. Let us assume, for example, that the absolute number of holdovers from t_0 to t_1 to t_2 to . . . t_k were constant. Calculated as a proportion of a *stable* quantity of total available positions, the figure would produce a relatively steady set of percentages that would suggest, in turn, little historical change. As a proportion of an *increasing* number of positions, it would produce declining percentages, with the concomitant implication of declining continuity—which would be partially misleading, since the expansion in available offices (in fact, a common pattern) might reflect a strategy of institutional cooptation on the part of a small and willful band of men. And as a proportion of a *decreasing* number of total positions, the unchanging number of holdovers would yield a series of rising percentages—also misleading in their way, since they would not reflect a growth in continuity so much as a shrinkage in the system (perhaps through a purge of some sort).

Within each of the nine resulting possibilities, shown by the cells in Table B-1, there exist some further questions. First, continuity of what? Of individuals or groups? It is one thing to study the personal fate of individual political actors, and it is quite another to analyze continuities or discontinuities in the representation of groups (cliques, families, factions, parties, even social classes) within the political system. Depending upon the choice of focus, results can vary widely: group continuity might be high while individual continuity is low, if different members of the groups rotate in office over time; group continuity might be low while individual continuity is high, if politicians shift allegiances; and, of course, group continuity and individual continuity might vary together.

TABLE B-1

A Classification of Frameworks for the Analysis of Continuity and Turnover within Political Elites

(p = prior, s = subsequent)

N Positions Available	Institutional Scope		
	Within One Single Office	Within a Pool of Selected Offices	Within an Entire System
Increasing	p / s	p / s	p / s
Stable	p / s	p / s	p / s
Decreasing	p / s	p / s	p / s

A second question deals with chronological direction: continuity from the past, or continuity into the future? That is, one could conceive of continuity as the proportion of a group at time t_0 that went on to hold positions at subsequent time t_1, and the "subsequent" continity rate (CR_s) would take the following mathematical form:

$$CR_s = \frac{N \text{ holdovers from } t_0 \text{ to } t_1}{\text{Total N officeholders at } t_0}$$

and it is represented by the letter *s* in each of the cells in Table B-1. But one could just as legitimately conceive of continuity as the proportion of officeholders at t_0 who were held over from a "prior" elite (say at t_{-1}), as indicated by the letter *p* in Table B-1, in which case the computing formula would be:

$$CR_p = \frac{N \text{ holdovers from } t_{-1} \text{ to } t_0}{\text{Total N officeholders at } t_0}$$

330

Obviously these approaches all concern the same phenomena, continuity and turnover, but they also tap different dimensions of them.

Then there is another question: What are the appropriate units of time? By definition the study of duration (as within an elite) and chronological trends must rest upon comparison between specified units of time. The periods may vary according to the problem at hand —days, years, or centuries—but they must be consistently comparable in some strict sense.

In my own approaches to these questions I have tried to temper my desire for methodological rigor with a concern for the realities of Mexican history and politics. For Chapter 6 I have focused on the careers of *individuals*, not on the representation of groups. This choice in part reflects necessity, since I have been unable to identify membership in the most relevant kind of group, the *camarilla*, with much consistency or thoroughness. But it also reflects a deliberate decision to view the political system from the standpoint of the individual, as drawn out in Chapter 9; here I might also add that individuals must pick their *camarillas*, that they often move from one group to another, so there is an empirical basis for focusing on the continuity of individuals rather than groups (although, in Chapter 3 and elsewhere, I do explore the continuity of social classes and other broad categories).

As to units of time, I have employed the *presidential term* as the basic object of analysis, on the assumption that the president has ultimate authority over the distribution of national office (though he may not choose to exercise it all the time). A presidential term, in turn, is considered to exist as long as an individual effectively exerts the power of the presidential office. Application of this criterion has required some delicate judgments (such as excluding the Carranza government in Veracruz in 1914-15, or putting the presidencies from 1928 to 1934 together in a single unit),[1] and one major disadvantage is that all terms from 1900 through 1971 are not equal in length. Nonetheless I have focused upon 19 separate presidential periods, ranging in duration from several months to six years. (See the list in Table 1-1.)

In general, individual incumbents have been identified with the presidential term *during which* they came into the office under study, even though their tenure may have stretched over into the following term (this has been especially true for some state governors). Uncertainty about the effective reach of presidential authority and the consequent control of offices at some points in time, such as in the eras of

---

[1] I have also been tempted to consider the Cárdenas presidency as dating from mid-1935, after his break with Calles, instead of from the formal inauguration in 1934. In fact the 1935-1940 period shows less continuity with previous regimes than does the 1934-1940 term, but the difference is not very great.

the Convention (1914-15) and the *Maximato* (1928-34), has furnished another rationale for collapsing some individual terms into chronological groups.[2]

The determination of institutional scope, as referred to in Table B-1, was made on various grounds. Because of the "no-reelection" rule (plus the substantive findings in Chapter 5, on patterns of interpositional mobility), I discarded the possibility of focusing on continuity within a single office. Confronted with the choice of working with a pool of offices or with the "entire system," I took an unabashedly empirical approach. Drawing upon the stratification scheme in the HIGHEST OFFICE variable (Table A-3), I created nine separate pools of offices. The smallest and most exclusive pool contains positions with the highest scale values (8) for HIGHEST OFFICE, mainly top cabinet positions. The next pool consists of offices with scale values of 8 or 7, thus including heads of selected decentralized agencies and state-supported companies. To this group the next pool adds offices with scale value 6, governorships of major states. And so on to the final pool, for offices with scale values from 8 through 0, incorporating just about every person who ever held any major national office in Mexico between 1900 and 1971—which represents, within the limits of my data, the "entire system" option.

For each of these nine pools, for each of the 19 presidential terms, I then computed an index of elite continuity from the percentage of incumbents in each term who had held office within the same institutional pool during *any* previous presidential term, not just the immediately prior one, thus obtaining a measure of the relative incidence of the "same old faces" on the national scene.[3] (Technically, this involved a variation on the formula for CR_p, since the numerator now consisted of N holdovers from $t_{<0}$ to t_0 instead of only those from t_{-1}

[2] I have counted legislators who were designated after the unveiling of a new presidential candidate—and governors who took office concurrently with the new candidate—as part of the incoming candidate's regime, although the outgoing president no doubt has some influence on the selection of these officeholders. For a good discussion of this question—and a justification of my procedure in relation to the Chamber of Deputies—see Rudolph O. de la Garza, "The Mexican Chamber of Deputies and the Mexican Political System" (Ph.D. dissertation, University of Arizona, 1972), p. 139, note 18. If my procedure results in any distortion, observe that it should produce an upward bias in the rate of continuity—for which reason the relatively low rates discovered in Chapter 6 are all the more impressive.

[3] But note that this index measures continuity *within the pools*. A person entering an exclusive pool (for instance, the scale 8-7 pool) from an inclusive pool (say the 8-3 pool) is *not* counted as a repeater in the exclusive pool, but he *would* be a repeater in the inclusive one.

to t_o.) As stated in Chapter 6, this is the calculation behind the data in Table 6-1.

The question then became: which pool is the most appropriate? The average rates of continuity through the 19 points in time were rather similar, ranging from 27.3 percent for the highest set of offices (with scale value 8) to 35.1 percent for the entire system (scale values 8 through 0). But were the trends over time the same?

Essentially they were. To illustrate this point, Table B-2 presents a matrix of product-moment correlation coefficients (Pearson's r) show- ing the relationships between the chronological trends in continuity as measured for each of the nine institutional pools. Since the pools have been constructed in an additive way, one might expect the correlations to be generally positive, as they all are here. What is particularly strik- ing, however, is the strength of the associations. The weakest correla- tion in the entire matrix, for pools 8-7 and 8-0, is .723, and fully half the correlations are .90 or greater!

TABLE B-2

Correlations between Trends in Continuity
(as measured for differing pools)

Scale Values for Pools[a]	Scale Values for Pools[a]								
	8	8-7	8-6	8-5	8-4	8-3	8-2	8-1	8-0
8	—								
8-7	.978	—							
8-6	.908	.934	—						
8-5	.885	.927	.988	—					
8-4	.916	.922	.932	.934	—				
8-3	.896	.886	.848	.844	.898	—			
8-2	.918	.921	.922	.915	.954	.971	—		
8-1	.778	.752	.865	.836	.820	.832	.876	—	
8-0	.749	.723	.842	.813	.805	.819	.857	.997	—

NOTE: Pearson's r for 19 observations (each observation being a presidential term).
[a] Scale values correspond to those for HIGHEST OFFICE variable. (See Table A-3.)

The practical implication is unambiguous: all the pools depict the same fundamental trend, so it would be justifiable to pick out any one of them for close analysis. To establish general continuity rates, de- picted in Table 6-1 and Figure 6-1, I elected to focus on the trend which has the highest average correlation with all the other trends and which therefore represents the most "typical" of trends. This rule has led me to settle on the pool with scale values 8 through 2 (mean coefficient = .917). This pool has the added advantage of offering a fairly stable number of positions, which usually hovered between 100 and 200 per term. For other purposes I employed other pools.

Aside from dealing with continuity from prior elites to current elites (CR_p), I have also attempted in Chapter 6 to measure rates of continuity from current elites to subsequent elites (CR_s). In this regard I employed the "entire system" option, including offices with values 8 through 0, in order to obtain as complete as possible a picture on elite repetition and career duration. The results of these efforts appear in Tables 6-4 and 6-5 which, given the number of appearances within the 8-0 pool, indicate the statistical chances of *re*appearing within the pool at any subsequent time.

Sadly enough, this raised the issue of mortality, since the chances of obtaining a subsequent position naturally (!) depended upon the chances of living through the current presidential term. Equally sadly, I have very spotty data on the dates of death, so it was impossible for me to eliminate individuals accordingly.

My first response to this problem was to screen out people according to the age at which they entered the national elite. In successive experiments for each of the officeholding cohorts, I screened out those who first reached elite status at age 60 or more, on the grounds that they were fairly near death's door and could not have survived too many subsequent regimes. Next I screened out those who reached office at age 50 or more. And to assure myself a bit of youth, I deleted those who came into office at age 40 or more.

The results of these maneuvers appear in Tables B-3 through B-5, which compare the reentry probabilities for all officeholders in the 8-0 pool, by cohort, with those for age-specific groups. The contrasts are startling. Once a person reached national office under Díaz, for example, the likelihood of repeating was .698 for the entire group, disregarding age, but it jumped up to .887 for those known to have entered under the age of 60, and it was .924 for those who entered under 40. Even more stunning is the same set of figures for the 1946-71 cohort (Table B-5), which shows a reentry probability of .356 for the entire group and .614, .666, and .815 for the respective age-specific groups.

What was happening? Could mortality have had such disastrous effects on Mexico's political leaders? I doubt it. For as the tables show, the introduction of controls for age brings about sharp reductions in the number of observations (that is, individuals) under analysis. Deleting those who entered the elite at 60 or more, for instance, reduces the available N for the prerevolutionary cohort from 610 to 150; for the revolutionary cohort, from 2,282 to 595; for the postrevolutionary

*Effects of Controlling for Age
on Probabilities for Reentering Political Elite:
Prerevolutionary Cohort, 1900-1911*

| Nth Presidential Regime during which an Elite Position Held | Probabilities for Reentering | | | |
	All Available Officeholders, Disregarding Age (N = 610)	Excluding Those Known to have Entered Elite at Age 60 or More (remaining N = 150)	Excluding Those Known to have Entered Elite at Age 50 or More (remaining N = 117)	Excluding Those Known to have Entered Elite at Age 40 or More (remaining N = 66)
1	.698	.887	.889	.924
2	.578	.790	.846	.869
3	.374	.581	.602	.585
4	.435	.508	.547	.581
5	.475	.548	.552	.556
6	.316	.235	.188	.100
7	.500	.500	.667	——[a]
8	.333	.500	.500	

[a] No member of this group appeared in more than seven presidential regimes.

TABLE B-4

*Effects of Controlling for Age
on Probabilities for Reentering Political Elite:
Revolutionary Cohort, 1917-40*

| Nth Presidential Regime during which an Elite Position Held | Probabilities for Reentering | | | |
	All Available Officeholders, Disregarding Age (N = 2,282)	Excluding Those Known to have Entered Elite at Age 60 or More (remaining N = 595)	Excluding Those Known to have Entered Elite at Age 50 or More (remaining N = 559)	Excluding Those Known to have Entered Elite at Age 40 or More (remaining N = 419)
1	.330	.590	.612	.668
2	.382	.544	.556	.600
3	.387	.435	.432	.435
4	.306	.361	.354	.329
5	.265	.267	.276	.333
6	.111	.125	.125	.125

TABLE B-5

*Effects of Controlling for Age
on Probabilities for Reentering Political Elite:
Postrevolutionary Cohort, 1946-71*

Nth Presidential Regime during which an Elite Position Held	All Available Officeholders, Disregarding Age (N = 1,239)	Probabilities for Reentering		
		Excluding Those Known to have Entered Elite at Age 60 or More (remaining N = 500)	Excluding Those Known to have Entered Elite at Age 50 or More (remaining N = 422)	Excluding Those Known to have Entered Elite at Age 40 or More (remaining N = 243)
1	.356	.614	.666	.815
2	.374	.417	.448	.520
3	.424	.430	.437	.437
4	.329	.346	.346	.356
5	.261	.263	.263	.313
6	.167	.200	.200	.200

cohort, from 1,239 to 500.[4] That is to say, I was controlling not only for age, I was also controlling for *whether or not the person's age was known*. Since the kind of sources available—biographical dictionaries, newspapers, and the like—tended to furnish data on only the major politicians, knowledge of age becomes a proxy indicator of prominence. The more prominent politicians necessarily held more positions, and appeared in more regimes, than did the less prominent ones. Hence a distortion in the results.

To remedy this situation I turned to the life table, a basic instrument of demographic analysis which typically contains data on life expectancy with controls for sex and age. Fortunately, Eduardo Arriaga has published an extensive set of life tables for Latin American populations in the nineteenth and twentieth centuries,[5] and from this study I took the tables for Mexican males in three separate census years: 1900, which I used in connection with the prerevolutionary cohort; 1930, for the revolutionary cohort; and 1960, for the postrevolutionary cohort. Beyond the age of 5, the data on expectancy and survival in the tables appear for five-year intervals.

To use the tables, I assumed that mortality took place at steady

[4] As in other instances, I have excluded from consideration all those who (a) first entered the elite under Díaz Ordaz, or (b) held any office under Echeverría.

[5] Eduardo E. Arriaga, *New Life Tables for Latin American Populations in the Nineteenth and Twentieth Centuries* (Berkeley: Institute of International Studies, University of California, 1968).

rates within each five-year interval, and thus obtained estimates of year-by-year survival rates for the Mexican male population as a whole. Then I took the average ages of entry into the 8-0 pool for members of known age in each chronological cohort (45 for the prerevolutionary group, 36 for the revolutionary group, 43 for the postrevolutionary group) and assumed that these accurately depicted the mean ages of entry for all members of each cohort. Next, I assumed that the average length of a presidential term during the careers of cohort members could be approximated by the average length of presidencies within the cohort-defining period (four years for 1900-1911, four years for 1917-40, six years for the post-1946 era). However tenuous in themselves, these assumptions enabled me to calculate the proportion of officeholders who, beginning at a specific age, would normally have died during the course of an average presidency. With this proportion I could compute an estimated number of survivors and, using this as a denominator, I could finally obtain an adjusted probability of elite reentry, allowing for mortality. (Tables B-6 through B-8 set out the procedures in full.)

It should be clearly understood that the adjusted probabilities are *estimates*, not unerringly accurate measurements. As shown in Chapter 3, in fact, Mexican political leaders have consistently come from the advantaged layers of society, so they almost certainly did not die at the same rate as the national average (which is conveyed in the life tables).[6] By overemphasizing the impact of mortality, the adjusted probabilities might well represent a kind of upper bound for continuity; similarly, by ignoring mortality, the raw probabilities represent a lower bound.[7] As is so often true in statistics, the real answer may lie somewhere in between.

[6] It could also be that the mortality schedule for the political elite of 1900-1911 was closer to the rate for the entire 1960 population than to the one for the 1900 population. Though the differences in life expectancy at birth are startling (25 for 1900, 33 for 1930, 56 for 1960), death rates in the 35-65 age brackets show rather little variation—so the selection of life tables has only minor implications for the adjusted probabilities.

[7] Ignoring mortality is almost like assuming that Mexican politicians were among the healthiest people in the world. Note the extraordinary survival rates within the relevant age brackets in the life table for Model "West," Level 24, in Ansley J. Coale and Paul Demeny, *Regional Model Life Tables and Stable Populations* (Princeton: Princeton University Press, 1966), pt. II, p. 25.

TABLE B-6

Procedures for Computing Raw and Adjusted Probabilities
for Reentering Political Elite: Prerevolutionary Cohort, 1900-1911

A	B	C	D
Nth Presidential Regime during which an Elite Position Held	Total N Individuals with Positions in Nth Presidential Regime	N Individuals with Careers Ending in Nth Presidential Regime	N Individuals Going on to Hold Positions in Subsequent Presidential Regimes
1	610	184	426
2	426	180	246
3	246	154	92
4	92	52	40
5	40	21	19
6	19	13	6
7	6	3	3
8	3	2	1
9	1	1	0

E	F	G	H
Raw Probability of Reentering Political Elite (D/B)	N Individuals (in Column B) Assumed to Have Died during Nth Presidential Regime	N Individuals Assumed to Have Been Available for Subsequent Positions B—F	Adjusted Probability of Reentering Political Elite (D/G)
.698	85	525	.811
.578	69	357	.689
.374	46	200	.460
.435	20	72	.556
.475	10	30	.633
.316	6	13	.462
.500	——————— no further adjustments made ———————		
.333			
——			

TABLE B-7

*Procedures for Computing Raw and Adjusted Probabilities
for Reentering Political Elite: Revolutionary Cohort, 1917-40*

A	B	C	D
Nth Presidential Regime during which an Elite Position Held	Total N Individuals with Positions in Nth Presidential Regime	N Individuals with Careers Ending in Nth Presidential Regime	N Individuals Going on to Hold Positions in Subsequent Presidential Regimes
1	2,282	1,530	752
2	752	465	287
3	287	176	111
4	111	77	34
5	34	25	9
6	9	8	1
7	1	1	0

E	F	G	H
Raw Probability of Reentering Political Elite (D/B)	N Individuals (in Column B) Assumed to Have Died during Nth Presidential Regime	N Individuals Assumed to Have Been Available for Subsequent Positions B—F	Adjusted Probability of Reentering Political Elite (D/G)
.330	164	2,118	.355
.382	60	692	.415
.387	26	261	.425
.306	12	99	.343
.265	4	30	.300
.111	———— no further adjustments made ————		
—			

TABLE B-8

Procedures for Computing Raw and Adjusted Probabilities
for Reentering Political Elite: Postrevolutionary Cohort, 1946-71

A	B	C	D
Nth Presidential Regime during which an Elite Position Held	Total N Individuals with Positions in Nth Presidential Regime	N Individuals with Careers Ending in Nth Presidential Regime	N Individuals Going on to Hold Positions in Subsequent Presidential Regimes
1	1,239	798	441
2	441	276	165
3	165	95	70
4	70	47	23
5	23	17	6
6	6	5	1
7	1	1	0

E	F	G	H
Raw Probability of Reentering Political Elite (D/B)	N Individuals (in Column B) Assumed to Have Died during Nth Presidential Regime	N Individuals Assumed to Have Been Available for Subsequent Positions B−F	Adjusted Probability of Reentering Political Elite (D/G)
.356	77	1,162	.380
.374	36	405	.407
.424	19	146	.479
.329	11	59	.390
.261	5	18	.333
.167	———— no further adjustments made ————		
—			

APPENDIX C.
PARTIES AND SECTORS IN
THE NATIONAL CHAMBER
OF DEPUTIES, 1964-67

Thanks to the cooperation of authorities at the Archivo de la Cámara de Diputados de la Nación in Mexico City, I managed to obtain information on the social background of deputies by party and sector for the legislative sessions of 1964-67 and 1970-73. Since the relationships between the variables tend to be the same for both sessions, however, Chapter 8 presents the data for only the 1970-73 group, which contains fewer missing observations than does the 1964-67 congress. In order to support my claim about the similarity in patterns, and also to make the material available to interested researchers, the following seven tables present the relevant data for the 1964-67 legislature.

TABLE C-1

Constituency, by Party and Sector, 1964-67

State and Region	Party							
	PRI							
	Peasant	Labor	Popular	PAN	PARM	PPS	Unknown	Totals
Pacific North:								
BC Norte	1	0	1	1	0	0	1	4
BC Sur	0	0	1	0	0	0	0	1
Nayarit	0	1	1	0	0	0	0	2
Sinaloa	3	0	0	0	0	1	0	4
Sonora	1	1	1	0	0	1	1	5
Subtotals	5	2	4	1	0	2	2	16
North:								
Chihuahua	1	0	2	1	0	0	2	6
Coahuila	1	1	2	0	1	0	0	5
Durango	1	0	2	0	0	0	1	4
Nuevo León	0	1	3	1	0	0	1	6
San Luis Potosí	1	1	2	1	1	0	1	7
Tamaulipas	0	1	2	0	1	0	2	6
Zacatecas	0	1	2	0	0	0	1	4
Subtotals	4	5	15	3	3	0	8	38

TABLE C-1 *(cont.)*

State and Region	PRI			PAN	PARM	PPS	Unknown	Totals
	Peasant	Labor	Popular					
Center:								
Aguascalientes	1	0	1	0	0	0	0	2
Guanajuato	4	1	3	2	0	1	0	11
Hidalgo	1	0	3	0	0	0	1	5
Jalisco	1	2	4	1	0	0	5	13
México	2	3	4	0	0	0	0	9
Michoacán	3	1	3	1	0	1	2	11
Morelos	1	1	0	0	0	0	0	2
Puebla	1	3	5	0	0	1	1	11
Querétaro	0	0	1	0	0	0	1	2
Tlaxcala	1	1	0	0	0	0	0	2
	—	—	—	—	—	—	—	—
Subtotals	15	12	24	4	0	3	10	68
Federal District:	1	7	13	11	1	3	3	39
Gulf:								
Campeche	0	1	1	0	0	0	0	2
Quintana Roo	0	0	1	0	0	0	0	1
Tabasco	1	0	1	0	0	0	0	2
Veracruz	3	3	7	0	0	1	1	15
Yucatán	0	0	2	1	0	0	1	4
	—	—	—	—	—	—	—	—
Subtotals	4	4	12	1	0	1	2	24
Pacific South:								
Chiapas	2	0	4	0	1	0	0	7
Colima	1	1	0	0	0	0	0	2
Guerrero	2	0	3	0	0	0	1	6
Oaxaca	4	0	4	0	0	1	1	10
	—	—	—	—	—	—	—	—
Subtotals	9	1	11	0	1	1	2	25
Totals	38	31	79	20	5	10	27	210

TABLE C-2

Membership on the Gran Comisión, by Party and Sector, 1964-67

Committee Status	PRI Peasant	PRI Labor	PRI Popular	PAN	PARM	PPS	Unknown	Totals
Nonmember	32	28	60	20	5	10	22	177
Member from small state delegation[a]	2	2	6	0	0	0	0	10
Member from medium state delegation[b]	2	0	6	0	0	0	4	12
Member from large state delegation[c]	2	1	7	0	0	0	1	11
Totals	38	31	79	20	5	10	27	210

[a] Delegations with 1 or 2 members.
[b] Delegations with 3 to 5 members.
[c] Delegations with more than 5 members (actual range: 6 to 24).

TABLE C-3

Urbanization of Birthplace, by Party and Sector, 1964-67

Level of Urbanization	PRI Peasant	PRI Labor	PRI Popular	PAN	PARM	PPS	Unknown	Totals
Rural[a]	19	11	35	2	4	2	11	84
Semirural[b]	2	4	13	1	0	0	2	22
Semiurban[c]	5	3	8	2	0	2	2	22
Urban[d]	2	3	12	2	0	1	4	24
Highly urban[e]	1	1	1	4	0	0	2	9
Unknown	9	9	9	9	1	5	6	48
Totals	38	31	79	20	5	10	27	210

[a] Communities with less than 10,000 inhabitants as of 1921 (according to Departamento de la Estadística Nacional, *Resumen del censo general de habitantes de 30 de noviembre de 1921* [Mexico: Talleres Gráficos de la Nación, 1928], pp. 166-182).
[b] Communities with 10,000-19,999 inhabitants as of 1921.
[c] Communities with 20,000-49,999 inhabitants as of 1921.
[d] Communities with 50,000-499,999 inhabitants as of 1921.
[e] Communities with 500,000 or more inhabitants as of 1921.

Table C-4

Level of Education, by Party
and Sector, 1964-67

		Party						
		PRI						
Level	Peasant	Labor	Popular	PAN	PARM	PPS	Unknown	Totals
None	0	0	0	0	0	0	0	0
Primary	2	6	1	0	0	0	0	9
Secondary	2	0	2	0	1	0	0	5
Special, trade, or normal school[a]	6	3	12	2	1	1	2	27
Preparatory	0	0	4	0	1	0	0	5
University[b]	22	7	53	14	1	4	18	119
Unknown	6	15	7	4	1	5	7	45
Totals	38	31	79	20	5	10	27	210

[a] Schools of commerce, agriculture, and technology; military academies; and normal schools.
[b] Includes all those who are believed to have attended a university, whether or not they are known to have received degrees.

Table C-5

Professional Title, by Party
and Sector, 1964-67

		Party						
		PRI						
Professional Title	Peasant	Labor	Popular	PAN	PARM	PPS	Unknown	Totals
Licenciado en derecho (lawyer)[a]	10	2	32	9	1	0	10	64
Licenciado (other or unknown)	2	0	2	1	0	0	1	6
Doctor (medicine)	2	0	8	1	0	2	3	16
Profesor	2	0	10	2	1	0	3	18
Ingeniero (engineer)	7	1	3	1	0	2	2	16
Other	1	1	2	0	0	1	0	5
None	14	27	22	6	3	5	8	85
Totals	38	31	79	20	5	10	27	210

[a] Includes some doctores en derecho (doctors of law).

TABLE C-6

Age, by Party and Sector, 1964-67

		Party						
	PRI							
Age[a]	Peasant	Labor	Popular	PAN	PARM	PPS	Unknown	Totals
20-29	4	1	2	0	0	0	1	8
30-39	4	3	8	2	0	1	8	26
40-49	14	11	34	12	1	3	7	82
50-59	14	11	33	4	1	4	8	75
60-69	1	4	2	0	1	1	1	10
70-plus	1	1	0	0	2	1	1	6
Unknown	0	0	0	2	0	0	1	3
	—	—	—	—	—	—	—	—
Totals	38	31	79	20	5	10	27	210

[a] As of 1964.

TABLE C-7

Age and Professional Title, by Party and Sector, 1964-67

	Peasant Sector				Labor Sector			
Age	None	Law[a]	Other	Totals	None	Law[a]	Other	Totals
Under 40	0	5	3	8	2	1	1	4
40-59	13	5	10	28	20	1	1	22
60 and over	1	0	1	2	5	0	0	5
Unknown	0	0	0	0	0	0	0	0
	—	—	—	—	—	—	—	—
Totals	14	10	14	38	27	2	2	31

	Popular Sector				PAN, PARM, and PPS			
Age	None	Law[a]	Other	Totals	None	Law[a]	Other	Totals
Under 40	2	7	1	10	2	0	1	3
40-59	19	27	21	67	9	9	7	25
60 and over	1	0	1	2	2	1	2	5
Unknown	0	0	0	0	1	1	0	2
	—	—	—	—	—	—	—	—
Totals	22	34	23	79	14	11	10	35

NOTE: Twenty-seven individuals with unknown sectoral affiliation are omitted from this table.

[a] Includes some *licenciados* who are not definitely known to have been lawyers.

BIBLIOGRAPHY
AND SOURCES

BIBLIOGRAPHY

SECTION A.
TRACKING DOWN POLITICAL ELITES

The location of biographical data on Mexico's political elites proved to be no easy task. When I started the research, in 1969, there was no comprehensive directory of politicians; there was no known investigative model to follow; there was no clear indication of where to begin. Eventually, of course, through persistence and luck, it became possible to get the data for this book. For students of Mexico, I present this bibliography as a selective guide to sources. More broadly, for scholars involved in collective biography of any sort, I offer this essay as a token of sympathy, solidarity, and encouragement.

Once the Mexican political elite had been defined, as set forth in Appendix A, my first task was to find the names of all the incumbents in all of the specified offices. In principle this seemed perfectly straightforward; in practice it was not.

To identify members of the *cabinet*, as well as some other positions, I relied heavily on such newspapers as *El Imparcial* (1900-1914) and, especially, *Excélsior* (1920–present), both of Mexico City. One of the most useful sources of all, the *Enciclopedia de México*, Vols. 1– (Mexico: Instituto del Enciclopedia de Mexico, 1966–present), contains a list of cabinet members from 1871 to 1971, but the relevant volume did not come out until well after the start of my research. For recent years, Roderic Ai Camp has published rosters of cabinet members (and many other officeholders) in his excellent *Mexican Political Biographies, 1935-1975* (Tucson: University of Arizona Press, 1976). Also helpful in tracing the movements of cabinet ministers and other politicians is the informative and fascinating book by Mariano Galván Rivera, *Colección de las efemérides publicadas en el calendario del más antiguo Galván desde su fundación hasta el 30 de junio de 1950* (Mexico: Antigua Librería de Murgía, 1950).

To locate missing names of some incumbents I leafed through the *Memorias* of some of the ministries, particularly for the early decades of the century. Some specialized sources provided further help, along with some biographical details on the ministers as well: the two books by Rafael Carrasco Puente, *Datos históricos e iconografía de la educación en México* (Mexico: Secretaría de Educación Pública, 1960), and *Iconografía de Hacienda: Secretarios y Encargados del Ramo, desde que se inició la Revolución Mexicana de 1910 hasta la fecha* (Mexico: Secretaría de Hacienda Pública, 1948); the anonymous "Biografías e iconografías de Secretarios de Hacienda," *Boletín Bibliográfico de la Secretaría de Hacienda* 3 (20 November 1954); Secretaría de Relaciones Exteriores, *Funcionarios de la Secretaría de Relaciones Exteriores desde el año 1821 a 1940* (Mexico: Talleres Gráficos de la Nación, 1940); and the extremely useful article by Francisco Naranjo, "México en la historia: gobernadores del Distrito Federal," *Novedades* (Mexico City), 18 May 1949.

To supplement such sources for the cabinet, and also to locate members of the *subcabinet* (subsecretaries and *oficiales mayores*), at least from the 1940s onward, I was able to consult a series of official directories, first published by the Secretaría de Bienes Nacionales e Inspeccion Administrativa as the *Directorio del Gobierno Federal de los Estados Unidos Mexicanos, 1947* (Mexico: Talleres Gráficos de la Nación[?], 1947). Subsequent issues of the *Directorio del Gobierno Federal*, sometimes with varying subtitles, appeared in 1949, 1951, and 1956. In 1961 a *Directorio del Poder Ejecutivo Federal* was published by the Secretaría del Patrimonio Nacional, which came out with updated revisions in 1963, 1965, and 1968. The following year the Secretaría de la Presidencia produced a *Manual de organización del Gobierno Federal, 1969-70* (Mexico: Talleres Gráficos de la Nación, 1969), and soon after that the *Directorio del Poder Ejecutivo Federal 1971* (Mexico: Secretaría de la Presidencia, 1971).

The identification of *official party leaders*—that is, the executive committee of the PNR-PRM-PRI—turned out to be relatively simple. Miguel Osorio Marbán's two-volume *El partido de la Revolución Mexicana (ensayo)* (Mexico: Impresora del Centro, 1970) provides much of the necessary information, especially for the period from 1929 to the 1940s. Other good sources have been two PRI magazines, *La República* (1949-66) and *Polémica* (1969-72), both of which occasionally offered profiles of party leaders.

To trace top-level directors in the *semipublic sector*, the managers of the most important decentralized agencies and state-supported companies, I relied, initially, on many of the sources most useful for the cabinet, since some of these posts are regarded as tantamount to ministerial positions. In some instances I consulted the annual reports submitted to the *asamblea general de accionistas*. Ferrocarriles Nacionales also put out a journal, *Ferronales*, which I consulted for 1944-63, and Benito Coquet has written a five-volume compendium on *La seguridad social en México* (Mexico: IMSS, 1964). Two directories contained comprehensive rosters for selected years: Secretaría de

Bienes Nacionales e Inspección Administrativa, *Directorio del Gobierno Federal: organismos descentralizados y empresas de participación estatal, 1951* (Mexico: Talleres Gráficos de la Nación, 1951), and Secretaría del Patrimonio Nacional, *Anuario de los organismos descentralizados y empresas de participación estatal, 1965* (Mexico: Talleres Gráficos de la Nación, 1965). In addition, staff members of the agencies and companies readily provided lists of current and past directors wherever necessary.

The names of national congressmen, both *deputies* and *senators*, were among the easiest to find. For each three-year session of the lower house I used Cámara de Diputados, *Directorio de la Cámara de Diputados* (Mexico: Imprenta de la Cámara de Diputatdos, 1900-1970). I found no such regular directory of the Senate, but I was able to obtain a typed list of all senators from a modest and anonymous functionary of the Archivo de la Cámara de Senadores; to him my heartfelt thanks. To identify members of the Aguascalientes convention, also included in my elite, I read the newspaper *La Convención* (1914-15). For the constitutional convention of 1916-17 I used the *Diario de los debates del Congreso Constituyente*, 2 vols. (Mexico: Imprenta de la Cámara de Diputados, 1922), and checked the data against a later edition, sponsored by the Comisión Nacional para la Celebración del Sesquicentenario de la Proclamación de la Independencia Nacional y del Cinquentenario de la Revolución Mexicana, also in 2 vols. (Mexico: Instituto Nacional de Estudios Históricos de la Revolución Mexicana, 1960).

The *ambassadors* posed almost no problem at all, since their names (plus some supplementary information) have been regularly published in the *Boletín Oficial* of the Secretaría de Relationes Exteriores (1900–present).

But if the diplomats treated me well, the *governors* of states and territories did not display the same consideration. Lists of state executives came to be exceedingly precious materials. Roger C. Anderson kindly provided me with a roster for the 1940-64 period, and the Oficina de Información Asuntos Económicos de los Estados y Territorios de México, in Mexico City, gave me a roster for 1969-70. Camp has since then published the names of governors from 1935 onward on his *Mexican Political Biographies*. Yet data remained extremely sparse for the prior years, especially for the periods of upheaval and turbulence. The Secretariat of Gobernación, whose task it is to deal with governors, could offer me no help.

So I turned to various places. Newspapers, particularly *El Imparcial* and *Excélsior*, frequently carried dispatches from the states. For presidential inaugurations, too, they would often list the names of banquet guests, usually including all of the governors. Every state government published a *Periódico Oficial*; since laws and decrees required gubernatorial signatures, these proved to be extremely valuable sources. Most states have also had local historians, dedicated amateurs, for the most part, whose love of their land has produced a rich, copious, and informative literature. Organized by state, these works include the following.

AGUASCALIENTES

Jesús Bernal Sánchez, *Apuntes históricos, geográficos y estadísticos del Estado de Aguascalientes* (Aguascalientes: A. E. Pedroza, 1928)

BAJA CALIFORNIA

Pablo L. Martínez, *Historia de Baja California* (Mexico: Libros Mexicanos, 1956)

CAMPECHE

Juan de Dios Pérez Galaz, *Diccionario geográfico e histórico de Campeche* (Campeche: Talleres Linotipográficos del Gobierno del Estado, 1944)

CHIHUAHUA

Francisco R. Almada, *Geografía del Estado de Chihuahua* (Impresora Ruiz Sandoval: Chihuahua, 1945), and, more explicitly, Almada, *Gobernadores del Estado de Chihuahua* (Mexico: Imprenta de la Cámara de Diputados, 1950)

COAHUILA

Pablo C. Moreno, *Galería de coahuilenses distinguidos* (Torreón, Coah.: Imprenta Mayagoitia, 1966)

COLIMA

Daniel Moreno, *Colima y sus gobernantes (un siglo de historia política)* (Mexico: Ediciones Stadium, 1953); Jose María Rodríguez Castellanos, "Lista de gobernadores del Estado de Colima," *Memorias de la Academia Mexicana de la Historia* 16, no. 3 (July-September 1957): 281-306; and Felipe Sevilla del Río, "Los gobernadores del Estado de Colima," *Memorias de la Academia Mexicana de la Historia* 16, no. 4 (October-December 1957): 361-365

DURANGO

Pastor Rouaix, *Diccionario geográfico, histórico y biográfico del Estado de Durango* (Mexico: Instituto Panamericano de Geografía e Historia, 1946)

GUERRERO

Héctor F. López Mena, *Diccionario geográfico, histórico, biográfico y lingüístico del Estado de Guerrero* (Mexico: Ed. Pluma y Lápiz,

1942), and Moisés Ochoa Campos, *Historia del Estado de Guerrero* (Mexico: Porrúa, 1968)

GUANAJUATO

Jesús Rodríguez Frausto, *Guía de gobernantes de Guanajuato* (Guanajuato: Universidad de Guanajuato, Archivo Histórico, 1965)

JALISCO

Gabriel Agraz García de Alba, *Jalisco y sus hombres: compendio de geografía, historia y biografía jaliscienses* (Guadalajara: n. p., 1958), taken from the same author's multivolume *Ofrenda a México: compendio de geografía, historia y biografía mexicana* (Guadalajara: n. p. 1958–); Anonymous, "Cronología de los gobernantes del Estado de Jalisco," *Memorias de la Academia Mexicana de la Historia* 20, no. 3 (July-September 1961): 303-324

MICHOACÁN

José Bravo Ugarte, *Historia sucinta de Michoacán*, 3 vols. (Mexico: Editorial Jus, 1964), and Jesús Romero Flores, *Diccionario michoacano de historia y geografía* (Morelia: Edición del Gobierno del Estado, 1960)

NUEVO LEÓN

Ricardo Covarrubias, *Gobernantes de Nuevo León, 1582-1961* (Monterrey: n. p., 1961)

OAXACA

Jorge Fernando Iturribarria, *Oaxaca en la historia (de la época precolombiana a los tiempos actuales)* (Mexico: Editorial Stylo, 1955)

PUEBLA

Enrique Gómez Haro, Enrique Juan Palacios, and Enrique Cordero y T., *Numeración cronológica de los gobernantes del territorio poblano y presidentes municipales de la heróica Puebla de Zaragoza*, 4th ed. (Puebla: Publicaciones del Grupo Literario Bohemia Poblana, 1961)

SAN LUIS POTOSÍ

Isaac Grimaldo, *Gobernantes potosinos, 1590-1939* (San Luis Potosí: Tip. Esc. Hijos del Ejército No. 10, 1939), and Primo Feliciano Velásquez, *Historia de San Luis Potosí*, vol. 4 (Mexico: Sociedad Mexicana de Geografía y Estadística, 1948)

SINALOA

Amado González Dávila, *Diccionario geográfico, histórico, biográfico y estadístico del Estado de Sinaloa* (Culiacán, Sin.: Gobierno del Estado de Sinaloa, 1959)

SONORA

Francisco R. Almada, *Diccionario de historia, geografía, y biografía sonorenses* (Chihuahua: Gobierno del Estado de Sonora, 1952);

Eduardo W. Villa, *Historia del Estado de Sonora*, 2nd ed. (Hermosillo: Editorial Sonora, 1951), and Villa, "Nómina de los gobernantes de Sonora desde la época colonial hasta el presente," *Divulgación histórica* 2, no. 8 (15 June 1941): [383]-390

TABASCO

Manuel Mestre Ghigliazza, *Apuntes para una relación cronológica de los gobernantes de Tabasco* (Mérida: Carlos R. Menéndez, 1934)

TAMAULIPAS

Juan Manuel Torrea, *Diccionario geográfico, histórico, biográfico y estadístico de la República Mexicana: Estado de Tamaulipas* (Mexico: Sociedad Mexicana de Geografía y Estadística, 1940)

VERACRUZ

Juan Zilli, *Historia sucinta de Veracruz*, 2nd ed. (Mexico: Editorial Citlaltepen, 1962)

YUCATÁN

Abelardo Barrera Osorio, *Próceres yucatecos: sintesis biográficas* (Mérida: [Talleres Gráficos del Sudeste], 1959), and Carlos Echánoue Trujillo, ed., *Enciclopedia yucatense*, 8 vols. (Mexico: Ediciones Oficiales del Gobierno de Yucatán, 1944)

I first learned of many of these directories through two MLS theses at the University of Texas at Austin: Vicente Javier Sáenz Cirlos, "Guía de obras de consulta sobre México, en el campo de las ciencias sociales" (1968); and José Adolfo Rodríguez Gallardo, "Guía de materiales de referencia sobre las humanidades mexicanas" (1970). I am happy to record my debt to both.

Such were the sources that allowed me to identify the 6,302 individuals who held any one of these offices—from president to deputy to governor—at any time between 1900 and 1971. By collating notes on all incumbents, as explained in Chapter 1, I was able (with allowances for human error) to construct complete dossiers on interpositional mobility within this pool of offices for the entire population.

But this was only part of the job. Having identified the Mexican elite, I was now confronted with the task of finding personal information about its members—date and place of birth, education, occupation, father's occupation, and so on. Some of the sources listed above provide some information of this kind, but, as shown repeatedly throughout the text, I was unable to get such data on much more than half the individuals. It was not for want of trying.

Several general sources were helpful, most particularly the monumental *Diccionario Porrúa de historia, biografía, y geografía de México*, 3rd ed., 2 vols. (Mexico: Editorial Porrúa, 1971). I have already mentioned the *Enciclopedia de México*. A third such source, among the most informative, is Editorial Revesa's *Diccionario biográfico de México*, 2 vols. (Monterrey: Editorial Revesa, 1968). Further help can be obtained from the *Diccionario Enciclopedia UTEHA*, 10 vols. (Mexico: Union Tipográfica Editorial Hispano Americano, 1950), and also from Juan López de Escalera, *Diccionario biográfico y de historia de México* (Mexico: Editorial del Magisterio, 1964).

Aside from these major reference works, there exist numerous other biographical collections. Most outstanding is the series of articles by Jesús Romero Flores, "Mil biografías en la historia de México," in the newspaper *El Nacional* (Mexico City), 1946-47. Other general sources, of somewhat lesser value, include:

Antonio Bustillos Carrillo, *Apuntes históricos y biográficos* (Mexico: Editorial Taranzas del Valle, 1954)

Ricardo Covarrubias, *Los 67 gobernantes del México independiente* (Mexico: Partido Revolucionario Institucional, 1968)

Manuel García Purón, *México y sus gobernantes (biografías)*, 2nd ed. (Mexico: Porrúa, 1964)

Heriberto García Rivas, *150 biografías de mexicanos ilustres* (Mexico: Diana, 1964)

Felipe Morales, *Doscientos personajes mexicanos* (Mexico: Ediciones "Ateneo," [1952])

Miguel Ángel Peral, *Diccionario biográfico mexicano*, 2 vols. plus Appendix (Mexico: Editorial P.A.C., 1944).

Other sources are specialized by period. Pride in the *Porfiriato*, especially at the 1910 centennial celebration, produced a number of congratulatory works about Díaz and his collaborators. Most useful among these are Ireneo Paz, ed., *Album de la paz y el trabajo* (Mexico: Imprenta de Ireneo Paz, 1910) and *Los hombres del centenario: obra consagrada el Excmo. Sr. General Porfirio Diaz* (Mexico: n. p., 1910); Alberto Leduc et al., *Diccionario de geografía, historia, y biografías mexicanas* (Mexico: Librería de la Viuda de C. Bouret, 1910); and, somewhat surprisingly, Mary Robinson Wright, *Mexico: A History of Its Progress and Development in One Hundred Years* (Philadelphia: George Barrie & Sons, 1911). There are also some biographical directories about the pre-1900 Díaz elite—by Federico M. Fusco, M. Félix Iglesias, and, most notably, Lázaro Paviá—which would make it entirely possible to analyze the social composition of the Porfirian regime from 1876 onward, an important study that still remains to be done.

The Huerta government, brief and unpopular, prompted no comparable outburst of self-congratulation. I know of only one usable source: Gregorio Ponce de León, *La paz y sus colaboradores* (Mexico: Secretaría de Fomento, 1914).

The Revolution, predictably, has created a whole tradition of hagiography, and this, in turn, has led to the publication of various directories. They are uneven in coverage and quality, however, and none is truly outstanding. They include:

Juan de Dios Bojórquez, *Forjadores de la Revolución Mexicana* (Mexico: Biblioteca del Instituto Nacional de Estudios Históricos de la Revolución Mexicana, 1960)

Juan de Dios Bojórquez, *Hombres y aspectos de México en la tercera etapa de la Revolución* (Mexico: Biblioteca del Instituto Nacional de Estudios Históricos de la Revolución, 1963)

Luis F. Bustamante, *Perfiles y bocetos revolucionarios* (Mexico: Tipogr. de "El Constitucional," 1917)

José Fernández Rojas and Luis Melgarejo Randolf, *Hombres y hechos del constitucionalismo*, vol. 2 (Mexico: Ediciones Vida Mexicana, 1916)

Arturo Langle Ramírez, *Vocabulario, apodos, seudónimos, sobrenombres, y hemerografía de la Revolución* (Mexico: Universidad Nacional Autónoma de México, 1966)

Alberto Morales Jiménez, *Hombres de la Revolución Mexicana: cincuenta semblanzas biográficas* (Mexico: Biblioteca del Instituto Nacional de Estudios Históricos de la Revolución Mexicana, 1960)

Daniel A. Moreno, *Figuras de la Revolución Mexicana: antología y breves semblanzas políticas y literarias* (Mexico: Ediciones de Andrea, 1960)

Daniel A. Moreno, *Los hombres de la Revolución: cuarenta estudios biográficos* (Mexico: Libro-Mex, 1960)

Francisco Naranjo, *Diccionario biográfico revolucionario* (Mexico: Imprenta Editorial "Cosmos," [1935]).

Naranjo later wrote a series of articles, iconoclastic and informative, not quite as rich in content as in the title: "Los millonarios de la Revolución," *Diario de Yucatán* (Mérida), July-September 1948.

Published sources for more recent years are, paradoxically, sparse. Marvin Alisky's *Who's Who in Mexican Government* (Tempe: Center for Latin American Studies of Arizona State University, 1969) is cursory and brief. Jesús Romero Flores included the *curricula* of his senatorial colleagues during the 1964-70 sexennium in *Mis seis años en el Senado* (Mexico: n. p., 1970). Sergio Serra Domínguez and Roberto

Martínez Barreda produced data on some other legislators in *Mexico y sus funcionarios* (Mexico: Litográfico Cárdenas, 1959). But that was all. It was not until 1976, with the publication of Roderic Ai Camp's *Mexican Political Biographies, 1935-1975*, that we have had a comprehensive reference work. Fortunately, Camp was kind enough to send me his typescript several years ago, and we have constantly traded notes and information; our collaboration has been a steady source of stimulus and pleasure.

Aside from biographical dictionaries, I found substantial amounts of information in newspapers, not only in *El Imparcial* and *Excélsior* but also in *El Demócrata* (Mexico City), 1916-20; *El Diario* (Mexico City), 1910-13; the *Diario del Sureste* (Mérida), 1936-49; the *Diario de Yucatán* (Mérida), 1933-38; *El Nacional* (Mexico City), 1916-58; *Novedades* (Mexico City), 1943-55; *La Prensa* (Mexico City), 1936-39; *Todo* (Mexico City), 1934-53; *El Universal* (Mexico City), 1917-76; the *Universal Gráfico* (Mexico City), 1933-60; plus a few others, usually spot-checked for only an article or two. In this I received invaluable guidance from Stanley R. Ross, ed., *Fuentes para la historia contemporáneo de México: periódicos y revistas*, 2 vols. (Mexico: El Colegio de México, 1965-67). The weekly newsmagazine *Tiempo* of Mexico City, with its foreign edition known as *Hispano Americano*, proved to be another informative source.

Several archives were of great help. At the Archivo de la Cámara de Diputados I was given access to two biographical directories, one for the 1964-67 session and the other for 1970-73, and these made it possible for me to write Chapter 8. At the library of the Asociación de Diputados Constituyentes de 1917, Tte. Corl. Ignacio Suárez permitted me to consult a biographical file on the men who wrote the constitution. At the Departamento de Archivo e Información, of the newspaper *Excélsior*, José Maldonado Flores allowed me to have access to data files that were particularly thorough on leaders of the 1950s and 1960s. And in 1971, colleagues at the Instituto Mexicano de Estudios Políticos, A. C., offered me complete access to the extensive biographical information they had compiled on the early Echeverría regime.

In 1970, near the end of the Díaz Ordaz *sexenio*, I mailed a brief questionnaire to approximately 300 officeholders, explaining my intent and requesting straightforward biographical data. About 80 responded—not an overwhelming number, but 79 more than some skeptical colleagues predicted. Several respondents volunteered words of encouragement, one declined to fill out the schedule on the grounds that public servants should not seek "publicity," and another—then the acting Secretary of Gobernación—invited me for an interview. All in all, I found the mail survey to be an extremely useful technique (and so, I might add, has Roderic Ai Camp; see his own discussion of sources on pp. 463-468 of *Mexican Political Biographies*).

I completed most of the data-gathering on the 6,302 officeholders from 1900 to 1971 in the latter part of 1971. The research entailed some wasted effort and a great deal of duplication, but this was part of my purpose: to obtain as much data as possible from separate and independent sources. The confirmation and reinforcement of information was an essential part of this entire enterprise, and it allowed me to assess the reliability of the material in a critical way.

With the basic data in hand, the summer of 1972 was devoted to the coding of more than 25,000 computer cards. The fall of that year was spent in punching and "cleaning" the dataset, and the first computer runs occurred in the spring of 1973. Off and on, I have been working on the project ever since.

Having used the computerized dataset extensively, I am confident that it is reliable and accurate. Copies of the magnetic tapes and the accompanying codebook, itself about 300 pages long, are on file and open to researchers at the Data and Program Library Service of the University of Wisconsin-Madison. Additional copies are located at the Colegio de México and the Instituto de Investigaciones Sociales of UNAM, both in Mexico City.

Research on elite changes from 1971 through 1976, and on the presidential succession of 1976, took place as the events themselves unfolded. This time I had a stroke of good luck: acting on a friendly tip, I requested, and promptly received, copies of the *curricula* of new cabinet members that had been distributed to the local press around inauguration day. To say the least, this simplified matters a lot.

Section B.
List of Works Cited

In addition to gathering the hard, quantifiable data as described in Section A, I have also consulted many other sources. The following list is highly selective, noting only those works cited in the text. It is organized into (*a*) books and theses, (*b*) articles and papers, and (*c*) newspapers and periodicals.

Books and Theses

Agor, Weston H., ed. *Latin American Legislatures: Their Role and Influence*. New York: Praeger, 1971.

Aguilar Camín, Héctor. *La revolución sonorense, 1910-1914.* Mexico: Departamento de Investigaciones Históricas, Instituto Nacional de Antropología e Historia, 1975.

Aguilar M., Alonso, and Fernando Carmona. *México: riqueza y miseria.* Mexico: Editorial Nuestro Tiempo, 1970.

Alemán, Miguel. *Miguel Alemán contesta.* Austin: Institute of Latin American Studies, University of Texas, 1975.

Almond, Gabriel A., and Sidney Verba. *The Civic Culture: Political Attitudes and Democracy in Five Nations.* Princeton: Princeton University Press, 1963.

Anderson, Roger Charles. "The Functional Role of the Governors and Their States in the Political Development of Mexico, 1940-1964." Ph.D. dissertation, University of Wisconsin-Madison, 1971.

Armstrong, John A. *The European Administrative Elite.* Princeton: Princeton University Press, 1972.

Arreola, Raúl C. *El tapado al desnudo.* Mexico: Costa-Amic, 1975.

Arriaga, Eduardo E. *New Life Tables for Latin American Populations in the Nineteenth and Twentieth Centuries.* Berkeley: Institute of International Studies, University of California, 1968.

Aubey, Robert T. *Nacional Financiera and Mexican Industry: A Study of the Financial Relationships between the Government and the Private Sector of Mexico.* Los Angeles: UCLA Latin American Center, Latin American Studies, vol. 3, 1966.

Bachrach, Peter. *The Theory of Democratic Elitism: A Critique.* Boston: Little, Brown, 1967.

Báez Villaseñor, José et al. *Doctor Salvador Zubirán: 50 años de vida profesional.* Mexico: Asociación de Médicos del Instituto Nacional de la Nutrición, 1973.

Balboa, Praxedis. *Apuntes de mi vida.* Mexico: n. p., 1975.

Barton, Allen H., Bogdan Denitch, and Charles Kadushin, eds. *Opinion-Making Elites in Yugoslavia.* New York: Praeger, 1973.

Beck, Carl et al. *Comparative Communist Political Leadership.* New York: David McKay, 1973.

Bell, Roderick, David V. Edwards, and R. Harrison Wagner, eds. *Political Power: A Reader in Theory and Research.* New York: The Free Press, 1969.

Bernstein, Harry. *Modern and Contemporary Latin America.* Chicago, Philadelphia, New York: J. B. Lippincott, 1952.

Blondel, Jean. *Comparing Political Systems.* New York: Praeger, 1972.

Bonilla, Frank. *The Failure of Elites,* vol. 2 of *The Politics of Change in Venezuela.* Cambridge: M.I.T. Press, 1970.

Bottomore, T. B. *Elites and Society.* London: Penguin Books, 1964.

Brandenburg, Frank R. *The Making of Modern Mexico*. Englewood Cliffs, N.J.: Prentice-Hall, 1964.

Brzezinski, Zbigniew. *The Permanent Purge: Politics in Soviet Totalitarianism*. Cambridge: Harvard University Press, 1956.

Brzezinski, Zbigniew and Samuel P. Huntington. *Political Power: USA/USSR*. New York: Viking Press, 1965.

Bulnes, Francisco. *El verdadero Díaz y Revolución*. Mexico: Editora Nacional, 1967.

Camp, Roderic Ai. *The Education of Mexico's Revolutionary Family* (forthcoming).

Cadena Z., Daniel. *El candidato presidencial 1976*. Mexico: n. p., 1975.

Carmona, Fernando et al. *El milagro mexicano*. Mexico: Editorial Nuestro Tiempo, 1970.

Coale, Ansley J., and Paul Demeny. *Regional Model Life Tables and Stable Populations*. Princeton: Princeton University Press, 1966.

Cockcroft, James D. *Intellectual Precursors of the Mexican Revolution, 1900-1913*. Austin: University of Texas Press, 1968.

Cornelius, Wayne A. *Politics and the Migrant Poor in Mexico City*. Stanford: Stanford University Press, 1975.

Cosío Villegas, Daniel. *Historia moderna de México. El porfiriato: La vida política interior, segunda parte*. Mexico: Editorial Hermes, 1972.

————. *La sucesión presidencial*. Mexico: Joaquín Mortiz, 1975.

————. *El estilo personal de gobernar*. Mexico: Joaquín Mortiz, 1975.

————. *La sucesión: desenlace y perspectivas*. Mexico: Joaquín Mortiz, 1976.

Cumberland, Charles C. *Mexican Revolution: The Constitutionalist Years*. Austin: University of Texas Press, 1972.

————. *Mexico: The Struggle for Modernity*. New York: Oxford University Press, 1968.

Dahl, Robert A. *Modern Political Analysis*. Englewood Cliffs, N.J.: Prentice-Hall, 1964.

————. *Who Governs? Democracy and Power in an American City*. New Haven: Yale University Press, 1961.

de la Garza, Rudolf O. "The Mexican Chamber of Deputies and the Mexican Political System." Ph.D. dissertation, University of Arizona, 1972.

del Río, Eduardo (Rius). *Pequeño Rius ilustrado*. Mexico: Ediciones de Cultura Popular, 1971.

————. *Rius en Política*. Mexico: Ediciones de Cultura Popular, 1974.

DeRossi, Flavia, *The Mexican Entrepreneur*. Paris: OECD, 1971.

Domhoff, G. William, and Hoyt B. Ballard, eds. *C. Wright Mills and the Power Elite*. Boston: Beacon Press, 1968.

Dulles, John W. F. *Yesterday in Mexico*. Austin: University of Texas Press, 1961.

Eckstein, Susan. *The Poverty of Revolution: The State and the Urban Poor in Mexico*. Princeton: Princeton University Press, 1977.

Eulau, Heinz, and John D. Sprague. *Lawyers in Politics: A Study in Professional Convergence*. Indianapolis: Bobbs-Merrill, 1964.

Facts on File, 1970 and 1976. New York: Facts on File, 1970, 1976.

Fagen, Richard R., and William S. Tuohy. *Politics and Privilege in a Mexican City*. Stanford: Stanford University Press, 1972.

Frey, Frederick W. *The Turkish Political Elite*. Cambridge: M.I.T. Press, 1965.

Fuentes, Carlos. *The Death of Artemio Cruz*, trans. Sam Hileman. New York: Farrar, Straus, and Giroux, 1964.

Gaxiola, Francisco Javier. *Memorias*. Mexico: Editorial Porrúa, 1975.

Gill, Clark C. *Education in a Changing Mexico*. Washington: U.S. Government Printing Office, 1969.

Godau, Rainer Horst. "Mexico: A Bureaucratic Polity." M.A. thesis, University of Texas at Austin, 1975.

González Casanova, Pablo. *Democracy in Mexico*, trans. Danielle Salti. New York: Oxford University Press, 1970.

González Cosío, Arturo. *Historia estadística de la Universidad, 1910-1967*. Mexico: UNAM, Instituto de Investigaciones Sociales, 1968.

Greenberg, Martin Harry. *Bureaucracy and Development: A Mexican Case Study*. Lexington, Mass.: D. C. Heath, 1970.

Grindle, Merilee Serrill. *Bureaucrats, Politicians, and Peasants in Mexico*. Berkeley and Los Angeles: University of California Press, 1977.

Gruening, Ernest. *Mexico and Its Heritage*. New York: D. Appleton-Century, 1928.

Guerrero del Castillo, Eduardo. "El reclutamiento y la selección del personal en la administración pública mexicana." Tesis de licenciatura, Escuela Nacional de Ciencias Políticas y Sociales, UNAM, 1963.

Hale, Charles L. *Mexican Liberalism in the Age of Mora, 1821-1853*. New Haven: Yale University Press, 1968.

Hansen, Roger D. *The Politics of Mexican Development*. Baltimore: Johns Hopkins University Press, 1971.

Hernández Enríquez, Gustavo Abel. "La movilidad política en México, 1876-1970." Tesis, Ciencias Políticas y Administración Pública, UNAM, 1968.

Hunter, Floyd. *Community Power Structure: A Study of Decision Makers.* Chapel Hill: University of North Carolina Press, 1953.

————. *Top Leadership, U.S.A.* Chapel Hill: University of North Carolina Press, 1959.

Instituto de Investigaciones Sociales, Universidad Nacional Autónoma de México. *Primer censo nacional universitario 1949.* Mexico: UNAM, 1953.

Iturriaga, José E. *La estructura social y cultural de México.* Mexico: Fondo de Cultura Económica, 1951.

Johnson, Kenneth F. *Mexican Democracy: A Critical View.* Boston: Allyn and Bacon, 1971.

Keller, Suzanne I. *Beyond the Ruling Class: Strategic Elites in Modern Society.* New York: Random House, 1963.

Kling, Merle. *A Mexican Interest Group in Action.* Englewood Cliffs, N.J.: Prentice-Hall, 1961.

Lasswell, Harold D., and Daniel Lerner, eds. *World Revolutionary Elites: Studies in Coercive Ideological Movements.* Cambridge: M.I.T. Press, 1966.

Lasswell, Harold D., Daniel Lerner, and C. Easton Rothwell. *The Comparative Study of Elites: An Introduction and Bibliography.* Stanford: Stanford University Press, 1952.

Laun, John I. "El reclutamiento político en Colombia: los ministros de estado, 1900-1975." Bogotá: Universidad Nacional de los Andes, 1976.

Lieuwen, Edwin. *Mexican Militarism: The Political Rise and Fall of the Revolutionary Army, 1910-1940.* Albuquerque: University of New Mexico Press, 1968.

Lozoya, Jorge Alberto. *El ejército mexicano (1911-1965).* Mexico: El Colegio de México, 1970.

Madero, Francisco I. *La sucesión presidencial en 1910.* Mexico: Ediciones Los Insurgentes, 1960. First published in 1908.

Maldonado, Braulio. *Baja California: comentarios políticos,* 3rd ed. Mexico: Costa-Amic, 1960.

Marvick, Dwaine, ed. *Political Decision-Makers.* Glencoe, Ill.: Free Press, 1961.

Matthews, Donald R. *The Social Background of Political Decision-Makers.* New York: Random House, 1954.

————. *U.S. Senators and Their World.* Chapel Hill: University of North Carolina Press, 1960.

Meisel, James H. *The Myth of the Ruling Class: Gaetano Mosca and the Elite.* Ann Arbor: University of Michigan Press, 1962.

MEXICO:

Departamento de la Estadística Nacional. *Resumen del censo general de habitantes de 30 de noviembre de 1921.* Mexico: Talleres Gráficos de la Nación, 1928.

Dirección General de Estadística, Secretaría de Industria y Comercio. *VIII censo general de población, 1960. Resumen general.* Mexico: Talleres Gráficos de la Nación, 1962.

———. *IX censo general de población, 1970. Resumen general.* Mexico: Talleres Gráficos de la Nación, 1972.

Secretaría de la Economía Nacional, Dirección General de Estadística. *Anuario estadístico de los Estados Unidos Mexicanos 1939.* Mexico: Talleres Gráficos de la Nación, 1941.

Secretaría de la Economía Nacional, Dirección de Estadística. *Compendio estadístico.* Mexico: Talleres Gráficos de la Nación, 1947.

Secretaría de la Economía Nacional, Dirección General de Estadística. *Quinto censo de población, 15 de mayo de 1930. Resumen general.* Mexico: Talleres Gráficos de la Nación, 1934.

Secretaría de Economía, Dirección General de Estadística. *Estadísticas sociales del porfiriato 1877-1911.* Mexico: Talleres Gráficos de la Nación, 1956.

Secretaría de Industria y Comercio, Dirección General de Estadística. *Compendio estadístico 1960.* Mexico: Talleres Gráficos de la Nación, 1960.

Secretaría de la Presidencia, Dirección de Inversiones Públicas. *México: Inversion pública federal, 1925-1963.* Mexico: Talleres Gráficos de la Nación, 1964.

Michels, Robert. *Political Parties: A Sociological Study of the Oligarchical Tendencies of Modern Democracy,* trans. Eden and Cedar Paul, ed. Seymour Martin Lipset. New York: Collier Books, 1962.

Miliband, Ralph. *The State in Capitalist Society.* New York: Basic Books, 1969.

Mills, C. Wright. *The Power Elite.* New York: Oxford University Press, 1959.

Molina Enríquez, Andrés. *Los grandes problemas nacionales.* Mexico: Carranza e Hijos, 1909.

Montemayor H., Andrés. *Los pridestinados.* Monterrey, N.L.: Avance Editorial, 1975.

Moreno Sánchez, Manuel. *Crisis política de México.* Mexico: Editorial Extemporáneos, 1970.

Moreno Sánchez, Manuel. *México: 1968-1972. Crisis y perspectiva.* Austin: Institute of Latin American Studies, University of Texas, 1973.

Mosca, Gaetano. *The Ruling Class,* trans. Hannah D. Kahn, ed. Arthur Livingston. New York and London: McGraw-Hill, 1939.

Moya Palencia, Mario. *La reforma electoral.* Mexico: Ediciones Plataforma, 1964.

Mueller, John H., Karl F. Schuessler, and Herbert L. Costner. *Statistical Reasoning in Sociology,* 2nd ed. Boston: Houghton Mifflin, 1970.

Nagle, John D. *System and Succession: The Social Bases of Political Elite Recruitment.* Austin: University of Texas Press, 1977.

Needler, Martin C. *Politics and Society in Mexico.* Albuquerque: University of New Mexico Press, 1971.

Niemeyer, E. V., Jr. *Revolution at Querétaro: The Mexican Constitutional Convention of 1916-17.* Austin: University of Texas Press, 1974.

Padgett, L. Vincent. *The Mexican Political System.* Boston: Houghton Mifflin, 1966.

Pareto, Vilfredo. *Sociological Writings,* trans. Derek Mirfin, ed. S. E. Finer. London: Pall Mall Press, 1966.

Poniatowska, Elena. *La noche de Tlatelolco.* Mexico: Ediciones Era, 1971.

Portes Gil, Emilio. *Autobiografía de la Revolución Mexicana. Un tratado de interpretación histórica.* Mexico: Instituto Mexicano de Cultura, 1964.

Portuondo, Alonso. "The Universidad Nacional Autónoma de México in the Post-Independence Period: A Political and Structural Review." M.A. Thesis, University of Miami, 1972.

Poulantzas, Nicos. *Political Power and Social Classes,* trans. Timothy O'Hagan. London: NLB and Sheed and Ward, 1973.

Purcell, Susan Kaufman. *The Mexican Profit-Sharing Decision: Politics in an Authoritarian Regime.* Berkeley and Los Angeles: University of California Press, 1975.

Putnam, Robert D. *The Comparative Study of Political Elites.* Englewood Cliffs, N.J.: Prentice-Hall, 1976.

Quandt, William B. *The Comparative Study of Political Elites,* Sage Professional Papers in Comparative Politics 01-004. Beverly Hills, California: Sage Publications, 1970.

———. *Revolution and Political Leadership: Algeria, 1954-1968.* Cambridge: M.I.T. Press, 1969.

Ramírez, Ramón. *El movimiento estudiantil de México: julio-diciembre de 1968,* 2 vols. Mexico: Ediciones Era, 1969.

Rendón Corona, Armando. "Los profesionales de la política en México 1940-1970." Mimeo, Instituto de Investigaciones Sociales de la UNAM, [1976].

Reyna, José Luis, and Richard S. Weinert, eds. *Authoritarianism in Mexico.* Philadelphia: ISHI, 1977.

Reynolds, Clark W. *The Mexican Economy: Twentieth Century Structure and Growth.* New Haven: Yale University Press, 1970.

Ross, Stanley R., ed. *Is the Mexican Revolution Dead?* New York: Alfred A. Knopf, 1966.

Ruiz, Ramón Eduardo. *Labor and the Ambivalent Revolutionaries: Mexico, 1911-1923.* Baltimore: Johns Hopkins University Press, 1976.

Santillán López, Roberto, and Aniceto Rosas Figueroa. *Teoría general de las finanzas públicas y el caso de México.* Mexico: Universidad Nacional Autónoma de México, 1962.

Schattschneider, E. E. *The Semisovereign People: A Realist's View of Democracy in America.* New York: Holt, Rinehart, and Winston, 1960.

Schlesinger, Joseph A. *Ambition and Politics: Political Careers in the United States.* Chicago: Rand-McNally, 1966.

Schumpeter, Joseph A. *Capitalism, Socialism, and Democracy,* 3rd edition. New York: Harper and Brothers, 1950.

Scott, Robert E. *Mexican Government in Transition,* 2nd ed. Urbana: University of Illinois Press, 1964.

Segovia, Rafael. *La politicización del niño mexicano.* Mexico: El Colegio de México, 1975.

Sepúlveda, Bernardo and Antonio Chumacero. *La inversión extranjera en México.* Mexico: Fondo de Cultura Económica, 1973.

Shafer, Robert J. *Mexican Business Organizations: History and Analysis.* Syracuse, N.Y.: Syracuse University Press, 1973.

Singer, Morris. *Growth, Equality, and the Mexican Experience.* Austin: University of Texas Press, 1969.

Sinkin, Richard N. *The Mexican Reform, 1848-1876: A Study in Nation-Building.* Austin: Institute of Latin American Studies, University of Texas, forthcoming.

Smith, Peter H. *Argentina and the Failure of Democracy: Conflict among Political Elites, 1904-1955.* Madison: University of Wisconsin Press, 1974.

Sung, George C. S. *A Biographical Approach to Chinese Political Analysis.* Santa Monica, California: Rand Corporation, 1975.

Tannenbaum, Frank. *Mexico: The Struggle for Peace and Bread.* New York: Alfred A. Knopf, 1964.

Tucker, William P. *The Mexican Government Today*. Minneapolis: University of Minnesota Press, 1957.

Vernon, Raymond. *The Dilemma of Mexico's Development: The Roles of the Private and Public Sectors*. Cambridge: Harvard University Press, 1963.

Wilkie, James W. *The Mexican Revolution: Federal Expenditure and Social Change since 1910*. Berkeley and Los Angeles: University of California Press, 1967.

Wilkie, James W., and Edna Monzón de Wilkie. *Mexico visto en el siglo XX: entrevistas de historia oral*. Mexico: Instituto Mexicano de Investigaciones Económicas, 1969.

Wilkie, James W. *Statistics and National Policy*, Supplement 3 (1974) of *Statistical Abstract on Latin America*. Los Angeles: UCLA Latin American Center, 1974.

Womack, John Jr. *Zapata and the Mexican Revolution*. New York: Alfred A. Knopf, 1969.

Articles and Papers

Anderson, Bo, and James D. Cockcroft. "Control and Cooptation in Mexican Politics," republished in Cockcroft et al., eds., *Dependence and Underdevelopment: Latin America's Political Economy*. Garden City, N.Y.: Doubleday, 1972.

Armstrong, Frances. "The Sovereign Revolutionary Convention in Mexico: Patterns in Leadership" (seminar paper, University of Wisconsin-Madison, January 1972).

Arriola, Carlos. "Los grupos empresariales frente al Estado (1973-1975). *Foro Internacional* 16, no. 64 (April-June 1976): 449-495.

Bachrach, Peter, and Morton S. Baratz. "Two Faces of Power." *American Political Science Review* 56, no. 4 (December 1962): 947-952.

Banco Nacional de México. *Review of the Economic Situation of Mexico* 47, no. 545 (April 1971).

Bernstein, Harry. "Regionalism in the National History of Mexico," in *Latin American History: Essays on Its Teaching and Interpretation*, ed. Howard Cline. Austin: University of Texas Press, 1967.

Barkin, David. "Mexico's Albatross: The U.S. Economy." *Latin American Perspectives* 2, no. 2 (Summer 1975): 64-80.

Bennett, Douglas, and Kenneth Sharpe. "The State in Late Dependent Industrialization: The Control of Multinational Corporations in Mexico," paper presented at the annual meeting of the American Political Science Association, Chicago, 1976.

Black, Gordon S. "A Theory of Political Ambition: Career Choices and the Role of Structural Incentives." *American Political Science Review* 66, no. 1 (March 1972): 144-159.

Blumin, Stuart. "The Historical Study of Vertical Mobility." *Historical Methods Newsletter* 1, no. 4 (September 1968): 1-13.

Brandenburg, Frank. "The Relevance of Mexican Experience to Latin American Development." *Orbis* 9, no. 1 (Spring 1965): 190-213.

Camp, Roderic Ai. "The Cabinet and the *Técnico* in Mexico and the United States." *Journal of Comparative Administration* 3, no. 2 (August 1971): 188-214.

————. "Education and Political Recruitment in Mexico: The Alemán Generation." *Journal of Interamerican Studies and World Affairs* 18, no. 3 (August 1976): 295-321.

————. "Losers in Mexican Politics: A Comparative Study of Official Party Precandidates for Gubernatorial Elections, 1970-75," in *Quantitative Latin American Studies: Methods and Findings*, ed. James W. Wilkie and Kenneth Ruddle, Supplement 6 (1977) of *Statistical Abstract of Latin America*. Los Angeles: UCLA Latin American Center, 1977.

————. "Mexican Governors since Cárdenas: Education and Career Contacts." *Journal of Interamerican Studies and World Affairs* 16, no. 4 (November 1974): 454-481.

————. "The Middle-Level Technocrat in Mexico." *Journal of Developing Areas* 6, no. 4 (July 1972): 571-581.

————. "The National School of Economics and Public Life in Mexico." *Latin American Research Review* 10, 3 (Fall 1975): 137-151.

————. "A Re-examination of Political Leadership and the Allocation of Federal Revenues in Mexico." *Journal of Developing Areas* 10, no. 2 (January 1976): 193-212.

————. "El sistema mexicano y las decisiones sobre el personal político." *Foro Internacional* 27, no. 1 (July-September 1976): 51-83.

————. "Women and Political Leadership in Mexico: A Comparative Study of Female and Male Political Elites." Unpublished paper.

Coatsworth, John H. "Anotaciones sobre la producción de alimentos durante el porfiriato." *Historia Mexicana* 26, no. 2 (October-December 1976): 167-187.

————. "Railroads, Landholding, and Agrarian Protest in the Early Porfiriato." *Hispanic American Historical Review* 54, no. 1 (February 1974): 48-71.

Cochrane, James D. "Mexico's New *Científicos*: The Díaz Ordaz Cabinet." *Inter-American Economic Affairs* 21, no. 1 (Summer 1967): 61-72.

Cockcroft, James D. "El maestro de primaria en la Revolución Mexicana." *Historia Mexicana* 16, no. 4 (April-June 1967): 565-587.

Cosío Villegas, Daniel. "Los llamados y los escogidos del PRI." *Plural* 5, no. 6 (March 1976): 47-49.

Creelman, James. "President Díaz: Hero of the Americas." *Pearson's Magazine* 19 (March 1908): 231-277.

Czudnowski, Moshe M. "Sociocultural Variables and Legislative Recruitment: Some Theoretical Observations and a Case Study." *Comparative Politics* 4, no. 4 (July 1972): 561-587.

de Navarrete, Ifigenia M. "La distribución del ingreso en México: tendencias y perspectivas," in *El perfil de Mexico en 1980*, vol. 1. Mexico: Siglo XXI, 1970.

Drake, Paul W. "Mexican Regionalism Reconsidered." *Journal of Interamerican Studies and World Affairs* 12, no. 3 (July 1970): 401-415.

Duncan, Otis Dudley. "Path Analysis: Sociological Examples." *American Journal of Sociology* 72, no. 1 (July 1966): 1-16.

————. "Social Stratification and Mobility: Problems in the Measurement of Trend," in *Indicators of Social Change: Concepts and Measurements*, ed. Eleanor Bernert Sheldon and Wilbert E. Moore. New York: Russell Sage Foundation, 1968.

Dye, Thomas R. and John W. Pickering. "Governmental and Corporate Elites: Convergence and Differentiation." *Journal of Politics* 36, no. 4 (November 1974): 900-925.

Edinger, Lewis J., and Donald D. Searing. "Social Background in Elite Analysis: A Methodological Inquiry." *American Political Science Review* 61, no. 2 (June 1967): 428-445.

González Cosío, Arturo. "Clases y estratos sociales," in *México: Cincuenta años de Revolución*, vol. II, *La vida social*, by Julio Durán Ochoa et al. Mexico: Fondo de Cultura Económica, 1961.

Granados Chapa, Miguel Angel. "Nayarit: consolidación del monopartido." *Foro Internacional* 16, no. 64 (April-June 1976): 429-448.

Grayson, George W. "Mexico's Opportunity: The Oil Boom." *Foreign Policy*, no. 29 (Winter 1977-78): 65-89.

Grindle, Merilee. "Patrons and Clients in the Bureaucracy: Career Networks in Mexico." *Latin American Research Review* 12, no. 1 (1977): 37-66.

Gruber, Wilfred. "Career Patterns of Mexico's Political Elites." *Western Political Quarterly* 24, no. 3 (September 1971): 467-482.

Herman, Valentine. "Comparative Perspectives on Ministerial Stability in Britain." Unpublished paper (University of Essex, 1973).

Katz, Michael B. "Occupational Classification in History." *Journal of Interdisciplinary History* 3, no. 1 (Summer 1972): 63-88.

Kautsky, John H. "Patterns of Elite Succession in the Process of Development." *Journal of Politics* 31, no. 2 (May 1969): 359-396.

————. "Revolutionary and Modernizing Elites in Modernizing Regimes." *Comparative Politics* 1, no. 4 (July 1969): 441-467.

Kochanek, Stanley A. "The Relation between Social Background and Attitudes of Indian Legislators." *Journal of Commonwealth Political Studies* 6, no. 1 (March 1968): 34-53.

Land, Kenneth C. "Principles of Path Analysis," in *Sociological Methodology 1969*, ed. Edgar F. Borgatta. San Francisco: Jossey-Bass, 1969.

Leal, Juan Felipe. "El Estado mexicano: 1915-1973 (Una interpretación histórica)," paper presented at the Primer Encuentro Latinoamericano de Historiadores (Universidad Nacional Autónoma de México, Centro de Estudios Latinoamericanos, 1973).

————. "The Mexican State: 1915-1973, A Historical Interpretation." *Latin American Perspectives* 2, no. 2 (Summer 1975): 48-63.

Leeds, Anthony. "Brazilian Careers and Social Structure: A Case History and a Model," in *Contemporary Cultures and Societies of Latin America*, ed. Dwight B. Heath and Richard N. Adams. New York: Random House, 1965.

Lerner Sigal, Bertha. "Partido Revolucionario Institucional," in Antonio Delhumeau A. et al., *México: realidad política de sus partidos*. Mexico: Instituto Mexicano de Estudios Políticos, 1970.

Lewis, Paul H. "The Spanish Ministerial Elite, 1938-1969." *Comparative Politics* 5, no. 1 (October 1973): 83-106.

Linz, Juan J. "An Authoritarian Regime: Spain," in *Mass Politics: Studies in Political Sociology*, ed. Erik Allardt and Stein Rokkan. New York: The Free Press, 1970.

————. "Continuidad y descontinuidad en la élite política española: de la restauración al régimen actual," in *Estudios de ciencia política y sociológica*. Madrid: n. p., 1972.

————. "Notes toward a Typology of Authoritarian Regimes," paper presented at the annual meeting of the American Political Science Association, Washington, D.C., 1972.

Lomnitz, Larissa. "Carreras de vida en la UNAM." *Plural* 54 (March 1976): 18-22.

Mabry, Donald J. "Mexico's Party Deputy System: The First Decade." *Journal of Interamerican Studies and World Affairs* 16, no. 2 (May 1974): 221-233.

Miliband, Ralph. "The Capitalist State: Reply to Nicos Poulantzas." *New Left Review* 59 (January-February 1970): 53-60.

——. "Poulantzas and the Capitalist State." *New Left Review*, 82 (November-December 1973): 83-92.

Nagle, John D. "A New Look at the Soviet Elite: A Generational Model of the Soviet System." *Journal of Political and Military Sociology* 3 (Spring 1975): 1-13.

——. "The Soviet Political Elite, 1917-1971: Application of a Generational Model of Social Change," paper presented at the annual meeting of the American Political Science Association, New Orleans, 1973.

——. "System and Succession: A Generational Analysis of Elite Turnover in Four Nations," paper presented at the annual meeting of the Southern Political Science Association, Atlanta, November, 1973.

Needleman, Carolyn, and Martin Needleman. "Who Rules Mexico? A Critique of Some Current Views on the Mexican Political Process." *Journal of Politics* 31, no. 4 (November 1969): 1011-1034.

Parsons, R. Wayne, and Allen H. Barton. "Social Background and Policy Attitudes of American Leaders." Paper presented at the annual meeting of the American Political Science Association, Chicago, 1974.

Payne, James E., and Oliver H. Woshinsky. "Incentives for Political Participation." *World Politics* 24, no. 4 (July 1972): 518-546.

Portes Gil, Emilio. "Sentido y destino de la Revolución Mexicana," in *México: Cincuenta años de Revolución*, vol. III, *La política*. Mexico: Fondo de Cultura Económica, 1961.

Poulantzas, Nicos. "The Problem of the Capitalist State." *New Left Review* 58 (November-December 1969): 67-78.

——. "The Capitalist State: A Reply to Miliband and Laclau." *New Left Review* 95 (January-February 1976): 63-68.

Purcell, John F. H., and Susan Kaufman Purcell. "Mexican Business and Public Policy," in *Authoritarianism and Corporatism in Latin America*, ed. James Malloy. Pittsburgh: University of Pittsburgh Press, 1976.

——. "El estado y la empresa privada." *Nueva Política* 1, no. 2 (April-June 1976): 229-250.

Purcell, Susan Kaufman. "Decision-Making in an Authoritarian Regime: Theoretical Implications from a Mexican Case Study." *World Politics* 26, no. 1 (October 1973): 28-54.

Ronfeldt, David F. "The Mexican Army and Political Order since 1940," in *Contemporary Mexico: Papers of the IV International*

Congress of Mexican History, ed. James W. Wilkie, Michael C. Meyer, and Edna Monzón de Wilkie. Berkeley and Los Angeles: University of California Press, 1976.

Rustow, Dankwart A. "The Study of Elites: Who's Who, When, and How." *World Politics* 18, no. 4 (July 1966): 690-717.

Ryder, Norman. "The Cohort as a Concept in the Study of Social Change." *American Sociological Review* 30, no. 6 (December 1965): 843-861.

Schleth, Uwe. "Once Again: Does It Pay to Study Social Background in Elite Analysis?" in *Sozialwissenschaftliches Jahrbuch fur Politik*, ed. Rudolf Wildenmann. Munich: Gunter Olzog Verlag, 1971, pp. 99-118.

Schmitt, Karl M. "Congressional Campaigning in Mexico: A View from the Provinces." *Journal of Inter-American Studies* 11, no. 1 (January 1969): 93-110.

Scott, Robert E. "Mexico: The Established Revolution," in *Political Culture and Political Development*, ed. Lucian W. Pye and Sidney Verba. Princeton: Princeton University Press, 1965.

Searing, Donald D. "The Comparative Study of Elite Socialization." *Comparative Political Studies* 1, no. 4 (January 1969): 471-500.

Segovia, Rafael. "La reforma política: el Ejecutivo Federal, el PRI y las elecciones de 1973." *Foro Internacional* 14, no. 3 (January-March 1974): 305-330.

Smith, Peter H. "The Making of the Mexican Constitution," in *The Dimensions of Parliamentary History*, ed. William O. Aydelotte. Princeton: Princeton University Press, 1977.

———. "La movilidad política en el México contemporáneo." *Foro Internacional* 15, no. 3 (January-March 1975): 379-413.

Spitzer, Alan B. "The Historical Problem of Generations." *American Historical Review* 78, no. 5 (December 1973): pp. 1353-1385.

Treiman, Donald J. "A Standard Occupational Prestige Scale for Use with Historical Data." *Journal of Interdisciplinary History* 7, no. 2 (Autumn 1976): 283-304.

Tucker, William P. "Las élites mexicanas." *Aportes*, no. 13 (July 1969): 103-106.

Tuohy, William S. "Centralism and Political Elite Behavior in Mexico," in *Development Administration in Latin America*, ed. Clarence E. Thurber and Lawrence S. Graham. Durham, N.C.: Duke University Press, 1973.

Wolf, Eric R., and Edward C. Hansen. "*Caudillo* Politics: A Structural Analysis." *Comparative Studies in Society and History* 9 (1966-1967): 168-179.

Womack, John, Jr. "The Spoils of the Mexican Revolution." *Foreign Affairs* 48, no. 4 (July 1970): 677-687.

Periodicals and Newspapers

In addition to the newspapers mentioned in Section A, I consulted a number of periodicals and papers for 1976 through early 1978 for material on the transition from Echeverría to López Portillo. They are:

El Heraldo (Mexico City)

Impacto (Mexico City)

Latin America

El Nacional (Mexico City)

New York Times

Novedades (Mexico City)

Proceso (Mexico City)

Siempre! (Mexico City)

El Sol (Mexico City)

Últimas Noticias (Mexico City)

¡Ya! (Mexico City)

Wall Street Journal (New York)

INDEX

Specific items in illustrations, tables, and figures are not included in this index; for guidance consult the List of Illustrations, the List of Tables, and the List of Figures on pages xi through xv. See also the List of Abbreviations on page xvi.

Administrative network: defined, 146; and revolutionary cohort, 147-48; and postrevolutionary cohort, 149, 153-54; located in Mexico City, 253; and López Portillo elite, 306-307; mentioned, 203, 251
Agachado, 262
Age: and elite recruitment, 97-101, 175-76, 183, 185; and relative political success, 128; and revolutionary tendency, 141; of exit from office, 204, 271, 273; by party and sector, 237-40; of prerevolutionary elite, 243; of revolutionary cohort, 244; effect on measurement of continuity, 334-37
Agrarian Reform, Secretariat of: under Gómez Villanueva, 269, 284, 289; under Rojo Lugo, 304, 307
Aguaciles, 246
Aguascalientes: site of convention, 35; as part of Center, 67; Olivares Santana as governor, 284, 304
Aguilar, Alonso: on power structure, 194-95; on social origins, 200; on wealth of politicians, 201
Aguilar, Luis, 60
Alamán, Lucas, 29
Alatriste, Sealtiel: path to office, 250-51; advice from Beteta, 261
Alegría, Rosa Luz, 307
Alejo, Francisco Javier: as member of *efebrocracia*, 281; in López Portillo regime, 303
Alemán, Miguel: as fox, 8; and reorganization of PRI, 37-38, 228, 232-33; election to presidency, 50, 225; in Ávila Camacho cabinet, 51; from state of Veracruz, 71; urbanization of elite, 74; and military, 95, 121; age structure of elite, 97-99; and elite continuity, 165, 167, 177, 180; subsequent fate of selected appointees, 166, 273-74, 303; capital accumulation, 201; recruitment of UNAM classmates, 250; mother, 255; move from Gobernación to presidency, 279; in López Portillo regime, 301. See also *Alemanistas*

Alemán, Miguel Jr., 283
Alemanistas: representation in Senate, 225; target of hostility, 273; in López Portillo regime, 301; mentioned, 50. See also Alemán, Miguel
Algeria, 60, 84
Allende, Salvador: visits with Echeverría, 280; mentioned by Echeverría, 296
Altos Hornos de México, 322
Amiguismo, 288
Antesalero, 274-75
Anti-Reelectionist Party, 33-34
Archivo de la Cámara de Diputados de la Nación, 341
Archivos políticos, 252
Argentina: change in composition of elite, 8-9; as authoritarian regime, 56; government expenditures, 60; division of elites, 192-93; under military rule, 276
Arredondo, Francisco M., 244
Arreola, Raúl C., 256
Arriaga, Eduardo, 336
Arriba y adelante, 263-64
Ataturk, Kemal, 20
Atlanta, Georgia, 317
Attorney General: Flores Sánchez, 303-304; Ojeda Paullada, 304
Auditorio Nacional, 298
Austria, 29
Authoritarianism: defined as limited pluralism, 3-4, 49-50; applicability to Mexico, 50-61; in ABC countries, 56; and forms of exit from office, 182-83; and elite structures, 216; and rules of game, 277
Ávila Camacho, Manuel: as transitional president, 21; selection of cabinet, 51-52; and Carrillo Flores, 166; and elite continuity, 167

Baillerés, Raúl, 60
Baja California Norte: as part of Pacific North, 67; Maldonado as governor, 269
Baja California Sur: as part of Pacific North, 67; representation on Gran

Baja California Sur (*cont.*)
Comision, 229; Cervantes del Río as governor, 283
Bakunin, Mikhail, 184
Balboa, Praxedis: promotion in PEMEX, 255; as enemy of Portes Gil, 260; as friend of López Mateos, 260; as governor of Tamaulipas, 260
Banco de México: founded, 135; floats peso, 294; under Romero Kolbeck, 301; in elite hierarchy, 322; mentioned, 270
Banco Nacional de Crédito Ejidal, 322
Banco Nacional Hipotecario Urbano y de Obras Públicas, 322
Barros Sierra, Javier, 307-309
Bermúdez, Antonio, 255
Beteta, Mario Ramón, 299
Beteta, Ramón: advice to Alatriste, 261; on political forgiveness, 268; on corruption, 270-71
Biebrich, Carlos Armando: ousted from office, 269-70, 289-90; mentioned, 271
Bojórquez, Juan de Dios, 225
Bonilla, Frank, 318-19
Bonillas, Ignacio, 37
Bracamontes, Luis Enrique: as *tapado*, 285; excluded from López Portillo regime, 304
Brandenburg, Frank R.: on revolutionary creed, 52; on rates of turnover, 159, 164; on role of PRI, 231-32; on Revolutionary Family, 319-24
Brazil: as authoritarian regime, 56; *panelinha* system, 276-77
Bremer, Juan José as member of *efebrocracia*, 281; in López Portillo regime, 303
Britain: change in composition of elite, 8, 79-80; investments in Díaz era, 30; degree of political apathy, 55; government expenditures, 60; lawyers in politics, 89; class structure of elite, 101; and law of increasing disproportion, 104, 130-31; career patterns, 157; "safe seats" in Commons, 157, 169; and elite continuity, 177; elite homogeneity, 192-93
Bulnes, Francisco, 105
Buscachambas, 248

Caballada, 244
Cabañas, Lucio, 262
Caciques, 245
California, University of, 32
Calles, Mario, 307

Calles, Plutarco Elías: *maximato* of, 17, 294; as president, 37; and *Cristero* revolt, 37; as party founder, 37; from Sonora, 71; and military, 95; age structure of elite, 97; in exile, 225. See also *Callistas*
Callistas: in Ávila Camacho cabinet, 51; representation in Senate, 225. *See also* Callas, Plutarco Elías
Camacho, Manuel, 281-82
Camarilla: defined, 50-51; in economic system, 59; formation of, 86, 91, 120-21; selection of, 255-56; resemblance to *panelinha*, 276-77; and presidential succession, 278; of Sánchez Taboada, 279, 283; of Olivares Santana, 284, 304; of López Portillo, 299, 301, 313; mentioned, 260, 281, 293, 331
Cambridge University, 130, 304
Camp, Roderic Ai: on role of UNAM, 250; on family ties, 254-55
Campeche, 67
Campesinos: migration toward cities, 44; low level of organization, 53-54; excluded from elites, 91-92; and public policy, 186; congressional representation, 218, 233-37, 240; representation on Gran Comisión, 229; as members of PRI, 231-32; land seizures by, 269. *See also* CNC
CANACINTRA, 210
Cananea Copper Company, 31
Carbajal, Gustavo, 307
Cárdenas, Cuauhtemoc, 307
Cárdenas, Lázaro: and reorganization of party, 37, 169; split with Calles, 37, 51; and military, 38, 95; oil expropriation, 41, 53; from Michoacán, 71; educational attainment of elite, 82; and turnover, 167; as mythological hero, 263; as example to Echeverría, 280. See also *Cardenistas*
Cardenistas: representation in Senate, 225; mentioned, 50. *See also* Cárdenas, Lázaro
Cargada, 288
Carrancistas: described, 34-35; as revolutionary movement, 36-37; representation in Senate, 225; mentioned, 24. *See also* Carranza, Venustiano
Carranza, Venustiano: resists Huerta, 34; triumph, 35; as revolutionary, 35-37; as president, 36; death of, 37; from Coahuila, 70; and military, 95; age structure of elite, 97; social

Subsecretary of Gobernación, 303; use of family ties, 307, 310

Echeverría Zuno, Rodolfo (son of Luis), 263

Echeverristas: in political office, 282; in control of congress, 290-91; exclusion urged by Laviada, 298; in López Portillo regime, 299-300, 303-304, 306; presence criticized, 303; age structure of, 305. *See also* Echeverría, Luis

Education: availability of, 45-49; and elite composition, 80-87; and military, 95-96; and relative political attainment, 113-16; and elite recruitment, 183, 185; of entrepreneurs and politicians, 199-200, 214; of parties and sectors, 234-35, 239-40; and prerevolutionary elite, 240; and revolutionary elite, 245; and postrevolutionary elite, 247, 249-50; and López Portillo elite, 313; mentioned, 62. *See also* UNAM

Efebrocracia: defined, 281; in Echeverría elite, 281-82; Biebrich as member, 389; ousted by López Portillo, 303-305

Eisenhower, Dwight D., 178

Ejidos, 35, 295

El Paso, Texas, 33

Electoral network: defined, 144, 146; and revolutionary cohort, 148; and postrevolutionary cohort, 149, 153-54; restrictions on career, 251; and López Portillo elite, 307; mentioned, 203

Engels, Friedrich, 52

Engineers: in political positions, 91; and relative political attainment, 118; and university careers, 200, 250; background of Bracamontes, 285

England. *See* Britain

Envoy Extraordinary and Minister Plenipotentiary, 322

Equipo, 255. *See also* Camarilla

Escuela Nacional de Jurisprudencia, 84. *See also* UNAM

Escuela Nacional Preparatoria, 46-47, 86n. *See also* UNAM

Europe: patterns of elite continuity, 177; ambassadorship for Beteta, 270

Excélsior: story on Biebrich, 269; management coup, 293-94

Executive network: defined, 146; and revolutionary cohort, 147; and postrevolutionary cohort, 153-54; access to uppermost offices, 247; location in Mexico City, 253; and Echeverría's career, 279; and López Portillo elite, 306-307; mentioned, 203, 251

Fábricas Militares, 321

Fagen, Richard R., 55-56, 61

Farell Cubillas, Arsenio: as director of IMSS, 300; ties with López Portillo, 306

Fascism: as epithet for Echeverría regime, 296-97

Federal District: defined as region, 67; representation in elites, 70-71; birthplace of Echeverría, 71; location of UNAM, 84; and relative political attainment, 111; deputyships, 219; importance to lawyers, 273; Martínez Domínguez ousted as head, 281; PRI organization, 289; Hank González appointed as head, 303-304, 310; and López Portillo regime, 306; place of department in elite hierarchy, 321. *See also* Mexico City

Ferrocarriles Nacionales: under Díaz, 30; place of director in elite hierarchy, 321

Flores Magón, Enrique and Ricardo, 24

Flores Sánchez, Oscar, 303-304

Foreign Relations, Secretariat of: under Carrillo Flores, 166; under Roel, 300

France: social background of elites, 79, 101, 193; lawyers in politics, 89; intervention in Mexico, 174; elite continuity, 177; apparent elite rivalries, 193; mentioned, 60

Franco, Francisco: and elite continuity in Spain, 182; mentioned, 20, 57, 90

Frey, Frederick W., 89-90

Fuentes, Carlos: novel quoted, 184-85; resigns ambassadorship, 312

Futurismo, 310, 312

Gabinetitis, 293

Gabinetomanía, 293

Gallo, 50

Gálvez Betancourt, Carlos: as *tapado*, 284, 287; excluded from López Portillo regime, 304

Gamboe Pascoe, Joaquín: as *politico*, 304; leader of Senate, 307; use of family ties, 310

Gamma coefficient: explanation of, 107-108; use of, 108-22 *passim*

García Barragán, Marcelino, 295

García López, Agustín, 273-74

García Téllez, Ignacio, 51

Garrido Canabal, Tomas, 245

Garza Sada family, 60

Gaxiola, Francisco, 51

Georgia (state), 317

Jiménez Ruiz, Eliseo, 262-63
Juárez, Benito, 29

Kautsky, John H., 21
Kennedy, John F., 178
Khrushchev, Nikita, 180
Kissinger, Henry, 298
Korea, 205
Kropotkin, Piotr, 184

La solución somos todos, 299
Labor, Secretariat of: under Muñoz
  Ledo, 284, 289; under Ojeda Paullada,
  300, 304
Labour Party (British), 79. *See also*
  Britain
Lara Pardo, Luis, 243-44
Lasswell, Harold, 6
Latifundistas: and revolution, 9; accused
  by Biebrich, 269
Lavalle Urbina, María, 307
Laviada, Iñigo, 297-98, 303
Lawyers: status of legal profession, 48;
  as political officeholders, 89-90, 103,
  183, 185; and relative political attain-
  ment, 118-20, 127-29; and university
  careers, 200, 250; practice after poli-
  tics, 204, 273; presence in congress,
  236-38; Echeverría as example, 279;
  as presidential precandidates, 283-84;
  in López Portillo regime, 306; mentioned, 175
Leal, Juan Felipe, 10-11
Leal, Luisa María, 307
Leeds, Anthony, 276-77
Legorreta, Luis G., 60
León, Luis L., 225
Limantour, José Yves: as fox, 8; and
  Madero family, 32
Linz, Juan J.: concept of authoritarianism, 3, 49-50; on authoritarianism in
  Spain, 57; on classification of authoritarian regimes, 61; on lawyers in
  politics, 90; on career patterns in
  authoritarian regimes, 157; on elite
  continuity, 182; mentioned, 53
Loaeza, Enrique, 301
López Mateos, Adolfo: election to presidency, 50; from state of México, 71;
  and *técnicos*, 91; and Carrillo Flores,
  166; and elite continuity, 168-69, 176;
  as friend of Balboa, 260; on leftism of
  regime, 263; Echeverría's role in campaign, 279; Moya Palencia's role in
  campaign, 283. See also *Lopezmateistas*

Lopezmateistas, 303. *See also* López
  Mateos, Adolfo
López Portillo, Guillermo, 301
López Portillo, José: and classmates at
  UNAM, 250; presidential campaign,
  263-64, 266, 289-91; praised by Biebrich, 269-70; as *tapado*, 283-84; as
  friend of Echeverría, 283, 288, 296;
  as presidential candidate, 287-89; election to presidency, 291; terrorist attack on sister, 294; rumored attack on
  wife, 295; comment on political crisis,
  296; urged to break with Echeverría,
  297-98; inauguration, 298-99; recruitment of political team, 299-312; cap-
  tures public confidence, 312; governmental policies, 312-14; mentioned,
  191, 278. See also *Lopezportillistas*
López Portillo, Margarita: victim of
  terrorist attack, 294; appointed to
  political post, 301
Lopezportillistas: relation to *echeverristas*, 290-91; in command of economic
  policy, 300; background of, 306. See
  also López Portillo, José
Los Pinos, 287

Macías, Pablo, 51
Madero, Evaristo, 32
Madero, Francisco: background, opposition to Díaz regime, 32-33; campaign,
  33; as president, 33-34; as revolutionary, 36; regional aspects of cabinet
  selection, 70; urbanization of elite, 72;
  age structure of elite, 97-99; and elite
  turnover, 163; as mythological hero,
  263; grandson as possible presidential
  candidate, 289; mentioned, 24, 278
Madrazo, Carlos, 309
Madrazo Pintado, Carlos Armando, 309
Maldonado, Braulio: on political discipline, 269; on self-abasement of
  politicians, 274-75
Marcelo Sada, Andrés: target of accusations, 296, 312; on investment climate,
  312
Martínez Domínguez, Alfonso, 281
Martínez Manautou, Emilio: as presidential precandidate, 284; in López
  Portillo regime, 300. See also *Martínez-
  manautuismo*
Martinezmanautuismo, 300. See also
  Martínez Manautou, Emilio
Marx, Karl: on determinants of elite
  composition, 10; mentioned, 7, 52
Matthews, Donald R., 10

LIBRARY OF CONGRESS CATALOGING IN PUBLICATION DATA

Smith, Peter H.
  Labyrinths of power.

  Bibliography: p.
  1. Elite (Social sciences)—Mexico. 2. Power
(Social sciences) 3. Mexico—Politics and government—
1910-1946. 4. Mexico—Politics and government—
1946-   I. Title.
HN120.Z9E47   301.44'92'0972   78-51191
ISBN 0-691-07592-1
ISBN 0-691-10065-9 pbk.